D0845142

PRESIDENT EDVARD BENEŠ

President Edvard Beneš during his exile in London.

PRESIDENT EDVARD BENEŠ

Between East and West
1938–1948

EDWARD TABORSKY

HOOVER INSTITUTION PRESS
Stanford University, Stanford, California

943.7
T11p

DB
2191
.B45
T3
1981

The Hoover Institution on War, Revolution and Peace, founded at Stanford University in 1919 by the late President Herbert Hoover, is an interdisciplinary research center for advanced study on domestic and international affairs in the twentieth century. The views expressed in its publications are entirely those of the authors and do not necessarily reflect the views of the staff, officers, or Board of Overseers of the Hoover Institution.

Hoover Press Publication 246

© 1981 by the Board of Trustees of the
Leland Stanford Junior University
All rights reserved
International Standard Book Number: 0–8179–7461–X
Library of Congress Catalog Card Number: 80–83829
Printed in the United States of America

To the memory of my mother

OCT 22 '81

UNIVERSITY LIBRARIES
CARNEGIE-MELLON UNIVERSITY
PITTSBURGH, PENNSYLVANIA 15213

Contents

Preface

In the annals of twentieth-century politics, there is hardly a more tragic figure than Edvard Beneš, the cofounder, longtime foreign minister, and second president of Czechoslovakia. Twice he regained freedom for his beloved country, each time against fantastically superior forces, only to see his life's work reduced to rubble and his cherished hopes of truly peaceful East-West coexistence smashed. Broken in body and spirit, he died haunted by agonizing doubts about the correctness of his course, doubts that never ceased to torture him in the desolate six-month interval between his exodus from Prague's Hradčany Castle on February 27 and the fatal stroke that felled him on September 3, 1948.

Over three decades have passed since Beneš's death, yet the controversy concerning his conduct remains unresolved. Judgments of his behavior and appraisals of his character and political acumen range from scathing condemnations to unconditional exonerations. Some see in him little more than an opportunistic fellow traveler, a "quartermaster of communism in central Europe" moved by "egoistic concerns and ambition unchecked by moral scruples." Others portray him as a Micawberish optimist obsessed with a naive belief in Stalin's promises and unrealistic dreams of lasting Soviet-Western collaboration. Still others claim that he was the unfortunate victim of an adverse confluence of circumstances and blame his fall on the absence of sorely needed Western support.

What is the truth, if it can be found at all? As a close associate of Beneš during the last decade of his life, I should like to offer my own analysis of his actions and their motivations.

For over six years, from 1939 to 1945, I served as Beneš's personal secretary and legal adviser, first during his political exile in England and later after his return to liberated Czechoslovakia. Even after I went to Sweden as Czechoslovak envoy extraordinary and minister plenipotentiary in 1945, I maintained close contact with the president and his collaborators throughout the crucial years of 1945–1948. In the six years of his exile in England, I saw Beneš literally every day of the week, either at his modest villa in the London suburb of Putney, at his country home at Aston Abbots in Buckinghamshire, or at his office in London. I accompanied him on his political journeys to the United States in 1943 and to the Soviet Union in 1943 and 1945.

Since the staff of the President's Office during his exile was very small and we were jointly involved, sharing the good and the bad, in an uphill struggle for freedom and political survival rather than in mere routine government operations, there was a sort of closeness and intimacy not found under ordinary circumstances. This gave me a unique opportunity to observe the president, to get to know him as a person and as a statesman, and to gain insight into his reasoning and modus operandi. Throughout those years I kept a diary. I also managed to preserve, and thus keep out of communist hands, a sizable archive of important documents illuminating Beneš's actions and motivations. (The Czechoslovak Ministry of the Interior seized the president's personal archive immediately after his death.) Following the communist coup of February 1948, I interviewed all who had played a role in, or had firsthand knowledge of, the crisis and had found asylum in the West. These materials, as well as other relevant sources, both published and unpublished, form the basis of this study.

The period of this study ranges from 1938 to 1948, encompassing the culmination of the appeasement of the 1930s—Munich, the Ides of March 1939, the Second World War; the outbreak and acceleration of the "cold war"; the communization of Czechoslovakia; and Edvard Beneš's resignation and death. This has been, thus far, the twentieth century's most fateful period, a period that profoundly affected the destiny not only of Czechoslovakia but of Europe and the whole world. It was a period of great hopes and even greater disappointments. It was also the period in which Beneš emerged as one of the foremost protagonists in the unfolding drama of fast moving world events, at times playing a crucial role, and wielding international influence disproportionate to his country's size. During this period, his reputation as a champion of democracy, accomplished East-West broker, and a prognosticator shot sky-high, only to fall flat again when his vision of East-West rapprochement turned, through no fault of his, into a mirage. He himself viewed this period, until everything around him began crumbling in 1948, as the crowning period of his political career.

I wish to thank my colleagues in the Department of Government of the University of Texas at Austin for their valuable linguistic and stylistic suggestions. I am greatly indebted to the Research Institute of the University of Texas at Austin, the Relm Foundation, the American Philosophical Society, and the American Council of Learned Societies for the financial assistance that enabled me to complete this study. I should also like to thank the editors of *Foreign Affairs* for allowing me to use parts of my articles "Beneš and the Soviets" and "The Triumph and Disaster of Edvard Beneš," which appeared in the January 1949 and July 1958 issues of that quarterly, and the editors of *East Central Europe (L'Europe Du Centre-Est)* for allowing me to use parts of my article "President Edvard Beneš and the Crises of 1938 and 1948," which appeared in the no. 2, 1978 issue of the journal.

1

The Man, the Diplomat, the Statesman

Hitler's annexation of Austria in 1938 was proof that the Führer's promise to unite all the Germans in one Reich was serious. With a substantial German minority, already gravely infected by the Nazi sickness, spread in a broad arc all along the border with Germany, Czechoslovakia was clearly next. No one was more aware of the dire threat Hitler's designs posed for the twenty-year-old republic than Edvard Beneš. Beneš assumed the presidency in 1935 from the hands of the ailing and venerable Tomáš G. Masaryk during a period of increasing international malaise, typified by the Spanish civil war, fascist Italy's invasion of Ethiopia, the eclipse of the League of Nations, and the debilitating Anglo-French appeasement. Thus, soon after he moved from the Czernin Palace home of the Ministry for Foreign Affairs to Hradčany Castle, the traditional seat of Czechoslovakia's presidents and before them of Bohemia's kings, events forced the new president to make decisions vital to the continued existence of his nation. With little room to maneuver, he watched first the Nazi occupation of Czechoslovakia and then its engulfment into the Soviet orbit.

What sort of a man was Beneš as he stood at the threshold of that unbelievable sequence of events that forced him first to capitulate to Hitler and go into his second exile, then enabled him to return triumphantly to the Hradčany Castle, and finally coerced him to surrender to the communists and withdraw a broken man to his beloved South Bohemian country house at Sezimovo Ústí, where a merciful death finally redeemed him from his torment a few months later? How prepared was he for the gigantic role he was called on to play in that crucial decade of 1938–1948? What were the convictions, beliefs, principles, and values that guided him and that affected his actions? What were his modus operandi, his methods, his ways of doing things?

Beneš appeared well equipped for the task that lay ahead of him on his ascension to the republic's presidency. As Tomáš Masaryk's chief collaborator in the struggle for his country's independence during the First World War, he was actively involved in the complex endeavors to secure Western support for his cause. He served as Czechoslovakia's perennial minister for foreign affairs from 1918 to 1935, playing a decisive role in the making of his country's foreign policy. Indeed, it would not be an exaggeration to speak of Beneš as the architect of Czechoslovak foreign policy. Although he was responsible as foreign minister constitutionally and politically to the cabinet as a whole, and through it collectively to the parliament, increasingly his became the deciding voice in foreign policy. He emerged as a major figure at the League of Nations, where he served six times as chairman of its Council, once as president of its Assembly, and several times as rapporteur on important issues brought before the League. In his seventeen years as head of the Foreign Ministry, he made meaningful contributions to most major international conferences. He was thus able to establish and maintain contacts with many prominent statesmen and diplomats; some of them became his friends and admirers, some his enemies. His well-deserved reputation for his ability to effect compromises prompted Lord Curzon to introduce him to Stanley Baldwin in 1923 as "the little man for whom we send when we are in trouble." "And," the British foreign secretary continued, "he always puts us right."[1]

But the rich experience gained from the conference rooms and antechambers of Western Europe that made Beneš superbly qualified to deal with the democratic statesmen of the Western world proved of little value in transacting business with the statesmen and diplomats of the Soviet Union. Beneš was not unaware of the Soviet leaders' ulterior motives. Indeed, the thought that under certain circumstances the Soviet Union might utilize the postwar chaos in Eastern Europe to dominate the area was always present in Beneš's mind, even when his trust in Stalin's word reached its apogee following his December 1943 visit to Moscow. But somehow he chose not to understand that the approach he used with Western statesmen would not produce the same results when dealing with Stalin and his associates.

In particular, he could not bring himself to believe that the Soviet recipient of a well-meant, voluntary concession might not consider it a gesture of goodwill, friendship, or trust to be reciprocated, but rather might view it with suspicion and wonder about the motives of a "bourgeois" statesman and "class enemy" who made unexpected gifts to the Soviet Union. The Soviets simply pocketed a concession advanced without insistence on a corresponding quid pro quo as an extra gain that did not reduce the offerer's debt. A classic illustration of a gratuitous concession on Beneš's part (discussed fully in Chapter Seven) was his implicit suggestion, made on several occasions beginning with Beneš's talk with the Soviet ambassador to Great Britain, Ivan Maisky, in September 1939, that he would be willing to let the Soviet Union have Ruthenia (subsequently called Subcarpathian Ukraine), Czechoslovakia's easternmost province.

Similarly, Beneš concluded that dealings with the Soviet leaders should be based on consideration and take into account the adverse effects of their long isolation. He did occasionally stress firmness in negotiating with the Russians, but for the most part he was either unwilling or unable to follow this precept.[2] Beneš felt that Soviet misbehavior, bad faith, and broken promises should be met not with plain, straightforward language but with tolerance. One should minimize the whole issue and even excuse it as a misunderstanding. An especially revealing example of this was Beneš's letter of January 29, 1945, to Stalin confirming Czechoslovakia's willingness to cede Ruthenia to the Soviet Union. The Soviet action in Ruthenia in the fall of 1944 and the winter of 1944–45 flagrantly violated the noninterference clause of the 1943 Soviet-Czechoslovak Treaty of Friendship, Mutual Assistance, and Postwar Cooperation and amounted to a forcible grab of territory that as late as December 1943 the Soviet Union had recognized as part of Czechoslovakia. Nonetheless, Beneš thought it appropriate to assure Stalin that neither he nor his government "thought even for one moment that the Soviet government would intend to solve unilaterally the question of Subcarpathian Ukraine or had the intention of violating the agreement between our states." And even though he had already learned that the opposite was much closer to the truth, he added: "I know well the principles of the policy of the Soviet Union, and I know that this is absolutely out of the question."[3]

Of course, by January 1945, with the Red Army and NKVD (the Soviet secret police) agents moving ever deeper into Czechoslovakia and helping native communists assume control in one area after another, Beneš was hardly in a position to use blunt language to protest Stalin's perfidy. But Beneš did resort to excessive euphemism in his communications with Soviet leaders, both oral and written, even when his position vis-à-vis the Soviet Union was much stronger. He even advised Western statesmen to handle their affairs with Stalin with similar circumspection. For instance, on January 27, 1944, when British Foreign Secretary Anthony Eden asked Beneš's opinion of a draft letter on the Polish question from Churchill to Stalin, Beneš told Eden that he considered the draft too sharp and recommended that the letter be couched in more moderate terms.

Beneš often used a similar approach with Western statesmen and even with his own people. He was convinced that quiet diplomacy was a more effective way to deal with thorny problems than blunt language. The best way to make a person keep a promise, Beneš used to say, is to believe that he means it and deal with him on that basis.[4] Also, he was basically a kind man who disliked chiding and rebuking others even when they deserved it. With Western statesmen and diplomats, Beneš's considerate approach was appreciated and often produced better results than a tougher stance might have. The adherents of dialectical materialism, however, view such an approach not as gentlemanly understatement prompted by the desire to facilitate a mutually satisfactory solution, but as a sign of timidity and weakness and a mere display of face-saving verbalism that can be disregarded with impunity.

In his dealings with Western diplomats Beneš did on occasion resort to tough language. On April 9, 1942, in one of his many discussions with Philip Nichols (the British envoy to the Czechoslovak government in exile) about British repudiation of the Munich agreement, he threatened to inform "our friends in the Liberal and Labour parties" of the Foreign Office's unwillingness to repudiate Munich and accused the British of a "lack of political imagination and foresight" in not realizing the possible consequences of their equivocation.[5] Yet he would not use such forceful language when dealing with Soviet diplomats, to say nothing of Molotov and Stalin.

Some critics hold that Beneš's softness in dealing with communists is attributable to his failure to understand the communist mentality, to grasp and evaluate the twisted workings of the Marxist-Leninist mind correctly. Even one of the president's closest associates, the late Jaromír Smutný (chief of the President's Office during Beneš's exile in London and later, until Beneš's resignation in June 1948, in Czechoslovakia), appears to have held this opinion. "Beneš had difficulty in reaching understanding with statesmen who differed from him psychologically," reads an entry in Smutný's unpublished notes.[6] Smutný also asserted that Beneš lacked knowledge of human nature because he had lost contact with people.[7]

Although by no means as ignorant of human nature as Smutný's remark suggests, Beneš did misread Stalin's psyche, place too much trust in his assurances, and misinterpret his real intentions. Beneš himself subsequently conceded this point. "Was I or was I not mistaken in my judgment and expectation [that the Soviet Union could be trusted]?" he wondered in his memoirs of the Second World War in reference to the 1943 negotiations over the Czechoslovak-Soviet Treaty of Friendship, Mutual Assistance, and Postwar Cooperation.[8] Similar ex post facto doubts about Stalin's trustworthiness are evident in several last-minute additions to the volume.[9] A few days before his death, he confessed: "My greatest mistake was that I refused to believe to the very last that even Stalin had lied to me, cold-bloodedly and cynically, both in 1935 and later, and that his assurances to me and to [Jan] Masaryk were all intentional deceit."[10]

Beneš's faith in Stalin's word and in Soviet good intentions regarding Czechoslovakia reached its highest point during and immediately following his visit to Moscow in December 1943 and coincided with the then flourishing spirit of East-West cooperation bolstered by the Teheran Big-Three Conference. The warmth, friendliness, and apparent sincerity of Beneš's reception in Moscow and, above all, Stalin's resounding *da* to all of Beneš's desiderata greatly impressed Czechoslovakia's president, especially when contrasted with the delays, evasions, and maybe's that some of his postulates (particularly recognition of Czechoslovakia's pre-Munich boundaries and the massive transfer of the Sudeten Germans to the Reich) encountered in Britain and the United States. Reporting to the Czechoslovak State Council in London after his return from Moscow, he described Stalin and Molotov as "great Soviet patriots" able "to esteem the patriotism of others since they are far-sighted political realists fully aware of what they want and what they can achieve."[11]

However, this highly favorable impression, though contributing to Beneš's faith in Soviet good intentions, was by no means decisive. To rely on subjective personal impressions would have been quite out of character for a man so dispassionate, scholarly, and coolly rational as Beneš. Although never underestimating the usefulness of personal contacts, he believed that they could not substantially change the policies of any nation.[12] Thus, he scoffed at the assertions of his political opponents after Munich that he might have obtained a better deal had he established personal contacts with Hitler. Beneš always maintained that Neville Chamberlain's confidence in his ability to influence Hitler by personal appeals was extremely naive.

Beneš's hopes were based on something deeper. The former professor of sociology held that politics was the main element of sociology and that the primary work of a good politician was to discover the nature of social reality—to determine the constants in a given society and to analyze and define them. "As a science," he wrote, "democratic politics must look at a society and the world objectively, must search for truly objective reality, must analyze society thoroughly and widely, and must, so to speak, dissect it alive."[13]

Having dissected and analyzed the Soviet system as he saw it in 1943, he concluded that its revolutionary era had ended and it was now passing through gradual transformation to a form of socialist democracy. The Soviet Union would move toward the right, permitting more and more political, cultural, and personal freedoms. Simultaneously, the Western democracies would move toward the left, toward socialism, or at least toward social welfare, economic planning, and economic regulation. As both systems converged, the sharp edges of their ideological and political antagonisms would be dulled and genuine peaceful coexistence would ensue.[14] Thus, Beneš became a firm believer in and an ardent advocate of what is now labeled the "theory of convergence."

The doctrinal thaw that Beneš had observed in the Soviet Union, Stalin's wartime appeals to patriotism rather than to communism, cultural relaxation, and other hopeful signs of change were, as he saw it, concessions that, once given to the Soviet peoples, could not easily be taken away. The wartime partnership with the United States and Britain appeared to help the Soviet Union escape its isolationist shell, converting the onetime international outcast into a highly respected great power, which would not wish to compromise this position by reverting to its earlier lawless behavior. Riding high on the prestige resulting from Soviet military victories, international communism would lose more than it could gain by a return to earlier practices. The colossal task of reconstructing the huge area of the Soviet Union devastated by the war would necessitate major aid from abroad, especially from the United States, and this consideration would induce Stalin to refrain from gravely antagonizing the West. "Soviet Russia will be interested in retaining, even after the war, the cooperation with the Anglo-Saxon democracies which is developing so promisingly," he wrote to his collaborators in Czechoslovakia as late as July 16, 1944.

> She will need their aid in many respects. The suffering of Russia and her devastation defy imagination, and the Soviet Union is guided by the effort to rebuild the country as soon as possible. That is also the guarantee which makes our treaty of alliance with the USSR so real and so vitally important for us. This is why the Soviets will not interfere with our internal affairs more than in the case of other states. We shall decide by ourselves how we will want to arrange our new life and order.[15]

Thus, the cornerstone of Beneš's hope in Soviet good conduct was his belief that even after the defeat of Germany the Soviet Union would need the West so much that it would resist its Bolshevist urge to renege on its wartime promises and install communist rule in East Central Europe by force.

So strong was Beneš's trust in Stalin that he clung to it even when alarming evidence of Soviet duplicity began mounting in the latter part of 1944. First, in August 1944, without informing Beneš, the Soviet authorities began negotiating with the commander-in-chief of the puppet Slovak army, Gen. Ferdinand Čatloš, who virtually offered Slovakia to the Soviet Union by suggesting quite bluntly that "the Slovak inner-political matters might be solved in accordance with the interests of the USSR."[16] One month later Beneš was gravely dismayed by Soviet procrastination in helping the Slovak divisions that rose against the Germans in central Slovakia when the Soviet army reached Slovakia's northern borders, even though Stalin had assured Beneš in December 1943 of prompt and effective aid if and when active resistance occurred. At that time both Stalin and Molotov had sharply criticized what they considered the low level of anti-German resistance in Czechoslovakia, urging that it be stepped up and promising aid.

But the worst breach of faith occurred in the fall and winter of 1944 after the Red Army had entered Czechoslovak territory and occupied Ruthenia. Almost immediately the Soviets began forcibly drafting Ruthenians into the Red Army and compelling mayors to sign "spontaneous" petitions asking to be "reunited with the Ukrainian brothers on the other side of the Carpathian Mountains." Radio Kiev broadcast similarly phrased telegrams sent to Stalin and Beneš. The Czechoslovak government delegation that, under the provisions of the Czechoslovak-Soviet agreement of May 8, 1944, was to administer the liberated territory was denied direct radio communication with its government in London, held virtually incommunicado, and robbed of its funds by Soviet-backed self-styled Ruthenian militiamen while Soviet authorities looked the other way.

Deeply shocked by these Soviet actions, Beneš began to wonder if he had put too much faith in Stalin's word. "Now we shall see," he told me on November 24, 1944, "whether Stalin meant what he said in 1943—or whether he only wanted to deceive us." Nonetheless, he continued to consider his earlier belief in Soviet reasonableness as essentially correct. When his biographer Compton Mackenzie asked Beneš on December 13, 1944, whether he believed that Stalin was "fundamentally reasonable," the president answered: "I think so. He may have at home many difficulties which prevent him from doing many reasonable things but I consider him to be fundamentally reasonable and rather constructive."[17] Hence, Beneš's rationalization for those aspects of Soviet behavior that failed to fulfill his expectations was to explain them as being caused by factors other than intentional disregard of given promises. The Soviet action in the Čatloš incident could easily be excused by military expediency, which demanded that any avenue be utilized, including temporary dealings with quislings, to hasten the Allied victory and save soldiers' lives. Nor was it necessary to view Soviet behavior during the Slovak uprising as intentional, even though the Soviet failure to aid Polish underground forces during the August 1944 Warsaw uprising might have raised doubts. Excessive caution, communications delays, bureaucratic red tape, or even logistic and technical difficulties were possible explanations.

But finding a credible excuse for Soviet actions in Ruthenia was much more difficult, even for someone as anxious to do so as Beneš. After racking his brain for a plausible explanation, he finally blamed Ukrainian nationalism and overzealous on-the-spot excesses of the Soviet military. On December 12, 1944, he wrote František Němec, chief of the Czechoslovak government delegation in Ruthenia:

> I believe that these things do not suit Moscow, that Moscow does not like it any more than does our government . . . It seems to me, however, that the Ukrainian government, the Ukrainian soldiers, and, in particular, the

Ukrainian communist party proceed differently, that they want to confront both Moscow and us with accomplished facts and that they have no regard for anyone, following ruthlessly their purpose. I do not think that it is double-dealing on the part of Moscow, and I have the impression that it is beginning to get out of the hands of the central government. It would be, of course, a serious phenomenon. One must not forget that Ukrainian nationalism is and will be dangerous for everybody and that Moscow must reckon with it.[18]

Although weakened (though by no means destroyed) by this display of Soviet misbehavior, Beneš's belief in Stalin's reasonableness vis-à-vis Czechoslovakia was strengthened by several countervailing instances of Soviet good behavior. The president was quite pleased by reports from Zdenek Fierlinger (Czechoslovakia's ambassador to Moscow) and František Němec on December 29, 1944, about Molotov's promises to Němec of direct radio communication with London and a halt in the recruiting of Slovak volunteers for the Red Army. Molotov apologized for the incidents in Ruthenia, blaming them on general war fatigue and excesses caused by "the atmosphere of high tension evoked by the strong Ukrainian nationalist movement."[19] A few weeks later, Stalin served Beneš another potent tonic in a personal letter that made the Soviet desire for Ruthenia clear but assured Beneš that "the Soviet government had no intention whatsoever of harming the republic of Czechoslovakia or its prestige." "On the contrary," it was "fully prepared to give the Czechoslovak republic every possible assistance for its liberation and reconstruction."[20] Yet another reassuring development was the unequivocal Soviet rebuff of some overzealous Slovak communists who assumed that the Soviet Union wished to establish a soviet Slovak republic. They were stupefied to learn that such was not the Soviet intention.

In March 1945, during our second wartime trip to Moscow (on the way back to Czechoslovakia), several events did much to restore Beneš's faith. Molotov was rather apologetic about Ruthenia, making it clear that the Soviets wanted the province mainly to satisfy the Ukrainians, and thanked Beneš for his understanding and help. He also confirmed that the prewar boundary between Ruthenia and Slovakia would be respected, thus allaying Beneš's fears that part of Slovakia might be included in the transfer. At the farewell banquet in the Kremlin, Beneš was greatly impressed by Stalin's public apology for "the many acts of wantonness" committed by Soviet soldiers in Czechoslovakia and his concern for the full independence of the Slav nations and promise of noninterference in their internal affairs. Beneš was even more impressed when Stalin was rather critical of Czechoslovakia's communists and told Beneš that communist representation in the new Czechoslovak government was larger than was proper. "The whole atmosphere of that evening," wrote Smutný in his notes, "seemed to me to be more cordial and more serious-minded than during the similar visit a year ago, as if both sides, that is, the president and Stalin, had gained more confidence in one another."[21]

Thus, despite his disappointments of fall and winter 1944, Beneš returned to Czechoslovakia confident that all would be well between him and Stalin. He was, of course, fully aware of Soviet activities in other East European countries already controlled by the Red Army. He knew that a few days after the Yalta Conference had promised the liberated countries of Europe "democratic institutions of their own choice," Stalin sent Deputy Commissar for Foreign Affairs Andrei Vyshinsky to browbeat King Michael of Romania into substituting a communist-controlled cabinet for one Stalin did not like. He knew that the Lublin government, unilaterally installed by and fully subservient to the Kremlin, was converting Poland into a Soviet satellite. But he continued to believe that Czechoslovakia's case would be different. Unlike the Poles, Romanians, and Hungarians, the Czechs and Slovaks had always been pro-Russian, seeing in Russia, whether tsarist or Soviet, a big brother ready to help them against their traditional German, Austro-German, and Magyar enemies. This big-brother complex was further strengthened by the bitter Munich experience with the West. Although the communist version of the Soviet Union's readiness to help Czechoslovakia in 1938 by fighting Germany even without French participation (had only Beneš asked Stalin to do so) is far from true, the Soviet stand was so superior to those of France and Britain that it could only fortify traditional Czechoslovak pro-Russianism.

Of all the East European governments exiled by Hitler's Wehrmacht, Beneš's government in exile in London was the only one genuinely friendly to the Soviet Union. No statesman had striven harder or longer to bring about rapprochement and cooperation between the Soviet Union and the Western democracies. As early as 1924 Beneš had stressed that without Russia there would be no peace in Europe and urged that Russia be introduced as a political factor in European politics at the earliest possible moment.[22] He continued to believe and work for this even during the trying 1939–1941 period when Soviet Russia was cavorting with Nazi Germany following the conclusion of the Nazi-Soviet Nonaggression Pact of August 1939. These endeavors and

Beneš's unswerving loyalty to Stalin resulted in much criticism of his policies. Some of Beneš's detractors saw him as an "ever-opportunistic statesman" who "was painstakingly getting in line to reap for Czechoslovakia all the possible advantages she might get by becoming a willing front-row Soviet-Russian satellite."[23]

As Beneš pointed out in his *Memoirs*, the Western world viewed the evolving relations between Czechoslovakia and the Soviet Union as a "test case" of Soviet intentions toward Eastern Europe.[24] Hence, from the viewpoint of a Western-bred, rational analyst, the expectation that Soviet Russia would in its own interest refrain from forcibly communizing Czechoslovakia seemed well-founded. It was inconceivable that Stalin would jeopardize his country's newly gained international status and the tremendous reservoir of goodwill that the Soviet Union had acquired in Czechoslovakia and the West by its heroic struggle against Nazi Germany, or that he would want to discredit a man who had loyally rendered the Soviet Union such invaluable service.

Some of Stalin's reasons can be deduced from the tenets, strategy, and eschatology of Marxism-Leninism, but the primary reason can be summed up in one word: mistrust. As his deeds and Khrushchev's revelations amply document, Stalin did not trust anyone, not even his closest associates. The slightest pretext, sometimes no pretext at all, sufficed to prompt his quasi-paranoid mind to detect disloyalty, plots, and conspiracy, even where none existed. He simply did not believe Beneš; the more the president endeavored to convince Stalin of his loyalty, the more suspicious Stalin became. Beneš was not unaware of this trait. "I believe them [Stalin and his associates], but they do not believe me," he said shortly after our return to Czechoslovakia in April 1945. "They do not believe anybody . . . They do not believe me, and that is why they want to check on my actions." Yet he attached little importance to this and did not "take it tragically," seeing in it merely a typical aspect of both the Russian and the communist mentalities.[25]

Stalin's mistrust was further enhanced by the fantastic welcome the returning president received in every hamlet, village, and town as our small, motorized caravan proceeded from Košice, the first seat of the Czechoslovak government on liberated Czechoslovak territory, toward Prague in April 1945. This display of Beneš's popularity among the Czechoslovaks and its unmistakable spontaneity could not have sat well with Stalin, who probably viewed it as an undesirable strengthening of the president's political stature that would encourage him in a more independent course of action and impede Czechoslovakia's satellitization.

Another factor in Beneš's relations with Soviet leaders was his wartime conduct of negotiations with Stalin and Molotov in Russian. Dispensing with interpreters tends, as Beneš knew, to create a more intimate atmosphere. However, since his knowledge of Russian was hardly adequate for such purposes, he put himself at a disadvantage and had to grasp occasionally for words, often seeking the assistance of others to find the correct term. Thus, he could not express himself as clearly, precisely, and eloquently as was desirable.

Furthermore, in whatever language he was speaking, Beneš talked more than he listened. He simply loved to discuss, explain, expound, elaborate. Beneš believed that he would persuade by the sheer weight, soundness, and logic of his arguments and that his openness and sincerity would favorably impress others and perhaps induce them to reciprocate. "I play with my cards on the table," he told Mackenzie, referring to his wartime negotiations with the Russians, the British, and the Americans.[26] Although this was not literally true—Beneš did keep some of his cards face down—he practiced open diplomacy more than any other statesman of World War Two fame did. Such behavior put him at a disadvantage, especially when dealing with so secretive a group as Soviet negotiators.

Moreover, Beneš's loquacity, coupled with his considerateness, tended occasionally to create uncertainty about his exact stand on an issue. His custom was to give a lengthy professorial exposé, interspersing it with various obiter dicta and enumerating all imaginable pros and cons (ticking them off one, two, three, on his fingers). Even when he disagreed with the other side's arguments, he did not always say so directly, but resorted to circumlocutions, such as "yes, but" or "on the other hand." Sometimes when the conversation was over, his interlocutor was left unsure of the precise meaning of what had been said or the nature of what had been agreed.

This method of conducting negotiations led, or at least contributed, to situations in which Beneš was convinced that he had fully explained his viewpoint and reached an agreement or obtained approval, while the other side thought otherwise. In a long talk with the French minister to Prague, Victor de Lacroix, on September 17, 1938, for example, Beneš remarked offhand that at the peace conference in 1919 he had been ready to let Germany have portions of northern and western Bohemia.

The French, who had already decided not to honor their obligation to aid Czechoslovakia, eagerly jumped to the conclusion that Beneš was willing to settle the Sudeten question by making territorial concessions.[27] A similar misunderstanding arose when Beneš informed the British in mid-1943 that the United States approved his plan to conclude a treaty with the Soviet Union; the U.S. State Department denied ever discussing the treaty. Several other misunderstandings, which are discussed in later chapters, also seemed to be caused, at least partly, by this particular aspect of Beneš's modus operandi.

One trait of Beneš's mentality that crept into his political analyses, evaluations, and decision making throughout that crucial 1939–1948 decade was his optimism. Beneš himself said: "By nature I am an optimist. In the most difficult position I have never despaired. In politics I always behave as though I were playing tennis. When my opponent is 'forty' and I am 'love' and the next ball may be the last, I am still convinced that I can win the game. To this attitude I attribute many political successes which at the time seemed beyond imagination."[28]

So pronounced and conspicuous did his optimism become, especially at ominous times, that all those who came into contact with him noted it. Speaking of Beneš's "world outlook" in 1934, an earlier biographer wrote of his "philosophical optimism [in] believing that this world, if it is not the best of all possible worlds, can become such."[29] Another biographer, who served as the president's secretary during Beneš's sojourn in the United States in the spring of 1939, recounted that "at every possible opportunity in his many and varied public appearances in the United States, Dr. Beneš voiced his optimism" and maintained that this was "no pose but a deep and sincere conviction."[30] (This was at a time when the mutilated post-Munich rump of Czechoslovakia had been administered the coup de grace by Hitler.) Writing in 1944–45, Mackenzie referred to Beneš's optimism as "famous" and "by now proverbial." "If he has made mistakes," he opined, "they have been mistakes of optimism; and even the opportunism of which his critics make so much play is usually to be traced to such optimism."[31]

Similar references to Beneš's optimism, mostly critical, recur in reports of conversations of various Western diplomats with the Czechoslovak president. "Dr. Beneš' enthusiasm rose to lyrical heights when he was describing his reception" (by Stalin during a 1935 visit to the Soviet Union), reported Sir Joseph Addison to Samuel Hoare of a June 1935 conversation in which Beneš told the British diplomat that "the Soviet

UNIVERSITY LIBRARIES
CARNEGIE-MELLON UNIVERSITY
PITTSBURGH PENNSYLVANIA 15213

Government had recognized the futility of encouraging communist propaganda abroad and would abandon all such efforts."[32] Other comments by high-level British diplomats (such as Sir Orme Sargent, Sir Charles Bentinck, and Sir Robert Vansittart) in 1936 and 1937, mainly in connection with the escalating Sudeten crisis, spoke of "Dr. Beneš' technique to practice an imperturbable optimism in all circumstances" and Dr. Beneš's "usual exaggerated optimism."[33]

Another instance, which I recall quite vividly, occurred on Beneš's birthday on May 28, 1940. The German army had already split the Franco-British armies in two, reached the English Channel, and seized Calais, and the entire Belgian army had just capitulated. The situation looked bleak indeed, and all of us around the president were worried and despondent. But not Beneš. "Oh, that does not matter," he told us with a comforting smile. "This is just one small episode. France must be punished, otherwise there would be no justice. The Western powers will have difficult times, but I have no doubt whatsoever about our ultimate victory. And if they face defeat, there are still two factors: (1) America, which will enter the war should it prove necessary to prevent the defeat of the West; (2) Soviet Russia, which will have to go to war should there be a danger of German victory." Well-known to his associates, as well as to all those who had contact with him, were his recurrent annual predictions, especially after 1942, that the war would soon be over, possibly "by Christmas or next spring."[34]

Although Beneš's optimism definitely ceased being imperturbable after the bitter 1944–45 experience with the Russians and the native communists, it stayed with him, in a more guarded fashion, almost to the very end. Indeed, developments in the first half of 1947 actually strengthened his confidence that all would be well in the end. After failing by a solid 12 percent to gain the coveted majority in the 1946 elections, the communists began to suffer their first setbacks, and their strength in local government began to recede. To the chagrin of the party and the pleasure of noncommunists, the Ministry of Justice, headed by one of Beneš's closest associates, Prokop Drtina, moved resolutely to prosecute the communist-dominated police for illegal practices. Noncommunist newspapers became more and more outspoken in their criticism of communist abuses. The Social Democrats began at long last to shake off the hold of their fellow-traveling left wing and to assert themselves more strongly against communist attacks on political freedoms. Popular morale was rising, and civic courage slowly began gathering momentum.

Thus, when Beneš received me in June 1947 before I returned to my diplomatic post in Sweden, I found the president confident that despite the many remaining difficulties, Czechoslovakia would avoid communization. His optimism evidently did not abandon him even after the Cominform's establishment and Stalin's veto in summer 1947 of Czechoslovak participation in the Marshall Plan negotiations (after the Czechoslovak government had already accepted the U.S. invitation). As late as November 1947, as reported by U.S. Ambassador Laurence Steinhardt, Beneš's optimism "reached the point of asserting that the turning point had been reached." The "Communists," he told Steinhardt, "will make one or two more efforts between now and May elections to intimidate and even terrorize non-communists to influence the outcome of the elections but they will not succeed."[35]

Most of Beneš's optimism was genuine. *"Gouverner, c'est prévoir,"* he used to say, and until the communist coup of February 1948 he firmly believed that his optimistic predictions would be proven essentially correct. His optimism stemmed from the conviction that his assessments of the relevant factors were correct and that his expectations were well founded. It was not just Micawberish wishful thinking that something would turn up. However, some of it was meant to build morale and counter the possible ill effects, on both his collaborators and the statesmen and diplomats of Czechoslovakia's allies, of what he considered temporary setbacks. Hence, when talking with Western statesmen and diplomats, addressing American or British audiences, sending messages to his collaborators in the Czechoslovak underground, or speaking over British radio to his compatriots at home, he often sounded more optimistic than he actually was, especially when discussing the prospects of Soviet behavior. Since he considered the continued cooperation of the Soviet Union and the Western powers as a sine qua non for the peace and security of Europe and therefore for the survival of Czechoslovakia as a free and independent country, he was determined to use any means in pursuing this paramount goal. He himself referred to this as the "alpha and omega" of his thoughts and actions after returning to London from his 1943 visit to Moscow.[36] Since the main obstacle to East-West cooperation seemed to him to be the accumulated legacy of deep-rooted mutual suspicions, he deemed it necessary to contribute to the removal of that obstacle by offering both sides as optimistic an interpretation as possible of their intentions and designs. In that sense he did tend to become overoptimistic, and his less charitable critics may have a point in accusing him of wishful thinking.

However, Beneš was by no means an exception in this respect. Virtually all statesmen and politicians indulge in excessive optimism if it suits their political needs, although they may be far less optimistic in private. Even a staunch anti-Bolshevik like Churchill could assure the House of Commons on his return from the Yalta Conference that "the Soviet leaders wish to live in honourable peace with Western democracies" and that he knew "of no government which stands to its obligations . . . more solidly." Yet in talking with Beneš three days earlier, the British prime minister had sounded much less optimistic. Although he expressed the hope that "the Russians would remain within the limits of their strength and possibilities," Churchill conceded that he could not "guarantee the future of [continental] Europe" and that "only the British would manage to defend themselves even if the Russians took everything and reached French territory and the Atlantic Ocean."[37]

Another element that affected Beneš's judgment and policies vis-à-vis the Soviet Union and the West was his commitment to socialism. Beneš's nondoctrinaire socialist beliefs are well documented by his own statements and writings. As a young student he even came under the influence of Marxism for a while. "I was very socialistic, Marxist," he confided to Mackenzie in discussing his 1906 sojourn in London. "I was a young enthusiastic boy; I went to the East End and saw the slums. I did not know too much about England and was disgusted with the great wealth on one side and the misery on the other, and I wrote a certain number of articles for a socialist paper in my country."[38] But he soon outgrew this passing flirtation with orthodox Marxism, spurning its dialectical materialism, anti-individualism, and lopsided emphasis on violence and class struggle, and embraced instead the ideology and methodology of West European democratic socialism. "I was always in favor of social justice, which ought to be realized by evolutionary methods and not by violent and sanguinary social revolutions or the dictatorship of the proletariat," he wrote in 1939 in his *Democracy Today and Tomorrow* when explaining his rejection of Marxism.[39] Thus, it was logical for him to join the non-Marxist and rather middle-of-the-road Czechoslovak Socialist party when leading politicians insisted that the young foreign affairs minister could not continue sitting in the cabinet as a nonparty expert. As he told me during our exile in London, he might have joined the somewhat more socialistic Czechoslovak Social Democratic party but felt it would have been inappropriate in view of that party's membership in the Second International. (Observing the nonpartisan status of the presidency established by Tomáš Masaryk,

Beneš resigned his party membership on election as president; but his commitment to democratic socialism continued.)

As a socialist, Beneš was, of course, no friend of capitalism; and in the expanded Czech edition of *Democracy Today and Tomorrow* (written in London in 1942–43), he took the Western democracies to task for their "lack of courage and ability to resolve more radically and more systematically the social problems and intervene more sharply in the economic structure of modern society." He expressed the conviction that "the economic system of classical liberalism and capitalism had outlived its usefulness" and declared that "the social legislation and social reformism of the end of the nineteenth and the beginning of the twentieth century . . . was no longer sufficient." Calling for "progressive collectivization of the means of production and private profit," he advocated replacing "*the capitalist 'free play of economic forces'* " by "*scientific economic planning.*"[40]

Beneš's critique of Western capitalism by no means implied that he supported wholesale collectivization of all means of production. His goal was a mixed system in which key and large-scale enterprises would be publicly owned and operated, but small and even medium-size enterprises would remain in private hands. "I imagine in the future most of these large enterprises will be taken out of the hands of individuals and placed in the hands of the community," he told Mackenzie in 1944. "I declare it is part of my programme to establish such a system in our Republic after the war."[41] Moreover, he urged that even this limited collectivization be carried out "gradually, in an evolutionary manner, empirically . . . without catastrophes and without violence, by agreement and through cooperation."[42] The nationalization decrees he signed on October 24, 1945, affected only 17.4 percent of Czechoslovakia's enterprises and 57.7 percent of the labor force, while factories employing no more than 150 to 500 workers (depending on the type of industry) remained in private hands.[43] Even so, the president thought that the decrees were too extreme, and he signed them only with grave misgivings and under communist pressure.

Thus, Beneš's anticapitalist bias was fairly slight, and his socialist leanings were quite moderate. Nonetheless, they were instrumental in predisposing him to a more rose-colored view of the Soviet experiment and aspirations than might otherwise have been the case, especially when coupled with his proverbial optimism. It was a foible he shared with many well-meaning socialists (and even liberals) during the popular-front era of 1934–1938 and again during the wartime grand alliance of 1941–1944. At least in part, it accounts for some of Beneš's highly eulogistic references, some bordering on naiveté, to Stalin, the Soviet Union, and Soviet life, made mostly after his return from Moscow in January 1944. Asked, for instance, whether mechanization had adversely affected the Soviet people, he asserted that, on the contrary, "mechanization has helped the development of the individual" and that "the establishment of the so-called Communist society has raised every human being to a higher level." Although critical of some Soviet methods, he praised "the higher moral conception of Russian communism," contrasting it with the "depreciation of moral standards" in Western Europe in the Munich era.[44] Describing his brief stop at Baku, the capital of Soviet Azerbaijan, during his return from Moscow to London in December 1943, Beneš drew an unbelievably romantic and impressionistic picture of Azerbaijani life, asserting that the Azerbaijani people "were as happy as any I have ever seen" (although he spent only one day and one night there).[45] A few years later, he spoke again of "the unforgettable impressions" of his 1943 visit to the Soviet Union and claimed that he had been able to "look well enough into the life of the Soviet Union" and had "further deepened his understanding of the peoples of the Soviet Union, characterizing the positive changes (in the direction of liberalization and democratization) in Soviet Russia as a natural development, "sociologically fully explainable."[46]

Furthermore, in analyzing in *Democracy Today and Tomorrow* the main weaknesses of prewar democracies, he concluded that in the future, democratic states would have to accept "*a certain augmentation of power and of several new functions of the state*" and that the state would have to "intervene in the future more in individual liberties than it did in classical prewar democracy." That did not mean, of course, that he wanted Czechoslovakia to follow the autocratic example of the Soviet Union, which he considered as having "*gone too far in this direction.*"[47] However, this attitude made the Soviet model seem less objectionable to him, especially in view of his firm belief in the inevitability and irreversibility of Soviet democratization.

Beneš's wartime pro-Russianism gained additional momentum when, shortly after the German invasion of the Soviet Union, the Kremlin concluded that its interests could be well served if it sponsored the idea of Slav cooperation. On Soviet initiative an All-Slav Congress, attended mostly by political exiles in the Soviet Union, convened in Moscow in April 1942, adopted a proclamation addressed to the "subjugated Slav brothers," and established an All-Slav Committee, headed by a Soviet general, Alexander Gondurov. To provide a central medium for exchanging ideas about Slav unity and cooperation, in June 1942 the committee began publishing the monthly *Slaviane* (The Slavs), run by an all-communist editorial board consisting of two Russians, one Czech, one Pole, and one Yugoslav.

Beneš saw in Soviet sponsorship of Slav cooperation a valuable political asset both for Czechoslovakia and the other Slav countries. "A new era will occur in the evolution of Slavdom after the Second World War," he predicted in his volume *Úvahy o slovanství* (Reflections on Slavdom), published in London in 1945. "It will be, I believe, an era of great realizations and substantial approximation of the ideas of Slav cooperation, mutuality, and unity such as a great many generations of Slavs had dreamed about in the past." He felt that the tendency in the West was to regard the Slavs as inferior: "Neither the Slavs as a whole nor individual Slav nations per se were valued as much as they rightfully deserved."[48] It was his firm hope that Slav cooperation, led by a powerful and influential Soviet Union, would change this view and that the Soviet Union would gain "for itself and for the other Slav nations an entirely new world status."[49] The assumption by the Soviet Union of "the traditional role that had always been conceded and ascribed to the Russian people by other Slav nations" filled him, he confessed, with "personal satisfaction."[50]

Beneš's commitment to all-Slav unity and cooperation was further reinforced during his journey to Moscow in December 1943. During our wait at the British air base at Habbanyiah in Iraq for clear weather over the Soviet Union, the president had a long conversation on the subject with the Soviet deputy foreign commissar, Alexander Korneichuk, who had been sent by Stalin to escort us. To Beneš's delight, Korneichuk told him precisely what he hoped to hear: the Soviet Union's Slav policy was genuinely democratic and was unrelated to the pan-Slavism and pan-Russianism of the tsarist era; its basic principle was the full equality of all Slav nations; and the Soviet Union, the Soviet communist party, and Stalin himself understood the Slav policy in this sense and considered it a permanent part of Soviet policy.

Beneš was pleased again when Stalin and Molotov reconfirmed these points. At the farewell banquet in the Kremlin, Stalin spoke extemporaneously on the desirability and necessity of Slav cooperation. Up to now, he said, the Germans had succeeded in dividing the Slavs, pitting one group against another. But now all Slavs must unite. Stalin then raised his glass to toast all the Slavs, even those, he stressed with an expressive twinkle in his eyes, who were still fighting alongside the Germans.

Beneš was firmly convinced that the Kremlin had committed itself to the kind of all-Slav unity he himself favored and that the Soviet commitment would benefit Czechoslovakia and the other small Slav nations. "I am certain that an era of great possibilities for the Slavs is about to come," he told us during our stay in Moscow.[51] His report to Jan Masaryk restated in no uncertain terms that Soviet Russia "will take over the leadership of the Slavonic nations and will acquire for herself and all Slavonic countries a completely new and strong position in European and world politics."[52]

Despite Beneš's elation over the advantages for Czechoslovakia from this Soviet-led all-Slav unity, he was not unaware of the potential pitfalls. His chief concern was the ability of the Kremlin to resist the temptation to utilize the idea of all-Slav cooperation to promote its own ideological and political goals. Such worries began to plague him in later 1944 when Soviet misbehavior in Czechoslovakia made him wonder for the first time whether his trust in Stalin had been misplaced. In December 1943 he could write from Moscow to Jan Masaryk that "it would be a fundamental mistake" to regard the Slav policy of the Soviet Union as "mere tactics."[53] However, in the chapter "Slavdom of the Future" in *Reflections on Slavdom*, completed late in 1944, he seemed less sure. "The question still remains," he wrote, "will not the Russian communist party and, under its influence, the Soviet Union return after the war to pure communist doctrine? And, as a result of this, will not its wartime Slav policy remain mere tactics?" The entire chapter bristles with warnings, implicit and explicit, lest the new all-Slav policy be tied to Russian and communist messianism, converted into "an instrument for inner-political objectives of one political party" and used for "the communization of the other Slav nations" or "the engulfment of smaller Slav countries in the large Soviet state system."[54]

However, the several gestures of Soviet goodwill (mentioned earlier in this chapter) during his second visit to Moscow in 1945 revived Beneš's hope that the Kremlin would avoid these errors and excesses. Beneš was particularly pleased by Stalin's rejection (at the farewell banquet) of the old pan-Slavism that sought to unify all Slavs under tsarist control and by the way he contrasted it with "Leninist neo-Slavism," which wanted all Slav nations "to retain their independence and to arrange their internal affairs according to their own ideologies and traditions."[55]

Another characteristic of Beneš's mentality and modus operandi was his habit of working alone, handling single-handedly even matters better left to others and often arriving at definitive conclusions and making decisions in the solitude of his study without consulting his collaborators. This habit was noted by all those who had frequent dealings with him.[56]

In part, this was due to the circumstances under which Beneš had to operate. In his first exile in 1915–1918 he had to rely mostly on his own judgment and act on his own since it was often impossible for him to consult Tomáš Masaryk, who was frequently on the move and beyond Beneš's reach. During the Munich crisis of 1938 the Council of Ministers virtually abdicated its responsibility, leaving Beneš no choice but to step in. "I had to assume the entire responsibility," he complained in one of his reminiscences of Munich, "because I realized that everything would have fallen apart had I left it to the cabinet. I did not want to play any role, but I simply had to do it as there was no one else who would have done it."[57] He spoke to me in the same vein on a number of occasions. Similarly, no one but Beneš could have assumed the leadership of the Czechoslovak liberation movement and the concomitant decision-making authority during the Second World War, as he was the highest-ranking Czechoslovak political exile, and possessed the greatest international stature.[58] He was the only one who had the complete confidence of the overwhelming majority of Czechs and Slovaks at home and at the same time the capacity for securing the largest possible degree of unity in the ranks of Czechoslovak émigrés. As Smutný noted in his diary: "Beneš is our luck. If he did not exist we would devour one another and perish in the power struggle among the individuals. We recognize Beneš because he stands high above us in intelligence, tenacity, and working energy."[59] Finally, at the time of the communist coup of February 1948, the leaders of Czechoslovakia's democratic parties left the hopeless task of coping with the communist onslaught to the gravely ill president.

To a large extent, however, Beneš's tendency to work alone and to rely primarily on himself stemmed from his rather low opinion of other Czech and Slovak politicians, including his own cabinet appointees. Ever tactful and considerate, he rarely directly criticized a minister or official. But afterward with Smutný, Drtina, or myself, the president often gave vent to his true feelings, though he never resorted to expletives. (The harshest terms I heard him use in referring to his ministers were bulls in a china shop and blockheads.) Not even Jan Šrámek, the venerable monsignor whom he selected to serve as his wartime prime minister, remained unscathed. "There is one good thing about Šrámek," I heard him say on several occasions, "he does little and so he cannot foul up much." Or: "When it is raining, he comes to hide under my umbrella."[60] Contrary to the assumptions of those who are fairly familiar with Czechoslovak politics of the Second World War, Beneš also had a rather low opinion of the political capabilities of his foreign minister, Jan Masaryk, the great Tomáš Masaryk's son.[61] The man whom Beneš rated highest among his wartime ministers was Hubert Ripka, whom he considered at one time as the best prospect for the post of foreign minister after our return to Czechoslovakia, though he subsequently angered and disappointed Ripka by retaining Masaryk. Yet not even Ripka could escape his share of criticism, for Beneš found him too impulsive and too ambitious. In particular, Ripka displeased the president by his initial zeal in fostering the Czechoslovak-Polish confederative project in 1941–42 and then his subsequent pro-Russianism.[62]

Beneš's low opinion of his own ministers made it only logical that he preferred to handle all important matters himself, for he believed that he could manage any political business better. This belief in his own superior political wisdom was well founded and shared by virtually all unbiased observers of his endeavors, at least during the Second World War. "Far away the most outstanding Czech figure in the world," "the only experienced and really able leader among the Czech exiles," "in courage and ability undoubtedly the outstanding Czech of today," are just a few evaluations of Beneš culled from British diplomatic papers from the Second World War.[63]

However, in such situations there is always the danger of overconfidence; and this Beneš did not quite manage to avoid. Indeed, the way events unfolded, the opposite would hardly have been human. All of Beneš predictions were gradually coming true. Instead of securing "peace in our time," the Anglo-French appeasement of Hitler led to war. Soviet Russia was drawn into the war on the side of the West and was paying a heavy penalty for its 1939–41 flirtation with the Nazis. Just as Beneš had anticipated, the United States came to the rescue of Europe. After initial difficulties, Beneš secured full diplomatic recognition for himself as president and for his government and eventually succeeded in persuading the Allies to repudiate Munich and its consequences. By 1943 it looked as though Soviet-Western cooperation, which Beneš persisted in predicting even after the signing of the Nazi-Soviet Non-aggression Pact in 1939 and for which he had worked so hard, was all but assured. "People saw in me a Russophile, almost took me for a

Bolshevik, some even for a fool when I kept telling them again and again that Russia would in the end be on England's side," he opined one day in July 1941. "Now all of a sudden . . . they are coming to see me and tell me: You were right. Eden told Masaryk that Beneš was the only statesman who saw the situation correctly."[64]

It is hardly surprising that having been right so often, Beneš became convinced that his expectations would continue to be fulfilled. Coupled with his proverbial optimism, Beneš's self-confidence reached its peak in 1943 and early 1944. It was also during this period that, somewhat to my surprise and dismay, self-serving hints about his own foresight began to slip into his conversation. "Everything came out to the very last iota just as I had anticipated," he told Smutný on September 28, 1943, when he handed him the manuscript of his book on Munich for review.[65] Similarly, in defending his behavior at the time of Munich in a heated discussion with Czech communist leaders in Moscow in December 1943, he could not resist stressing the correctness of his prescience: *"I claim the merit that I anticipated in 1938 that certain events would take place and other events would not . . . to carry out a correct policy means also to be right in anticipating events— gouverner, c'est prévoir!* And that happened in our case!"[66] In late spring 1944, he told Mackenzie that if he retired from public life after his return to his liberated homeland (and stayed out of political controversies that were bound to develop later), he would be "considered as a saint."[67]

Beneš's habit of working alone and reaching decisions on his own was hardly conducive to grooming capable collaborators (let alone a potential successor) who could have eased his burden, especially when his health began to wane. The problem was further compounded by Beneš's overall relations with people, which are difficult to describe. "Dr. Beneš' picture is a difficult one to draw," remarked Lockhart, who knew him better than any other foreigner, in reporting on Beneš to his superiors in the British Foreign Office.[68] I cannot agree more. Basically, Beneš was a loner, almost a recluse, for whom politics meant everything. Sociability, let alone conviviality, joviality, and gregariousness, was a trait he definitely did not possess; and his sense of humor was rather restrained. "He does not like other people's company," noted Smutný in his diary. "He likes to have around him people to whom he can expound politics, discuss it with them, but he does not care gathering around him people for social entertainment."[69] He was kind and considerate, but he lacked personal warmth, being rather reserved and impersonal in his contacts with people. He was, however, not a formalist and certainly was not "as stiff as a poker," as Lockhart's report referred to him.

A fairly fitting description of Beneš's personal relations (though a bit too harsh and somewhat unjust) is provided by one entry in Smutný's diary:

> Beneš is an outstanding tactician and strategist, the greatest Machiavelli of the present time, but he does not know how to capture the masses, how to generate in them pleasure in their work, the sense of unity, togetherness in struggle, suffering and joy. He does not arouse confidence. People who come to him feel instinctively that something remains unsaid, that Beneš is using them for some kind of a plan about which he won't tell them, that he may be tacitly scolding them but won't say openly. People leave him persuaded, but not truly converted, assured but not loving him . . . Collaboration with Beneš forces people often to think about how his character is lacking in everything human. It is a machine for thought and work, without human feeling, but with human weaknesses.[70]

As Lockhart rightly pointed out, Beneš was indeed "without a real friend in the world."[71] Some of his collaborators were loyal out of sheer devotion to his cause, some because they admired his fortitude, and a good many because of the rewards they hoped to derive from their association with him. But none of them could be called a friend in the proper meaning of the word, even Jan Masaryk. As the son of Tomáš Masaryk, who had chosen Beneš as his successor in the presidency, Jan was always given special attention by the Benešes, especially Madame Beneš. A special "Jenda's room" was always reserved for him, and him alone, in the president's household, and he could spend a weekend with the Benešes anytime he wished. He could even get away with some of his less lascivious jokes in the president's presence, although, as Lockhart remembers, in Beneš's presence "even the exuberance of Jan Masaryk was subdued."[72] The Beneš-Masaryk relationship was really one between a wise protector and a lighthearted protégé, rather than one between two friends. Although both men were virtually the same age and had known each other for at least a quarter of a century, Beneš always called Jan Masaryk by the diminutive "Jenda" and Masaryk invariably addressed Beneš as "Mr. President," even when he was a weekend guest in Beneš's private residence.

Another aspect of Beneš's relations with people was his reluctance to support his collaborators and protect them if political expediency demanded that they be dropped. It was not that he was indifferent to their fate. He would defend them or at least try to secure them another position and even possibly reward them financially. But once he reached the conclusion that political pressure was too strong and further resistance on his part might be injurious to his cause, he gave in. "I cannot permit that people who were with me should suffer because of me," he once told Smutný. But he also made it clear that he might not be able to retain Smutný as chief of the President's Office after the war against strong political pressure to the contrary.[73]

No problem developed in Smutný's case, and he could cling to the position he coveted so much. Such was not the case, however, of two other top-level wartime collaborators, the minister of defense, Gen. Sergei Ingr, and the chief of the intelligence service, Gen. František Moravec. Since the communists heartily disliked the two generals, they were forced into premature retirement. Beneš, as was his custom in such situations, wrote to Fierlinger (who had meanwhile been made premier by the communists) highly praising the two men for their valuable work in the liberation movement and asking for "a just and reasonable solution."[74] Yet the tenor of the letter made it obvious that the president was already resigned to the communist vendetta against two of his foremost collaborators.

Even worse was the treatment encountered by Prokop Drtina, one of Beneš's closest associates throughout the Munich era and his exile in Britain and subsequently the postwar minister of justice. After having been forcibly ejected from his ministry during the communist putsch in February 1948, Drtina went to see the president, hoping to get some explanation why Beneš broke his promise not to accept Drtina's and the other democratic ministers' resignations and to consult with Beneš about his future. (Drtina was on leave from his previous position as Beneš's political secretary.) But he was turned away. He then attempted to commit suicide by jumping out of a window to protest, as Drtina wrote in his unpublished memoirs, "against Beneš's capitulation by sacrificing his own life when there was no other way to let the nation know about his attitude."[75] Although one cannot be sure, the shock caused by the president's failure to receive Drtina was probably a major factor in triggering his suicide attempt.[76]

On the other hand, political pressure, or the fear of such pressure, sometimes induced Beneš to appoint or retain people in positions where they did more harm than good to his cause. The worst example was Zdeněk Fierlinger, whom Beneš appointed as Czechoslovakia's envoy to Moscow in summer 1941 after the Soviet Union re-established diplomatic relations with the Czechoslovak government following the Nazi invasion of the Soviet Union. Although at the time no one knew that

Fierlinger was a crypto-communist, Beneš was aware of his pro-Soviet bias, which ordinarily would have precluded his appointment to that post. However, Beneš thought that by reappointing Czechoslovakia's prewar envoy to the Soviet Union, he would underline and strengthen the concept of the legal and political continuity of the pre-Munich republic and his own presidency, a concept that he considered important politically. Moreover, he also wanted to please the Soviet regime by having his country represented by someone of undoubted sympathy toward the Soviet Union.

Fierlinger soon began behaving as if he represented the Soviet Union's rather than Czechoslovakia's interests, fawning on Stalin as well as on Klement Gottwald, the main leader of the Czechoslovak communists, who had found refuge in Moscow after the collapse of Czechoslovakia in 1938–39. Because of this, Beneš became very angry with Fierlinger. "I cannot believe that someone can be such a blockhead," he complained bitterly in October 1943 after reading one of Fierlinger's telegrams urging him to disregard British objections and come to Moscow to sign the Czechoslovak-Soviet Treaty of Friendship, Mutual Assistance, and Postwar Cooperation.[77] In January 1945, after Fierlinger insisted that Beneš withdraw recognition from the Polish government in London and immediately recognize the communist-controlled Lublin government, he commented: "As soon as they [the Russians] whistle, Fierlinger would want me to dance at once without regard for what would happen here [in England]."[78]

Yet, Beneš refused the unanimous request of his cabinet to recall Fierlinger, fearing that both the Soviet regime and the Czechoslovak communists might interpret that step as an anti-Soviet gesture and cause him trouble. I thought then, and I still think today, that recalling the man and replacing him with someone willing to defy the Soviet regime when necessary to defend Czechoslovakia's interests would have been infinitely better. The Soviet Union replaced its ambassador to Czechoslovakia twice between 1941 and 1945 and thus could hardly have objected to a change in Czechoslovakia's representation in Moscow. Moreover, Beneš had available a tactful as well as a tactical way of doing it: giving Fierlinger a cabinet post, such as that of minister of economic planning—Fierlinger had always imagined himself an accomplished economist.[79]

Beneš's monopoly over decision making and his ability to make his views prevail began to ebb in late 1944 when the Soviet-backed leaders of Czechoslovakia's communist party initiated the power play that eventually installed Gottwald in Hradčany Castle. These were already all but nonexistent during the fateful negotiations for a new Czechoslovak government held in Moscow in March 1945; and they disappeared completely after the president's return to liberated Czechoslovakia in April 1945.

The primary reasons for Beneš's precipitous political emasculation lay in factors beyond his control, such as the overwhelming Soviet support for local communists, the absence of any meaningful Western counter-measures, and the lack of civic courage on the part of the demoralized masses. But Beneš's failure to provide the leadership that the situation demanded also contributed to the result. At the time all of us close to him believed that he should have been even more forceful in the immediate postwar era than he had been in prewar days. I personally felt that for a while he should have acted more authoritatively, capitalizing on his tremendous prestige with the Czechoslovak people and their absolute, almost mystical trust in him. "What we will need in those chaotic days, Mr. President," I told him in one of our many discussions on this topic, "is not a head of state who will stay above the parties, a sort of umpire over the interparty game, but a strong man who will nip communist trickery in the bud." "Yes, you are right," he answered. "This time I shall have to use all my authority and start stepping on communist toes. People will be demoralized, and I am afraid that there will be no strong democratic leaders. I shall have to take a much more active part in government than in normal times."[80]

But he chose to stay out of the 1945 Moscow negotiations about the formation of the new Czechoslovak government, leaving the democratic parties to grapple with the communists on their own. Although the tremendous ovations that he received on his return demonstrated that the populace revered him more than ever, Beneš neglected to exploit this invaluable political asset to underpin his sagging power base. Rather, he reverted to his old habit of negotiating, arguing, and compromising, techniques well suited to a functioning democracy, but inadequate for coping with the disciples of Marxism-Leninism, ever ready to promote the dictatorship of the proletariat by any available means. Instead of taking resolute action against the communist leaders' worst abuses of power, he preferred to plead, warn, and admonish patiently, biding his time and hoping that, somehow, the slow pressure of public opinion would induce the communists to mend their ways. He persisted in this behavior, remaining above the parties and seemingly striving for a solution by parliamentary means, even during the February 1948 crisis when he surely must have become fully aware that these means were irrelevant. While the communists were seizing the headquarters of the noncommunist parties and setting up communist-controlled "action committees" in all government agencies, the president told Ripka (on February 23, 1948): "It is up to you to defend yourselves. As far as I am concerned, I must remain above the conflict (*au-dessus de la mêlée*), above the parties."[81]

Pointing to Beneš's capitulation to Hitler in 1938 and his surrender to the communists in 1948, some critics contend that he was not a fighter. Although he was an assiduous debater and a tough negotiator who did not take no for an answer and sought to wear down his adversaries by bombarding them with memoradums, his critics maintain that he never took a final, irrevocable stand. There is a good deal of truth in this criticism. Both in 1938 and 1948, it was up to him to make the final decision to give up or to fight—that is, to wage a defensive war against Nazi Germany in 1938 and to call on the army and civilian groups loyal to him to prevent or to suppress the communist coup in 1948. In both instances he in fact began by insisting that he would resist with all available means; yet in both cases, for reasons explained later in this volume, he eventually changed his mind and surrendered. In June 1947, in the very last conversation I had with him, he told me that, should the communists attempt to seize power by violence, he was determined to fight them to the bitter end and that he would call on the Sokols (a patriotic gymnastic organization), the Legionnaires (the Czechs and Slovaks who had fought on the Allied side in WWI), and even the army if necessary. "The communists think that I would try to avoid an open clash with them at any cost," the president continued with a smile. "I know what they are saying: 'If you succeed in pushing Beneš into a tight corner and if you keep pressing him hard enough, he will yield in the end.' But they are wrong. I wish to avoid trouble, that's right, but my patience and my willingness to make deals with them have their limits. I shall make no compromise that would destroy democracy in this country. The communists could seize power only over my dead body." I also know that in the months preceding the communist putsch he talked to a number of people in the same spirit of defiance and resolve.[82] As late as February 23, 1948, he remarked: "I would rather die than yield to terror and betray Masaryk's ideals."[83] Yet, when the communists managed to push him into that tight corner, Beneš did yield. Despite his repeated assurances that they would win only over his dead body, he capitulated to their demands after five days of desperate opposition and signed the death warrant of Czechoslovak democracy.

Finally, no study of Beneš's mentality and behavior in the 1938–1948 decade would be complete without mentioning his "Munich complex." It is not surprising that the tragedy that befell his country and him personally in September and October 1938 was bound to affect him very deeply. He was betrayed and abandoned by France, the country he most cherished, a country that was committed by treaty to come unreservedly and unconditionally to Czechoslovakia's aid. His country and he personally were sacrificed by France and Great Britain in a futile attempt to satisfy the insatiable greed of Czechoslovakia's worst enemy. This feeling of betrayal was to color his relations with the Western democracies throughout the war years, and the opinions he developed at the time of Munich affected his subsequent actions and policies.

2

Munich and the Western Powers

Beneš's calvary began with the September 1938 crisis, its tragic consummation in the Munich diktat, and the ensuing liquidation of post-Munich Czechoslovakia in March 1939. There is, of course, no dearth of literature about that ugly period of world history, which facilitated the communization of Eastern Europe and much of Asia and so profoundly affected the world order. Many historians, writers, and students of international politics have published monographs and scholarly articles devoted to Munich and its aftermath. Munich figures prominently in books on twentieth-century history. Most political and diplomatic protagonists of the Munich tragedy have written memoirs or accounts, and the governments involved have issued collections of important papers and documents and, with the exceptions of the Soviet Union and communist Czechoslovakia, opened their official archives of the Munich era to scholarly research.

For a long time, however, the chief dramatis persona, Edvard Beneš, remained silent. After leaving Czechoslovakia for exile in London in October 1938, Beneš declined several lucrative offers to publish his memoirs about Munich, partly because he did not want to create any problems for his successor or impede the effort to reach a bearable modus vivendi with Nazi Germany. He did not want to give Hitler any pretext for treating post-Munich Czechoslovakia more harshly than he did.[1] But mainly, he thought that any public recriminations would be politically imprudent and counterproductive. Hence, he continued to refrain from any public criticism of Britain and France, even after Hitler's liquidation of the Czechoslovak rump in March 1939 exposed the futility of Anglo-French appeasement. He also urged his collaborators to do likewise. "No attacks on England and France because of Munich," he cautioned in a letter to Hubert Ripka from Chicago (where he served as a visiting professor at the University of Chicago) on March 21, 1939. "I myself did not say one word publicly, and I will not . . . Let us maintain a dignified silence about it, let us not inadvertently offend even those who know and see what has happened and who are the opponents of the regimes in those countries [referring to critics, such as Churchill and Eden, of appeasement], but who could not even themselves tolerate attacks on their countries and nations."[2]

However, as early as December 1940, Beneš began preparing a report on Munich.[3] He completed the first draft in September 1943 and asked a few of his collaborators, including myself, for their reactions and comments.[4] Beneš intended to deliver the report to Czechoslovakia's National Assembly after his return to liberated Czechoslovakia. But when he finally had an opportunity to address the assembly, in a solemn session held on October 28, 1945, commemorating the twenty-seventh anniversary of Czechoslovakia's birth, he allowed the occasion to slip by, "primarily because of considerations of an international nature," he told the assembly, for he "would not be able even today to say all that ought to be said so that all the events could be fully and correctly clarified." He promised, however, that as soon as the situation permitted, he would "tell the full truth and all the truth" about it "as he had seen it and as he had lived through it."[5] He reiterated this promise in his *Memoirs*, which covered his activities during the war but deliberately omitted the Munich period.[6]

Beneš himself never fulfilled this promise, for the suitable situation never materialized. In his literary legacy, he left four versions of the report, but none was in a completely finished form, ready for publication.[7] The second version of the manuscript was published in mimeographed form by the Institute of Dr. Edvard Beneš in London in 1955 and reprinted in 1958. When the fall of Antonín Novotný and the advent of Dubček's Czechoslovak Spring in 1968 enabled more liberal-minded historians to gain temporary control of the Czechoslovak Committee for the History of the Antifascist Struggle and the Institute for the History of Socialism, Beneš's Munich report was published in Czechoslovakia.

With the posthumous publication of Beneš's authoritative *Mnichovské Dny* (The days of Munich), the public record on Munich is virtually complete. Each side has had its say. The roles of all participants, both major and minor, have been adequately revealed and explained, defended, praised, excused, or condemned. The sequence of events and their consequences have been determined, and their relative importance evaluated.[8] Hence, there is no need to retell the story of Munich in its entirety here. What must be done, however, is to assess the effects of the Munich trauma as a whole and the roles played by France, Britain, the United States, and the Soviet Union on Beneš's actions and policies vis-à-vis the East and the West in the fateful years of 1938–1948.

The important aspects of Franco-British behavior throughout the Munich crisis are well known. Despite the self-serving endeavors of a few apologists, the Anglo-French record has been set straight in a multitude of unbiased works by distinterested historians and political scientists with no prescribed ideological dicta to follow. Their virtually unanimous verdict is devastating. France has been found guilty of flagrantly violating its treaty obligation to aid Czechoslovakia, and Great Britain of encouraging and abetting France. Less than six months after Munich, both countries once again failed to honor their pledges, this time to guarantee the post-Munich boundaries of Czechoslovakia, when Hitler administered the coup de grace to the then utterly defenseless country. In both instances they ignored not only their commitment to Czechoslovakia but also their solemn undertaking under the Covenant of the League of Nations to "respect and preserve against external aggression the territorial integrity and existing political independence" of members of the League. Unable or unwilling to grasp Hitler's megalomania and disregarding their own national interests, they connived to use a small, pro-Western country as ransom to buy off an international extortionist.

Adding insult to injury, the French Foreign Ministry subsequently began spreading the calumny that Beneš and his government had requested the Anglo-French ultimatum to justify their capitulation to the Czechoslovak people.[9] They further asserted that Beneš himself suggested that the crisis be resolved by ceding the Sudetenland to Germany.[10]

Hitler's liquidation of the post-Munich remainder of Czechoslovakia and the incorporation of the Czech lands into the German Reich as a protectorate could only intensify Beneš's Munich trauma. In submitting to the Munich diktat, he had no reason to suppose that within six months Hitler's Reich's Protector would sit in Prague. Indeed, there was every reason to believe that after gaining a tremendous victory at Munich on the pretense that all he wanted was to unify the Germans in one Reich and not to acquire any Czechs, Hitler would not explode a myth that could still serve him well in the case of Poland. With the strict Cartesian logic that dominated Beneš's thinking, he assumed that Hitler would ignore the crippled torso of Czechoslovakia and turn to the next victim. Beneš hoped that post-Munich Czechoslovakia would thus be able to cling to its imposed neutrality until war erupted between Germany and the West and gave Czechoslovakia a second chance.

One factor in Beneš's assumption was the Anglo-French guarantee of Czechoslovakia's post-Munich frontiers. Despite his bitter experience with France and Britain in September 1938, Beneš did not consider the Anglo-French guarantee altogether valueless. Of course, he did not believe that those who had refused to fight in September and October 1938 would do so should the Führer send his Wehrmacht to seize the rest of the country. But he thought that Hitler would hesitate to flaunt his contempt for the Western cosigners of the Munich agreement so soon and so blatantly. "Even I who had been through Munich did not suppose," he confided to Mackenzie, "that the guarantee given to Czechoslovakia by the Western Powers was morally worthless; even I thought that Germany in her necessity would retain the pretence of respecting that guarantee."[11] (Beneš was unaware, of course, of the whole grim truth about Chamberlain's peculiar and downright dishonest interpretation of the "guarantee," which the published minutes of British cabinet sessions have subsequently revealed.)[12]

Hitler's unexpected action exploded overnight a major assumption of Beneš's Munich surrender. The very existence of his people, which he had paid such a high price to preserve, was now in mortal danger. "What will happen if Hitler delays his next blow against Poland, and we have to wait several more years for a war against Germany?" he asked himself. "Will our people survive that hell? Will they remain firm in their resistance and morally untouched?"[13]

Nor were Beneš's worries alleviated by what he found in post-Munich England and France or his treatment by the politicians and bureaucrats of those countries during his political exile in England between October 1938 and January 1939 and again after his return to London in July 1939 following the completion of his professorial assignment at the

University of Chicago. The British and French publics, convinced that their governments' wisdom had saved them from war and secured "peace in our time," seemed to support wholeheartedly their leaders' appeasement policies. So did their elected representatives, who gave resounding votes of confidence to the respective premiers and cabinets in the British House of Commons and the French Chamber of Deputies. Neville Chamberlain and Edouard Daladier became instant saviors and heroes. "No conqueror returning from a victory on the battlefield had come adorned with nobler laurels," declared the *London Times* on Chamberlain's triumphant return from Munich.[14] In France subscriptions were started to give country homes and works of art to Daladier, Bonnet, Chamberlain, and Halifax, and *Le Petit Parisien* promptly collected over one million signatures for a book in gold in which the names of grateful Frenchmen were to be inscribed.[15] In an endeavor to strengthen the appeasement policy with economic underpinnings, Britain attempted in the months following Munich to broaden trade and economic relations with Nazi Germany and even expressed a willingness to grant credits for that purpose.[16] The brief interval separating the Munich diktat of September 30, 1938, from the Ides of March, 1939, was a moment of euphoric smugness. In the words of Wheeler-Bennett in his classic *Munich: Prologue to Tragedy*, it was "the 'Golden Age' of appeasement" in which "Mr. Chamberlain and his intimate advisors" (and, one must add, their French colleagues) "pursued the path of appeasement with unruffled complacency, perverse intransigence, and complete disregard of every warning of disaster."[17]

Hitler's unexpected liquidation of the post-Munich rump of Czechoslovakia on March 15, 1939, shocked Chamberlain and his English and French associates just as much as it shocked Beneš, though for very different reasons. Having persuaded themselves and the vast majority of their people that Hitler could be trusted when he said he wanted only the German-inhabited areas, they now found themselves publicly humiliated for allowing themselves to be deceived by Hitler's duplicity. Chamberlain, who truly believed that he had preserved peace by acquiescing in Czechoslovakia's mutilation, admitted that Hitler's action had "shattered the confidence which was just about beginning to show its head" and cautioned that Great Britain would resist "to the uttermost of its power" a challenge (meaning Hitler's) to its liberty.[18]

Responding to an upsurge of public indignation at Hitler's perfidy, the French and British governments lodged formal protests with the German government on March 18, 1939, denouncing the German action as a flagrant violation of the Munich agreement and refusing to recognize its legality. Furthermore, anxious to serve public notice on Nazi Germany that Britain would not tolerate any more unilateral faits accomplis, the British government took the unprecedented step of committing Britain to aid Poland, Romania, and Greece should they become victims of German aggression.

This promising departure from the Anglo-French prostration of the Munich era pleased Beneš. The British and French refusal to recognize the validity of Hitler's destruction of Czechoslovakia, coupled with parallel protests from the United States and the Soviet Union, provided the legal and political bases for Beneš's subsequent struggle to nullify the Munich agreement and restore pre-Munich Czechoslovakia.

Unfortunately, it soon became apparent that the British and French protests did not imply the abandonment of appeasement. The Munich agreement had been flagrantly violated by its German cosigner and beneficiary and was apparently dead, but the spirit of Munich remained very much alive. Less than two weeks after Hitler's takeover of post-Munich Czechoslovakia, Chamberlain's government chose to look the other way when the Bank of England handed over to the German Reichsbank 23,000 kilograms of gold bullion deposited for safekeeping in the Bank of England for the Czechoslovak National Bank by the Bank of International Settlements.[19] The post-Munich endeavors to strengthen Anglo-German economic ties, interrupted by the Ides of March, began gathering momentum again. When Helmuth Wohltat, a high-ranking German official reportedly close to Göring, came to London in July 1939 to attend a meeting of the International Whaling Commission, Robert Hudson, the secretary of the British Department of Overseas Trade, sought to interest him in British proposals for expanded Anglo-German cooperation in world trade.[20] There were also persistent rumors in connection with Wohltat's visit that Britain was willing to offer Germany a large loan to enable it to convert its economy from a wartime to a peacetime basis.

Furthermore, by June 1939 it looked as though the British and French governments were about to recognize the validity of Hitler's action of March 15, 1939. Faced with the German decision that exequaturs granted foreign consuls by the Czechoslovak government would not be honored after May 25, 1939, both Britain and France applied to Berlin for new exequaturs for their consuls in Prague. As Chamberlain and British Under-Secretary of State Richard Butler conceded in a heated debate in Parliament in June 1939, the action implied de facto recognition of the new status of Bohemia-Moravia as part of the German Reich. De facto recognition was also conferred on the German-controlled puppet state of Slovakia, which complied with the British request to issue an exequatur for the British consul at Bratislava and was granted in return an exequator for the Slovak consul in London.[21]

Beneš was dismayed by these unexpected developments, for de facto recognition often precedes recognition de jure.[22] Indeed, information was leaked to us that Chamberlain was considering closing the Czechoslovak legation in London. That prospect, coming in the wake of a report that Wohltat had linked the granting of the exequatur with such a closing, prompted Beneš to write a personal letter to the British foreign secretary, Lord Halifax, which I delivered to Halifax's residence at Eaton Square.[23] Halifax's evasive reply confirmed Beneš's apprehensions. (When the British Foreign Office subsequently opened its files to researchers, it became clear that only the outbreak of war had saved the Czechoslovak legation. "We had intended to liquidate it in the autumn," reads an internal note of Sir Orme Sargent, dated September 4, 1939.)[24] Beneš would have been even more alarmed had he known in 1939, as we know now from subsequently published British and German documents, how close Chamberlain was to another Munich-type deal, this time at the expense of Poland, a deal thwarted only by Hitler's arrogance and his conviction that the men he had met in Munich were "not the kind that would start a new world war."[25]

Beneš's presence could not but embarrass the British and French Munichites, with appeasement dominating their thinking and shaping their actions. Here was the foremost victim of their deal with Hitler, a living reminder of their guilt and their political myopia; a man who had told them in 1938 that the question was much greater than the fate of the Sudeten Germans; a man whose warning had been proven right less than six months later; a man who had cautioned that concessions to Hitler would only whet his appetite for more and would eventually lead to war. Such a man was bound to be thought a stumbling block on the path of appeasement. Any public activity on his part was highly undesirable, even if he avoided criticism of British and French policies.

When Beneš was granted permission to reside in Britain, the British Foreign Office made it amply clear that it did not want him to engage in any public activity.[26] Writing on Beneš's behalf, Jan Masaryk thought it necessary to assure the British government on October 28, 1938, that "he will live here as an absolutely private individual, make no public or political contacts, grant no interviews and in no way make difficulties for

HM's or Czechoslovak Governments."[27] On his return to England from America in July 1939, the Foreign Office promptly cautioned Beneš "not to abuse British hospitality" and to refrain from political activity.[28]

One can thus well appreciate what it meant for Beneš when a group of some forty prominent Britons, headed by Winston Churchill and Anthony Eden and representing the anti-Munich segment of the British political elite, demonstrated their appreciation by giving a private luncheon in Beneš's honor on July 27, 1939. In a series of short but emotional addresses, speaker after speaker commended Beneš for his self-abnegation, courage, and foresight, attacked Chamberlain's appeasement policy, and pledged to do everything in their power to restore a free, democratic Czechoslovakia. Typical of the tenor and the atmosphere of that memorable afternoon was Churchill's opening speech, which he concluded, his eyes filled with tears, with the promise: "I do not know how matters will now develop and I cannot say that Great Britain will go to war for Czechoslovakia. But I am quite certain that the peace which will be created will not be made without Czechoslovakia. I promise that as long as I live I will work to redeem the terrible sin committed against your country."

I still remember vividly the president's and Madame Beneš's exultation when they returned to their Putney home after the luncheon. As was his habit, Beneš immediately wrote a full account of the proceedings.[29] His elation is all the more comprehensible because of his firm conviction, even at that early stage, that Churchill would eventually become prime minister and Eden foreign secretary.

Although Beneš by no means believed that the outbreak of war would sweep "the guilty men of Munich" from their high offices, he did expect that his position and that of the Czechoslovak liberation movement in the West would improve. He thought that with no further need to accommodate Hitler, the British and French would want his cooperation, would welcome the creation of a Czechoslovak army in exile, and would even recognize a Czechoslovak government in exile. In April 1939, while in the United States, Beneš sent Roosevelt (through Hamilton Fish Armstrong, the editor of *Foreign Affairs*) a seven-page memorandum in which he wrote: "Upon the outbreak of war in Europe a new Czechoslovak Government will at once resume its normal functioning in so far as possible outside the territory of the Republic. It will place troops on the fighting front, will conduct propaganda behind the front, and will work in every way possible to defeat Germany and recover its homeland." And he gave vent to his conviction that "political and military exigencies will encourage France and Great Britain" to give their approval.[30]

Beneš's expectations, however, were too optimistic. To be sure, his offer to organize a Czechoslovak army to fight alongside the French and the British was accepted, and the earlier British objections to public activity on Beneš's part were lifted. As revealed in subsequently released British documents, the British Foreign Office, even before the war, had decided to "use" and "back" Beneš in the event of war. On August 23, 1939, one official advocated "some form of cooperation with the Czechs in time of war," for he thought that "the Czechs would probably, if encouraged, do as much or more to embarrass Germans as Abyssinians could do to embarrass Italy."[31] But Beneš's endeavors to obtain British and French recognition of a Czechoslovak government in exile were strongly rebuffed. After protracted negotiations, in November and December 1939, the French and British governments agreed to recognize only a Czechoslovak National Committee "qualified to represent the Czechoslovak peoples" (rather than Czechoslovakia as a state) and to manage the "reconstitution of the Czechoslovak Army.[32] Besides his unhappiness over the Anglo-French refusal to recognize his team as a government, Beneš was displeased with the narrow definition of the committee's function. But the British Foreign Office ignored his request to include at least a phrase acknowledging that the objective of the committee was "to carry on the struggle for the liberation of the Czechoslovak Republic."[33] So disappointed was Beneš with the meager results of his endeavors that he wondered whether it would not be better to keep secret the precise wording of the recognition.[34]

The French even urged Beneš's elimination from any role in the Czechoslovak liberation movement. Daladier told the Czechoslovak envoy to France, Štefan Osuský, on October 2, 1939 (on the occasion of the signing of the Franco-Czechoslovak agreement providing for the formation of the Czechoslovak army in France), that if Beneš were involved, "all that was done would crumble within a fortnight." Even more incredible, Daladier suggested that "a statesman who had committed so many mistakes" as Beneš ought to retire into private life. Referring to his own endeavors to separate Italy from the Nazi-fascist axis, the French premier suggested that Beneš's participation would cause difficulties for French diplomacy since "Mussolini would resist everything bearing Beneš's name."[35] Daladier clearly wanted nothing to do with Beneš; he did not even bother to reply to Beneš's telegram pledging Czechoslovak cooperation when France declared war on Nazi

Germany on September 3, 1939.[36] Moreover, he refused to receive Beneš when the latter came to Paris in October 1939 to take part in the negotiations about French recognition.

Beneš had to wait until Daladier's resignation in March 1940 and Chamberlain's in May 1940 before making any headway in his efforts to obtain recognition as a government for the National Committee. Even then, the British recognition of July 21, 1940, was marred by three serious flaws.[37] First, the British letter of recognition spoke only of a *provisional* Czechoslovak government. The meaning of this qualifying epithet (rarely used in diplomatic practice) was by no means clear. But it implied temporariness, transiency, and revocability and was clearly not the same as full-fledged recognition.[38] Both theoretically and practically, it relegated the Czechoslovak government to a status inferior to that of other exiled governments, such as those of Poland, Norway, Belgium, and the Netherlands, which had also found refuge in England.[39] This status was also reflected in the British failure to appoint a regular diplomatic agent, either an envoy extraordinary and minister pleni-potentiary or a chargé d'affaires, to maintain liaison with the newly recognized government. Instead the British chose to continue using Robert B. Lockhart, whose vague title was "British representative."

Second, the British government informed Beneš that its recognition of the provisional government did not imply British recognition of or support for any future boundaries in Central Europe.[40] This meant that Great Britain still wished to retain discretion over the disposition of Czechoslovak territories seized by Germany, Poland, and Hungary as a result of Munich and its aftermath.

Third, the British took exception to Beneš's cherished thesis of legal continuity. Holding that all that had happened in and concerning Czechoslovakia since September 19, 1938 (the date of the Anglo-French proposals that Czechoslovakia cede the Sudeten areas to Nazi Germany), had been imposed by "threats, terror, and violence" and was therefore illegal and unconstitutional, Beneš took the position that pre-Munich Czechoslovakia had never ceased to exist legally and that he, having been forced from office by Hitler's threats, had never legally ceased to be president.[41] Wishing to record his stand in an important official document, he included a reference to his thesis in a letter of July 9, 1940, to the British secretary of state for foreign affairs, in which he requested British recognition of his new government. In thanking the British government for its refusal to acknowledge the validity of Hitler's takeover and for its continued recognition, even after March 15, 1939, of the Czechoslovak legation, he expressed the opinion that the British government had emphasized thereby "the political and legal continuity of the Czechoslovak Republic."[42] Moreover, in listing the officeholders in his new government, he described himself as the "second" rather than the "former" president of the Czechoslovak republic.[43] Although not rejecting Beneš's contention outright, the British government made it clear that its protest against the German military action in Czechoslovakia in March 1939 should not be understood as an adoption of any definitive stand on the legal continuity of the Czechoslovak republic.[44]

It took another year of pleading, arguing, and imploring before Beneš managed to persuade the British to discard the disparaging epithet of provisionality, grant him and his government full de jure recognition with a status equal to that of other exiled governments, and replace the British representative with a duly accredited envoy extraordinary and minister plenipotentiary.[45] It would have taken even longer had it not been for Winston Churchill. On April 20, 1941, Churchill and his wife paid an official visit to the Czechoslovak armed forces in Britain. In farewell, the Czechoslovak soldiers sang "Rule Britannia." Hearing these men, who were ready to fight and die for Britain, singing to the glory of the country that had abandoned them to the Nazis in 1938 and 1939, deeply moved the British prime minister and brought tears to his eyes. Beneš, frustrated by the incessant procrastination of the British Foreign Office over full recognition, handed over to Churchill a brief memo asking him to expedite the matter.[46] As Lockhart told us a few days later, Churchill passed the memo on to Eden with a handwritten comment wondering why the Czechs could not be granted the same status as the other allies. "It had a tremendous impact," Lockhart reported when he saw the president on April 23, 1941, "and the Foreign Office was ordered to set things straight."[47] Nonetheless, it took another three months before full recognition was finally conceded on July 18, 1941. By some four hours, this delay permitted the Soviet Union to become the first power to extend full de jure recognition to Beneš's government, despite Beneš's repeated warnings to Lockhart that it would be detrimental to British interests should the Soviets recognize the Czechoslovak government first.[48]

Although removing the objectionable "provisional" label, the British adamantly refused to adopt Beneš's thesis of juridical continuity or to recognize Czechoslovakia's pre-Munich boundaries. On these two matters, so crucial to Beneš's all-out effort to erase Munich and its aftermath, Eden's note of July 18, 1941, simply restated the evasive neither-nor position taken by Halifax in his letter of July 18, 1940.[49] Since Beneš did not expect any change in Britain's policy in that respect, the refusal did not bother him too much. Moreover, his concern on that account was overshadowed by the simultaneous conclusion of the Soviet-Czechoslovak agreement on cooperation. That agreement established full-fledged diplomatic relations, which implied, as Beneš understood it and as it was subsequently interpreted by the Soviet government, not only full de jure recognition of his government in exile but also recognition of the pre-Munich boundaries of Czechoslovakia.[50] Molotov confirmed this in talks with Beneš on June 9, 1942.[51]

Beneš's anger was directed at the last paragraph of Eden's letter in which the British government exempted, at least for the time being, "certain categories of former Czechoslovak nationals" from the Czechoslovak government's jurisdiction.[52] Those former Czechoslovak nationals were the Sudeten Germans, and the jurisdiction that was denied was the right to draft them into the Czechoslovak army in Britain. Beneš saw this as another attempt to meddle in a strictly internal Czechoslovak concern. Moreover, neither side had mentioned the question during the protracted negotiations preceding full recognition. Beneš immediately suspected that one of Eden's Foreign Office subordinates known for his pro-Sudeten German sympathies had smuggled the obnoxious paragraph into the letter.[53] Visibly annoyed, the president told Lockhart, who, together with Jan Masaryk, had brought him Eden's letter, that he could not accept this and that it must be corrected. Indeed, a few days later Eden apologized for the incident, and the original letter was replaced with a new one that omitted the contested paragraph.[54] It was typical of Jan Masaryk, to whom Eden's letter was actually addressed and delivered, not to suspect that something might not be in order. When Beneš asked Masaryk about it, his excuse was that Eden had handed him the letter at 3:55 P.M. and that he had had time only to thank him.[55] The president's annoyance increased further when the British censor deleted a passage in which Beneš said that the areas lost at and after Munich would be returned from the radio address in which the president reported the British de jure recognition to his countrymen in Czechoslovakia.[56]

Although Beneš was not overly concerned when the British act of de jure recognition failed to recognize Czechoslovakia's pre-Munich boundaries or accept Beneš's thesis of juridical continuity, he did not give up. Within a few months, he was at it once again, as energetically as ever.

Beneš launched the new offensive in earnest in December 1941, following America's entry into the war, when he sent a note to all Allied governments clarifying in no uncertain terms not only the refusal of the Czechoslovak government to recognize the validity of any territorial changes imposed on Czechoslovakia since the September 1938 crisis but also its claim of the uninterrupted juridical continuity of pre-Munich Czechoslovakia.[57] Between January and July 1942, a long series of meetings with Eden and Nichols, the British envoy to the Czechoslovak government in exile, was devoted, either wholly or predominantly, to the twin issues of juridical continuity and pre-Munich boundaries.[58] In his *Memoirs*, Beneš described these sessions as "sometimes very lively and tough."[59] That is an understatement, especially with regard to his talks with Nichols, who repeatedly had to withstand the brunt of the president's unceasing verbal barrage chastising the British for their short-sightedness, reminding them of their heavy share of responsibility for Munich and its aftermath, warning them of the undesirable political consequences of their stubborn refusal to set things right, and cautioning them that it was in Britain's interest to resolve these matters before he undertook his trip to Russia, which might, he suggested, occur as early as the summer of 1942.[60] Nichols often emerged flushed and chastened from the president's study after these heated and rather one-sided altercations.[61]

When, at a luncheon with Eden on January 21, 1942, Beneš began his final assault on Munich, the prospects of a breakthrough seemed brighter. Anxious to document as graphically as he could the nonsensical mutilation of Czechoslovakia perpetrated at Munich, Beneš handed Eden a map of Czechoslovakia showing its post-Munich boundaries. Eden passed it to Nichols with the remark: "Look at that criminal absurdity!"[62] As Beneš soon realized, his optimism, prompted by Eden's apparently positive response to Beneš's arguments, proved premature. To expedite the agreement, Beneš decided to set aside the issue of juridical continuity and to concentrate on the boundary question. Eden's response was to bring a new formula to another luncheon meeting on June 25, 1942. But when the president told him that the Soviet Union had already recognized Czechoslovakia's pre-Munich boundaries, Eden pocketed his formula, saying that it would obviously fail to satisfy Beneš, and promised to devise a new one. The new formula, which he produced at another session with Beneš on July 7, 1942, stated that "as Germany has deliberately destroyed the arrangements concerning Czechoslovakia reached in 1938, in which His Majesty's Government in the

United Kingdom participated, His Majesty's Government regard themselves as free from any engagements in this respect"; and that "at the final settlement of the Czechoslovak frontiers to be reached at the end of the war, His Majesty's Government will not be influenced by any changes effected in and since 1938."[63]

Not even this final formula gave the president what he wanted; namely, unconditional recognition of Czechoslovakia's boundaries as they existed before Munich and a declaration that the Munich agreement was invalid *ab initio*. But he accepted it because he concluded that it was the best he could get. At least he had obtained an official British proclamation of nonrecognition of any and all territorial changes to the detriment of Czechoslovakia as a result of Munich and its aftermath.

Having settled, as best he could, the Munich issue with Britain, Beneš quickly moved on to France. On August 6, 1942, just one day after Eden had informed the House of Commons and the British public about Britain's rejection of Munich, Beneš suggested to Maurice Dejean, the commissioner for foreign affairs in General de Gaulle's French National Committee, that France should repudiate Munich and start a new chapter in Franco-Czechoslovak relations. Since there were no "Munichois" in de Gaulle's committee, Beneš expected that he would encounter no problems like those with the British and that the matter would be resolved speedily and satisfactorily. His expectations turned out to be correct; and the French repudiation of Munich was embodied in an exchange of letters between General de Gaulle and the Czechoslovak premier, Jan Šrámek, on September 29, 1942, the fourth anniversary of the signing of the Munich agreement.[64]

The Franco-Czechoslovak negotiations, however, were not entirely trouble free. The first formula proposed by the French was rather vague and fell far short of what Beneš envisioned.[65] Beneš felt compelled to reject it, and it took some additional prodding by Beneš and Ripka to make the French deliver an acceptable text.

Beneš found the final version of the French statement highly satisfactory, for it complied with all of his desiderata. Unlike the British repudiation, the French letter solemnly proclaimed that the Munich agreement, as well as all its consequences, had been invalid from the very beginning (*nuls et non-avenus*). It refused to recognize any territorial changes concerning Czechoslovakia that had taken place in 1938 or thereafter (*en 1938 ou depuis lors*) and made it clear that the French considered Czechoslovakia's "frontiers prior to September 1938" the only valid boundaries.

The United States was not, of course, a party to the Munich agreement. Nor was it under any legal obligation to help Czechoslovakia in 1938 and 1939 since it was neither a member of the League of Nations nor an ally of Czechoslovakia. Yet it did choose to become involved, and in a manner detrimental to Czechoslovak interests. On September 26, 1938, President Roosevelt sent Beneš and Hitler telegrams in which he urged them "not to break off negotiations looking to a peaceful, fair and constructive settlement of the question at issue" and expressed the hope that the negotiations would be brought to a "successful conclusion."[66] He was instrumental in inducing all countries in Central and South America to do likewise. Similar telegrams were also sent to Chamberlain and Daladier.

Beneš was deeply aggrieved by this action, which he saw as a concerted effort by the New World to lend support to a "peaceful" solution of the Sudeten problem whatever the cost to his hapless country.[67] In his *Munich Days*, he referred to it as "the *last* event of the entire September crisis that took away from us the last hope for a more favorable solution" and as "the last heavy blow of the September conflict."[68] He particularly resented Roosevelt's failure to differentiate between the aggressor and his victim and to consider the origin of the conflict. He realized immediately that Chamberlain and Daladier would welcome and interpret the telegrams as American approval of appeasement. It was "a decisive help to Chamberlain's policy and tactics and to the endeavors of Bonnet and Daladier," he said in evaluating Roosevelt's involvement in the Munich crisis.[69] Moreover, Beneš was, with good reason, quite unhappy with the attitudes of the U.S. ambassadors to Britain, France, and Germany, Joseph Kennedy, William Bullitt, and Hugh Wilson, all of whom were strong supporters of appeasement.[70]

However, Beneš's bitterness about Roosevelt's intervention quickly faded once he came to the United States on February 9, 1939. As a visiting professor at the University of Chicago for the spring semester, 1939, Beneš fully intended to adhere—even in America—to his self-imposed policy of avoiding publicity. But he immediately realized that this would be impossible. Hardly had his ship docked at New York than he was overwhelmed by the boisterous American welcome and caught in a web of publicity from which he found it impossible to escape—hordes of photographers and reporters refusing to take no for an answer; an automobile parade through the city with police on motorcycles, sirens screaming; a warm official reception given by New York's sprightly Mayor Fiorello LaGuardia, followed by the mayor's fiery welcoming speech; the stormy applause of thousands upon thousands of New Yorkers assembled in front of the City Hall. What a sharp contrast with the Old World's chilly indifference that Beneš had left only a few days before.

America's warm embrace boosted Beneš's morale tremendously. "I would have never believed," he reminisced in his *Memoirs*, "that there was so much genuine interest in us among all the strata of the American people and that they would manifest so truly and selflessly their sympathies for a small country smashed to the ground by the Munich policy."[71] Thus, it was hardly surprising that the resentment caused by Roosevelt's telegram was soon forgotten. Another substantial element was the forceful American protest against Hitler's rape of Czechoslovakia in March 1939. Not only was the United States the first country to condemn the German action publicly, using the strongest terms to do so,[72] but Beneš concluded that the firm U.S. action prompted Chamberlain to issue a similar protest. What else, he wondered, could have induced the British prime minister, who had told the House of Commons on March 15, 1939, that Czechoslovakia's "disintegration" through "internal disruption" absolved Britain from its obligation to guarantee Czechoslovakia's frontiers, to authorize a mere two days later a strong formal protest refusing to recognize the legality of Hitler's *coup de force*? We know now that a repentant Lord Halifax prevailed on his chief to change his mind. But in 1939 Beneš believed that Chamberlain's about-face had to be credited primarily to Roosevelt. Furthermore, Roosevelt's letter of March 27, 1939, was the most personal and the friendliest of the replies that Beneš received to his telegrams protesting the German action, dispatched on March 16, 1939, to Roosevelt, Chamberlain, Daladier, Litvinov, and the president of the Council of the League of Nations.[73]

Yet less than three weeks later, Beneš's faith in the U.S. commitment not to recognize the extinction of his country suffered a setback. On April 15, 1939, Roosevelt sent a telegram to Hitler and Mussolini asking the two dictators to guarantee the independence and security of 29 countries in Europe, Asia, and Africa, including tiny Luxembourg, but saying nothing about Czechoslovakia. He also promised the two dictators free access to world markets and raw materials as a reward. The

American president's appeal gravely dismayed Beneš, for he saw in it America's approval of, and in fact active participation in, the Anglo-French appeasement policy. Most of all, he knew and dreaded the implications of even a limited and temporary success of such a policy for his unfortunate country.

But Beneš could hardly protest an action meant to promote the cause of peace and international security, even though a favorable response from Hitler would have spelled disaster for the cause of a free Czechoslovakia. So on April 16, 1939, he composed and sent Roosevelt a telegram that was yet another classic example of Beneš's handling of such delicate matters. Although he heartily disliked Roosevelt's action, he began by expressing "most sincere thanks" for Roosevelt's message to the heads of the German and Italian governments, and he concluded by thanking him once again for his "new, far-reaching step for the peaceful settlement of European conflicts." But in the main body of the telegram he cautiously expressed his true concern, coupling it with a carefully camouflaged reprimand:

> The present unfortunate situation of my country, which is now under the temporary occupation of German military forces, has, of course, made it impossible for you to enumerate the Czechoslovak Republic among those free countries which could now be involved in the immediate negotiations for the conclusion of Non-Aggression Pacts. I understand perfectly the situation. But I believe that in your mind and in that of other governments which have not recognized the illegal occupation of Czechoslovakia and the establishment of the German protectorate, is the idea that the other unsettled questions—and of course, also those connected with Czechoslovakia—will during the eventual further negotiations inevitably be presented and settled according to the principles of justice and in the spirit of international agreements which have been made with Czechoslovakia and which continue legally to exist.[74]

As Beneš prayed and hoped, nothing came of Roosevelt's peace initiative. Moreover, shortly thereafter, in May 1939, Beneš attained what he considered the political climax of his 1939 visit to America—a personal meeting with President Roosevelt. Beneš took steps toward that end (through the Czechoslovak envoy to the United States) the moment he learned of the American protest against Hitler's destruction of Czechoslovakia. But Roosevelt was not yet ready to receive him and instructed the State Department to tell Beneš (through the Czechoslovak envoy) that "he hopes very much that in view of the present situation Dr.

Beneš will not come to Washington at this time nor ask for an appointment with him."[75] What Roosevelt meant by "present situation" was not spelled out. Most probably, the American president felt that meeting Beneš at that time might blemish his forthcoming appeal to Hitler and Mussolini and that it would displease Chamberlain and Daladier, as well as America's own advocates of appeasement.[76] As Beneš wrote in his *Memoirs*, he found on his arrival in the United States in February 1939 that "even in North America isolationists and appeasers were fairly powerful."[77] Furthermore, Nazi Germany's two partners in the 1938–1939 pillaging of Czechoslovakia, Horthy's regime in Hungary and Smigly-Rydz's regime in Poland, both of whom had strong supporters in the United States, also frowned on Beneš's political activity in the United States.[78]

In relaying Roosevelt's message to the Czechoslovak envoy in Washington, however, the State Department official in charge made it clear that under different circumstances, Roosevelt would be happy to receive Beneš. Thus, the door remained open, and a meeting between the two presidents was finally arranged with the help of Beneš's good friend, Hamilton Fish Armstrong. It took place at Roosevelt's summer residence at Hyde Park on May 28, 1939, and was meant to be strictly private and confidential. Beneš was instructed to travel to Hyde Park incognito under the alias of Dr. E. Brown; his American secretary, Edward Hitchcock, who accompanied him, was rechristened E. B. Hamilton for the occasion.[79] Many statesmen might have felt offended by being received so clandestinely, but not Beneš, to whom prestige and form mattered very little.

The contents of the talk, which lasted over three hours and ranged over virtually every important aspect of the international situation, need not be recounted here in full, for much of it went well beyond Munich and its consequences.[80] But a portion of the talk did deal with Munich, its prelude and its aftermath. According to Beneš, the American president sharply condemned Anglo-French appeasement, told Beneš that he considered Beneš the president, and stated that "for him Munich did not exist."[81] He said that he would never recognize Czechoslovakia's annexation by Nazi Germany and expressed the conviction that Beneš was right in not letting himself be provoked into going to war in 1938. After Beneš informed Roosevelt that he planned to establish a provisional government in exile after the outbreak of the war and that he would then turn to the American president for help in having it recognized, Roosevelt reportedly answered: "We have helped you once [during the First World War]; so we will help you the second time as well . . . we will certainly not do less for you in this new war than we have done for your cause in the last war."[82]

Beneš was highly satisfied with his talk with the American president, which dispelled the last residue of bitterness left by Roosevelt's appeal to the German and Italian dictators in April 1939. "It was for me the decisive conversation," he wrote in his *Memoirs*, "a conversation that co-determined my entire future policy during the war."[83] In particular, Beneš was delighted by Roosevelt's remark that he still considered Beneš president and by what Beneš thought was Roosevelt's implicit commitment to recognize the Czechoslovak government in exile when the time came. Indeed, the visit with Roosevelt was the best birthday present Beneš could have received, for May 28, 1939, happened to be his fifty-fifth birthday. (Shortly before leaving the United States, Beneš also had talks with Secretary of State Cordell Hull, and Undersecretary of State Sumner Welles.) He was also pleased that, unlike Great Britain and the Soviet Union, the United States had not granted any form of recognition to the puppet state of Slovakia. Beneš departed for Britain on July 12, 1939, convinced that relations between him and the United States were fine and that he could count on Roosevelt's fullest support in his struggle to undo Munich and liberate Czechoslovakia from the Nazis.

Once again, however, he was to discover that his expectations were too optimistic. On learning that Roosevelt was sending Sumner Welles to Europe in February 1940 to examine the situation (evidently to evaluate the prospects for ending the "phoney" war), Beneš telegraphed the Czechoslovak envoy in Washington instructing him to find out whether Welles could meet with Beneš in London. When Beneš read in the papers that, on his way from Rome to London, Welles had met in Paris not only with French statesmen but also with the Polish premier, Gen. Wladyslaw Sikorski, and Polish foreign minister August Zaleski, he quickly wrote (on March 9, 1940) to the American ambassador in London, Joseph Kennedy, asking him to help arrange a meeting with Welles to "present our case after six months of war" and deliver "a memorandum about the Czechoslovak case and our conception of the future peace." Beneš stressed that this would be "of fundamental importance for Czechoslovakia." After several days of impatient waiting, Beneš received a reply (signed by H. Johnson, a member of the U.S. embassy staff), expressing Welles's regrets that circumstances made it "impossible" for him to see Beneš "during this particular visit to London," but that he would give "very careful study" to any statement Beneš sent him.[84]

Beneš was disappointed and somewhat piqued by Welles's refusal to meet with him. If the U.S. undersecretary of state found time to see the exiled Polish leaders, why could he not spare one hour to hear Beneš? Moreover, when he had met with Welles in Washington on June 30, 1939, they had agreed to see each other again in London (though this was to occur during a trip planned for August 1939 that did not materialize). To Beneš, it looked as though Welles wanted, or was instructed, to avoid a personal meeting with him, probably because Welles or his Washington superiors feared that this might disrupt an upcoming meeting with Mussolini. Beneš sent Welles a ten-page memo (entitled "Czechoslovakia After the War: Her Claims and Plans"), which he had prepared especially for the occasion. But he did not abandon his effort to see Welles in person. If "some explanations concerning the ideas expressed in the document would be necessary," he wrote in a letter accompanying the memo, "I should be glad to give them either in writing or personally." He also inserted in the letter a sentence intended to show Welles that Beneš understood the reasons for Welles's reluctance to receive him : "I realize how busy you must be here in London and that there may be some difficulties concerning a personal talk with me at the present time."[85] Beneš wanted the letter to reach Welles quickly and safely; since he suspected that this would be doubtful if the letter and the memo were channeled through the Kennedy-run U.S. embassy, he asked me to deliver them personally to Welles's secretary at the Dorchester Hotel, where Welles was staying. But Welles chose to ignore Beneš's subtle hint and departed without replying to the letter. Nor did we learn what he did with the memo. Welles's book *The Time for Decision*, which deals with his 1940 mission to Europe, does not mention it.

Welles's unwillingness to receive Beneš clearly indicated that relations between Czechoslovakia and the United States would not be as smooth as Beneš's talks with Roosevelt, Hull, and Welles in May and June 1939 had led him to believe. This became obvious when, after Great Britain recognized the provisional government in July 1940, Beneš decided to initiate negotiations to obtain U.S. recognition.[86] At first he did not push the matter, for he realized that such action would not be politic at a time when Roosevelt faced an election campaign and had to grapple with strong isolationist forces at home. Although Beneš had no particular reason to distrust Wendell Willkie, he felt that the cause of Allied victory and the liberation of Czechoslovakia would be better served by Roosevelt's re-election. "Roosevelt's victory must be viewed as a culmination point in the development of the war," he said in a report to the

Czechoslovak underground on November 18, 1940. "His defeat would have amounted to a gain of some six months [for Germany], during which internal chaos in the United States would have enabled Germany to take decisive steps toward victory."[87] Thus, Beneš decided to wait, even though reports from Czechoslovakia expressed puzzlement and unhappiness about the continued absence of U.S. recognition, especially since Goebbels's propaganda machine exploited this to disparage the importance of Beneš and his liberation movement.

But when two months passed after the election with no sign of progress, Beneš became impatient and fired off a telegram to the Czechoslovak envoy, Vladimír Hurban, on January 23, 1941, instructing him to consult the State Department and uncover the problem. The result was rather disconcerting. "Atherton told me," Hurban reported, "that they recognized the full legal existence of Czechoslovakia. Should they now recognize a revolutionary provisional Czechoslovak government, he asserted, their firm attitude would in reality be thereby weakened and various complications would arise. They are aware of the detrimental psychological effect of that, but they consider their recognition of the Czechoslovak Republic in the old form to be better." A delegation of the Czechoslovak National Council in America that called on Cordell Hull's political secretary, Mr. Dunn, to plead for U.S. recognition of Beneš's government received a similar explanation. In an effort to overcome the negative position of the U.S. Department of State, Beneš tried to see Harry Hopkins, who happened to be in London at the time. But when I telephoned Hopkins's secretary on February 5, 1941, to arrange a meeting, I received an evasive answer. Hopkins was obviously as eager to avoid a personal talk as Welles had been almost a year before. Moreover, Anthony Drexel Biddle, the U.S. ambassador to the Polish government in exile, was appointed in February 1941 to serve simultaneously as ambassador to the exiled Belgian government and as minister to the exiled governments of Norway and the Netherlands. The U.S. failure to accredit Biddle to Beneš's government was blamed on the "lack of continuity surrounding his 'Government' or Committee at London, a condition that does not exist in connection with our relations to the other governments to which Mr. Biddle is accredited."[88]

I seldom saw Beneš as indignant as he was when he learned that an American diplomatic representative was accredited to every government in exile in London except his. "Are we a kind of black sheep or what?" he exclaimed. He was obviously deeply hurt by the American action, which virtually stigmatized the Czechoslovak government as inferior to the other governments in exile. Beneš had been displeased, but not unduly surprised, at the similarly discriminatory treatment of the Munich-infested British Foreign Office. But he did not expect it from the United States, not after his encouraging talk with President Roosevelt in May 1939. His bitterness showed quite clearly in a telegram he sent Hurban on February 10, 1941:

> I regard the legal position of the U.S.A. as a fundamental mistake. In any case, it harms us here in Britain and with all the Allies, it harms us with France, Turkey, and Russia, it harms us everywhere. The most serious matter is that our people at home resent this very much and draw serious conclusions from it regarding our situation . . . the case of Biddle's appointment is downright provocative. The U.S. behavior toward us is closely followed by Germany, which exploits this for purposes of gross abuse. In one word, the position of the United States is not advantageous for us; quite to the contrary, it poses an ever-growing political and diplomatic handicap for us and actually helps Hitler in Czechoslovakia and everywhere. I understood their reticence up to the time of the presidential election. But I do not comprehend their policy today.
>
> I should add that their attitude is intentional. Here in London all their official representatives avoid relations with us and do not show any interest in information regarding our affairs. After a really splendid and promising beginning, when I was in America, I cannot grasp at all their present policy. It is clear that there are deeper reasons behind it.
>
> Should anything happen in Europe, should it come to any negotiations, the present attitude of the U.S. would prove catastrophic for us. The recognition of a legation is valuable and has a fundamental importance; but according to what I see myself, it amounts to a recognition of Munich, which we ourselves rejected and which the British government—that is Halifax himself—rejected in a special letter addressed to me on November 11. It is our provisional government that represents and defends the legal continuity of the first Republic, as everything that happened after September 19, 1938, was unlawful violence and was never approved by the post-Munich Republic. The Polish government is no more legal than that of Czechoslovakia, for the nomination of the Polish president and government after the fall of Poland in September 1939 in Paris was as unconstitutional as ours. I give you all these reasons in order that you may use them in your argumentation.[89]

Fortunately, amid these setbacks an event occurred that greatly pleased Beneš and provided him with a new and promising opening in his struggle for U.S. recognition. John Winant replaced Joseph Kennedy, a die-hard supporter of Chamberlain's appeasement policy, as U.S. ambassador to Britain. Beneš was well acquainted with the former director of the International Labour Office at Geneva, whom he knew to be one of Czechoslovakia's best friends, and was confident that the chances of securing recognition had improved considerably. Since leaving the United States in July 1939, he had had to rely almost exclusively on Hurban to convey his views to Washington. Although Hurban was loyal to Beneš and was an affable and congenial person, Beneš was quite aware that he was not as efficient, as forceful, and as persuasive as he should have been in pressing Beneš's quest for recognition. But now Beneš had available to him right in London a sympathetic and influential American diplomat on whom he could turn the full weight of his eloquence. In a long talk with Winant on March 28, 1941, Beneš stressed the unfavorable repercussions in Czechoslovakia of the negative American attitude and pointed out how cleverly Nazi propagandists were exploiting the U.S. failure to recognize his government. Though in a more moderate form than in his telegram to Hurban, he expressed his profound disappointment with U.S. policy. Winant showed great understanding for Beneš's situation and promised to inform Roosevelt and to do everything in his power to help. They also agreed that the details and legal intricacies of recognition should be discussed with Winant's legal adviser, Benjamin V. Cohen. I therefore prepared for Beneš all the relevant documents, which he handed to Cohen before discussing the matter with him in three sessions on April 1, 8, and 29, 1941.

Beneš's faith in Winant's goodwill was not misplaced, and he later wrote that Winant "from the very beginning adopted a very positive attitude toward us and very effectively helped Czechoslovakia in Washington."[90] The two reports the ambassador sent to Washington (on April 2 and April 10, 1941, together with the documentation given by Beneš to Cohen) amply revealed his support for Beneš's request. "I personally feel very deeply about Czechoslovakia and hope very much that we might recognize the Czechoslovak government in exile," Winant wrote. "No government with which I dealt at Geneva seemed more genuinely eager than the Czechoslovak to pattern their way of life on American standards."[91]

Yet, despite Winant's support, weeks passed with no indication of progress. To expedite matters, Beneš used the occasion of Churchill's official visit to the Czechoslovak army on April 20, 1941, to ask the prime minister (in the presence of Averell Harriman and Gen. Henry

Arnold, who happened to be in England at the time) for help. This Churchill promised to do. Indeed, on May 12, 1941, Lockhart told the president that recognition was already being discussed with the Americans.

However, when no word came by month's end, Beneš, frustrated by the continuous red tape and suspecting that the matter might have gotten bottlenecked once again in the State Department, decided to make one final appeal directly to President Roosevelt. In a long, emotion-laden (and somewhat repetitive) letter dated June 4, 1941, he pointed out that Great Britain, all the Dominions, and a number of other countries had recognized his government. He explained that the Nazis were using the absence of the U.S. recognition "in order to break down the resistance of our people in their struggle to renew freedom and democracy in our country, to weaken them morally, and to destroy all their hopes for a better future." He stressed that a "really far-reaching step would be taken against the Nazi dictatorship" if recognition were accorded and that this action would correspond with the spirit of U.S. policy "for the support and protection of the freedom and dignity of modern man, for the preservation of the democratic institutions in Europe, and for the elimination of the barbarous regime which is today personified by the Nazi dictatorship which is destroying the small peoples of Europe." "Should assistance be afforded," he concluded, "history will demonstrate that it was not given to those who did not deserve it. And, what is most important of all, it will have been afforded to a nation to whom a great injury was done and whose cause is a just one."[92]

Considering the factor of geographical distance, the effect of Beneš's letter was almost immediate, even though the Soviet-German war, which broke out in the meantime, must have kept Roosevelt quite busy. On July 30, 1941, Roosevelt, in a very cordial personal letter, announced that he had appointed Mr. Biddle as envoy extraordinary and minister plenipotentiary to the provisional Czechoslovak government in London.[93] One day later Ambassador Winant officially notified the Czechoslovak minister for foreign affairs.[94]

Still, the U.S. recognition was not without flaws. Oddly enough, the United States recognized a *provisional* Czechoslovak government even though the British government had dropped the qualifier and granted full de jure recognition earlier in the same month. Also, Roosevelt's letter was addressed to Dr. Beneš as "president of the provisional Czechoslovak government," although Beneš was not president of the government, but president of the republic. Furthermore, like the initial British recognition, a confidential aide-mémoire attached to Winant's letter of recognition entered a reservation regarding Czechoslovakia's future boundaries and the issue of juridical continuity: "The relationship between our two Governments does not constitute any commitment on the part of the American Government with respect to the territorial boundaries of Czechoslovakia or the juridical continuity of the Czechoslovak Government headed by His Excellency Dr. Beneš."

Despite these stipulations, Beneš was quite satisfied with the result. Since he was aware of the Anglo-American policy of noncommitment regarding future boundaries in Europe (having already had a similar experience with the British), he had reckoned in advance that the United States would make some reservation in that respect as well. He had not asked the Americans for any commitment, for the United States, not being a party to the Munich agreement, bore no responsibility for Czechoslovakia's dismemberment. As for the issue of legal continuity, it did not escape Beneš that the U.S. reservation made more sense and was less obnoxious than the British reservation since it referred to the continuity of Beneš's *government* and not to the continuity of the Czechoslovak *republic* as the British reservation had done. Moreover, the American recognition was granted while the United States was still neutral, but the corresponding British recognition had been conceded only some eleven months *after* Britain's entry into the war.

Beneš did not expect, however, that the U.S. act of recognition would refer to his government as provisional. He knew that the British and the Americans had worked together on the appropriate recognition formula and that, as Lockhart had told him on May 17, 1941, the details of their respective notes were being discussed jointly by Mr. William Malkin of the British Foreign Office and Mr. Johnson from the U.S. embassy. Thus, after obtaining a full de jure recognition from the British on July 18, 1941, he had every reason to believe that the U.S. recognition would take an identical form. Its failure to materialize was never explained to us, and it took another fourteen months for the United States to set the matter right. On October 26, 1942, Ambassador Biddle informed Jan Masaryk of Roosevelt's decision to consider U.S. recognition as full and definitive and to address Beneš as the president of the republic in his message of greetings for Czechoslovakia's National Day (October 28).

In a letter to Roosevelt dated November 4, 1942, Biddle gave a moving description of Beneš's reaction to the good news:

On Czechoslovakia's National Day, when Dr Beneš received all the Chiefs of

Missions accredited to his Government, he made it a point to come across the room to shake my hand warmly and to ask me to convey to you an expression of his deep gratitude. As he went on to tell me how profoundly touched he and his associates were and how much this would mean to his countrymen in Czechoslovakia, I could discern that he was sincerely moved. As formerly in the case of Minister Masaryk, Dr Beneš did not attempt to conceal his tears. I never before saw him show so much emotion. I only regret that you yourself could not have witnessed how much your message meant to these two men and their associates.[95]

3

Munich and the Soviet Union

Compared with the Western attitude, the Soviet stand during the September 1938 crisis looked much better. The terms of the Czechoslovak-Soviet Alliance Treaty of 1935 obligated the Soviet Union to aid Czechoslovakia in case of German attack, but only in conjunction with France. Moreover, as a member of the League of Nations, the Soviet Union was bound under Articles 16 and 17 of the Covenant to help if the Council of the League determined that Czechoslovakia was the victim of aggression.

Throughout the crisis, the Soviet government maintained that it stood ready to honor these commitments. On September 19, 1938, immediately after receiving the Anglo-French proposals demanding that Czechoslovakia cede the Sudeten areas to Germany, Beneš asked the Soviet minister in Prague, Sergei Alexandrovsky, to have Moscow answer two questions: (1) Would the USSR render Czechoslovakia immediate and effective assistance in accordance with the Soviet-Czechoslovak treaty if France did likewise? (2) If, in the event of a German attack, Czechoslovakia requested the Council of the League of Nations to implement Articles 16 and 17 of the Covenant, would the USSR help as a member of the League of Nations?[1] According to Soviet documents, the Soviet answer was transmitted to Beneš by telephone the next day, during a meeting of the Czechoslovak cabinet.

The replies to both questions were affirmative.[2] Beneš himself confirmed this. Without mentioning Alexandrovsky's telephone message, he wrote in *Munich Days* that the Soviet envoy personally delivered the Soviet answer on the morning of September 21 and that the Soviet Union promised to aid Czechoslovakia even if only a majority rather than all of the Council members voted to invoke Articles 16 and 17 (an unlikely possibility).[3] Beneš's version thus portrays the Soviet government as willing to exceed its legal obligation under the Covenant (the concurrence of all members of the Council other than the parties to the dispute was required for a legally binding decision, especially on military actions).

Moreover, according to Beneš, he persuaded the Soviet government to commit itself further.[4] After informing the Soviet envoy of the Anglo-French ultimatum delivered personally by the British and French envoys in the early morning hours of September 21, Beneš told Alexandrovsky that, in view of the French defection, the Soviet promise, contingent as it was on obtaining at least a majority decision in the League's Council, was no longer adequate. Some Council members, Beneš argued, would intentionally delay the proceedings, and thus any decision, even a favorable one, would come too late to help Czechoslovakia. "Therefore, it would be necessary that the Soviet Union act faster," he allegedly told Alexandrovsky, who returned later the same day with an improved version of the Soviet commitment, which stated that "the Soviet Union would feel authorized to come to Czechoslovakia's aid" the moment Czechoslovakia "lodged its complaint with Geneva against the aggression and so informed the Soviet Union."[5] It is to the credit of the Soviet Union that, unlike France and Britain, it repeatedly pleaded, forcefully and publicly, for firmness toward Germany and called for representatives of the Soviet, Czechoslovak, and French armed forces to meet without delay to coordinate Czechoslovakia's defense.[6] Furthermore, when Poland, taking advantage of Czechoslovakia's prostration, began applying military pressure to back its claim to Czechoslovakia's Těšín (Teschen) territory, the Soviet government promptly complied with a Czechoslovak request and warned Poland on September 23 that it would renounce the Soviet-Polish Non-Agression Pact should Polish troops cross Czechoslovakia's boundaries.

Beneš was grateful for the Soviet stand, which seemed to affirm the Soviet government's continued willingness to honor its obligations and even to exceed them. This contrasted favorably with the faithlessness of the French and the collusion of the British. The Soviet Union "alone stood with us in those difficult moments and offered more than was its obligation," he wrote in *Munich Days*.[7] Nonetheless, he was not unaware of certain factors that made him wonder what "immediate and effective aid" the Soviet Union would offer if Czechoslovakia decided to fight Nazi Germany.

First, and most important, since the two countries did not share a common border, Soviet forces could link with the Czechoslovak army only by crossing Polish or Romanian territory. But both countries made it clear that they would never allow Soviet troops on their soil, and the Soviet government insisted that the Red Army would not enter them without permission. (The Soviet attitude was that it was the responsibility of France, which had good relations with both nations, or the Council of the League of Nations to secure the necessary permission.)[8] The Polish regime's attitude toward Czechoslovakia was so hostile that there was no way of changing its mind.[9] Thus, efforts to secure transit for Soviet troops centered on Romania, which was friendly to Czechoslovakia and its partner in the Little Entente. But the Romanians were as adamant as the Poles, claiming that "once the Russians came they would never leave." Moreover, the Romanians argued, there was only one single-track railroad that could be used for this purpose; the transportation of a single division would take at least four to five days and perhaps longer.[10] The only concession that the Romanians were willing to make was to "look the other way" or, as King Carol put it, to close "all three eyes" should Soviet planes fly over Romania.[11]

As Beneš painfully realized, under these circumstances the immediate and effective aid promised by the Soviet Union dwindled to whatever it was able and willing to provide by air. The Soviet foreign commissar himself conceded this in an address to a plenary meeting of the League of Nations on September 21, 1938. Litvinov stated that the Soviet Union intended to fulfill its "obligation under the Pact, together with France, to afford assistance to Czechoslovakia *by ways and means open to us*."[12] Beneš suspected that the Soviet intent was to supply the kind of help it had provided the Spanish Republican government. "I feared lest the Soviet Union get into a situation where it could assist us only to the extent it helped the Spanish Republic in the civil war," he wrote in *Munich Days*, adding: "For us that would have been a catastrophe."[13] He frequently expressed similar sentiments during his exile in London.[14]

Furthermore, even if the transit of Soviet troops could have been resolved, the fear that the Red Army was no match for the *Wehrmacht* remained. In the opinion of Beneš and his military advisers, in 1938 the Soviet Union was incapable of winning a war against Nazi Germany and, therefore, was in no position to deliver the promised immediate and effective aid. "I was well acquainted with Germany military preparations, and judging from reports of our experts on the state of Soviet preparedness, I deemed Soviet preparations not to be equal to those of Germany," Beneš wrote in *Reflections on Slavdom*.[15] He concluded that Czechoslovakia and the Soviet Union would lose a war with Germany,[16] which would lead to the worst for his country: a catastrophe, as he put it, "for long decades if not entire centuries."[17] "Hitler would have become master of Russia," he said in July 1941, "and we would not have gotten out of the yoke."[18]

Finally, the question arose, after France had reneged on its treaty obligations, of the Soviet desire to tangle with Nazi Germany. To be sure, the Soviet promise delivered orally by Alexandrovsky on September 21, 1938, implied that the Soviet Union would aid Czechoslovakia as soon as the Czechoslovak government lodged a complaint against German aggression with the League of Nations. But was this a definitive Soviet commitment to confront Germany with Czechoslovakia alone? The wording of Alexandrovsky's statement, as cited by Beneš, is far from clear. To say that one "feels authorized" to aid someone does not necessarily mean that one will do so. Nor were doubts about the real meaning of the Soviet commitment clarified by Litvinov's equivocal speech on September 23, 1938, to a meeting of a political committee of the League of Nations. Litvinov indicated that although the Soviet Union had no obligation to help Czechoslovakia if the French failed to respond, it might "come to the aid of Czechoslovakia only in virtue of a voluntary decision on its part or in virtue of a decision of the League of Nations" but that "no one can insist on this help as a duty."[19] This indeed sounded like a retreat from Alexandrovsky's assurance of two days earlier.

Diplomatic documents that became available after the war leave little doubt that, Soviet promises to Beneš notwithstanding, the Soviet Union never seriously considered fighting Germany without Western participation. Soviet diplomats, in talks with their French and British colleagues, invariably urged firmness and intransigence toward Germany and insisted that the Nazi demands be rejected. While dodging all questions of how the Soviet Union would meet its commitment, they never wavered in their stress on its readiness to fulfill its obligation to join France and Czechoslovakia in a war against Germany should that be the only way to stop Hitler. Indeed, as one historian of Munich points out, the harder France tried to extricate itself from its commitment, "the harder the Soviet leaders could claim that they were standing by their treaty."[20] As Litvinov told Heidrich at Geneva in May 1938, he did not believe that France would help Czechoslovakia.[21] Fierlinger also reported to Prague from Moscow at the end of August 1938 that the Soviets did not believe that France would fulfill its treaty obligations.

But when talking to the Germans, the Soviets expressed themselves much more circumspectly, so much so that as early as May 1938, Ernst von Weizsäcker, state secretary of the German Foreign Ministry, was able to note that "Russia hardly exists in our calculations today."[22] The British ambassador to Berlin, Sir Neville Henderson, also commented that German Foreign Ministry officials did not believe that the Soviet Union would intervene on behalf of Czechoslovakia, except perhaps with aircraft and some technical assistance.[23] Reporting to Berlin about conversations with Litvinov in August 1938, the German ambassador to Moscow, Count Werner von Schulenburg, opined that in case of a war between Germany and Czechoslovakia the Soviet Union would do as little as possible and would probably stay out of it altogether.[24] The counselor at the U.S. embassy in Moscow, Alexander Kirk, came to the same conclusion.[25]

Since the relevant documents on German-Soviet relations at this period came to light only after the war, Beneš and his associates were unaware in 1938 and throughout the war of the Soviet double-talk. But there were some early warning signs. In a conversation between Heidrich and Litvinov on May 11, 1938, the Soviet foreign affairs commissar complained that the West wanted to liquidate Hitler through Stalin and Stalin through Hitler; therefore, the Soviet Union did not intend to enter the war (which he considered inevitable) at the very beginning. Rather, it would intervene only toward the end in order to produce "a just and lasting peace."[26] On September 15, 1938, Heidrich reported from Geneva that Romania's foreign minister, Nicholas Comnen, had gained the impression from Litvinov that "the Romanians were actually complying with Soviet wishes when they opposed the transit of Soviet land armies."[27]

Did Beneš believe that the Soviet Union would, without French participation, risk war with Germany on Czechoslovakia's behalf on the sole condition that Czechoslovakia lodge a complaint with the League of Nations? A perusal of *Munich Days*, in which the president promised to "tell the full truth and all the truth," yields no clear answer. Describing his tormented thoughts on the night of September 20–21, 1938, after the British and French envoys delivered their countries' ultimatum, he wrote: "But what will happen if we are forced to wage this war alone? . . . what shall we do in this case when it becomes clear that France and England will not help and will be disinterested? And, above all, what will Soviet Russia do? At that time it was not yet clear to me what action it would *actually* take, but I definitely expected that, in principle, it would be with us." The chief of the General Staff and the inspector general of the Czechoslovak army, Generals Ludvík Krejčí and Jan Syrový, expressed themselves similarly, according to Beneš: "What the Soviets will actually do from the military standpoint cannot as yet be said." Another passage reads: "I myself never had any doubt about the attitude of the Soviet Union. I was certain that it would fulfill its obligations." Concluding the chapter devoted to the Soviet stand, he stated: "We had no apprehensions whatever regarding the [Soviet Union's] course of action; we were certain that it would fulfill its commitments and promises and would carry out its preparations for the eventuality of the war."[28]

Although giving the Soviet Union all possible credit for its behavior during the crisis in his *Munich Days*, Beneš never tackled the crucial question of whether, after France had reneged on its commitment, the Soviet Union was still prepared to give Czechoslovakia immediate and effective aid. Nor was this an oversight on his part. As he said, he wanted to tell the full truth about Munich and, in particular, about the role played by the Soviet Union. After the crisis, he came under sharp communist attacks charging that he preferred to capitulate to Hitler in order to save the Czechoslovak bourgeoisie rather than to accept the generous offer of Soviet aid, which "virtually guaranteed" ultimate victory. Thus, he had all the more reason to reveal how inadequate the Soviet offer really was. But he wanted to proceed as considerately and as diplomatically as possible to avoid offending the Soviet Union, whose goodwill he deemed so vitally important for his country.

The full truth as I see it, unadorned by diplomatic niceties and undiluted by considerations of political expediency, is that Beneš did not believe that, after France's defection, the Soviet Union would fight on Czechoslovakia's side. He suspected that the Soviets were bluffing and that their aid would boil down to fiery protests in the League of Nations and on the Comintern's airwaves, coupled perhaps with an ostentatious recall of the Soviet ambassador from Berlin, but not to military action against Germany. That was, at least, the impression I gained from a number of talks with the president during my tour of duty as his personal aide from 1939 to 1945. I want to stress the word impression because even in private conversations with his closest associates the president habitually qualified his statements with "ifs," "on the other hands," "maybes," and "perhapses," especially when talking about things Russian. This was also the impression of Smutný, who wrote in October 1943: "He [Beneš] believed that Russia would have stood firmly by its word if France would have, but no more. It would not have come to our aid alone."[29]

There is now available another important piece of evidence revealing Beneš's true thoughts about Soviet behavior at the time of Munich after he subsequently learned certain facts not known to him in 1938. It comes from the noted Czech editor, the late Ivan Herben, son of a prominent Czech writer whose family had been intimate friends of both Tomáš Masaryk and Edvard Beneš. On August 22, 1945, President and Madame Beneš paid a private visit to Herbens' family home in southern Bohemia, not far from the Benešes' own country home. Among the topics of discussion was Munich: "The President repeated again and again that he was now in possession of documents showing that the Soviets had betrayed us as had Daladier and Chamberlain and that they had no intention whatever of helping us. Their willingness to do so was sheer pretense; it was merely the usual communist trick. 'I shall prove it! I shall unmask that fraud of Soviet diplomacy as well as the legend of the communists,' the president virtually shouted, with fists clenched above his head. I had never seen him like that before." As the president came back again and again to the Munich scheme, Herben finally asked him why he did not publish the documents. "Beneš hesitated for a moment," Herben reports, "then he calmed down and answered with his typical diplomatic, cool, and colorless voice: 'You know, my dear colleague, that is the *absolute* truth. But the *political* truth is something else. Therefore, I cannot.' "[30]

It would be unfair, of course, to fault the Soviet leaders for their unwillingness to aid Czechoslovakia if it meant involvement in a war with Nazi Germany while the West stood idly by. In the conduct of foreign policy, especially in deciding whether to go to war, all nations are guided by conceptions of national interest. Although it was clearly in the Soviet Union's national interest in 1938 to stop Hitler's *Drang nach Osten,* (the reason for the alliances with such "bourgeois" countries as France and Czechoslovakia in the first place), it was not in its interest to shoulder that awesome burden without Western cooperation. As Litvinov complained in May 1938, there were indeed those in the West who desired to "liquidate Hitler through Stalin and Stalin through Hitler." The Soviet Union had good reasons for not becoming entangled (and probably defeated) in a one-sided war that many in the West might have hailed as a crusade against the menace of bolshevism. Hence, the Soviet leaders insisted that France, which (unlike the Soviet Union) was bound by an unconditional treaty obligation to help Czechoslovakia, must declare war first. France's refusal to honor its commitment and the decisions of the Czechoslovak government not to lodge a complaint against Germany with the League of Nations exonerated the Soviet Union, legally and politically, from any further action. Moreover, the Czechoslovak government never directly requested unconditional aid from the Soviet government irrespective of French or League of Nations actions. Beneš came close to raising this question on September 30, 1938. On learning of the heartbreaking results reached at the Munich conference, he told Alexandrovsky that Czechoslovakia was "confronted with the choice either of beginning war with Germany . . . or capitulating to the aggressor" and wanted to know "the attitude of the USSR to these two possibilities, that is, of further struggle or capitulation."[31] However, before the telegram could be deciphered in Moscow, Alexandrovsky informed Moscow that Beneš no longer insisted on an answer to his last question because Czechoslovakia had accepted the Munich diktat.[32] Thus we will never know what answer Stalin and his Politburo would have given.

While the Soviets can hardly be blamed for not wanting to fight Germany single-handedly, they must be faulted for the dishonest manner in which they and their comrades in Czechoslovakia exploited the Munich tragedy to ease Czechoslovakia's communization and to malign Beneš, his policy, and his actions. To serve their purposes, they conjured up the following scenario: After being shamefully betrayed and deserted by the West, Czechoslovakia was left with only one loyal friend, the Soviet Union. Only the Soviet Union stood selflessly and unshakably prepared to help Czechoslovakia, immediately, effectively, and unconditionally, by placing its enormous land, air, and naval forces at Czechoslovakia's disposal. It thus went far beyond its legal commitment, for it was ready to fight even if no one else did, and this on the sole condition that Beneš ask for help. Had he done so, Czechoslovakia and its big Slav brother would have won, thus sparing the Czechoslovak people the horrors and humiliation of the German occupation. But Beneš refused to accept the generous Soviet offer and instead capitulated to Hitler because he wanted to save capitalism and to protect the class interests of Czechoslovakia's bourgeoisie and was afraid of the political, economic, and social consequences that a joint Soviet-Czechoslovak victory over Nazi Germany would have entailed.[33]

In concocting this scenario, communist propagandists mix distorted half-truths with assumptions and hypotheses that can be neither proved nor disproved, supplementing them heavily with a one-sided Marxist-Leninist interpretation of Beneš's motives. Although relying for effectiveness primarily on emotional impact, they occasionally try to support their thesis with references to facts designed mainly to overcome the argument's principal weakness: the absence of any truly convincing evidence that the Soviet Union was willing to fight even without French participation and that it was militarily strong enough to prevail. After all, even after it became known that France would not honor its obligation, the Soviet government continued to make its offer to help contingent on French participation.[34]

To lend credibility to these assertions, Soviet and Czechoslovak communist sources rely primarily on testimony by Klement Gottwald published in Moscow's *Pravda* on December 28, 1949, concerning a conversation between the Czechoslovak communist leader and Stalin in mid-May 1938. "Stalin told me clearly," Gottwald wrote, "that the Soviet Union was prepared to give military assistance to Czechoslovakia even if this was not done by France." The only condition was that Czechoslovakia "would defend itself and would request Soviet assistance." Gottwald also claimed that he passed Stalin's statement on to President Beneš.[35] Similar statements concerning Stalin's message to Beneš through Gottwald are included in the book *Angliia i miunkhenskii sgovor*, written by the Soviet historian V. G. Poliakov, and in a German-language volume, *Wer half Hitler*, authored by Ivan Maisky.[36] But each mentions a different date for the Gottwald-Stalin meeting: Poliakov, September 18; and Maisky, "sometime around September 2."

This confusion regarding the date and the use of such vague terms as "mid-May" and "sometime around" is rather strange, especially since it concerns a statement crucially important to both Czechoslovakia and the Soviet Union. Equally strange is the manner in which Stalin's message was allegedly conveyed to Beneš, through a member of an opposition party with no official standing in Beneš's administration rather than through normal diplomatic channels. Most damaging to the credibility of Gottwald's assertion is an official Soviet document: a telegram in which Alexandrovsky reported Gottwald's conversation with Beneš on September 19, 1938: "Beneš asked Gottwald's opinion about the course of action of the USSR. He [Gottwald] replied that it was not his business to answer for the USSR, but nobody had any grounds to doubt that the USSR would meet its obligations. If it was a question of *something over and above the obligation,* then Beneš should formulate exactly what and put an inquiry to the government of the USSR."[37] If Stalin had really told Gottwald in "mid-May" 1938 that the Soviet Union was prepared to give military assistance to Czechoslovakia even if France was not, and if Gottwald had transmitted this message to Beneš, why did he not remind the president of this on September 19, when the crisis reached its climax and when Beneš asked him quite specifically about the Soviet Union's probable course of action?

Perhaps even more puzzling in this context is the silence of the official collection of documents about the Munich crisis (published in both Moscow and Prague in 1958) about the *second* message, which Beneš reported Alexandrovsky delivered on September 21, that implied that the Soviet Union would help Czechoslovakia even if France did not. The collection contains a mass of other documents, including Alexandrovsky's telegram transmitting to Moscow the two questions posed by Beneš on September 19, 1938, as well as the Soviet reply to them.[38] In asserting that the Soviet Union was ready to help even without France, why would Soviet propagandists rely on an obscure and unsubstantiated ex post facto statement of Gottwald rather than utilize Beneš's own testimony virtually conceding the point? Was there really such a message? In the hectic confusion of the crisis, did Beneš misunderstand the Soviet minister? Or did Alexandrovsky, in his struggle to persuade the Czechoslovak government to resist German demands, say something he should not have said? We may never know. (The late Milan Hodža, Czechoslovakia's premier at the time of the Munich crisis, reportedly told the historian George Vernadsky that the Soviet Union did offer to "help Czechoslovakia even if France did not act," but according to Hodža the offer was made "after Godesberg terms had been made known," which would have been on September 23 or 24.[39] Most probably Hodža got his information from Beneš and may well have been mistaken with regard to the meaning of Alexandrovsky's second message as well as the exact date of its delivery.

Communist utilization of the legend that Beneš and the Czechoslovak bourgeoisie preferred capitulating rather than winning with Soviet help has varied according to the prevailing communist strategy and tactics. The first wave of communist criticism in the wake of the Munich debacle soon subsided. In July 1941, Beneš opined that this was the result of a conversation he had had with the Soviet ambassador to the United States, K. A. Umansky, in the spring of 1939 about his policy at the time of Munich. After consideration of Umansky's report on his talk with Beneš by "the highest Soviet in the presence of the Czech communists," Beneš told us, the campaign against him was discontinued.[40] After the conclusion of the Nazi-Soviet Non-Aggression Pact in August 1939, the legend reappeared in vitriolic anti-Beneš statements issued by the communist underground in German-occupied Czechoslovakia and in the pamphlet *Guilty Men of Czechoslovakia.*[41]

The Soviet volte-face brought about by the June 1941 Nazi invasion of the Soviet Union and the era of East-West cooperation that followed in its wake put an abrupt end to the communists' public censure of Beneš's handling of the crisis. But the communists by no means abandoned their Munich legend. Indeed, it resurfaced in full force in discussions the president had during his visit to Moscow in December 1943 with the top four leaders of the Czechoslovak Communist party, Klement Gottwald, Rudolf Slánský, Jan Šverma, and Václav Kopecký, who had found wartime refuge in the Soviet capital. Gottwald and his associates rejected in no uncertain terms Beneš's explanation of his behavior in September 1938. Although they refrained from the standard communist charge that Beneš's motivation was to save the Czechoslovak bourgeoisie, they censured him for not accepting the help of the heroic Red Army and for endangering the very existence of the Czechoslovak people by his capitulation. The controversy became so loud, so excited, and so heated that the harsh voices of the communist accusers, particularly Kopecký's, could be heard throughout our *osobniak*, the villa that Stalin assigned us as our quarters in Moscow. "Our Moscow politicians disputed my views very hotly," remarked Beneš in describing the conversation somewhat euphemistically in his *Memoirs.*[42] It was obvious that Gottwald and his cohorts were preparing to use the Munich issue as a major tool to undermine Beneš's prestige and influence after their return to Czechoslovakia.

Nor were the Czechoslovak communist leaders the only ones who took exception to Beneš's Munich surrender. Stalin raised the delicate issue himself, although much more circumspectly. The subtle confrontation occurred at the official welcoming banquet given in Beneš's honor on our arrival in Moscow on December 11, 1943. As we sat at the long table in the Kremlin's dining hall, Stalin suddenly hit Beneš, who was facing Stalin across the table, with the straightforward question: "And why didn't you fight in 1938?" Sitting only a few seats away from Beneš, I could not fail to notice that the president froze for a few seconds and blushed slightly as he began feverishly organizing his thoughts to parry what he recognized at once as a veiled reproach. What could poor Beneš reply? Surely he could not offend his host by telling him, in front of the Politburo members and generals who attended the banquet, that he had deemed the Red Army no match for the Wehrmacht in 1938 and that he had even had serious doubts that any meaningful Soviet aid would be forthcoming? So he listed, counting them on his fingers as was his custom, the other reasons he chose not to fight. In particular, he mentioned his fear that Chamberlain and Daladier might have succeeded in presenting a war fought by Czechoslovakia and the Soviet Union alone as an attempt to promote the bolshevization of Europe.[43] This would have played directly into the hands of Nazi Germany, which zealously portrayed its action against Czechoslovakia as an anti-Bolshevist crusade. Moreover it was possible that reactionary circles in Western Europe might have eventually persuaded their regimes to assist Germany in such a crusade. That development would have spelled disaster not only for Czechoslovakia but also for the Soviet Union and would have doomed any chance of the East-West cooperation that was so crucial for the preservation of peace and security in Europe and the world.

Stalin listened attentively to Beneš's arguments, watching closely how the president ticked off his reasons, but said nothing in rebuttal. Yet it was evident that he either remained unconvinced or feigned disbelief. Later at the traditional performance in Stalin's private cinema in the Kremlin, he showed us a film of Red Army operations, and remarked to Beneš with a tone of reproach: "Well, this army was at your disposal in 1938." Sitting just behind them, I could notice, as Stalin turned to Beneš, how his penetrating eyes tried to measure Beneš's reaction. Clearly the question was premeditated, as premeditated as his reference to Munich during the banquet. Beneš remained silent. He could not very well ask Stalin how this army could have saved Czechoslovakia in 1938 when a few years later, in 1941 and 1942, it was still not only not advancing toward Czechoslovakia, but was being pushed hundreds of miles in the opposite direction by the Wehrmacht.

Was it only coincidence that during that fateful visit to Moscow in 1943 both Stalin and the Czechoslovak communists chose to raise the issue of Beneš's Munich surrender and expressed, in their respective ways, their disapproval? Both the Czechoslovak communists and their Soviet mentors were fully aware of the paramount importance of Munich and their Munich legend to advancing the cause of communism and overthrowing Czechoslovak democracy.

Another sad factor greatly facilitating the one-sided communist utilization of the Munich tragedy was that not even after the liberation could the Czechoslovak people be told the truth about Soviet behavior in 1938. The dire necessity of not angering the Soviet dictator made it imperative to avoid even mild public deprecation of Soviet intentions or actions. While communist-controlled media freely publicized the communist legend of Soviet willingness to aid Czechoslovakia selflessly and unconditionally, those who knew better had to keep silent. For this reason, the president felt compelled to abandon his original intention of publishing his report on Munich as soon as possible after returning to his liberated homeland, and that was why he told Herben he could not publish the documents revealing the Soviets' duplicity.

However, as long as Beneš was alive, communist propagandists refrained from using the portion of the scenario that claimed that Beneš had capitulated in order to save the Czechoslovak bourgeoisie. Anxious to minimize the adverse worldwide publicity triggered by the 1948 putsch, the Czechoslovak communists and their Soviet mentors wanted to retain Beneš as a figurehead president. It would not have served their purpose to impugn Beneš's honesty by casting aspersions on his motives. But Beneš's resignation and subsequent death in September 1948, as well as the world's refusal to accept the communist version of the 1948 takeover, released the communists from the self-restraint. Once again, as during the Nazi-Soviet accommodation of 1939–1941, the communists supplemented their version of Munich with strident anti-Beneš invective blaming the surrender on his "counterrevolutionary anti-Soviet policy," his conspiracy with Western capitalists, and his fear that acceptance of Soviet aid would mean suicide for Czechoslovakia's bourgeoisie.[44]

When the liberalization trend of the sixties, which culminated in the Czechoslovak Spring of 1968, loosened the straitjacket of communist censorship, a refreshing note of objectivity crept into some Czechoslovak accounts of the Munich era and Beneš's role. Writing in a widely circulated popular Czechoslovak magazine, a noted Czech historian gave a surprisingly well-balanced account of the reasons that prompted Beneš to yield in 1938, duly stressing Beneš's fear that a war with Germany with the help of the Soviet Union alone might have strengthened the "anti-Soviet front of imperialist powers" and possibly even led to their military involvement on Germany's side.[45] In comparing Beneš's standpoint with that of the Czechoslovak communists, not only did the author maintain a meticulously neutral attitude (in itself a striking innovation for a communist-ruled country), but the tenor of her article seemed more sympathetic toward Beneš's views than toward Gottwald's.

As was to be expected, the Soviet-ordained "normalization" that followed Dubček's ouster in 1969 inevitably ended such "extravaganzas." The orthodox one-sided clichés of the early fifties became once more the rule in the seventies whenever Munich was discussed.[46] In 1973 the Czechoslovak film industry even turned out a "historical" movie about Munich with the suggestive title *Dny zrady* (Days of treason). In reviewing and commenting on the movie, *Rudé právo*, the party daily, did not neglect to point out that "even the treacherous Western imperialists were brothers to Beneš, whereas in the USSR, which could and did want to save him, he saw such a long-term danger that he chose rather treason and capitulation."[47]

What was the impact of the Munich crisis on Beneš? Understandably, as all of us close to him in those trying times can confirm, the trauma of Munich and its aftermath left a lasting scar in Beneš's mind and emerged as an important determinant of his thought and action. Eradicating Munich and its consequences became his foremost preoccupation. "From September 30th, 1938, I never stopped thinking, day and night, how to achieve the repudiation of that despicable Munich Dictate," he told Mackenzie in 1944. "I lived with one single aim in my life—the repudiation of Munich and the reconstitution of the Czechoslovak Republic."[48]

Considering the humiliating French and British treatment of Beneš in 1938–1939 and the rebuffs and frustrations he suffered in his efforts to get the French and British cosigners to repudiate the Munich diktat and obtain recognition for his government in exile, it would have been only natural for Beneš to develop a good measure of hatred and bitterness toward them. Yet to the best of my knowledge, that was not the case. Perhaps the only person among the French and British Munichites he truly hated was Georges Bonnet, mainly for his hypocritical behavior during the September 1938 crisis and his deceitful insinuation that Prague had requested the Anglo-French ultimatum.[49] Beneš's feeling toward the others can be described as a combination of varying degrees of dislike and pity. Nor did the French and British appeasers' treatment of him cause any feeling of bitterness or antipathy toward France and Britain as such. Writing about Britain's and France's responsibility for Munich in his *Memoirs*, he urged his readers not to forget how both these powers, especially France, had helped Czechoslovakia gain independence in the First World War.[50]

Nonetheless, Munich was instrumental in convincing Beneš that Western democracies were not reliable allies and that Czechoslovakia's security vis-à-vis Germany must be based primarily on an alliance with the Soviet Union. To that extent, his Munich complex contributed toward pushing him closer to Moscow and welcoming the Soviet Union's becoming Czechoslovakia's immediate neighbor. At the same time, however, Beneš never ceased striving for the retention of close ties with Britain and their re-establishment with France. Even before the conclusion of the 1943 alliance with the Soviet Union, he was very unhappy when his offer to conclude a similar treaty with Great Britain was declined. After his return to Czechoslovakia, he did all he could to conclude a new treaty of alliance with France, and in a fruitless effort to overcome communist objections, he even sent Stalin a forceful memorandum in support of the treaty.[51] To demonstrate his country's continued commitment to friendship and cooperation with the West, he planned to pay an official visit to Paris immediately after the conclusion of the treaty. Even at the height of his slavophile stance, Beneš insisted that Czechoslovakia's foreign policy must be neither solely Eastern nor solely Western. "We are in the middle of Europe and we can seclude ourselves neither from the East nor from the West," he stressed in the introduction to *Reflections on Slavdom*. "Our neighborhood with Germany and the danger of its *'Drang nach Osten'* forces us to seek support not only in the East but to reckon also with its Western neighbors."[52] As he used to tell his collaborators, including myself, he advocated a well-balanced policy equally oriented toward the East and the West.[53]

Thus, Beneš's "Munich complex" influenced his views on Czechoslovakia's East-West relations considerably less than is generally believed, especially after the success of his protracted efforts to obtain British and French repudiation of Munich. Strange as it may sound, rather than resenting Munich as a humiliation and defeat he subsequently began to view his actions as a great achievement of which he could rightly be proud. "I consider that my behaviour over Munich was the greatest achievement of my life," he told Mackenzie. "I can say with complete sincerity that I won a victory over my own self and was able to sacrifice that self for the sake not only of the Czechoslovak nation but also of Europe and, indeed, of human peace."[54] In recounting the gist of this conversation to Smutný, he added: "I am proud of Munich, and I do not deny that the Great Powers are still indebted to us."[55]

4

The First Soviet Veto

"Without a free Poland there will be no free Bohemia. Without a free Bohemia there will be no free Poland," wrote Tomáš G. Masaryk in 1918 in his *New Europe*. Beneš fully shared his great mentor's view, whose correctness he saw confirmed by the tragic events of 1938–1939. In a March 1940 letter to his brother in the United States, Beneš wrote: "Their [the Polish] cause is clearly linked with our cause. Without our freedom they shall not be able to exist. But without their restoration we cannot be restored either."[1] Hence, he decided to utilize the disaster that had befallen the two countries to bring them closer together. Indeed, for Beneš this was an integral part of his struggle to undo Munich and to prevent its recurrence. He was convinced that cooperation between the two Slav neighbors in 1938 would have prevented their collapse. "I saw in this war a unique opportunity once and for all to end what had been and to embark on a new era of Polish-Czechoslovak relations based on true friendship between our two nations and on a close mutual political, military, and economic cooperation in the future," he wrote in the chapter "Czechoslovakia and Poland During the Second World War," which was meant to be included in the second volume of his *Memoirs*.

> The history of both our Western Slav countries has been interwoven by a difficult struggle for national survival against the Germans. Both stand in the traditional path of German expansion to the East, to the Danubian

Basin, the Ukraine, and the Black Sea. Both of them are the first outpost against German *"Drang nach Osten."* Thus they would always become the first victims of every new German attempt at expansion. I was convinced that it was necessary to spare no effort to counter this perpetual menace by building in the East a lasting Polish-Czechoslovak association backed by the strength of the Soviet Union. This powerful bloc of three Slav countries—and only such a bloc—was and is capable of quenching Germany's thirst for new conquests, or defeating it, thoroughly and decisively, should it try again.[2]

Furthermore, Beneš hoped that other small countries of East Central Europe, such as Austria, Hungary, and perhaps Romania, would eventually join the association. Thus, the prewar jumble of small entities quarreling with and conspiring against one another would be replaced by a larger regional association capable of providing a measure of much-needed stability in that notorious danger spot of international politics and of asserting East Central Europe's independence vis-á-vis both Germany and the Soviet Union.

Unfortunately, after promising beginnings, which in January 1942 culminated in the adoption of a protocol spelling out the basic principles of a planned Czechoslovak-Polish confederation, a Soviet veto halted further work on Beneš's ambitious project. Left with the hapless alternative either of persevering in his pursuit and incurring Soviet enmity or remaining on good terms with the Soviet Union by abandoning the project, Beneš felt compelled to opt for the latter. His decision, reached only after all efforts to persuade the Soviet leaders had proved fruitless, subjected him to a good deal of adverse criticism, especially from the Poles and some right-wing opponents among the Czech, Slovak, Hungarian, and Austrian refugees. They accused him of abandoning his own project the moment the Soviets expressed displeasure. The criticism gathered momentum after it became obvious that Beneš's policy of seeking an accommodation with the Soviets had failed and the countries of East Central Europe had fallen one by one under Soviet domination.

Although some of this criticism is justified, much of it is mere hindsight and based on one-sided or incomplete evidence (partly because Beneš himself never published his own account of the Czechoslovak-Polish negotiations and the Soviet role). In 1944, on his request, I prepared the chapter "Czechoslovakia and Poland During the Second World War." Even so, anxious as he was to disturb the Soviets as little as possible, he deliberately described and characterized Soviet interference in Czechoslovak-Polish affairs in the mildest and least onerous terms he could without distorting the facts. Knowing his predilections in this respect, I was careful in preparing the account to avoid any pronounced criticism of Soviet behavior. Nonetheless, when the president handed the chapter back for retyping, I could see that his revisions and insertions tended to de-emphasize Soviet responsibility for the abortion of his project even more and to lay the blame more on the Polish side. Because of his official position and the political environment, Beneš could never tell, at least not for public consumption, the full story of this venture. Least of all could he reveal publicly his true feelings about the project, his endeavors to keep it alive, and his resentment of the crude Soviet intervention.

Before World War II, Polish-Czechoslovak relations had fallen to a sad state. In the fateful years of 1932–1933, which witnessed Hitler's rise to power, Beneš (then minister for foreign affairs) attempted to reach an understanding with the Polish foreign minister, Col. Jozef Beck, and thus achieve some measure of Czechoslovak-Polish cooperation in the face of the Nazi threat.[3] Instead, in January 1934 Poland concluded a nonaggression treaty with Nazi Germany. When in 1936 French Foreign Minister Paul Boncour sent the French ambassador to Warsaw, Léon Noel, to Beneš to inquire whether Czechoslovakia would join France in helping Poland in case of a German attack, Beneš's answer was an unequivocal yes. But the French effort to induce the Polish regime to undertake the same obligation in case of a German attack on Czechoslovakia remained fruitless.[4] In mid-August 1936 when the French chief of staff, Maurice Gamelin, passed through Prague on the way to Poland, Beneš tried once more. He sent Gen. Louis Faucher, the chief of the French military mission in Czechoslovakia, to Gamelin with a written offer urging joint Polish-Czechoslovak military preparations against a possible German attack on Poland or Czechoslovakia. But once again Beneš's indirect approach to the Polish regime was rebuffed. As General Faucher subsequently informed Beneš, General Gamelin handed the Czechoslovak proposal to the Polish premier, Edward Smigly-Rydz, whose reply was, however, evasive and noncommittal.

But Beneš's bitterest disappointment regarding Polish policy toward Czechoslovakia came when, at the height of the September 1938 crisis, the Polish regime took advantage of Hitler's action against Czechoslovakia to lay claim to the Těšín area. On September 22, 1938, a deeply shocked Beneš wrote a dramatic personal letter to Polish President Ignacy Moscicki, offering to cede the area to Poland in exchange for nothing more than Polish neutrality. "Knowing the delicacy of our mutual relations," he concluded his appeal, "knowing how difficult it has always been to change them for the better in normal times and through normal diplomatic and political means, I attempt to use the present crisis to break the obstacles of decades and to create in one stroke a new atmosphere. I do this in all sincerity. I am convinced that the future of our two nations and their future collaboration will thereby definitely be assured."[5] The letter was sent on September 25, just after the British and French ceased discouraging Czechoslovakia from a general mobilization, which the president thereupon immediately ordered. It looked as though the war might break out—this occurred after the unsuccessful meeting between Chamberlain and Hitler at Godesberg—and Beneš hoped that by giving the Polish government what it wanted, he might be freed from worries about the long Polish-Czechoslovak border and would be able to concentrate on the expected German attack. Moscicki replied on September 27 that he had handed the letter to the Polish cabinet, which would try to reach an agreement. The nature of the agreement the Polish cabinet contemplated became clear when, on September 30, the Polish minister in Prague delivered an ultimatum to the Czechoslovak minister for foreign affairs demanding that a major portion of the Těšín area be surrendered within 24 hours and the remainder within ten days.

The Polish government also lent its full support to Hungary's territorial claims against Czechoslovakia. In its eagerness to obtain a common frontier with Hungary, it ordered the Polish press to launch a concerted campaign for the transfer of Ruthenia to Hungary. Colonel Beck even journeyed to Bucharest to offer a portion of Ruthenia to King Carol of Romania (who declined the offer). The Polish regime was anything but displeased when its desire for a common Polish-Hungarian frontier was fulfilled by the Hungarian takeover of Ruthenia after Hitler's liquidation of post-Munich Czechoslovakia in March 1939. The simultaneous creation of an "independent" Slovak state also met with the Polish government's wholehearted approval. The Polish president could rightly boast that "Poland was the first power to recognize the new Slovak republic" when he received the first accredited Slovak minister to Warsaw. Smigly-Rydz's regime even stooped so low that in a futile attempt to dissuade Hitler from moving against Poland, it did not hesitate in March 1939 to claim credit for helping Germany dismember Czechoslovakia in 1938. "Finally it is well known that in autumn 1938 the determined Polish attitude [*Polens entschlossene Haltung*] contributed to an important extent to prevent war [*einer kriegerischen Auseinandersetzung*] in connection with the fulfillment of German claims." So reads the memo that the Polish ambassador in Berlin, Jozef Lipski, handed the German foreign minister on March 26, 1939.[6] Ashamed of its predecessor's attempt to appease Hitler by referring to Polish merits at the time of Munich, the Polish government in exile omitted this passage when publishing Lipski's memo in the *Polish White Book* in Great Britain during the war.[7]

After the Polish government finally realized that Poland was to be the next victim of Hitler's *Drang nach Osten* and that no amount of Polish accommodation could change that, its policy and behavior became somewhat less anti-Czech. The Czechoslovak legation in Warsaw and the Czechoslovak consulate in Cracow were unofficially allowed to assist Czechoslovak refugees coming to Poland; Radio Katowice began Czech-language broadcasts; and a camp for the military training of Czechoslovak refugees of military age was established. However, when the Czechoslovak minister to Poland, Juraj Slávik, returned to Warsaw in August 1939 from a visit to the United States, Colonel Beck's *chef de cabinet* told him that he would no longer be recognized as such. The Poles would "tolerate" the activities of the legation, he was told, but they could no longer recognize it after they had recognized Slovakia.[8]

Moreover, the Polish government continued to behave with cold haughtiness toward the Czechoslovak liberation movement that Beneš was organizing in Great Britain and the United States. It supported an anti-Beneš group in Poland led by Gen. Lev Prchala, who wanted to locate the central headquarters of the liberation movement in Poland. The movement was to be led by a National Committee of Czechs and Slovaks in Poland headed by a presidium consisting of Prchala and two of his anti-Beneš associates. This, as Prchala wrote in a memo sent in August 1939 to the chief of the Polish General Staff, Gen. Waclaw Stachiewicz, would be "the guarantee that Poland itself and the participants in the Czechoslovak struggle in Poland would be able to exert real influence on the final solution of the Czechoslovak case and thus to secure a lasting Czechoslovak-Polish friendship and alliance."[9] What made the Polish government's attitude even more reprehensible in Beneš's eyes was that it was not based solely on its dislike of Beneš, but was closely connected with its cherished idea on the proper reorganization of Central Europe after (as the Polish government took for granted) Poland had defeated Germany. The Polish scheme did not contemplate the restoration of prewar Czechoslovakia, not even in boundaries that would leave the areas seized by Poland and Hungary in 1938 and 1939 in their respective hands and preserve the common Polish-Hungarian frontier. Rather, Slovakia and "Czechia," both presumably liberated by the Polish army, were to come, as two separate countries, under the Polish eagle's protective wings, preferably in some form of a tripartite union led by Poland.

This unhappy legacy of discord and animosity hardly boded well for an early improvement of relations between the two Slav neighbors. Deeply hurt by Poland's unfriendly behavior, especially by the "stab in the back" (as Beneš always referred to it) at the time of Munich, most Czechs got a malicious satisfaction from the crushing of the Poles by their accomplices in the dismemberment of Czechoslovakia one year earlier. Beneš was, of course, well aware of his countrymen's harsh feelings toward Poland. Yet he hoped that the terrible fate that had befallen both nations would make them rise above their old quarrels and misunderstandings and would open a new and happier era in their mutual relations. Having become the two foremost victims of the German *Drang nach Osten*, it seemed logical for them to seek new and better modi vivendi and cooperandi. "I believed that in this new war . . . Poland would eliminate the leftovers of its reactionary, fascist-behaving [*fašisující*] system and would progress toward a truly popular democratic government that would not be blinded by illusions of *grandeur* and would better understand the value of the Czechoslovak-Polish friendship," wrote Beneš in the unpublished chapter on Polish-Czechoslovak relations.

When, after a few weeks of war, Poland collapsed, the regime of Smigly-Rydz and Colonel Beck was swept aside, and a Polish government in exile headed by Gen. Wladyslaw Sikorski was formed in France, Beneš concluded that the time had come for yet another attempt to bring about a lasting rapprochement between the two nations. Beneš, who had met the new Polish premier in prewar days, knew that Sikorski was one of the main opponents of the Pilsudski regime and of Colonel Beck's policy. So he had every reason to believe that the new Polish government would receive his endeavors sympathetically. After sending Sikorski a telegram of congratulations on his appointment as Polish premier, Beneš had two personal meetings with him while visting Paris in October 1939. These two meetings brought the two statesmen close to each other. I cannot speak for General Sikorski, but Beneš was very satisfied with their talks. As the president told me, Sikorski strongly condemned the foreign policy of Pilsudski and Beck since 1926 and conceded that Poland and not Czechoslovakia bore the responsibility for the bad relations between the two countries. "We shall now establish a special commission," Beneš quoted Sikorski as saying, "which will thoroughly examine the guilt of Beck and of his followers." Sikorski's determined criticism of his predecessors pleased Beneš, who returned to London firmly convinced that the way was open for fruitful Czechoslovak-Polish collaboration.

Indeed, when Sikorski repaid Beneš's Parisian visit by calling on him in London on November 18, 1939, the Polish premier suggested, and Beneš gladly concurred, that cooperation between their countries should in principle be fashioned along federative lines. Shortly thereafter, on December 2, Beneš had an opportunity to discuss the matter with the Polish ambassador, Count Edward Raczynski. The president reaffirmed his positive attitude toward the idea of a Czechoslovak-Polish federation. Having learned, however, of speculations in some Polish émigré circles in London that the Czech lands and Slovakia would join such a federation as separate units, he stressed that Czechoslovakia would join only as one country. In answer to Raczynski's question whether other Central European countries might join the federation, Beneš agreed that the eventual inclusion of Austria, Hungary, and Romania could be considered. He made it amply clear, however, that Czechoslovakia would find it impossible to enter any union with Poland if Poland sought territorial expansion in Lithuania and the Ukraine. "I know," he told Raczynski, "that there are many Poles desiring a Great Poland, including also parts of the Ukraine, and federated with Lithuania. With such a Poland, Czechoslovakia could not enter into a kind of federation, since complicated problems would arise that would be extremely difficult to solve."[10]

Raczynski thanked Beneš for his "frank statement" and his "friendly attitude" and said that he would report the conversation to Polish Foreign Minister August Zaleski. A short time later, a proposal for mutual cooperation came from the Polish side in answer to Beneš's request for Polish recognition of the Czechoslovak National Committee, which France and Great Britain had just recognized. In its answer, the Polish government expressed the desire that its act of recognition be accompanied by an agreement on future Czechoslovak-Polish cooperation. This was unacceptable to Beneš because it would have seemed that Polish recognition was conditional on political promises by Czechoslovakia. Moreover, the Polish proposal contained a suggestion that ran contrary to Beneš's whole conception of a Polish-Czechoslovak union. The Poles wanted to include a clause of mutual support in negotiations regarding frontiers, especially those between Czechoslovakia and Germany and between Poland and the Soviet Union. Such a clause would necessarily have drawn Czechoslovakia into the Soviet-Polish frontier controversy, the last thing Beneš desired.

The inevitability of this approach's failure must have been clear to the Polish government—if Raczynski had correctly reported the contents of his discussion with Beneš. Yet this first setback by no means weakened Beneš's commitment to the idea of a Czechoslovak-Polish union and its eventual enlargement to include East Central European countries. He restated it in no uncertain terms in the confidential memorandum to Sumner Welles, the U.S. undersecretary of state, during Welles's visit to Europe in March 1940.[11] "Another important question," Beneš wrote in the memorandum,

> will be *the problem of the relations of the future Czechoslovak State to her neighbours.* A possible federal organisation in Central Europe is being spoken of. As Foreign Minister for 17 years I attempted to prepare the progressive building up of a federal Central Europe, i.e., of a close economic and political collaboration between Czechoslovakia, Yugoslavia, Rumania, Austria, and Hungary on the basis of some kind of federation . . . In the present circumstances it is our intention to solve these matters in collaboration first of all with Poland, as of course also with the other small Central European States. As far as we are concerned, there will definitely be no difficulties of principle in these questions.[12]

When, after the collapse of France, the Polish government transferred its seat to London and Beneš's National Committee was recognized as Czechoslovakia's provisional government, the Czechoslovak-Polish negotiations moved quickly from tentative exchanges of views to positive results. In two long meetings in October 1940, Beneš and Sikorski explored in depth the question of wartime and postwar cooperation between their two countries. To avoid any possible misunderstanding, Beneš also used the occasion to review the main problems that he feared might create certain difficulties and to state quite frankly what he expected from the Polish side. He stressed in particular: (1) that the Poles must permanently abandon any idea of a tripartite federation that Slovakia and the Czech lands would join as separate states; (2) that the Polish-Czechoslovak boundary issue brought about at the time of Munich had to be settled amicably between the two countries; (3) that the social systems of the two countries must converge; (4) that a rapprochement must take place in Polish-Soviet relations. In the unpublished chapter on Polish-Czechoslovak relations, Beneš wrote that he gained the impression that Sikorski agreed with his arguments, except that he wanted the boundary issue shelved until Polish-Czechoslovak cooperation had made more headway and a better atmosphere had thus been created for its amicable solution.

Anxious to get things going, Beneš sent Sikorski a twelve-page memorandum on November 1, written in French and entitled "Exchange of Views Concerning Polish-Czechoslovak Cooperation After This War," in which he expounded in detail his views about the shape of the future Polish-Czechoslovak confederation and means of bringing it about.[13] In the first part of the memo, "Basic Principles and General Purposes," Beneš suggested that Polish-Czechoslovak cooperation take the shape of a "confederation sui generis," naturally established on a flexible basis that would permit the gradual development of a common political and economic organization based on past experience. The guiding principles of the confederation were to be:

1. The sovereignty of Poland and Czechoslovakia would not be disturbed by the bond of confederation, each country keeping its own head of state, cabinet, parliament, army, etc.
2. Restriction of sovereignty would be chiefly directed to economic measures. There would be a common commercial policy and a transport, customs, and currency union.
3. There would be a common foreign policy, but separate diplomatic representatives would remain.
4. Armaments and army equipment would be identical, and war production would be standardized accordingly.
5. The common organs of the confederation would be:
    a) A council composed of delegates of both countries, including especially their prime ministers and ministers for foreign affairs, foreign trade, finance, and transport. This council would direct the entire foreign and military policy of the confederation and would coordinate the principles of economic policy, trade, finance, and transport. Its resolutions would be approved and carried out by both governments.
    b) A common general staff, but the general staffs of each country would remain.
    c) A joint committee of both parliaments whose decisions must be submitted for approval to each parliament.
    d) An economic and trade council.

In the second part of the memorandum, "Some Conditions for

Achieving the General Purpose," Beneš reviewed the prerequisites that he felt had to be fulfilled in order to create the Czechoslovak-Polish union. He stressed, in particular, two of them: (1) adjustment of social structure of the two countries (Beneš's conviction was that postwar Poland would have to be thoroughly democratized); and (2) good relations between Poland and the Soviet Union.

The latter was the crux of the whole issue. The settlement of the Polish-Soviet dispute and the establishment of at least a correct mutual attitude between those two antagonists was for Beneš a sine qua non for any Polish-Czechoslovak union.

> We shall easily agree on a common line of policy that our union ought to pursue toward the United States and the British empire (both during and after the war) as well as toward western and northern Europe and toward Germany. We shall encounter some difficulties, which, however, will be easy to overcome, in establishing our common relations toward the Danubian countries. But the most difficult problem will be to find a common line of policy toward Soviet Russia. Poland is at war with Russia; Czechoslovakia is not. The Czechoslovaks suffer from a sort of Russian mystique [*une sorte de mystique russe*], which could become even stronger at the end of this war. A social and economic revolution in Central Europe after this war, a revolution that would assume in Czechoslovakia a predominantly national and anti-German character, might in certain circumstances make popular sympathy for Russia even more pronounced . . . It is neither a question of opinion nor of general political ideologies. On one side it is a question of sentiment, on the other a question of national interests as the Czechoslovaks conceive of them. In general, all of them are of the opinion that to be able to stop more or less definitively the German *Drang nach Osten*, i.e., a life-and-death struggle of the Germans against the Poles and the Czechs, a struggle that is carried on today in the name of the Nazi revolution but could be led tomorrow by the Germans in the name of a social revolution, *we must not have the Russians against us.*[14]

Finally, in the third part of the memo, "Forms of Immediate Cooperation," Beneš proposed that a special directing committee be established for the further study of all questions concerning Polish-Czechoslovak cooperation. Furthermore, accepting a suggestion made earlier by Sikorski, he proposed in the concluding paragraph of the memo that controversial questions (meaning, without singling it out, mainly the issue of the Těšín territory seized by Poland in 1938) be left for later when "the atmosphere of friendship and confidence between the Poles and the Czechoslovaks had been definitely established."

While Beneš was writing to Sikorski, negotiations were proceeding between the foreign ministers of Poland and Czechoslovakia with a view toward making a public declaration on the new phase of Polish-Czechoslovak relations. It was thought that at that time of great trial, when the British empire alone was resisting the Nazi onslaught, it would be appropriate to manifest Polish-Czechoslovak solidarity publicly and thereby underline the two nations' unshakable trust in a better future. On November 11, 1940, the Polish and Czechoslovak governments in London issued a joint declaration pledging themselves to end "once and for all the period of past recriminations and disputes" and after the war "to enter as independent and sovereign states into a closer political and economic association which would become the basis of a new order in Central Europe and a guarantee of its stability." The declaration also expressed the hope that their cooperation would be "joined by other countries in that part of the European continent."[15]

Sikorski answered Beneš's memorandum on December 3, 1940. In the ten points of his memorandum (written in French), which, as he pointed out, "expressed the unanimous opinion of the Polish government," the Polish premier agreed in general with Beneš's standpoint. He concurred with Beneš that it would be "highly desirable to establish the best relations of good neighborliness between the Polish-Czechoslovak confederation and Russia." But he thought that this could only be achieved provided Russia "saw in the middle of Europe a solid bloc, formed by Poland and Czechoslovakia, with which it would have to reckon as with a serious partner." Sikorski spoke frankly of the "realism and lack of ideological scruples" in Soviet policy and expressed his fears that Russia might be tempted to "establish a communist regime not only in Warsaw and Prague, but also in Berlin." He also stressed that "Poland maintained integral rights to the territory of the republic" and that he counted on "recovering their possession through an agreement that he hoped to conclude with Russia at an opportune moment."[16]

Pleased with Sikorski's attitude, Beneš wrote back on December 23, 1940, that he noticed "with the greatest satisfaction that there was an agreement on the main principles and that there was no serious obstacle to setting to work without delay." He announced at the same time that Jan Masaryk, Hubert Ripka, and Juraj Slávik were appointed the Czechoslovak members of the Committee of Coordination, which was to direct further negotiations and supervise and coordinate further work.

However, Beneš's satisfaction proved of short duration. On January 26, 1941, Sikorski, on an official visit to the Czechoslovak army in

Britain, stayed overnight at the president's country home at Aston Abbots. During and after dinner the Czechoslovak president and the Polish premier had their longest and most detailed talk. Not surprisingly, a substantial part of their conversation dealt with the Soviet Union. Beneš carefully explained to Sikorski his thesis on the probable development of the war. He argued, in particular, that the war could not be won without U.S. and Soviet help and that, therefore, Poland and Czechoslovakia must reckon with, and even welcome, Soviet participation in the war and must make their plans and adjust their policies accordingly.[17] Sikorski listened to Beneš's reasonings with ever-growing misgivings. As Beneš described Sikorski's reaction in his *Memoirs*, the Polish premier rose and began to pace nervously about the room. Then he came to a halt in front of Beneš and declared with extreme gravity: "What you are saying would be catastrophe for us all."[18] He then countered by explaining to Beneš his own expectations. The Soviet Union was too weak and too fearful to enter the war. It would like to participate in the war at "about five minutes to twelve," but then no one would want it to become involved, least of all the British. Anyway, Great Britain would hold out against Nazi Germany and would later be joined by the United States. Thus, the war would be won and the ensuing peace would be dictated by the Anglo-Saxons.

The Polish premier also tried, as had previous Polish negotiators, to enlist Czechoslovakia's help in the Polish-Soviet frontier controversy. "General Sikorski requested," wrote Beneš in his account of the conversation, "that in negotiations about the future Czechoslovak-Polish union, Czechoslovakia accept the standpoint that the union should be based on the principle that Poland would have its original boundary in relation to Russia and that we should mutually agree on our frontiers in relation to others and would thereafter stand jointly and firmly behind them." As Beneš had done earlier during the negotiations leading to Polish recognition of the Czechoslovak National Committee, he declined Sikorski's request and countered with a formula suggesting that the two countries join in the confederation without stipulating boundary settlements.

Another noteworthy divergence in their talk concerned Hungary. When Beneš explained that Czechoslovakia intended to reclaim all Czechoslovak areas annexed by Hungary in 1938–1939, including Ruthenia, Sikorski seemed surprised. As he told Beneš, he thought that Czechoslovakia had already surrendered its claim to Ruthenia.

Although the two statesmen parted in friendship and agreed that work on the confederative project should continue, Beneš was deeply disturbed by Sikorski's attitude. For the first time he wondered whether, in view of the fundamental difference in their conceptions of the war and its probable outcome and the contrast in their evaluations of the international situation, the close association with Poland that he so ardently desired would be attainable. "This conversation with General Sikorski, though clear, open-minded, sincere, and friendly," he wrote, "made me fear for the first time that, under the circumstances, we might not be able to reach agreement even with Sikorski's government."[19] Thus, Sikorski's official visit to the Czechoslovak army—planned as a solemn public display of cooperation between the two countries— brought into sharp focus precisely those elements that were most divisive.

The situation worsened when the two statesmen, feeling that their positions should be made a matter of record, chose to register them in another round of letters. Writing in Polish on February 10, 1941 (in line with a new Polish-Czechoslovak resolution providing for the use of the native languages in mutual intercourse rather than the traditional French), Sikorski stated bluntly:

> As I have already had the opportunity to state orally, the Polish govern-ment firmly adheres to the point of view that our frontiers as they were before September 1939 may in no case undergo any changes detrimental to us. Poland, which had those frontiers, entered the war in which it made tremendous sacrifices in the defense of a common cause. Therefore, we cannot even admit any thought that Poland would emerge smaller from this war. Without precluding any favorable changes that could take place with regard to the western frontiers, the Polish government will defend with determination its present possessions in the east. It will never and nowhere allow its indisputable rights to the frontiers of 1939, many times recognized by Russia, to be curtailed. If we do not put forward these questions at present, we do so for tactical considerations only, as I had the honor of informing you on a previous occasion. Nevertheless, the Polish government officially states this standpoint, which is one of the bases of its work, whenever it is necessary. It rightly considers that if it acted differently, it would not be fit to represent the nation.[20]

Sikorski reiterated his view that Poland and Czechoslovakia ought to support each other in their territorial claims. He called for a "positive attitude" and "utmost solidarity" on the part of Czechoslovakia and, in an implied criticism of Beneš, opined that the future boundaries of Czechoslovakia were not a matter of indifference to them. "That is why I emphasize so strongly everywhere Czechoslovakia's right to the Sudetenland, without which, in my opinion, there would be no western boundary suitable for an effective command defense."

In disbelief Beneš repeatedly read Sikorski's letter, measuring with nervous steps the length of his spacious Aston Abbots study. Suddenly noticing me, he commented bitterly:

> So he had a mouth full of condemnation for Beck's policy, but he is not in the least ashamed to claim the fruits of Beck's criminal robbery. Why, it was his idea as well as mine that we ought to leave that thorny question of our mutual boundaries for later, after we have made more progress on the way toward general understanding and had created a better atmosphere for their solution. I accepted that. And now he turns around and raises the question. Well, I cannot remain silent now, for my silence might be interpreted as consent. I shall have to write back.

Only after I read Sikorski's letter did I fully realize what Beneš meant, for Sikorski's statement about "our frontiers as they were before September 1939" clearly applied to the Těšín territory seized by Poland in 1938.

Two weeks later Beneš's reply (dated February 25, 1941) was ready. In addressing the boundary issue posed in Sikorski's letter Beneš wrote:

> I say sincerely that we do not consider the question an easy one for us. If I had to express myself generally in response to your letter, I would have to say as you did, that the Czechoslovak government simply insists on the frontiers that Czechoslovakia had before September 1938 because otherwise my government would not be fit to represent the nation. But I think that it is premature and almost impossible today to formulate a definitive standpoint in regard to frontiers in all the details. This question depends on the final outcome of the war and on the present and future attitude of individual nations and states that are involved in this war. There is no doubt that in the course of the following months we will formulate various questions in a different manner than we would formulate them today. Therefore, from our side we do not wish to discuss these most delicate matters today and are waiting until events themselves will help us solve a number of these questions. But when, nevertheless, we have to speak of the frontiers, we do so in a very general form, just as I did during our last discussion.
>
> Therefore, I proposed to you, in connection with our present negotiations, not to define precisely and in all detail the frontier questions of one or the other country at present, but to accept immediately the following fundamental formula: *We have agreed to form in Central Europe a new*

international political body whose forms we are just beginning to discuss, whatever the ultimate frontiers of our countries may be.

I would consider the agreement concerning the above-mentioned formula to be essential. Each of us can state his frontier demands, according to his needs and conceptions, and the other partner will simply take note of it and will respect it without interfering in the matters of the other, but will never and in no way undertake anything that will be against the demands of the other partner. This procedure would secure unity and mutual loyalty. It would also alleviate the difficulties of both governments, because neither of the governments would otherwise be able to prevent, in either the Polish or Czechoslovak camp, the formation of hostile groups that would attack their governments, forcing them to act differently and to adopt another standpoint. The acceptance of the above-mentioned standpoint would be so firm, objective, and thoroughly mutually loyal that both governments could always resist any pressure and could always under any circumstances adhere to it. It could never cause quarrels and difficulties between them.[21]

Beneš also restated his desire that the Soviet army not enter Polish or Czechoslovak territory:

The second principle about which we have already reached a fundamental agreement may be formulated as follows : It is in the interest of both our states that an agreement be reached in time among all the interested countries, that is, Poland, Czechoslovakia, Britain, the United States, and the Soviet Union, that in case of a German collapse the Soviet army will not cross the line that it is now holding and will not penetrate further westward into Polish or Czechoslovak territory. I confirm that it is as much in the interests of Czechoslovakia as it is of Poland.

Finally, Beneš felt it necessary to take exception to the passage in Sikorski's letter that seemed to reaffirm the Polish intention of retaining the Těšín territory:

In my memorandum of November 1, 1940, I have proposed that we ought not to discuss controversial Czechoslovak-Polish problems now but ought to defer their solution to such time when we agree on our future cooperation. In your memorandum of December 3, 1940, you have fully approved of this. Therefore, I assume that the clause of your letter of February 10, 1941, stating that "the Polish government firmly adheres to the point of view that our frontiers as they were before September 1939 may in no case undergo any changes detrimental to us," does not apply to the action of Colonel Beck against Czechoslovakia in September 1938 and to all the consequences that arose from his ultimatum and his military action directed against Czechoslovakia . . . I think that all those matters are reserved for a later discussion.

Beneš did not expect that the Polish government would give up its claim to the Těšín area. But he hoped that his formula would allow Sikorski to set the delicate issue aside until further progress on their confederative project had made the issue somewhat less relevant and less emotional. As mentioned earlier, that seemed to be Sikorski's original standpoint. However, the Polish premier's reply, dated June 18, 1941 (after his return from a journey to the United States and Canada), made it clear that the Sikorski government considered the matter nonnegotiable. Stressing the importance of the speediest possible settlement of the boundary controversy for the "atmosphere" of Polish-Czechoslovak cooperation, Sikorski expressed his conviction that Poland and Czechoslovakia would arrive at a "satisfactory solution." His conception of that solution was revealed in the ensuing paragraph in which he referred to the letter that Beneš had sent to the then Polish president, Ignacy Moscicki, at the height of the 1938 Munich crisis. He was convinced, Sikorski wrote, that a satisfactory solution would be reached "particularly by the fact that when speaking about matters concerning Těšín Silesia [Sląska Cieszynskiego]," Beneš allegedly had recognized "the need to correct the mistakes committed against Poland."[22]

Nor did Sikorski like Beneš's proposal that Czechoslovakia and Poland not become involved in one another's boundary issues with regard to third countries. He labeled Beneš's formula as a "principle of *désintéressement*" and a bare minimum. "For me it is self-evident," he added in a clear tone of reprimand, "that the regard for the durability and resistance power of the [Polish-Czechoslovak] association, as well as the regard for its own security, must automatically evoke a like interest in each partner both for matters of frontiers and in respect of the relations with the neighbors of the other partner."

What was most surprising in Sikorski's letter of June 18, 1941, was that, a mere three days before the outbreak of the Soviet-German war, he still seemed to believe that Germany and the Soviet Union might cooperate against Britain. "The encirclement of Russia, which the Germans have accomplished," wrote Sikorski, "neither excludes the possibility of a Russo-German conflict in the future, nor the possibility that Germany will impose on Russia a cooperation that will be inimical to Britain." Were Sikorski and the Polish General Staff so misinformed, or was this only wishful thinking? The latter would seem to be the case. Since March 1941 we had received reports from our agents, stationed at the Führer's headquarters, that the Germans had definitely decided to attack the Soviet Union and that all preparations were being accelerated to that end. (First reports gave mid-May as the zero hour for the invasion. Later the deadline was postponed until the second half of June.) Because the British had similar information, Polish ignorance is inconceivable, especially since the major German military preparations were taking place in the Nazi-occupied areas of Poland.

But what angered and hurt Beneš most was Sikorski's unwarranted allegation that Beneš's 1938 letter to Moscicki, written under extreme duress, was prompted by "the need to correct the mistakes committed against Poland," when it was in reality nothing more than a desperate last-ditch attempt to avert a threatened Polish invasion by sacrificing a portion of Czechoslovak territory. To clarify the matter, Beneš decided to send Sikorski a special memo detailing the reasons and the circumstances surrounding his 1938 offer of the Těšín territory. But the extremely heavy demands on his time caused by the hectic pace of events following the German invasion of the Soviet Union forced him to postpone writing the memo until October 1941. After reviewing the highlights of Polish-Czechoslovak relations between the two world wars, Beneš said about his letter to Moscicki:

> At the most critical moment of all, I wanted to make, both in the interest of Poland and ourselves, a sacrifice that would have made it possible for Beck's regime not to go against us, to change its policy at the fateful moment, and to protect also its own general interests against expansionist Nazism ... It was not a question of admitting mistakes—I myself have always considered the frontier matter between Poland and Czechoslovakia as having been definitely and justly settled. But at that critical time it was a question of our not looking back to what had happened in the past, but of attempting together to save both our peoples and countries. Colonel Beck answered with an *ultimatum* and the dispatch of a number of divisions to our border. This was the final blow against us in the September crisis, and *it was a fundamental factor in inducing me to decide not to go to war and to wait.* I was quite certain—and I said so at the time to all my generals—that within a few months it would come to an attack on Poland.[23]

When the German invasion of the Soviet Union on June 21–22, 1941 converted the biggest Slav country from a partial accomplice of Nazi Germany into an active partner of the West in the anti-Nazi coalition, it looked as though the main problem confronting the Czechoslovak and Polish negotiators on the confederative project had been resolved. That was, at least, what Beneš thought and hoped. On July 30, 1941, Poland and the Soviet Union concluded an agreement ending the state of war that had existed between them since September 1939, and the two enemies became allies. Diplomatic relations between the two were restored, a Polish army under a commander appointed by the Polish government was to be formed from among Polish citizens in the Soviet Union, and the two governments pledged to render one another "aid and support of all kinds" in the war against Hitlerite Germany. The Soviet government declared "the Soviet-German treaties of 1939 as to territorial changes in Poland have lost their validity," and the Polish government stated that it was not bound by any agreement with any third power that was directed against the USSR.

The prospects for a fair and reasonable settlement of the outstanding issues between Poland and the Soviet Union seemed considerably brighter, and Beneš's cherished dream of a Czechoslovak-Polish confederation backed by the might of a friendly Soviet Union appeared close to realization. He was, of course, under no illusion that Polish-Soviet relations would henceforth be smooth. He knew that the Polish government interpreted the Soviet-Polish agreement of July 30, 1941, as implicit Soviet recognition of Poland's eastern boundary before September 1939, and he suspected (correctly, as it turned out) that such was not the Soviet intention. Furthermore, he was greatly dismayed when many Poles displayed malicious joy over Soviet setbacks during the initial phase of the fighting and once more began propagating their favorite thesis that Germany would defeat the Soviet Union and then succumb to the West. He was afraid that this attitude (which he considered nothing more than foolish wishful thinking) would impede Polish-Soviet rapprochement and thereby create new difficulties for Czechoslovak-Polish relations. Nonetheless, he viewed the new situation as a great improvement. Replying on October 6, 1941, to Sikorski's letter of June 18, 1941, he wrote: "I consider, Mr. Premier, your conduct of negotiations with the Soviet Union as a political act of true statesman-like foresight and as an act of great political importance for you as well as for us. I know that it is only the *first* step, but the first step is often the most decisive."[24] Beneš decided to take advantage of the opportunity provided by the improvement in Soviet-Polish relations in the wake of their momentous agreement of July 30, 1941 (which Sikorski himself characterized as "the turning point in history") to speed up and, if possible, bring to completion the work on the Polish-Czechoslovak confederation.

With that idea in mind, Beneš invited the Polish foreign minister, Count Raczynski (successor to Zaleski) to lunch on September 4, 1941, and had a long talk with him. He began by stressing that this was "the historic moment," which neither Poland nor Czechoslovakia should let slip by without doing all they could to come to an agreement "once and for all" and promised to do everything in his power to bring it about. He assured his guest that Russia's involvement in the war changed nothing and would change nothing in Czechoslovakia's policy vis-à-vis Poland, not even if the Soviet Union became Czechoslovakia's neighbor. Aware of the threat that the unresolved boundary controversy between Poland and Soviet Russia posed for Czechoslovak-Polish cooperation, he virtually urged the Poles not to insist on their prewar boundary with the Soviet Union. "I told him quite frankly," Beneš wrote in his memo of the conversation, "that they should have courage to discuss the matter directly with Russia and settle it. Only by such an agreement can they reach as advantageous a settlement as can be achieved, that is, get back the largest possible territory and get rid of the largest possible number of Ukrainians."[25]

Beneš and Raczynski agreed that the work of the Czechoslovak-Polish committees and subcommittees that had been set up earlier to arrange the details of the confederation should be speeded up. The result of their efforts was the Czechoslovak-Polish protocol of January 19, 1942 (signed on January 23), which embodied in fourteen points a number of fundamental principles on which the Czechoslovak-Polish confederation was to be based.[26] The protocol envisaged common policy in foreign affairs, defense, economics and finance, social questions, transportation, and posts and telegraphs; coordination of foreign trade and custom tariffs, leading eventually to a customs union; a unified monetary policy; cooperation in the field of education and culture; unrestricted movement and the right of citizens of the member-states to pursue any gainful occupation throughout the entire confederation; and mutual recognition of diplomas, documents, and court judgments. Common organs of the confederation were to be established to ensure common policy in these areas. The two governments also expressed their desire "that the Polish-Czechoslovak confederation should embrace other states of the European area with which the vital interests of Poland and Czechoslovakia are linked." Finally, the protocol carefully enumerated the rights that the constitutions of the member-states were to guarantee to their citizens; namely, "freedom of conscience; personal freedom; freedom of the spoken and written word; freedom of organization and association; equality of citizens before the law; free admission of all citizens to the performance of all state functions; the independence of courts of law; and the control of government by representative national bodies elected by means of free elections."

Simultaneously, the Polish and Czechoslovak governments passed a resolution expressing their satisfaction with the conclusion of the Greek-Yugoslav agreement of January 15, 1942, on the creation of a Balkan union and their conviction that the prosperity and security of the area of Europe between the Baltic and the Aegean seas depended primarily on the collaboration of the two confederations.

Beneš was pleased with the protocol, which he viewed as a well-balanced and soberly conceived summary of basic principles for building the confederation. Most of all, he was gratified by the virtually exhaustive listing in the protocol of the civil and political rights that the member-states were obligated to grant their citizens. Discussing the protocol in the unpublished chapter on Czechoslovak-Polish relations, he labeled this particular provision as "especially important" and reminded his readers that "it was one of the conditions that he had laid down from the very beginning for Czechoslovak-Polish cooperation in the future." Since he believed that Polish-Soviet relations had improved, he concluded that his primary sine qua non was being implemented. Thus, in an article in *Foreign Affairs* entitled "The Organization of Postwar Europe," he felt confident enough to state that "the creation of this new political unit [the Polish-Czechoslovak confederation] can already be considered an accomplished fact."[27] He used the same language in a talk, "The Present War and the Future Peace," at the University of Aberdeen on November 19, 1941.[28] Unfortunately, Beneš's expectation proved overly optimistic. Before the basic principles of the protocol could be elaborated further, a Soviet veto halted the project.

Beneš had no intention of presenting the British and the Russians with an accomplished fact. He resolutely declined a suggestion to that effect from the Polish side (Raczynski suggested this at a luncheon with Beneš, and Sikorski at the Dorchester Hotel in London on August 17, 1942, after Beneš had informed them of Soviet opposition to the confederation). He was a man of caution, and caution bade him first make sure that no great power opposed the idea.

He found out quickly that Great Britain and the United States were favorably inclined to the closest possible cooperation between Poland and Czechoslovakia and that they blessed all attempts to build an even broader union in Central and Southeastern Europe. He suspected, however, that memories of the "cordon sanitaire" might make the Soviets suspicious of closer unions of countries along their western borders. His apprehensions were enhanced by Fierlinger's reports on talks with Maisky. After Stalin had ordered the Czechoslovak legation in Moscow closed in December 1939, Fierlinger moved to London, where he paid several visits to the Soviet ambassador. From what he told Beneš, it was clear that the Soviet Union's stand toward Sikorski and his government was harshly antagonistic. For instance, in reporting a conversation with Maisky on March 31, 1941, Fierlinger stated: "He admits that President Beneš most probably will enter Prague again. But he cannot guarantee that Sikorski will ever make his entrance into Warsaw."[29] This is why Beneš was most anxious to explain to the Soviets in good time the purpose of the confederation, to allay misunderstandings, and hammer into their suspicious minds that the confederation was not directed against them. At first he seemed quite successful. In July 1941 as Fierlinger was leaving for his post in Moscow, the president instructed him to raise the issue of Polish-Czechoslovak relations with the Soviet Foreign Commissariat. On August 25, 1941, Fierlinger wired back:

> According to your instructions, I explained to Vyshinsky for the first time in detail our view of cooperation with Poland and of the establishment of a Polish-Czechoslovak confederation, completely independent but at the same time in friendly relations with the Soviet Union. He vividly expressed to me his personal approval, adding that he would inform me of the exact official attitude. He assumed that no objection or difficulties would arise.[30]

To confirm this, Beneš invited Maisky to see him on August 28, 1941. "I would like to know," Beneš asked the Soviet ambassador,

> whether Moscow has any objections concerning our plans of cooperation with Poland. I sent you some time ago, through Fierlinger, full information about this cooperation and explained to you my point of view and what were our conditions for that policy: (1) The internal structure of Poland must coincide more closely with ours—no dictatorship, real democracy, no aristocratic or great landowners' policy; (2) agreement of Poland with Russia and peaceful cooperation. We do not wish to enter into negotiations with Russia concerning Poland or any other matters; we wish

to be loyal to all as we were previously, but we wish also to be loyal to Russia and inform it. I asked Fierlinger to speak about this in Moscow. He has already telegraphed me that he has spoken to Vyshinsky, who told him that he personally assumed that Russia would in all probability not raise any objections to Polish-Czechoslovak cooperation if this cooperation is based on conditions explained by Dr. Beneš.

"I was informed about that, and I understand my information in the sense you mentioned," Maisky replied with an affirmative nod. "I have reported to Moscow all your previous talks, and I shall now write again and seek to obtain information."[31]

It was after he had obtained these Soviet assurances that Beneš invited the Polish foreign minister, Count Raczynski, to the long talk mentioned earlier in which it was agreed that work on the project be speeded up, resulting in the protocol of January 23, 1942. So optimistic was Beneš about the ultimate outcome that at a luncheon given by Raczynski on the occasion of the signing of the protocol, he told Sikorski, "We must conclude all our work on the confederation in two to three months." Sikorski nodded approvingly and, departing from his earlier stand, reciprocated by agreeing with Beneš's oft-repeated warning that the Poles ought not in their political calculations reckon on a Soviet defeat: "Yes, I say this everywhere. I say that we need a Russian victory; otherwise it would be our destruction as well . . . I came back from Russia [which he visited in December 1941] fully convinced of the necessity to reach an agreement with Russia. I shall now work for that as much as I can. The old Polish romanticism must disappear."[32]

Everything seemed in the best order. At a luncheon in honor of Beneš at the Soviet Embassy four days after the publication of the Czecho-slovak-Polish protocol, Maisky heartily assured the president that "in Moscow there were no objections against the Polish-Czechoslovak agreement." "We want to reach a direct agreement with the Poles as well," added Maisky, "but we have no intention of giving up our rights to Western Ukraine and Western Belorussia."[33]

Yet the real troubles soon began. Hardly one week elapsed after the Czechoslovak-Polish protocol was signed before the first hint of Soviet misgivings appeared. Fierlinger reported from Moscow at the beginning of February 1942 that "Soviet circles" were of the opinion that the Czechoslovak policy of cooperation with the Poles "runs ahead of events and does not take a realistic view of the future" and that "at a moment in which we are fighting to recover our independence, we are giving it up in favor of some kind of a political union whose consequences cannot

today be assessed."[34] Simultaneously, the Soviet envoy to the Czechoslovak government, Alexander Bogomolov, started a curious whisper
campaign. In striking unison, he and his associates from the Soviet
embassy began seeking out Czechoslovak politicians and expressing to
them their "personal" doubts whether it was sound policy to confederate
with the Poles and to welcome the Greek-Yugoslav Balkan union.

When Beneš heard of this from several people, he at once sensed the
danger, for he knew that Soviet diplomats would start such a campaign
only on the direct orders of Moscow. He asked Bogomolov to see him,
explained the entire matter once again, and gave him a number of
documents concerning the Czechoslovak negotiations with the Poles,
including extensive excerpts from his correspondence with Sikorski.
The Soviet envoy seemed satisfied with these explanations, and Beneš
began to believe that the entire campaign might have been meant only as
a Soviet warning that his government should not go too far and, in
particular, not push for a broader union embracing other countries of
Eastern Europe. Beneš's belief was further confirmed by a long conversation with Molotov on June 9, 1942, in London. The conversation, held
at the Soviet Embassy, dealt with a number of important topics, but
Polish-Czechoslovak relations figured high among them. According to
Beneš's account of the conversation, it was Molotov who brought up the
subject. While emphasizing that the Soviet Union wanted friendship and
cooperation with the Poles, Molotov complained that the Poles were
engaging in propaganda against them and were even attempting to use
the project of the Czechoslovak-Polish Confederation against the Soviet
Union. He wanted, therefore, to learn more about the Czechoslovak
attitude in this matter.

Beneš did his best to allay Molotov's misgivings. He gave the Soviet
foreign commissar a detailed account of his negotiations with Sikorski,
dwelling in particular on three conditions that had to be met:

> a. We could not decide definitely anything as long as we were outside
> our own country. It was only possible to prepare it; the people at home
> would have to approve it before a common organization could commence
> to function.
> b. The social structure of both states must coincide more closely because
> we could not make a confederation with Polish aristocrats.[35]

Replying to Molotov's question whether this meant that a friendly
relationship between Poland and the Soviet Union was a condition for
the Czechoslovak-Polish Confederation, Beneš assured him

clearly and categorically that this was indeed so and could not be otherwise. In the intended confederation we wish to become guarantors of good relations with the Soviets. There are no differences between the Soviet Union and us, and I presume there will not be any. In view of our geographical position and our relations with the Germans and Hungarians, we could not burden ourselves with the differences and difficulties of a third party. Therefore I stated quite frankly that we did not want to become involved in the Soviet differences with Poland, though we presumed that in all probability we would become neighbors of the USSR.

Molotov in turn declared that "he now fully understood why we wished to be on friendly terms and in agreement with the Poles. Therefore, they had no objections." But he expressed misgivings about the plan for a larger confederation stretching from the Baltic to the Mediterranean. "They did not trust it," he said, "in substance those plans were always directed against us." To put his mind at ease, Beneš told Molotov that he himself was somewhat reluctant in that respect:

We do not wish to build castles in the air and especially not with countries that today are on the other side of the front, not knowing what would happen to them after the war, as, for instance, Hungary, Romania, and Bulgaria. I told him that our participation in any such negotiations would only be possible after we reached full agreement with them [the Soviet Union] and on the condition that all the countries participating in such negotiations had all their affairs fully in order with regard to the USSR.[36]

After receiving what he thought to be approval from the Soviet foreign commissar and Stalin's right-hand man, Beneš was profoundly shocked when, on July 16, 1942, only five weeks after his talk with Molotov, Masaryk informed Beneš that Bogomolov had told him that the Soviet Union opposed the negotiations with the Poles. To make quite sure, Beneš invited Bogomolov to lunch on July 31, 1942. With the very first mouthful, the Soviet envoy began an exhaustive philippic against the Poles and enumerated at length the reasons that in his "personal" opinion spoke against the confederation with the Poles. "Besides," he added, "you Czechoslovaks do not need any union with the Poles to make you safe. Germany will be beaten so that it might never rise again. And if it did rise, no association with Poland could save you. The Soviet Union, which will be your neighbor, will give you all the help you need."

Here Beneš interrupted Bogomolov's harangue:

All the reasons that you are quoting against our union with the Poles fail to

convince me. But one reason, and one reason alone, would suffice: that is
to say, if the Soviet Union objects to it. I am and I must be a realist in
politics. Even if I do not recognize the right of anyone to command us, I
know that after this war we shall be Russia's neighbor; and if the Soviet
Union considers the Polish-Czechoslovak union detrimental to its interests, then it has the right to say so.

Then for the first time, the Soviet ambassador hesitantly admitted that
the opinions he had just expressed were not his own or those of the
"Soviet circles" that he had so often quoted, but the actual views of the
Soviet government.[37]

Once again Beneš gathered all his arguments in a last-ditch effort to
sway the stubborn Soviet envoy and through him the Kremlin. "The
world believes in confederations, in greater unions of states and the idea
of a Polish-Czechoslovak confederation had met with great sympathy
both in America and Britain. How shall one now explain the sudden
retreat? We must tell the British and the Poles the actual facts. You
realize that this will be grist for the mill of those who oppose you and
us." But it was a lost battle. The Soviet Union had pronounced its first
veto and perpetrated its first act of political blackmail since it had
become an ally of the West. Stalin's best friend among the leading Allied
statesmen was the first to suffer humiliation at the hands of those whom
he had attempted to help. Although bitterly disappointed by the
shocking and unexpected Soviet about-face, Beneš knew that as long as
Stalin persisted in his opposition, any further work on the Czechoslovak-Polish confederation had to be halted. Due to Soviet disapproval,
what Beneš saw as the basic purpose and the raison d'être of the
confederation—namely, the creation of a solid bastion against any
recurrence of the German *Drang nach Osten*—could not be achieved.
Beneš did not underestimate the strengthening of Poland's and Czechoslovakia's positions vis-á-vis the Soviet Union resulting from confederation—provided the Poles gave up their claim to the prewar Soviet-
Polish boundary and thereby deprived the Soviets of their main pretext
for opposing Polish-Czechoslovak cooperation. But the Soviet-Polish rift
kept broadening rather than narrowing, and all hope that the Polish
London government would ever be less intransigent in its frontier
controversy with the Soviet Union was vanishing. This being so, Beneš
felt that buying Polish cooperation at the price of Soviet enmity would be
a very bad deal.

Beneš, however, did not abandon his original scheme. Suggestions that Beneš "was ready to give up all his ideas of European federation and . . . sacrifice them all to pro-Soviet opportunism" are utterly wrong and contrary to fact.[38] His proposal to Sikorski in November 1940 was the result of careful thought and not an opportunistic gesture. As Beneš made clear to Bogomolov in their talk of July 31, 1942, despite the Soviet *nyet* he still continued to believe confederation the best solution. Having duly informed the Poles and the British about the sad development and seeing that, at least for the time being, any further progress toward confederation was barred, Beneš wondered how the Soviet opposition could be overcome. If confederation was unacceptable to the Soviet Union, perhaps a treaty of mutual assistance was not, he thought. Eventually this might develop into a closer union when circumstances were more propitious.

The British immediately accepted Beneš's idea, and on November 19, 1942, Eden confirmed in a letter to Masaryk that "a very simple treaty of alliance and friendship between the Czechoslovak Government and the Polish Government, approved both by His Majesty's Government and the Soviet Government, might be appropriate and timely" and "should have the blessing of His Majesty's Government and the Soviet Government."[39] Immediately Beneš prepared a brief draft (in French) of a simple treaty in which Czechoslovakia and Poland agreed to "assist one another in all cases where their national interests were threatened or impaired by Germany . . . afford one another full political, diplomatic, and military assistance in case of an unprovoked attack by Germany . . . support one another in the defense of their interests against Germany in regard to all questions that might arise from the liquidation of this war . . . [and] help one another in the work of reconstruction in their countries."[40]

Unfortunately, the Soviet had not the slightest intention of granting their blessing, even to such a tame and innocuous ersatz. On January 29, 1943, Beneš received Bogomolov on the occasion of Bogomolov's promotion to ambassador. Normally, such audiences are strictly formal, and no delicate political issues are discussed. But the former Russian philosophy teacher did not bother about such diplomatic usages. Barely had he handed over his new credentials when he plunged head first into his favorite pastime of attacking the Poles. This time he declared quite bluntly that the Soviet Union was opposed not only to a Czechoslovak-Polish confederation, but also to any alliance with the present Polish government. This was too much even for the otherwise infinitely patient

Beneš. After Bogomolov left, I witnessed one of the rare instances when the president could not contain his anger. Why, it was Bogomolov himself who had suggested, in one of their earlier talks, that the Polish-Czechoslovak confederation be replaced by a treaty of alliance. In the course of one of their heated arguments about the whole problem of Polish-Czechoslovak relations, Bogomolov had asked Beneš: "Why do you insist on having a confederation? Would not an alliance be sufficient for the time being?"[41]

On the same day Bogomolov had his audience, Beneš lunched with Eden and Nichols and informed the British of the new complication. Needless to say, Eden was extremely displeased by this latest display of Soviet intransigence. But he understood our difficulties and, as Beneš told me, expressly declared that under such circumstances it was impossible for us to enter an alliance with the Poles. It was agreed that Eden would discuss the matter with Maisky.

Seeing that there was no chance of gaining Soviet assent to the creation of a Czechoslovak-Polish confederation and that the idea of a Polish-Czechoslovak alliance also met with resolute Soviet opposition, Beneš continued to rack his brain in an attempt to devise some way to allay Soviet suspicions. At that time he still thought that the persistent Soviet opposition to any kind of closer Polish-Czechoslovak association was caused by Soviet apprehension that a nucleus of a new cordon sanitaire would thus be created rather than by a premeditated design to establish Soviet hegemony in Central Europe. He realized that the communists would exploit the chaos caused by the war in order to secure and strengthen their position, but he still was not convinced, as of 1943, that this would be the main purpose of Soviet foreign policy in the immediate postwar years. Moreover, he thought, the Western powers, which had been taught a terrible lesson at Munich, would surely realize that Soviet domination of Central Europe would be almost as bad for Western Europe and for world peace as domination by Nazi Germany and would resist such an attempt.

Beneš quickly seized the new opportunity that emerged during the 1943 negotiations for the conclusion of a Czechoslovak-Soviet treaty of friendship and alliance. Since the Soviets rejected a bilateral Czechoslovak-Polish alliance, he proposed a tripartite alliance of Soviet Russia, Poland, and Czechoslovakia. That, he thought, would give him an alliance with the Poles as well as with the Russians. A common Slav bulwark would be set up on the eastern frontiers of Germany, and Czechoslovakia could feel all the safer against a possible German lust for revenge. Because the Soviet Union would be a partner both of Czechoslovakia and of Poland and the main member of the triple alliance, Stalin need have no more suspicions that a Czechoslovak-Polish bloc hostile to the Soviet Union would emerge on its western border. At the same time, the Poles and the Czechoslovaks would be better able to guard their independence vis-à-vis the Soviet Union within such a tripartite bloc than they would if each of them had only bilateral relations with Soviet Russia.

Without delay Beneš began preparing the ground for the realization of his new plan. An excellent occasion presented itself when Bogomolov, having just returned from Moscow, invited Beneš to lunch on March 19, 1943, and, as instructed by his Kremlin bosses, asked Beneš certain questions. He was interested mainly in learning exactly what Beneš meant by a tripartite treaty. The Soviet initiative was a welcome surprise for Beneš, who took advantage of the unexpected opportunity to plead vigorously for his cherished idea. When he returned from the luncheon, the president looked very pleased. "It seems that they cooled his head in Moscow," he told me. "I had the impression that this time he spoke more positively than ever before, and perhaps some formula will be found after all." Beneš's renewed optimism was apparent in the concluding paragraph of his account of their conversation:

> On this occasion our conversation was of a quiet character, more open-minded from Bogomolov's side than previously and very friendly. This time he did not abuse the Poles and was rather mild-mannered. I had the impression that a conciliatory change of attitude had taken place. From the discussion and questions it also *appeared* as if Bogomolov were not excluding the possibility that something might be done with the Poles. It seemed as if they wanted my explanation perhaps in order to give more favorable answers than before, both in respect to the negotiations between us and the Poles and between us and them. *But I am not absolutely certain of that.*[42]

Beneš's hopes seemed to be reinforced by a letter from Bogomolov dated April 23, 1943: "Concerning the tripartite treaty in the sense that the president spoke of it, the Soviet government *fundamentally* agrees with the president's proposal. Of course, given the present relations existing between Poland and the Soviet Union, it is impossible to discuss the matter in a definitive manner now. It is necessary to gain time."[43]

At that time Beneš did not know that Stalin would continue biding his time until the communist-controlled Lublin Committee could be changed into the government of the Polish "people's democracy," which Beneš himself would be forced to recognize. In 1943 it looked, on the contrary, as if the Soviets had yielded at last. Without further difficulties Beneš secured Soviet approval of an additional protocol to the Soviet-Czechoslovak Treaty of Friendship, Mutual Assistance and Postwar Cooperation, signed during his visit to Moscow in December 1943. This protocol reserved a place for Poland, as Beneš had proposed in talks with Bogomolov in March 1943: "The USSR and the Czechoslovak Republic agree that if any third state that has common frontiers with the USSR or with the Czechoslovak Republic and in the present war has been the object of German aggression desires to become a party to this agreement, that state will be given the opportunity with the sanction of the USSR and the Czechoslovak Republic of signing this treaty, which thereby would acquire the quality of a tripartite treaty."

A place for Poland in a tripartite alliance was not the only thing Beneš achieved in Polish affairs during his visit to Moscow in 1943. He also did his best to further Polish-Soviet understanding. Indeed in no period of the war did the final settlement of the Polish-Soviet dispute seem so close as when Beneš left Moscow with Stalin's proposals for the new Polish premier, Stanislaw Mikolajczyk.

When Mikolajczyk, who had succeeded Sikorski as Polish premier after the general's tragic death, learned about Beneš's impending departure for Moscow, he came to see him at Aston Abbots. In my diary on November 13, 1943, ten days before our departure for Moscow, I wrote:

> These days the Poles are our constant visitors. On Wednesday, our last day in London before our departure to Russia, [Adam] Tarnowski [Polish envoy to the Czechoslovak government] visited the president. Yesterday Minister [of Labor and Social Affairs Jan] Stanczyk came to lunch to Aston Abbots and today Mikolajczyk. It is evident that the Poles feel that matters are moving toward a climax and that it is essential to obtain some acceptable form of settlement of Polish-Soviet relations. No wonder. Considering the present speed of the Soviet advance, the Red army will very soon be at the Polish frontier.
>
> Mikolajczyk explained in detail his point of view of how Polish-Soviet differences could be solved. He would want to reach agreement with the Soviets whatever the cost because he considers it essential for the survival of Poland; and he would like to visit Moscow to reach a final settlement. Principally he is striving to make sure that the Soviet government will not

interfere in the internal affairs of Poland. Regarding the crucial frontier dispute, he is prepared to go to the absolute limit acceptable to the Poles. He would like to save only Lwow and a part of eastern Galicia for Poland. They would become reconciled to the loss of the rest. He authorized Beneš to inform the Soviet statesmen about all this during his visit to Moscow. In short, the Poles are in a tight corner and are seeking a way out. How much easier and simpler matters would have been for them had they done in 1941 what they are so willing to do now!

As is clear from this entry, Mikolajczyk wanted Beneš's help in bringing about a serious rapprochement between him and Stalin. Both Stanczyk and Mikolajczyk evidently believed that Beneš was, thanks to his excellent relations with the Soviets, the right person for such a task. Beneš gladly accepted this delicate mission since it was in Czechoslovakia's prime interest that Polish-Soviet relations be improved. Thus, he scribbled yet another item on the sheet listing the subjects he wanted to discuss in Moscow. It read: The settlement of Polish-Soviet differences.

As it turned out, the opportunity to embark on his mission on behalf of the Poles presented itself even before he reached Moscow. To welcome us on Stalin's behalf and to serve as our official escort, the Soviet government sent Alexander Korneichuk, a Ukrainian writer and Soviet deputy foreign commissar, to meet us in Iraq. Beneš began his talks about Polish-Soviet relations with this affable emissary from Moscow while we awaited better weather to fly to Moscow. Beneš took great pains to explain to Korneichuk the necessity of a Polish-Soviet understanding. He told him about the message he was bringing from Mikolajczyk for Marshal Stalin. He stressed the importance the British and the Americans attached to a reasonable solution to this question and urged a quick settlement since this was of paramount importance for removing once and for all the threat of the German *Drang nach Osten*.

Korneichuk's reaction to Beneš's arguments revealed a strong bias against the London Poles. But we thought that this was due at least in part to his Ukrainian origin and perhaps to the influence of his wife, Wanda Wasilewska, a fanatical Polish communist, and that it was not necessarily indicative of Stalin's attitude. On December 2, 1943, I wrote in my diary:

> Very energetically and brusquely Korneichuk condemned the methods and intentions of the London Poles. "They became absolutely alienated from the Polish nation, and they follow only their narrow reactionary power-political goals. I exclude the possibility of any collaboration with

them and do not believe one can find among the London Polish émigrés a single politician who would be able to cast off the fetters of their general reactionary conceptions. Not even what you told me concerning your conversations with Mikolajczyk convinces me. On the contrary, it only substantiates my opinion that one cannot be under any illusion regarding the intentions of even the best of the London Poles. The Soviet Union naturally desires an independent and strong Poland, nationally consolidated and sincerely democratic. We also desire that Poland take everything from Germany to which it has a proper claim and that it join the family of Slav nations as a strong and equal partner. The Soviet Union has not the slightest intention of interfering in Polish internal affairs and is fully in favor of Soviet-Polish-Czechoslovak agreement expressed in the tripartite treaty concerning friendship and alliance you have in mind. This is the only way in which German aggression against the Slavs can be prevented in the future."

From what Korneichuk has said one can see that Mikolajczyk's message will hardly find appreciative ears in Moscow. But who knows? After all, Korneichuk is a Ukrainian and as such he undoubtedly has a more sentimental attitude toward the whole matter than a Great Russian would have. And then his wife Wanda Wasilewska is a Polish communist and a fanatical enemy of the Polish government in London. Personally I have noticed that when he became excited, his usually delightful childish smile disappeared from his face and his voice became suddenly harsh whenever the Polish government in London was mentioned in the conversation. It may well be that a somewhat better mood for some form of reconciliation may prevail in the Kremlin.

Korneichuk's anti-Polish sallies notwithstanding, Beneš refused to give up. His resolve to bring about some sort of a reasonable Soviet-Polish modus vivendi is clearly apparent from what he told Smutný:

I want to bring back with me for the Poles in London a principled Russian position regarding Poland, a position that could serve as a basis for a well-balanced future relationship among all three of us. I explained to Korneichuk in great detail the way I envisage it and what it means for both of us to have a strong and satisfied Poland as a neighbor. Korneichuk understands this. I want from them [the Soviets] written confirmation of their position, which I visualize as follows: Russia will declare or will authorize me to tell the Poles:

1. that it wants Poland to be independent and strong;

2. that it has no interest in interfering in internal Polish affairs, but that Poland must be a truly democratic country;

3. that it accepts the Soviet-Czechoslovak-Polish tripartite treaty as the basis of its policy toward Poland and that it would be willing to carry it out in the future;

4. that, under such conditions and for the purpose of righting the wrongs committed by Germany against Poland and Czechoslovakia, it wishes to reach an agreement with Poland and Czechoslovakia with regard to the boundaries of the two countries vis-à-vis Germany.

I shall formulate these four points in writing and will give them to Korneichuk as a basis for discussion. I believe that the Russians are sincere in their policy toward Poland.[44]

Indeed, it seemed to Beneš in December 1943 that the mood in the Kremlin was better—much better. The opportunity to discuss Polish-Soviet problems and to convey to Stalin Mikolajczyk's message offered itself on the second day of our stay in Moscow. We arrived by train from Baku on December 11, 1943, the weather not having improved enough to allow us to fly as originally planned. That evening Stalin gave an official banquet in Beneš's honor. Next day the Czechoslovak-Soviet treaty was signed, and our Soviet hosts took us to the Bolshoi Theater to attend a brilliant performance of Rimsky-Korsakov's *Snegurochka* (The Snow Maiden).

But the president did not see the entire performance. During the intermission he left the central box and went to another at the side of the stage where he was expected by Stalin, who came to the theater incognito. There, in a corner hidden from the audience, they sat with Kalinin, Molotov, Voroshilov, Korneichuk, Fierlinger, and Smutný and entered full steam into the Polish question. Stalin wished to know the president's opinion regarding the London Poles and Beneš's opinion of the possibilities of improving Soviet-Polish relations. Beneš was delighted that an opportunity to help improve Soviet-Polish relations had presented itself so soon. He informed Stalin of the contents of his talks with Mikolajczyk and of the Polish premier's desire to re-establish contacts with the Soviet leaders and to visit Moscow to settle Polish-Soviet controversies. He described at some length conditions among the London Polish émigrés and strongly recommended Mikolajczyk as a man who was sincere, well-intentioned, and anxious to reach an agreement. Beneš did not conceal from Stalin the power of the followers of Pilsudski among the Polish refugees and governing circles in London, but he insisted forcefully that some agreement between the Soviet Union and Poland could and should be achieved. Hence, he wished to reserve a place for Poland in the Soviet-Czechoslovak alliance.

Stalin listened attentively to the president's arguments and asked a number of questions. He then summed up their discussion, explained his own views, and finally agreed that the president might tell Mikolajczyk this as the official standpoint of the Soviet government. Stalin's point of view, as Beneš understood it, was essentially as follows: renewal of diplomatic relations with the Polish government was conditional on a change of government and removal of inveterate opponents of the Soviets. Mikolajczyk was acceptable to the Soviets as head of the new Polish government. Attacks on the Soviet Union must cease. As for frontiers, the Soviet Union insisted on the present eastern boundary and at most was willing to cede a few minor pieces to Poland. But it would support a substantial enlargement of Polish territory westwards, even as far as the Oder River. The Soviet Union favored a strong, independent Poland and had no intention of interfering in its internal affairs. It wished to conclude an alliance with Poland similar to the Soviet-Czechoslovak treaty and did not intend to make a deal with a new revolutionary Germany, should one result from this war, against Poland or any other country.

At the beginning of this long discussion, Stalin seemed rather skeptical. When the president assured him that the Poles would see reason after the war and everything would be all right, Stalin remarked: "Yes, but that will be after the third war." Beneš immediately countered that he did not believe there would be a new world war. When Voroshilov also began to doubt the prospects for future peace, Stalin interrupted: "You won't change the Germans. After a while there will be another war with them."

It was evident that Stalin knew very little about Mikolajczyk, or else deliberately pretended ignorance, hoping that he could thus compare his own information with the president's views. During the conversation a humorous incident occurred that surely made the ears of the Polish premier tingle—on Stalin's suggestion everyone drank a toast to Mikolajczyk.[45]

The president was fully contented with his talk with Stalin and evidently did not regret missing part of the performance. In his conversations with us, we could notice the satisfaction of a man who believed that he had successfully completed a mission of goodwill. He hoped that at long last the gaping abyss between the Soviets and the Poles might be bridged. "If only the Poles come to their senses and if Mikolajczyk has sufficient courage to give up what in any case is lost for them in the east," he remarked pensively.

The Polish issue was also discussed in talks between the president and Molotov on December 14 and 16, 1943. When Molotov mentioned that the Russians as well as the British and the Americans had brought to the Teheran Conference maps on which the Curzon line was marked as the postwar boundary between Poland and the Soviet Union, Beneš told Molotov about Mikolajczyk's fear that the Soviet Union might claim areas west of the Curzon line. The Soviet foreign commissar assured Beneš that they had no such intention and suggested that the Curzon line might be negotiable. After Beneš had pointed out that the Poles would like to regain at least Bialystok and Lomza, Molotov seemed prepared to concede Lomza but not Bialystok, which, he said, was overwhelmingly Belorussian.[46]

Beneš returned from Moscow to London full of high hopes that the Soviet-Polish deadlock would soon be resolved and that this in turn would allow him to resume, at least in a less ambitious form, the pursuit of his cherished project of Czechoslovak-Polish cooperation. In this spirit of expectation he reported on his talks in Moscow to Churchill on whom he called on his way back from Moscow at Marrakesh in Morocco where the British prime minister was convalescing after an attack of pneumonia. "He thinks that what the Russians propose is the maximum they are prepared to concede," Beneš told us. "He recommends that the Poles accept it. He asked me to inform both Eden and Mikolajczyk as soon as possible after my return to England—and help persuade the Poles to accept the Soviet offer."[47]

Two days after his arrival in Great Britain, on January 8, 1944, Beneš saw Eden, whose reaction was the same as the prime minister's. "That's the best chance the Poles can get," he said. "Mikolajczyk should be wise enough not to let it go unused."[48] Unfortunately, the Polish premier thought differently. "Today we had a real Polish Day here," I wrote in my diary of the visits that Mikolajczyk and Stanczyk paid Beneš on January 10, 1944:

> Mikolajczyk came in the morning and Minister Stanczyk in the afternoon. The president informed both in detail about his talks with Stalin concerning Polish-Soviet relations as well as about his talks with Churchill at Marrakesh. He told them that Churchill was sending them the message that they ought to come to an understanding with the Russians on this basis. Mikolajczyk and Stanczyk admitted that they ought to do so, realized that such an opportunity to reach Soviet-Polish agreement should not be wasted, and felt that they would not be able to save the prewar eastern

frontiers of Poland no matter what they did. Both personally agreed on this but were convinced, especially Mikolajczyk, that they would not succeed in persuading their colleagues. "If the Russians would at least give up Lwow, then perhaps I could attempt it," said Mikolajczyk. "But as matters now stand it is absolutely hopeless. Even as we know that we will be losing our eastern territories, we can never give our consent to it." Stanczyk was more emphatic than Mikolajczyk in his desire to utilize the opportunity to reach agreement and was critical of Mikolajczyk's hesitation. But not even he was under the illusion that it would be possible to induce the present Polish government to do so.

It is a terrible dilemma. They know that by their behavior they are digging a grave for themselves; they know that they are aggravating the position of the future Poland; they know that they will lose the eastern territories in any case whether they do or do not come to an agreement with the Russians. They realize that by coming to an agreement now they could save quite a lot and that for their loss in the east they would be able to secure a more than equivalent compensation at Germany's expense. They know that in this way they could substantially facilitate the internal development of postwar Poland and, in cooperation with us, would feel stronger and more secure even against the communists, should they attempt to resolve the situation in Czechoslovakia or Poland to their advantage. But no! They prefer to let everything collapse rather than allow the odium to stick to them that they had appended their signature to an act that could corroborate the loss of the territory that once belonged to Poland.

Thus, the joint effort of Beneš, Churchill, and Eden to resolve the Soviet-Polish deadlock came to naught. Whether Stalin and Molotov were earnest about their proposals of December 1943 may, of course, be doubted in the light of subsequent developments. But if an agreement had been reached at that time, cosponsored as it would have been by Great Britain and the United States, it might well have hindered Soviet plans for domination. At least the Soviets would have lost the main argument against a Polish-Czechoslovak association. The way might thus have been reopened for closer Czechoslovak-Polish cooperation, and both nations might have resisted the Soviet policy of divide and conquer more resolutely.

Efforts to settle the Soviet-Polish dispute continued despite the failure of the Anglo-Czechoslovak attempt of January 1944. But each month of delay further weakened the Polish position. Public dissatisfaction in Great Britain and the United States with the Poles' intransigence over their eastern boundary was growing. The Western democracies clearly considered the Curzon line the reasonable dividing line between the Soviet Union and Poland. The London Poles could no longer treasure any illusions regarding this matter, and bitter controversies over policy developed even in their inner governmental circles. Finally, a Polish governmental group boldly attempted to salvage as much as possible from an increasingly more serious and more desperate situation. Toward the end of May 1944, these Poles decided to contact the Soviet Ambassador Lebedev, who in the meantime had replaced Bogomolov. Beneš learned about it firsthand from Lebedev on June 2, 1944. As soon as the Soviet ambassador left, Beneš instructed me to connect him with Mikolajczyk, who hurriedly came to see the president that afternoon. "A new chance that agreement between the Russians and the Poles might be reached after all," the president told me when he finished his telephone conversation with the Polish premier. "Ring up Lebedev and tell him: '*Vsë v poriadke*' [Everything is in order]."[49] Lebedev seemed very pleased by the message. That was the beginning of the last good offices that Beneš was able to offer the Poles and the Russians during the war. According to Beneš's written account, the events unfolded as follows:

On June 2 Lebedev asked urgently to be received by Beneš.[50] He came to tell him that, with Moscow's approval, he had met in the last two weeks once with Gen. Izydor Modelski, undersecretary of war in the Polish government in exile, and twice with Stanislaw Grabski, president of the Polish National Council, and that later in the day he would in all probability meet with Mikolajczyk. What he wanted Beneš to do was to inform the Polish premier how Moscow viewed the situation so that Mikolajczyk would know about it prior to their meeting. The message that the Soviet ambassador wanted Beneš to convey to Mikolajczyk was as follows:

a. From the government with which the Soviets are prepared to negotiate, the following four persons must be dismissed: [Minister of Defense Gen. Marion] Kukiel; [Minister of Information Stanislaw] Kot; [Commander-in-Chief of the Polish Armed Forces Gen. Kazimierz] Sosnkowski; and [Polish President Wladyslaw] Rackiewicz.

b. Mikolajczyk would be accepted with pleasure should he decide to visit Moscow to complete negotiations on the other matters.

c. Moscow understands the difficulties of the Polish government in respect of the acceptance of definite frontiers. Therefore, without abandoning its demands, it would do everything possible to avoid aggravating the situation of this new government friendly to it. It thus gives the assurance that an agreement would be reached during this visit to Moscow. Moscow does not exclude agreement on a mere demarcation line, leaving the question of the definite frontiers to settlement in the future.

When Beneš told Mikolajczyk, whom he invited to see him that same afternoon, about the Soviet desiderata, the Polish premier, visibly surprised, had this to say:

> In respect to Kukiel there will be no conflict; he will resign whenever I desire it. With Kot it will be more difficult. He is my party colleague, faithful to me, and it is just he who supports me in my Russian policy. A legend has been created that he is anti-Russian. It is not true. With Sosnkowski it will be extremely difficult, but even that could be arranged. He has made so many enemies that his dismissal could be brought about, especially if I can promise my people that if Sosnkowski leaves the government, we shall obtain this and that. But to expel him without knowing what for is very difficult. The most difficult undertaking will be with Rackiewicz—if it is possible at all. He is president, covered by the constitution. I do not know.

Beneš expressed his understanding of the problems the Soviet demands posed for Mikolajczyk and assured him that he by no means wished to interfere in Polish affairs. Nevertheless, he advised him to meet with Lebedev. But the meeting did not take place since Mikolajczyk left hurriedly to see President Roosevelt.

On June 13 Lebedev called again on Beneš and told him that Grabski came to see him in lieu of Mikolajczyk and requested that the Soviet demands be modified. "Everything could perhaps be arranged, but Moscow should retreat from the demand concerning Rackiewicz," Lebedev quoted Grabski as having told him.

> The quarrel among the Poles still continues, and a strong group has already been formed that works for resolving matters according to the stated demands. Even President Rackiewicz himself was won over to this policy. It is also agreed that Mikolajczyk would go to Moscow accompanied by Grabski and [Polish Minister of Foreign Affairs Tadeusz] Romer. Grabski reconnoitered whether it would be possible to undertake the journey first and change the government afterwards. Lebedev warned that this would not be possible because in the first place Moscow could only negotiate with a new government, and then should Mikolajczyk want to force a change after the journey, a campaign would again commence that

it was a dictate of Moscow and that Moscow was interfering in their internal affairs. And Moscow did not wish for a second time to lay itself open to such comment.[51]

The final event in this sad chapter of lost opportunities was the Czechoslovak recognition of the Lublin government. It constitutes a classic example not only of Beneš's desperate endeavors to maintain equilibrium between the East and the West, but also of his growing impotence once Stalin decided to use the Red Army to spearhead communist expansion in Central Europe.

The resignation of Mikolajczyk on November 24, 1944, shortly after his return from Moscow, and Grabski's on November 29 were signs to Beneš that the London Poles had been defeated. Those who favored rapprochement with Soviet Russia and were ready to facilitate this by surrendering territories east of the Curzon line (such as Mikolajczyk, Stanczyk, and Grabski) were discarded and their policy rejected by their colleagues and Polish President Rackiewicz. Not only did this foreclose any possibility of rapprochement with Moscow, but even the British deeply resented the development and almost unanimously blamed the new Polish government. Mikolajczyk's attempts at friendship with Russia, said a December 1 editorial in the *Times*, "were thwarted and finally defeated by those who failed to recognize that such a settlement was necessary and that it demands the frank abandonment of some past mistakes and of some misguided ambitions for the future." "In throwing over their former Prime Minister, Mr. Mikolajczyk," wrote the *Spectator* on January 5, 1945, "they have parted with the one man who could have bridged the gulf between the Polish Government and Russia." The general dissatisfaction of the British public with this new failure, attributed to Polish territorial intransigence, gave rise to a bitter declaration by the British prime minister, mercilessly condemning the attitude of the Polish government. Laying before the House of Commons on December 15, 1944, the "grim, bare bones" of the Polish situation, Churchill said bluntly that if Mr. Mikolajczyk had been able to return to Moscow with the assent of his colleagues, he would at that moment be at the head of a Polish government on Polish soil, recognized by all the United Nations and assured of the friendship of Marshal Stalin. And, Churchill declared, at the peace conference the British government would proclaim the Soviet claim to the Curzon line as right and just.

After this, Beneš did not doubt that the communist-controlled Lublin Committee would soon constitute itself as a government, would be recognized as such by the Soviet Union, and would then want to be recognized by the Czechoslovak government as well. Once again Beneš confronted a dilemma. His recognition of the Lublin Committee would be very unpopular in the West and would be exploited against him. Should he refuse to do so, trouble would arise in relation not only to the Lublin government but also to the Soviet Union. By the end of 1944 Beneš's trust in Soviet good intentions had suffered its first serious setbacks. The full story of his gradual disillusionment with Stalin is told in a later chapter; here it suffices to state that when the Red Army began in autumn of 1944 to liberate Czechoslovakia from the east, the Czechoslovak governmental delegate arrived in the liberated part of Czechoslovakia according to the understanding between Beneš and Stalin and according to the May 1944 Soviet-Czechoslovak agreement about the administration of liberated territories. But Beneš soon discovered that Stalin's pledge was not what he had thought. Despite the Soviet recognition of the pre-Munich frontiers of Czechoslovakia, repeated on so many occasions, the Soviet agents who came to Czechoslovakia with the Red Army started a campaign to annex the easternmost Czechoslovak province, Ruthenia, to the Soviet Union. They forced local mayors to sign petitions asking to be reunited with the "Ukrainian brothers on the other side of the Carpathians," organized "spontaneous" meetings, and caused telegrams advocating "reunion" to be sent to Stalin and Beneš. Radio Kiev in the Ukraine propagated the same line. The Czechoslovak governmental delegate protested but to no avail. Could one expect, the Soviets replied, that the Soviet Union would oppose the "will of the people"?

Since Beneš felt that Ruthenia was lost and, what was worse, feared that a similar procedure might be used in Slovakia, he was reluctant to increase this grave risk by opposing Stalin too vehemently by not recognizing the Lublin Committee, should it declare itself a government. Moreover, Fierlinger regularly bombarded him with dispatches insisting on a radical change of policy toward the Polish government in London. "The Kremlin is not satisfied with our foreign policy," Fierlinger telegraphed, for instance, on December 28, 1944. "After the signing of the treaty [of Friendship, Mutual Assistance, and Postwar Cooperation on December 12, 1943], they expected a more active policy on our part. But we are stressing a policy of fifty-fifty too much. Constant demands for supplying our territory with foodstuffs are also not accepted sympathetically. We must adapt our policy in accordance with Soviet demands."[52]

Despite this constant pressure and difficulties, Beneš defended himself as best he could and played for time. On December 30, 1944, he telegraphed back to Fierlinger:

> With regard to Poland I state the following: a). I aided the Soviets on all sides as no one else, under difficult political conditions existing here. I worked hard for a Polish-Soviet agreement . . . Everyone here knows that, especially the local Poles. I have never used this as an advertisement or for the purpose of propaganda. b). We cannot undertake anything in regard to the Lublin Committee insofar as we are not requested to do so by the Soviets or the Lublin Committee itself and as long as the Lublin Committee is not proclaimed as the government. It is unthinkable that we should begin to break off diplomatic relations with the Polish government [in London] when, as far as we are concerned, it is giving us no cause to do so. c). We expect with certainty that the Lublin Committee will proclaim itself as the government, that the Soviets will recognize it, and then the matter will be laid before us. In that case I deem it necessary to arrange preliminary negotiations with the Lublin government in which some form of declaration will be made that will mean the repudiation of Beck's policy against us in 1938 and 1939, disavowing all his actions and agreements with Germany, Hungary, and Romania against us, and the mutual promise of friendly relations in the future. Since, until now, the London Polish government has refused to undertake anything of the kind, it would be a strong manifestation that would make a deep impression both here and in America, would be of great help to Lublin, would deal a fresh blow to Germany, and would have very beneficial effects in Czechoslovakia and in Poland. Therefore, I entreat you to communicate all this to the Moscow government and possibly to ask their opinion. In this sense, you can, if the possibility permits, sound out the opinion of the Lublin Poles. It would be best if all this were accomplished simultaneously at the time when I will be moving from London eastwards, but I am not making this a condition.[53]

One day later Beneš's anticipation proved correct: the Lublin Committee renamed itself the provisional government of Poland and five days later was recognized by the Soviet Union. That, of course, was grist for Fierlinger's mill. In reply to Beneš's dispatch of December 30, 1944, he triumphantly telegraphed that the Russians were deeply dissatisfied with our Polish policy and considered Beneš's desire to obtain a Polish repudiation of Beck's aggressive policy an evasion. Three days later another telegram came, even more impatient. Valerian A. Zorin, head of the Central European section of the Soviet Commissariat of Foreign Affairs, had told him, Fierlinger wrote, that Chichayev had reported that Beneš promised to recognize the Lublin government as soon as it had been constituted. Therefore, Fierlinger asked to be allowed a free hand.[54] It was quite obvious from Fierlinger's dispatch that he intended to proceed to Lublin and settle the question of recognition on the spot.

It was as if Gottwald himself, if not a member of the Soviet Politburo, had dictated to Fierlinger what to write and what to do. Chichayev was an agent of the Soviet state security clad in diplomatic uniform and attached to the Soviet embassy in London. Beneš never told him what Chichayev reported to Moscow. "I told Chichayev exactly what I telegraphed to you," Beneš wired back to Fierlinger on January 9, 1945.

> I told him that through the Soviet recognition of the Polish Lublin government the problem is automatically placed before us; that is, we must solve it, which does not mean that we automatically recognize the government. I told him further that we wished to discuss the matter because at the same time we desire to settle frontier and other questions. Nothing more was said, and thus there was no difference between what I told you and what I told Chichayev. If Chichayev reported something else, I have no explanation for that.[55]

Obviously, Chichayev either misunderstood Beneš or, eager to please Moscow and to report a success to his superiors, distorted what Beneš had actually said.

Once again this was too much even for the patient Beneš. "How can one make any policy when one has to work with such people," he exclaimed when he finished reading Fierlinger's dispatch. He then angrily grabbed his pen and without hesitation wrote a sharp and indignant reply instructing Fierlinger not to go to Lublin:

> Evidently, in Moscow they do not see that the Polish case is shaking public opinion in Great Britain, that here it is a problem of great importance that causes crises . . . We will not change our opinion, but we will not present a fait accompli to anyone, especially not to Britain at a moment when we are about to leave . . . although you very often complain that London does not comprehend the conditions in Moscow, it appears as if Moscow wished to proceed in every question without the slightest comprehension of conditions in England. This cannot continue. There must be complete harmony . . . As I see it, a conflict concerning this matter will take place between England and the Soviets as well as between England and ourselves . . . I entertain no covert thought, neither do we want this matter delayed or prolonged. But we do not wish to become once again the object of anyone's diplomatic maneuvers.[56]

In another telegram sent a little later the president told Fierlinger: "You must understand that here, and even more after we have returned to Prague, we cannot act as if we were under a protectorate. We can only act as good and sincere allies."[57]

But Fierlinger evidently did not mind being under a Soviet protectorate. He urged and urged, and almost threatened, faithfully following instructions received from Zorin and Gottwald. Beneš saw that his desperate race with time was lost. The early international conference to solve the Polish problem he hoped for was not in sight. There was no sign of an early reunion between the Lublin government and Mikolajczyk and his group. So, after duly informing the British that he could no longer resist without seriously endangering Czechoslovakia's position vis-à-vis the Soviet Union, Beneš finally capitulated. On January 30, 1945, the Czechoslovak government recognized the Lublin government, and on February 5, 1945, the following explanatory circular, approved by the president, was sent to Czechoslovak legations throughout the world:

On January 30, 1945, the Council of Ministers unanimously adopted a resolution by which the Czechoslovak government recognized the provisional Lublin government and established diplomatic relations with it. The Russians, British, Americans, and the French have been informed. Thus ended the negotiations conducted from the time the Lublin Committee proclaimed itself as a provisional government. The Soviet government has repeatedly shown interest in respect to our decision in a matter to which it attached great importance. We requested Lublin to clarify all matters that remained unsettled between us and the Poles from the past, especially with regard to all the consequences resulting from the 1938 aggression. We emphasized to the Russians that we had to insist on the pre-Munich frontier vis-à-vis *any* Polish government. The English have asked us for a consultation and have suggested that the matter should be postponed. We explained to them the difficulty of our situation and found, in the end, a friendly understanding of our standpoint. To our suggestion that controversial frontier matters of 1938 and 1939 should on this occasion be settled, no answer was received from the Lublin government. When the Soviet government again insisted that we should not postpone the recognition as it would prolong uncertainty, we decided to accord recognition immediately, without concluding our negotiations with Lublin. But we still insist on our standpoint with regard to the pre-Munich frontiers (Beck's aggression in 1938, aggression of the so-called Slovak government in 1939). And according to a suggestion of the Soviet government, we will negotiate controversial questions later.

By doing this we wanted to secure full and active Russian aid in respect to all unresolved questions. Besides, the Soviet government stands by the

UNIVERSITY LIBRARIES
CARNEGIE-MELLON UNIVERSITY
PITTSBURGH, PENNSYLVANIA 15213

treaty [of Friendship, Mutual Assistance, and Postwar Cooperation] and by the pre-Munich boundaries. The Lublin representatives repeatedly condemned Beck's aggression. British official circles and the public on the whole realize that in the given situation we could not have acted otherwise, especially as we need Soviet aid when the Red Army is liberating our territory.

We have to reckon with a certain campaign of London Poles who have issued a proclamation in which one day later they broke off relations with the Czechoslovak government. This Polish proclamation makes the parting with the former Polish regime easier. We request that the Polish attacks, if they come, be answered only in the most necessary instances, reservedly but decisively.[58]

Thus ended Beneš's efforts to ensure the postwar security of Central Europe through an alliance of the smaller nations. The Soviets had served notice on Beneš that they intended theirs to be the dominant voice in East Central Europe and that his and his country's roles in postwar Europe were to be subservient to Soviet interests.

5

Beneš and Roosevelt

From the very outset Beneš's wartime political strategy comprised paying official visits, at appropriate times, to the two men who, as he knew, would play the decisive role not only in the conduct of the war but also in the shaping of the world's postwar order: U.S. President Franklin D. Roosevelt and Soviet dictator Joseph V. Stalin. While Beneš intended from the beginning that the two trips closely follow one another, he definitely wanted his visit to Washington to precede his journey to Moscow. This, he thought, would offset his critics' allegations of excessively pro-Soviet leanings. Hence, he quickly and eagerly accepted Roosevelt's December 1942 invitation to visit him. "I decided," he wrote in his *Memoirs*, "that politically I would link my visit with my already planned journey to the Soviet Union. The whole policy of the Allies was for me one united whole because in World War II all world problems were more than ever intertwined and it was quite impossible to solve one independently of the others. I therefore mapped out a comprehensive plan for myself. In the spring I would go first to Washington and then soon after my return I would go from London to Moscow."[1]

The visit was officially presented as primarily a courtesy visit, a thank-you gesture for U.S. actions to liberate Czechoslovakia. "I shall ask for absolutely nothing from them," said Beneš repeatedly in talking about the visit. "I shall simply say that I am coming to thank them for all they have done for us and to answer any questions they may have about our matters.[2] However, no busy statesman, least of all one so averse to ceremonial platitudes as Beneš, would travel thousands of miles just to shake hands with and deliver personal thanks to another extremely preoccupied statesman. In effect, Beneš intended to do much more than pay Roosevelt a mere courtesy visit. Although no new difficulties had emerged in U.S.-Czechoslovak relations following the two-step U.S. recognition of Beneš and his government in July 1941 and October 1942, several aspects of American policy and behavior caused Beneš some concern.

First, Beneš had some misgivings about the possible political implication of the Atlantic Charter, the declaration of principles agreed on by Roosevelt and Churchill on August 14, 1941. In particular, he disliked point 2, which criticized "territorial changes that did not accord with the freely expressed wishes of the peoples concerned." Beneš worried that this broadly phrased clause might be misused by the Sudeten Germans and the Hungarians, as well as by their supporters in the United States and Great Britain, to prevent Czechoslovakia from regaining its pre-Munich boundaries. As he knew from reports of the Czech underground, the average Czech in the Protectorate shared this worry. "The result of the meeting between Churchill and Roosevelt is unfavorably criticized by the people," read a radio message received from the Czech underground on August 25, 1941. "One again sees in it concessions to the Germans."[3] "The whole nation wants and desires to retain the historical frontiers," pleaded another message. "No one can understand . . . why the terrible injustice committed on us in 1938 could not be righted."[4] In order to allay his countrymen's fears, Beneš sent home a long message on September 6, 1941, minimizing the action and explaining that Roosevelt needed the charter to prevail over isolationists at home and to ease America's eventual entry into the war. He conceded, however, that there would be difficulties and conflicts over boundaries with the Germans, Hungarians, and Poles, and even disagreements among the Allies themselves.[5] Also, in a note of August 29, 1941 (addressed to Anthony Eden), the Czechoslovak government qualified its rather lukewarm acceptance of the Atlantic Charter by stressing its "understanding" that "the final interpretation and application of these principles will be in accordance with the circumstances and needs of the different parts of Europe and the world" and that "the vital interests and sovereign rights of the Czechoslovak Republic, as internationally acknowledged by the whole civilized world and temporarily disturbed by

Germany's acts of aggression beginning in September 1938, will be reinstated and safeguarded."[6]

Another of Beneš's concerns on the eve of his departure for the United States was the frigid and rather overbearing American attitude toward France in general and Charles de Gaulle in particular. Despite his traumatic experience with France in 1938, Beneš believed that the cause of peace and security in Europe would be well served by a strong, reborn France standing guard on Germany's western flank. He harbored no illusions that France could reclaim the leadership it had enjoyed on the European continent after the First World War. "After this war France shall not be able even after twenty years to play a leading role in European politics," he opined in July 1941.[7] But he felt that with American help and understanding, France could still make an important contribution to the postwar European balance of power. He also had a very high opinion of de Gaulle and anticipated that the overwhelming majority of the French people would welcome the general as their new leader. "Unlike other people," he wrote in his *Memoirs*, "I immediately saw in Charles de Gaulle after the fall of France the man who would play an important part in the military renovation of France and who would, at least for some time, be the mouthpiece of postwar France.[8] Hence, he thought that disregarding de Gaulle's notorious abrasiveness and treating him with more consideration would better serve the Allied cause and improve postwar cooperation between the French and the British and Americans.

Thus, Beneš's dismay at the American dealings with Admiral Darlan at the time of the U.S. invasion of North Africa was hardly surprising. He simply did not believe that a temporary advantage gained by cooperation with an unsavory turncoat could outweigh the undesirable consequences that the action would have in metropolitan France and other countries under German occupation.

Nor did Beneš feel as assured as he would have liked about relations between the United States and the Soviet Union. He was delighted by the Roosevelt administration's reaction to the Nazi invasion of the Soviet Union and the degree of Soviet-American cooperation thus far attained. But he knew that this cooperation was not to the liking of certain groups and influential persons in the United States. He was also keenly aware of the German efforts, greatly accelerated after the Wehrmacht's catastrophic defeat at Stalingrad, to persuade the United States and Britain that the only way to prevent the bolshevization of Europe was for the two countries to conclude a separate peace with Germany. Since, as he saw it in 1943, only the total defeat of Nazi Germany and sincere and friendly cooperation between the Soviet Union and the Anglo-Saxon powers could restore Czechoslovakia to its pre-Munich boundaries and guarantee its safety and independence, anything and anybody threatening such cooperation was necessarily on Beneš's blacklist.

Besides a number of conservative American isolationists, such as Joseph Kennedy and William Bullitt, another man high on the list was Archduke Otto von Hapsburg because of his endeavors to convince America that a Central European federation under his "presidency" was the best and perhaps the only alternative to communist domination of the area. Beneš felt that, far from being helpful, the Hapsburg involvement only made the attainment of close cooperation among the countries of East Central Europe more difficult. He had similar misgivings about the activities of the Hungarian politician Tibor Eckhardt and his group, who sought to gain American support for Hungary's retention of the territories seized from its neighbors in 1938–1939 and attempted to portray Hungary as an important link in the anticommunist bulwark in Eastern Europe and Beneš as virtually a Soviet agent.

Beneš was all the more apprehensive about such activities, and especially their impact on the United States, for yet another reason. He knew that the Soviet Union's postwar influence in Czechoslovakia and throughout East Central Europe would be strong and that native communists would do their utmost to profit from this. He felt that to cope with this threat and to preserve democracy, major economic and social reforms, including substantial nationalization of large industrial and commercial enterprises, would be necessary. Aware of America's firm commitment to capitalism and its dislike of socialism, he wondered whether the United States would view it as a rejection of the Western way of life and write off Czechoslovakia as an ungrateful and misguided godchild that had opted for the Soviet way.

Finally, Beneš was rather uncertain about the durability of America's commitment to postwar Europe. Since the outbreak of the war in 1939, he had never doubted that America would become involved as a full-fledged belligerent. But he was doubtful whether the United States would assume long-term commitments to safeguard the settlement reached at the end of the war. Will not isolationism once again prevail, he wondered, and Roosevelt's plans for world security be frustrated like Wilson's in 1919? His doubts were anything but relieved by a personal warning from John Foster Dulles in July 1942. Dulles, whom Beneš knew from earlier days and whose judgment he valued, expressed strong doubts about America's determination to become involved in postwar Europe's problems. "Do not rely too much on any considerable American participation in the postwar reorganization of Europe," he told Beneš quite frankly. "In America there is very little idealism, and the United States will stand firm only where it has its own direct interests."[9]

Thus, when he boarded the U.S. Armed Forces aircraft on May 6, 1943, for his first trans-Atlantic flight, Beneš carried with him a sheet on which he had jotted down the main topics he wanted to discuss. Naturally, first and foremost, he wanted to inform the American president fully and frankly of specific Czechoslovak problems, wishes, and expectations and to secure America's political support. In particular, he wanted to obtain Roosevelt's approval for solving the Sudeten German problem by transferring most of the Sudeten Germans into the Reich and to make sure of U.S. backing for Czechoslovakia's claim to its pre-Munich boundaries. He also wanted to tell Roosevelt his views on Czechoslovakia's international situation and its relations with the Soviet Union and to acquaint him with the purpose of his forthcoming visit to Moscow and with the Soviet-Czechoslovak Treaty of Friendship, Mutual Assistance, and Postwar Cooperation that was to be signed during that visit.

Second, he intended to convince Roosevelt of the crucial importance of good U.S.-Soviet relations for the recovery and stability of Europe. Believing that the best way to preserve the countries of East Central Europe from communism was through sincere understanding and cooperation between the Soviet Union and the West, he put this topic high on the list of his Washington agenda. Churchill himself had asked Beneš to support during his American visit the British thesis about the necessity of collaborating with the Soviet Union.[10] "While I was in America I intended to work for a closer *rapprochement* with Russia," he told Mackenzie in 1944. "I wanted to remove the suspicions between the Great Powers and establish that atmosphere of goodwill and co-operation which was to prove so important and effective at the great conference at Teheran."[11]

Beneš was also anxious to learn Roosevelt's ideas about the postwar reorganization of Europe, especially with regard to Germany, and the extent the United States was prepared to help maintain peace after the war. In that context he planned to say a few words in favor of France and the place that he thought should be assigned it in Europe.

Finally, Beneš took with him an eighteen-page memorandum for the Holy See that he wanted the American president to send to the pope. Beneš turned to Roosevelt with this rather unusual request only with great reluctance. In view of the complications that had plagued relations between Czechoslovakia and the Vatican in the past, including the Vatican's recognition of the puppet state of Slovakia, he felt that normalizing Czechoslovakia's relations with the Holy See before the end of the war was politically very important. In November 1940, soon after his government had been recognized, he wrote a letter to the Vatican's apostolic delegate in London, Archbishop W. Godfrey, suggesting the establishment of unofficial contacts between his government in exile and the Vatican. To keep this delicate approach absolutely secret, he directed me to deliver the letter personally. But the pope's reaction was evasive and noncommittal, and Beneš hoped that the Vatican might be more responsive if it received the memo through the American president.[12]

During Beneš's sojourn in the United States, which lasted from May 7 to June 9, 1943 (except for a short official visit to Canada), he had ample opportunity to discuss these topics, and even some he did not intend to raise. The highlights of his visit were two long conversations with Roosevelt, the first one on May 12, 1943 (following the official dinner at the White House and lasting until 2:00 A.M.), and the second one on June 7, 1943. On the morning of May 13, he also attended, at Roosevelt's request, the first part of a conference between the American president and Churchill, who had just arrived in Washington for talks with Roosevelt.

Strange as it may seem, the first topic of discussion at the initial meeting of the two presidents on May 12, 1943, was France.[13] Beneš found Roosevelt even more anti–French and anti–de Gaulle than he had anticipated. The U.S. president was sharply critical of the French colonial regime and its ineptitude as he had seen it during his recent visit to the liberated part of North Africa. "France ought not to be given back Indo-China, for example," he told Beneš. "Indo-China should be placed under the mandate of the great powers and administered by a committee, composed of one American, one Chinese, and one Filipino, which would prepare it for independence." He was also skeptical about the possibility of France's recovery after the war: "It will take a very long time for France before it recovers. I think that it would have to remain occupied for one year or even two after the liberation."

As had been his intention, Beneš rose to France's defense. "On the continent of Europe," he argued, "it is necessary in the interest of Europe and the rest of the world, and having in view the future situation of Germany, that there should be again, in addition to the Soviet Union, one other strong democratic great power—France."[14] He stressed that from the very beginning, France should be invited to participate actively in the new system of European and world security. Although Roosevelt appeared outwardly unmoved by his pleadings, Beneš felt, as he told me and repeated in his subsequent report to his Council of Ministers in London, that his arguments did have a certain impact.[15]

The next subject the two statesmen considered at some length and to which they returned again in their second conversation, was the issue of Polish-Soviet relations. In the spring of 1943, relations between the two nations, none too good even after the two countries became allies following the German invasion of the Soviet Union in June 1941, worsened. In April 1943 the Germans announced that in a forest near Katyn they had uncovered collective graves of thousands of Polish officers taken prisoner by the Soviet army in September 1939 and claimed that they had been massacred by the Russians. When the Poles requested an International Red Cross investigation, the Soviet Union indignantly broke off diplomatic relations with the Polish government in exile. Differences between the two countries reached a critical stage, and something had to be done. Beneš was anxious to exchange views with Roosevelt on what had become the main political impediment to good East-West relations. Both Roosevelt and Beneš were convinced, as was Churchill and most everyone except the Germans and most of the Poles, that the Katyn massacre had been perpetrated by the Germans, who then contrived a devilish Goebbelsian scheme to blame the Russians. In reporting to his cabinet, Beneš quoted Roosevelt as saying : "The Poles have been deluded; this is definitely untrue." And Beneš added: "I have a similar categorical confirmation from the English. This, gentlemen, has been a terrible delusion. An American informant gave me the details and told me who among the Poles was mainly responsible for it."[16]

Believing that the Germans were responsible for the Katyn massacre, the two presidents could easily agree that the Poles were to blame for the impasse and that if they resolved their boundary controversy with the Soviet Union by accepting a somewhat improved version of the Curzon line, all would be well. "The Russians are demanding nothing more than what rightly belongs to them," said Roosevelt. "Perhaps they could be a little more generous and concede to the Poles a few small areas east of the Curzon line. But we are not going to wage war on Russia because of Poland." On the other hand Roosevelt wanted Poland to be compensated by being given East Prussia.

In this connection Roosevelt also mentioned the Baltic states. He made it clear to Beneš that it was a very disagreeable problem for him, primarily because of American public opinion. Therefore, he could not recognize the incorporation of the three Baltic republics into the Soviet Union, at least not just yet. On the other hand, he did not want this question to continue to harm Soviet-American relations. "My belief is that he would like to resolve the matter somehow and that he searches for the least painful way to dispose of it." Such was Beneš's conclusion. Roosevelt asked Beneš to explain his attitude and the delicateness of the situation to Stalin during Beneš's forthcoming visit to Moscow. As Beneš understood it, Roosevelt wanted him to assure Stalin that the United States had no intention of opposing the Soviet annexation of the Baltic states, but that Roosevelt's concern was to handle the issue so as to make it palatable to the American public.

As could have been expected, the talks kept returning to the Soviet Union. "Russia was the center of all our discussions," said Beneš in his report to the Council of Ministers. Pursuing his intention to impress on Roosevelt the need for close Soviet-American cooperation in the postwar reconstruction of Europe, Beneš did his best to promote the objective he deemed so vitally important. "There will be no peace," he told Roosevelt, "unless there is a firm long-term agreement between the United States and the Soviet Union. The isolation of Russia as it occurred after the First World War must not be repeated. Russia must be accepted as an equal partner participating fully in world affairs and, in particular, sharing on an equal footing with the United States and Britain in all major policies affecting the destiny of Europe." Asked by Roosevelt if one could believe in the Soviet Union's good intentions, Beneš replied in the affirmative, citing as an example the good relations that had evolved between the Soviet Union and Czechoslovakia. He told Roosevelt about the assurances (reiterated by Bogomolov before Beneš's departure for the United States) that the Soviet Union would respect Czechoslovakia's sovereignty and territorial integrity, was firmly committed to the principle of noninterference in Czechoslovakia's internal affairs, and was willing to accept Poland as the third party to the proposed Czechoslovak-Soviet Treaty of Friendship, Mutual Aid, and Postwar Cooperation. He emphasized the elaborate Soviet publicity given to these promises of good behavior and interpreted this as a clear indication of genuine Soviet commitment to a new course.

Beneš's arguments met with a sympathetic reception, for Roosevelt's views on the necessity of Soviet-American cooperation and his desire that the Soviet Union be trusted coincided with those of the Czechoslovak president. After the first meeting with Roosevelt, Beneš told me:

> He is already committed to the idea of long-term cooperation with Russia. He just wants to find out if one can really believe in Russia's good intentions. But I have the impression that he trusts it and wishes to continue to trust it, and that he only wanted to have his own belief confirmed by my answer. In this respect he is definitely more positively inclined than Churchill. If similar trust develops on the other side, then all will be well. I have to tell Stalin about it, and he *must* believe that Roosevelt has sincere intentions and has sufficient power to carry out his intentions against whatever opposition may confront him.[17]

Roosevelt's hopes regarding Soviet conduct and his trust in Beneš's assurances were further boosted by Stalin's dissolution of the Comintern on May 23, 1943. During talks between Beneš and Cordell Hull on May 18, 1943, reference had been made to the Comintern. Beneš had told the U.S. secretary of state that in discussions with Maisky, Bogomolov, and other Russians, he had insisted that the Comintern should be dissolved and had gained the impression that it would be. The disbanding of the Comintern less than one week later could not but enhance Beneš's prestige and credibility as a statesman whose predictions frequently came true.

In discussing the Soviet Union, Beneš explained to Roosevelt his views on the further development of Czechoslovak-Soviet relations and the vital importance for his country of being on friendly terms with the Soviet Union and guaranteeing its safety by an alliance with the Soviet Union, hopefully also joined by Poland. He did not hide from Roosevelt that this new relationship with the Soviet Union would influence Czechoslovakia's political life and economic order. He also mentioned that after his return to London he would visit Moscow and conclude an alliance with the Soviet Union. As Beneš told me and as he reported to Jan Masaryk after this first conversation, Roosevelt "took note of this with visible satisfaction."[18] After reviewing his plans regarding the Soviet Union in his final meeting with Roosevelt, he sent another telegram in which he reiterated that Roosevelt "confirmed our former discussion and again took note of and agreed with my intention of concluding all the agreements on the occasion of my next journey to Russia."[19]

When Roosevelt asked Beneš's opinion on the desirability of a personal meeting between himself and Stalin, Beneš advised Roosevelt to do so and use the occasion to clarify frankly and openly all outstanding problems and to reach an early agreement on their solution. To a further question on the advisability of a meeting involving Roosevelt, Stalin, and Churchill, Beneš replied that Roosevelt should first see Stalin alone since negotiations between two are easier than between three. (In answering Roosevelt's question, Beneš was aware that Roosevelt had already decided to confer with Stalin.)

A sizable portion of the Roosevelt-Beneš conversations was devoted to the postwar security system. As Beneš found out, Roosevelt opposed reviving the League of Nations. Stating that, unlike Wilson, he was a realist, the American president expressed instead a preference for a loose association of united nations, a sort of world council led by the four great powers (the United States, Great Britain, the Soviet Union, and China), and meeting once a year. In addition, he favored appointing a person of recognized international standing as a world mediator who would visit troublespots and try to settle controversies by conciliation. Roosevelt mentioned South Africa's Jan Smuts as the kind of person he had in mind.

Although Beneš generously gave his opinions and volunteered advice on most matters discussed, he handled one subject with great restraint and circumspection; namely, the postwar disposition of Germany. The subject came up in both meetings with Roosevelt; it was also *the* subject on which Roosevelt solicited Beneš's opinion at the conference with Churchill on May 13, 1943. Roosevelt and Churchill were interested in Beneš's view concerning the partition of Germany into several countries, which they then regarded as possibly the best solution of the German problem. Not wishing to commit himself in advance and not knowing the position of the Soviet Union on this matter, Beneš did not express his views with any definiteness. He mainly stressed the need for broad decentralization, a profound re-education of the German people, substantial changes in social structure, and the strict punishment of all war criminals.[20] "It does not matter so much whether or not Germany will be partitioned," he told the two chief executives, "but much more important will be to defend, if need be, the solution that will be decided. Only a durable peace is a good peace. The peace of Versailles was not good because it did not last, because those who had created it were not willing to defend it when the critical moment had arrived." As Beneš subsequently learned in his final meeting with Roosevelt, the American president favored partitioning Germany into several states, perhaps as many as five or six.

Beneš had excellent reasons for not indicating his opinion of this scheme. To be sure, the dismemberment of Germany seemed at first glance to be advantageous since it would paralyze Czechoslovakia's historical enemy for years to come. But he figured that sooner or later the Germans would push for reunification and doubted that in the long run the Allies would have the willpower to keep the Germans divided. "We must never forget," he said in his report to the Council of Ministers, "that when Germany will begin to unify and others will not defend the peace settlement [providing for Germany's partition], all the pressure will then be on us, as was the case in 1938." Moreover, some of the partition schemes suggested in 1943 provided for Austria to be joined with Bavaria into a south German federation; this Beneš definitely opposed, for he deemed it better for his country if Austria remained independent.

There was one issue, however, affecting Germany on which Beneš was quite outspoken: the transfer of the Sudeten Germans to the Reich. In fact, he began discussing it while we were still sitting in the White House dining room. He raised the issue again in both conferences with Roosevelt on May 12–13 and June 7. Securing U.S. support for transferring a substantial number of Sudeten Germans to the Reich figured high on Beneš's American shopping list. Beneš had already gained Churchill's approval. As he told me after returning from a luncheon with Churchill on April 3, 1943, the British prime minister approved "in principle the transfer of population as the only possible solution of minority problems in Central Europe after the war."[21] But Beneš also knew that many influential Britons abhorred the very thought of enforced massive resettlement. Furthermore, by the time Beneš left for the United States, the Soviets had not replied to his request (made through Bogomolov on March 19, 1943) that Moscow inform him of its position on the transfer.[22] Thus, he was even more anxious to secure Roosevelt's backing—and he got it more easily than he expected. During their first conversation Roosevelt told Beneš that he ought to expel as many Sudeten Germans as possible. To confirm America's help in this matter, which he considered vital to Czechoslovakia's security, Beneš raised the transfer issue again in his final talk with Roosevelt. The American president reaffirmed, in no uncertain terms, his unconditional support for the transfer of Germans to the Reich, both from Czechoslovakia and Poland. He even expressed the belief that population transfers should be used to resolve the minority problem in Transylvania. As Beneš wrote to his colleagues in London: "He [Roosevelt] agrees to the transfer of minority population from Eastern Prussia, Transylvania, and Czechoslovakia. *I asked again expressly whether the United States would agree* to the transfer of our Germans. He declared plainly that they would."[23]

Roosevelt's unequivocal approval for the transfer of the Sudeten Germans may well have been instrumental in prompting Stalin to do the same, or at least in speeding up Soviet action on the matter. In the telegram about the first conversation with Roosevelt that Beneš sent to London on May 13, 1943, he mentioned Roosevelt's approval of the transfer idea. Masaryk and Ripka told Bogomolov, who immediately informed his superiors in Moscow. Shortly thereafter he returned to Czechoslovakia's Foreign Ministry with a statement that the Soviet Union accepted the principle of transfer and insisted quite peremptorily that this message be wired immediately to President Beneš. After delaying for three months, Stalin evidently made up his mind very quickly once he learned of America's positive attitude.

Finally, Beneš informed the American president about his problems with the Vatican and asked for Roosevelt's help. Roosevelt gladly accepted Beneš's memo and promised to have it delivered with his recommendation. He, too, thought that the Vatican had not behaved correctly toward Czechoslovakia.

In addition to the meeting with Roosevelt, Beneš also had fruitful talks with U.S. Secretary of State Cordell Hull; his number-one and number-two deputies, Sumner Welles and Adolf Berle; and the president's right-hand man, Harry Hopkins; as well as with several cabinet members, senators, congressmen, and other prominent Americans.

Next to the talks with Roosevelt, the most important were two long conversations on May 17 and May 30, 1943, with Sumner Welles. Naturally enough, the topics they discussed paralleled those covered in Beneš's meetings with Roosevelt. Welles turned out to be a resolute believer in the necessity of U.S.-Soviet cooperation and displayed full understanding of Czechoslovakia's policy vis-à-vis the Soviet Union. "We in America fully comprehend your line of cooperation with Russia," he told Beneš. "After what happened at Munich you must look to your own security." In particular, Welles seemed to understand Beneš's anxiety to conclude an alliance with the Soviet Union. As Beneš reported in a telegram to London on May 30, 1943, Welles "also stressed that the treaty we intended to conclude with Russia could be regarded as proof that the independence of Poland, Romania, and other neighbors would also be respected and that in this way we would be emphasizing that our policy was European, not binding us to an exclusively Eastern or an exclusively Western policy."[24]

On the other hand, Welles was highly critical of the Poles: "Polish policy for the last twenty years has been a failure. What the Poles have done—the balancing between Russia and Germany, their so-called great power policy—was simply intolerable. This must not recur. Poland is not a great power and cannot be one. Also, the Ukrainian problem definitely has to be solved. The Ukraine is connected with the *Drang nach Osten* and has always been the object of imperialist desires, first of Germany and then of Poland."

Furthermore, the U.S. undersecretary of state showed a sympathetic understanding of the Czechoslovak position on confederation with Poland: "We are for it and would wish it could be achieved. We in America always have had a liking for federative schemes. But we know your difficulties and understand them. We know that nothing can be done until Soviet-Polish relations have been settled." Also, Roosevelt had authorized Welles to add to the discussion Beneš had with the president that "it was not the intention of the United States to undertake anything in Central Europe that would in any way force their will on us." Finally, Beneš was quite pleased to learn that Welles opposed Churchill's idea of an Austro-Bavarian south German federation.

Unlike his conversation with Welles, which turned into true working sessions, the two talks Beneš had with Cordell Hull on May 13 and May 18 were primarily courtesy visits. The two statesmen did discuss politics, but not nearly as thoroughly as was the case with Roosevelt and Welles. The secretary of state was interested mainly in Beneš's opinion of the Soviet Union and its trustworthiness. But it was obvious that, like Roosevelt, he had almost decided that the Soviet Union would have to be trusted and that he wanted confirmation of his opinion from Beneš. Referring to the Soviet Union, he told Beneš: "We must have confidence. We have confidence. We shall show confidence." As if to indicate his positive attitude toward the Soviet Union, Hull pointedly recalled his 1932 negotiations with Litvinov, which led to the de jure U.S. recognition of the Soviet government. In a telegram to London about these talks (dated May 19, 1943), Beneš mentioned that "Hull, like the others, is chiefly interested in getting guarantees that Russia will not interfere in their [the United States'] internal affairs and will not deliberately support communism and communistic programs."[25]

One pleasant surprise for Beneš was his ninety-minute talk with Berle on May 31, 1943. According to reports, Berle was a die-hard conservative on good terms with the Hapsburgs, the Vatican, and Tibor Eckhardt. Furthermore, he was allegedly sympathetic toward Milan Hodža, the Slovak politician and former Czechoslovak premier, who had quarreled with Beneš and was actively inciting Americans of Slovak extraction to oppose Beneš and his government. Aware of this, Berle used the occasion (without being asked) to clear himself of such accusations: "I do not know why Eckhardt and Hodža are said to be in my circle of friends. I had not and have not anything in common with them. Hodža was your premier and he is now a refugee. We respect him as such, but we will not enter into a political bargain with him—this I can say categorically. We consider the Slovaks to be your internal affair, which does not concern us."[26] He also commended Beneš's government for refraining from using Czech ethnic groups in America to influence U.S. policy, which, he said, was not the case with the Poles. "I was agreeably surprised by Berle," Beneš told Smutný and myself while we were waiting at the Washington airport for the plane back to London. "We have heard so much about his reactionary attitude, favoring the Hapsburgs, Eckhardt, Hodža, and the Vatican, and about his alleged support for the Darlan deal. But when I talked to him, he emphatically denied all this without even being asked about it. I believe that much of what is attributed to him in this respect is without foundation. I have noticed that attacks by the press against him make him nervous. Besides, his recent speech about Russia suggests that he views matters correctly."[27]

Beneš and Berle also touched on the problem of Yugoslavia. Berle wondered whether, in view of the continuous ethnic strife in prewar Yugoslavia, it would be possible for the country to remain united. However, as Beneš had told Roosevelt, he insisted that the various ethnic groups must not be allowed to separate into different countries, for this would only increase the number of disputable frontiers in the Balkans and lead to even more quarreling. If the Yugoslavs stayed in one country, their quarreling would at least be done at home and would not become automatically an international dispute.

Finally, there was the message from Roosevelt brought by Harry Hopkins when he called on Beneš at Blair House on May 18, 1943.

"Roosevelt esteems your sound advice and judgment on European matters," Hopkins told Beneš. "Although he himself carefully follows European affairs, he cannot know all the details and he would appreciate keeping in constant contact with you very much. Roosevelt knows how Eden and Churchill trust you."[28] Needless to say, the president was visibly flattered by the message.

Beneš returned from America to England in high spirits, convinced that his American mission was even more successful than he had hoped. "The Washington talks surpassed all our expectations," he wired his foreign minister after the completion of the first round of talks on May 19, 1943. "The first thing I would like to state," he told his cabinet in the opening remarks of his report about the trip, "is that I am completely satisfied with my visit, I would say 100 percent satisfied." Evaluating the visit a few years later in his *Memoirs*, he described it as "wholly successful" and as "another great milestone in our war policy," characterizing it as "almost a demonstrative confirmation and ratification of our international position in the United States and the rest of the world . . . Between us and the U.S. government everything was quite straightforward; there were no misunderstandings or legal obscurities. Neither was there at that time any difference of opinion concerning our basic problems."[29]

Beneš was also gratified by the progressive consolidation of American public opinion in what he considered the right direction. He noted with profound satisfaction that there was no longer any need to fear that America might revert to isolationism after the war. He was delighted that not only Roosevelt and his collaborators but also leading Republicans and the bulk of the American public seemed to understand and accept the necessity of loyal and friendly cooperation with the Soviet Union. He was pleased that America was determined to force Germany to its knees and that a half-baked peace short of a total German defeat was no longer a danger.

Beneš was deeply impressed by the examples of America's tremendous war effort he saw at Ford's and Chrysler's assembly lines in Detroit, which had been converted to the production of planes and tanks, and by the tough military training at Fort Knox. He was grateful that despite the endeavors of autonomist and separatist groups among Slovak-Americans, no attempt was made to influence him in that respect and that official U.S. circles considered the Czech-Slovak issue as strictly and exclusively an internal Czechoslovak matter. As he reported to the

Council of Ministers, Roosevelt's only reference to the Slovaks was a question about Beneš's intentions regarding the Slovak quislings. And Cordell Hull had referred to "some Slovaks" who had sent him an anti-Beneš letter as "mischief-makers."[30]

Beneš even modified his earlier critical attitude toward the U.S. State Department, an attitude caused by the difficulties he had encountered in the matter of U.S. recognition of his government. "We have heard many complaints about the State Department, and even I had them," he told his ministers. "I want to state that I have found out firsthand that things are much better than they appeared to be from a distance, from here."

Finally, Beneš became convinced that he had Roosevelt's complete confidence, that the American president trusted him and valued his political judgment highly, and that he himself in turn had successfully gained an insight into Roosevelt's thought processes. After his last conversation with the American president on June 7, 1943, he told me: "When he is with people whom he trusts, Roosevelt tells quite a lot and very candidly; he tells virtually everything that is on his mind. I think that I could obtain a clear picture of his thoughts. I am almost sure of it."[31] He reported in much the same vein to his cabinet after his return to London.

The most serious accusation leveled against Beneš in connection with his 1943 American visit has been that he was instrumental in persuading Roosevelt that the Soviet Union could and should be trusted. Because Beneš was considered by Roosevelt and many other Western statesmen the foremost expert on European politics in general and the Soviet Union in particular, it has been argued, his opinion carried extra weight and he therefore bore an especially heavy share of responsibility in this respect.[32] Beneš's preoccupation with Soviet affairs during his visit to the United States was also subsequently criticized by one of his wartime collaborators, Ladislav Feierabend, the minister of state in Beneš's government in exile.

Writing in 1966, Feierabend upbraided Beneš for devoting more time to the Soviet Union in his discussions with the American representatives than to Czechoslovakia. He blamed Beneš for having wanted to reinforce the convictions of those who already believed Soviet professions of noninterference in internal affairs of other countries and for having sought to convert to such beliefs those who doubted them. He asserted that Beneš, "instead of taking care only of Czechoslovak problems, devoted much time to international questions, that he wanted to be a bridge between the East and the West and to play a greater role in world politics than the one that belonged to a representative of the Czechoslovak republic."[33]

Beneš did believe in 1943 that the Soviet Union, if accorded proper treatment by the West, would in its own interest refrain from subversion and would abide by its commitments not to interfere unduly in the internal affairs of other countries, especially its allies. He did not hesitate to affirm this whenever the topic of the Soviet Union and its prospective behavior arose in his American talks. Persuading the Americans and the British that the Soviet Union must be treated as a trustworthy ally was to him a prerequisite for the continued East-West cooperation that he considered a sine qua non of lasting peace and security for Europe and, above all, for his tormented country. The equally indispensable corollary of this was to convince Soviet leaders that they could and should trust the West, a mission he intended to accomplish during his subsequent visit to Moscow.

However, it is a gross exaggeration to assume that Beneš's role was as important as his critics credit (or debit) him. By the time of Beneš's first talk with Roosevelt, the American president and his associates already recognized the value of long-term Soviet-American cooperation and had already decided for the sake of such cooperation to trust the Soviet Union. Thus, Beneš's contribution toward making Roosevelt trust the Russians was relatively small. He simply reinforced a resolution that had already been made and allayed a few lingering doubts about its correctness.

Feierabend's ex post facto criticism is all the more reprehensible because he, as Beneš's minister and a visitor to the United States at the time of Beneš's visit, knew quite well the reason for Beneš's behavior. Moreover, the verbatim minutes of the meeting of the Czechoslovak Council of Ministers that heard the president's report on his visit reveal that in the subsequent discussion Feierabend, far from expressing any misgivings, had nothing but lavish praise for Beneš's conduct in the United States.

Nonetheless, Beneš lived to regret that he had assured Roosevelt of Soviet good intentions. During the visit Beneš paid the Herben family on August 22, 1945, he discussed his 1943 visit with Roosevelt. Beneš told Herben "with a certain shade of apology" that he had told Roosevelt that the Soviets were becoming more democratic, that they were coming closer to the West, and that they would loyally cooperate with the

Western democracies after the war. "So, as can be seen, I did persuade Roosevelt, and well!" concluded Beneš. According to Herben, none of those present had the impression that Beneš was boasting. On the contrary, they all felt that he was apologizing.[34]

Beneš's conviction that he had reached full understanding on all matters discussed in Washington (save for the issue of France and its future role) proved wrong in one important aspect; namely, Beneš's plan for the Czechoslovak-Soviet Treaty of Friendship, Mutual Aid, and Postwar Cooperation.

On learning, shortly after his return to London, of British opposition to his plan (the British claimed that there was a British-Soviet agreement not to conclude such treaties with any smaller allies during the war), the president countered by telling the British that he already had American approval to proceed with his plan. But when the British sought to verify Beneš's assertion, the U.S. State Department flatly denied that this was the case. Answering an urgent inquiry by Eden (made through Halifax on June 28, 1943), Sumner Welles stated that Beneš had never mentioned to him any desire to enter into a treaty with the Soviet Union, but merely the desire to reach an "understanding" with Stalin concerning the position of Czechoslovakia in Europe.[35] On August 24, 1943, the State Department supplemented Welles's communication by stating that the memos on Beneš's conversations with Hull, Welles, and Berle "contained no reference whatever to any proposed treaty between the Soviet and Czechoslovak governments."[36]

These State Department denials directly contradict Beneš's statement in his telegram to Masaryk on May 30, 1943 (the day of the second Beneš-Welles conversation), in which Beneš cited Welles as referring to the proposed treaty "as proof that the independence of Poland, Romania, and other neighbors would also be respected."[37] Moreover, the State Department's assertions did not address Beneš's claim that he had informed Roosevelt in both of their conversations of his intention to conclude an agreement during his visit to Moscow and that Roosevelt expressed his approval. As was the case in his talk with Welles, Beneš prepared telegrams to Masaryk immediately after his conversations with Roosevelt.[38] Also, I noted in my diary that Beneš spoke to me in much the same words on his return to Blair House, and he spoke in the same vein when he reported to his Council of Ministers a mere ten days after his return from America. Furthermore, when he talked with U.S. Ambassador Biddle in London about his conversations in Washington, he told Biddle that he had "expressed [in his Washington talks] the hope that during his contemplated visit to Moscow he might succeed in effecting a Czechoslovak-Soviet treaty."[39]

Each of these diametrically opposed versions is supported by official documents. Yet Beneš's version is probably the correct one or at least a closer reflection of events. A very substantial portion of Beneš's Washington conversations did deal with the Soviet Union, and Czechoslovak-Soviet, U.S.-Soviet, Polish-Soviet, and Polish-Czechoslovak relations. Furthermore, even U.S. sources concede that Beneš told Roosevelt and Welles about his intended journey to Moscow.[40] It is inconceivable that Beneš would have uttered not one word about the envisaged Czechoslovak-Soviet agreement. Nor could he have had any reason to keep it secret. As clearly revealed by his refusal (discussed in the next chapter) to sign the Soviet-Czechoslovak agreement until the British approved, he was determined to present neither Britain nor the United States with a fait accompli. Moreover, since in 1943 he wanted the United States to trust the Soviet Union, he had every reason to acquaint the U.S. president and his associates with the contents of the proposed agreement, especially with its clauses concerning noninterference in internal affairs and the possible admission of Poland to the alliance. Blamed as he was for abandoning the Czechoslovak-Polish confederation, he could only gain by showing the extent of his endeavors to salvage for Poland what he could. "Good, do it, I agree," Beneš quoted (in his report to the Council of Ministers) Roosevelt as commenting about his plan for a tripartite Czechoslovak-Polish-Soviet alliance to stop Germany's *Drang nach Osten.*

Although I have no doubt that Beneš did reveal in his Washington talks his intention of concluding a Czechoslovak-Soviet agreement, with a provision for the subsequent admission of Poland, during his visit to Moscow, I cannot be as certain about Roosevelt's approval. Anxious to secure American approval, Beneš may have interpreted as such gestures and statements that were meant merely to take note of Beneš's intention without necessarily giving him America's blessing. Or Roosevelt may have agreed with the idea of a treaty between Czechoslovakia and the Soviet Union without approving its signing before the end of the war. However, be that as it may, Beneš believed that the Americans agreed with his intention to conclude an agreement during his visit to Moscow later in 1943.

Beneš and Polish Premier Gen. Wladyslaw Sikorski watching a parade of the Czechoslovak brigade in England.

Beneš and Churchill inspecting the Czechoslovak Army Brigade in England.

Beneš receiving an honorary doctor's degree from the University of Aberdeen in Scotland.

A wartime visit to Scotland. *From left to right:* the lord mayor of Aberdeen; Beneš; Jaromir Smutný, head of the President's Office; the wife of the lord mayor; Madame Beneš; Jiřinka Beneš, the president's niece; and the author.

The author receiving instructions from Beneš during World War II.

Beneš in a U.S. tank at the
Army Training Center at
Fort Knox, 1943.

Beneš entering the Capitol to address the U.S. Congress in 1943.

Beneš meeting with Roosevelt during his 1943 visit to the United States. Shaking hands with Roosevelt is Czechoslovak Ambassador to the U.S. Vladimír Hurban.

Beneš during his triumphant return to Czechoslovakia in May 1945.

President and Madame Beneš at Prague's Hradčany Castle on the day of their return to Prague, May 16, 1945.

6

Beneš and Stalin

No event did more to convince Beneš of Stalin's trustworthiness than his 1943 visit to Moscow. The three weeks in December Beneš spent in the Soviet Union made him discard any lingering doubts about the Soviet leaders' intentions. The timing of the visit gave the Soviets a perfect opportunity to create a favorable impression. Our arrival in Moscow coincided with the conclusion of the Big Three Teheran Conference, which seemed to lay a solid foundation for harmonious East-West cooperation, and Stalin missed no opportunity to extol to Beneš the results of his meeting with Roosevelt and Churchill. With obvious pleasure he recounted how "Vinston" had presented him with the sword dedicated by Coventry to Stalingrad and how they had embraced, overcome with emotion, and kissed each other. He narrated how they had exchanged jokes, what a fine time they had together, and how highly he esteemed Roosevelt and Churchill. While we were in Moscow, the Soviet government announced that a new patriotic national anthem would replace the "Internationale," as it "no longer expressed the fundamental changes that the Soviet lands had undergone."[1] All this seemed perfectly natural and sincere, particularly to those like Beneš who were convinced that there was no reason why Soviet communism and Western democracy could not find a fair and sensible modus vivendi despite the differences in systems and ideologies. It is hardly surprising that Beneš concluded that his cherished dream of genuine rapprochement and mutual understanding between the Russians and the Anglo-Saxons was becoming a reality that he could rely on in his plans for the future.

This favorable image was further reinforced by all that Beneš was shown during his visit. We entered the country through Baku, the bustling capital of oil-rich Azerbaijan, poised impressively beside the Caspian Sea and studded with hundreds of derricks in hectic operation. For four days and nights we traveled by train through towns and villages that had only recently been scenes of terrific battles. We passed by veritable mountains of German armor half buried in the snow, impressive monuments to the Soviet victories over the Nazi Wehrmacht. We paid a dramatic moonlight visit to Stalingrad. We were taken to factories where we saw feverish effort and a high degree of efficiency. Beneš kept comparing these sights with those of his previous visit in 1935. He was amazed at the tremendous progress that he found and saw in it confirmation of his belief that the Soviet system, having successfully withstood the difficult test of a massive invasion, was now passing through a gradual transformation to a liberalized form of socialism. As a sociologist, he knew that a revolution could be victorious only if it could in due time become evolution. That was what he thought was happening in the Soviet Union. "Masaryk persistently refused to believe that the Soviet regime could last," was one of Beneš's comments. "I wonder what he would have said now. A regime that can improve the living standards of 90 percent of the people is bound to maintain itself. That is what so many people in the West fail to realize." Wherever he went and no matter with whom he talked, he found what he believed to be warm sympathy, an avid curiosity about the outside world, a genuine desire for friendship with the West, and a profound respect and admiration for Roosevelt and Churchill. Ideological orthodoxy seemed to have melted under the warmth of surging patriotism; the petulant dogmatism of earlier days seemed to be losing out to the sobering necessity of practical realism. "Progress here in the development of ideas since 1935 and especially since the war is great, real, and definitive," he wrote to Jan Masaryk from Moscow.

> To imagine that the present outlook toward the "Internationale," religion, *co-operation with the West*, Slav policy, etc., is merely tactical would be a fundamental error. The growth of a new Soviet empire, a decentralised one, with a firm place for the other Soviet nations, in the spirit of a new popular democracy, is undeniably and definitely on the march. A new

Soviet Union will come out of the war. Economically and socially it will retain the Soviet system in its entirety, but it will be quite new politically.[2]

A visit to Moscow at the proper time, coupled preferably with the conclusion of a new treaty with the Soviet Union, had been an integral part of Beneš's political strategy ever since Hitler's liquidation of post-Munich Czechoslovakia in March 1939. It was a logical outgrowth of Beneš's conviction that sooner or later the Soviet Union would become involved in the holocaust of the Second World War. He had told Roosevelt this as early as May 1939 in their talk at Hyde Park. In a message sent on August 20, 1939, Beneš assured his collaborators in the Czech underground: "With regard to Russia we cannot say anything today about its definitive stand and behavior, but *in the end it will certainly come out against Germany and will* hold with us and support us in any case."[3] He clung to this conviction throughout the weird Nazi-Soviet honeymoon that followed the conclusion of the Nazi-Soviet Nonaggression Pact of August 24, 1939. "Do not pay any attention to Hitler's words that there is an eternal peace between Germany and Russia," he cautioned his collaborators in a message sent on September 1, 1939.[4] "Our attitude toward the USSR remains on the lines of Czechoslovak foreign policy of the last years: loyalty, mutual sympathy, and friend-ship; and the expectation that the USSR will do nothing to harm us," read another message, sent on October 28, 1939. "We on our part do not wish to do anything in our activities that could, whenever and however, make amicable cooperation with the USSR more difficult. We shall probably become its next-door neighbor. We leave the way open for cooperation."[5]

Beneš's belief that the Soviet Union would eventually become involved in the war against Germany was not wishful thinking. It was based not merely on the fundamental irreconcilability of Nazism and communism but on solid evidence that the Soviets had no illusions about their chances of avoiding the war for as long as they would have desired. In November 1939, for example, the Soviet authorities surprised Beneš by allowing the Czechoslovak army units organized in Poland in the summer of 1939 among Czechoslovak refugees, which had subsequently been interned in the Soviet Union, to be gradually transferred to France. The Soviet Union even asked Romania to allow these men passage and supplied them with Soviet passports for this purpose. (Since Romania did not dare to do this, the transit was finally arranged through Syria.) Only a few groups were able to join the Czechoslovak army in

France, but this was a striking example of how the Russians began double-crossing the Nazis after a mere two months of Soviet-German partnership. Soviet authorities even compelled communist members of the Czechoslovak military units to be transferred, although most of them wanted to remain in the Soviet Union.

As early as May 1939 contact was established between our underground movement and Soviet intelligence agents in Czechoslovakia. These contacts continued and gradually increased after the conclusion of the Nazi-Soviet pact. The Soviets grew especially insistent after the French collapse in the summer of 1940 on collaborating as closely as possible with the Czechoslovak underground. They claimed that the German-Soviet conflict was near and inevitable, that Soviet Russia counted on Czechoslovakia as the most developed component of Central Europe, and that the two nations had a grand future ahead of them.[6] In May 1940 our intelligence officer in Bucharest, Col. Heliodor Pika, was allowed to proceed to Moscow and establish contact with our soldiers still remaining in the Soviet Union. Soviet agents also sought the cooperation of our intelligence agents in Bucharest and Istanbul. On December 22, 1940, a special Soviet emissary using the alias Dorn met in England with Col. František Moravec, chief of our intelligence service, and told him that he had instructions from Moscow to discuss with us the exchange of military intelligence, particularly reports on the location of German armies in Poland, Finland, Norway, and Romania. On January 18, 1941, the Soviets proposed that the untransferred Czechoslovak military units should remain in the Soviet Union and become the nucleus of a Czechoslovak army on Soviet territory in the future.

Beneš's expectation of Soviet involvement in the war on the side of the West was reinforced by conversations with the Soviet ambassador to Britain, Ivan Maisky. Beneš saw Maisky's willingness to maintain contacts with him after the conclusion of the Nazi-Soviet pact as a clear indication of Soviet sympathy for the Czechoslovak cause because the Soviet ambassador would not have done so without Kremlin approval. Moreover, Maisky's explanation of the Soviet policy of apparent cooperation with Germany seemed sensible and consonant with Beneš's own thesis.

In a meeting on August 23, 1939, the very day Nazi Foreign Minister Joachim von Ribbentrop arrived in Moscow to sign the pact, Maisky described the treaty as a Soviet reprisal for France's and Britain's anti-Soviet stance at the time of Munich. He suggested that the pact would drive a wedge between Nazi Germany and Japan and break up the Anti-Comintern Pact. They knew, the Soviet ambassador conceded, that Germany would violate the pact when it was to its advantage to do so. But that gave the Soviet Union the right to do the same and to choose the most suitable moment to enter the war.[7]

In a second meeting, held in September 1939 after the Soviet army had already overrun eastern Poland, Maisky felt it necessary to counter rumors then circulating in London that the Soviet action was pre-arranged. He denied this emphatically and claimed that the Soviet action had not been coordinated with the German invasion. He justified it by the Soviet desire to protect the Ukrainian population of eastern Poland and prevent it from falling under Nazi control.[8] At that time Beneš was unaware of the secret protocol to the German-Soviet pact, which came to light only after the war and revealed that the Soviet Union had acted in collusion with Nazi Germany. The question arises whether Maisky deliberately lied to Beneš or whether knowledge of the protocol had been withheld from him so that he would believe what he was telling Beneš and thus sound even more convincing. In view of the Kremlin's notorious secretiveness, I am inclined to believe that the latter was probably the case.

At a luncheon with Beneš at the Soviet Embassy in London on November 21, 1939, Maisky assured the president that the liberation of Czechoslovakia remained among the main objectives of Soviet foreign policy, even though, as he conceded somewhat apologetically, for tactical reasons they had to appear to "zigzag."[9]

Some Soviet actions were anything but indicative of Soviet sympathy for Czechoslovakia's cause, as Beneš conceived it. As mentioned previously, in September 1939, the Soviet government recognized the Nazi-created puppet state of Slovakia and established diplomatic relations with the Slovak government headed by the quisling monsignore, Jozef Tiso; and in December 1939 it ordered the Czechoslovak legation in Moscow closed. Moreover, the Soviet foreign commissar took the unprecedented step of denying the Czechoslovak minister the farewell audience customarily given an ambassador or minister at the end of his mission. Thus, the Soviet Union completely reversed its March 1939 stand of refusing to recognize the validity of Hitler's dismemberment of Czechoslovakia. Furthermore, as described earlier, with the Comintern's blessing the Czechoslovak communists unleashed a slanderous campaign against Beneš and his liberation movement abroad in 1939–1940 and ceased to cooperate with the noncommunist underground inside Czechoslovakia. Furthermore, Slovak communists began calling for a Soviet Slovakia.

Nor was Beneš pleased with Soviet economic aid to Germany or Soviet actions in Latvia, Lithuania, Estonia, Finland, and Romania in 1939–1940. In particular, he deplored the abortive Soviet attempt to impose on Finland a people's democratic regime headed by the veteran Comintern agent and Soviet citizen of Finnish nationality, O.V. Kuusinen. He was also displeased by various Soviet statements professing friendship for Nazi Germany, such as Molotov's speech of August 1, 1940, in which the Soviet foreign commissar lauded the "good-neighborly and friendly [Soviet-German] relations" and claimed that they were not based on fortuitous or transient considerations but on the fundamental interests of Germany and the Soviet Union. Beneš feared that such statements might be misunderstood by his countrymen at home and cause despondency.

However, these Soviet actions and pronouncements in no way weakened his ingrained belief in Soviet Russia's eventual participation in the war on the Allied side. Some of them, such as the closing of the Czechoslovak legation in Moscow, the recognition of Slovakia, and the various pro-German utterances by Soviet leaders, he viewed as the sort of zigzagging Maisky mentioned at their luncheon in November 1939. "It was clear to me that the Soviet Union was bribing Germany to prolong the period of neutrality," he wrote in his *Memoirs*.[10] Others, such as the Soviet territorial demands on Finland, he thought were prompted primarily by the Soviet Union's effort to improve its strategic position vis-à-vis Germany.[11]

The fact that, as Beneš proudly claimed in his *Memoirs*, he did not allow himself to be misled by *"the seeming rapprochement"* of Germany and the Soviet Union served him well when, on June 22, 1941, Nazi Germany unleashed its blitz on the Soviet Union.[12] What he had been predicting ever since 1939 as a logical climax in the development of the war had become a reality. The Soviet colossus had joined the depleted ranks of the anti-Hitlerite front. The prospects for East-West cooperation had increased. The anti-Beneš propaganda that portrayed the Czechoslovak president as a naive dupe and incurable optimist prone to self-delusions about the Soviet Union suffered a severe blow, while Beneš's prestige as a statesman endowed with unique foresight rose to unprecedented heights.

Beneš had every reason to be profoundly satisfied with this great turning point of the war on that memorable day of June 22, 1941. As I sat with him in his Aston Abbots study on that fateful Sunday, celebrating the event and listening to news bulletins about the German invasion,

I could discern in his face, especially in his expressive eyes, a satisfaction more serene and more intense than I had seen since the outbreak of the war in September 1939. Yet, as his occasional comments revealed, his joy was tempered by two worrisome concerns: (1) whether Great Britain and the United States would support the Soviet Union and do whatever they could to help it; and (2) whether the Soviet Union was strong enough to repulse the Nazi hordes, especially if Western aid was too small or too slow in coming.

As Beneš wrote in his *Memoirs*: "On Sunday, the 22d, when the crossing of the Soviet frontier by the German armies was reported, we in London were all in a state of extreme tension and expectation as to how Great Britain and the United States would react."[13] Beneš hoped that both Churchill and Roosevelt would decide in favor of helping the Soviet Union. He had had an opportunity to discuss the anticipated Soviet involvement in the war and its ramifications with Churchill during the latter's official visit to the Czechoslovak brigade in England on April 19, 1941, and had gained the impression that the British reaction would be positive. But he knew that there were in Britain and especially in the United States influential circles that might succumb to the temptation of letting Russia bleed under the German onslaught to repay it for its connivance with Hitler and to liquidate the communist threat for good. He was somewhat apprehensive lest these circles adversely affect British and American policy at such a critical juncture. But Beneš's worries were quickly calmed when, in a broadcast to the nation on the evening of June 22 (which Beneš labeled as "one of the most important documents of the Second World War" in his *Memoirs*),[14] Churchill committed Britain to all-out aid to "Russia and the Russian people" and solemnly promised to appeal to Britain's "friends and allies in every part of the world" to follow the same course and pursue it as Britain would, "faithfully and steadfastly to the end."

Churchill's forceful commitment and Roosevelt's corresponding decision also helped allay Beneš's concern whether the Soviet Union could withstand the German assault. Whenever he talked with the British or the Americans in the months preceding the German invasion about Soviet military preparedness, he always stressed that the Soviet army was well prepared, its fighting morale high, and its officers up to their task. An especially thorough discussion on this subject occurred during Churchill's visit to the Czechoslovak army on April 19, 1941. As Beneš reminisced in his *Memoirs*:

During the discussion he [Churchill] returned three times to the question:

"And you believe that the Soviet Union will really fight, that it will hold out, that its officers' corps is of sufficiently high caliber?" I assured Churchill that I had full confidence in the Soviet Union and its power to hold out against a German assault. After lunch we drove to our army in Churchill's car and discussed in detail the state of the Red Army: its preparedness, its morale, the conditions of the officers' corps. This last question especially—the memories of Tukhachevsky's and the officers' purges of 1936 and 1937 were still alive— constantly occupied Churchill's mind. And he added other questions concerning the moral and political state of the Soviet population, the country's economic preparedness, communications, etc. I tried honestly and truthfully to dispel his doubts and to strengthen and confirm his hopes.[15]

However, when talking privately with Smutný, Drtina, and myself, Beneš was not as certain of the Soviet ability to contain the Wehrmacht as he professed to be in discussing the matter with foreigners and outsiders. "I would have wished that the German attack took place later than this, perhaps next spring," he told me on the morning of the invasion, for he thought that the Soviet Union could not as yet have completed all necessary preparations. He had sounded even more skeptical the evening before, on June 21, when in a conversation with Smutný he had admitted that the Russians might be defeated and possibly be compelled to conclude a separate peace with Germany.[16] Thus, Beneš's actual belief was that the Soviet army would give a good account of itself; that the Kremlin would spare no lives, throwing into the battle and sacrificing huge numbers of soldiers; and that the Soviet generals would conduct a protracted war "in the Russian way," retreating and forcing the Germans to disperse over vast areas and overextend their lines of supplies and communications.[17] Nor did he think that the invasion could trigger a revolution or coup. The Kremlin "will saturate the hinterland with GPU [the Soviet secret police], who will kill anyone attempting a coup," he told Smutný on June 23, 1941.[18] Furthermore, he expected that Soviet forces would eventually stop the German advance somewhere deep inside Russia, but only if they got prompt and substantial Anglo-American aid. It was only after the Wehrmacht failed to take Moscow and Leningrad, however, and got bogged down in the bitter Russian winter that Beneš shed all his worries in this respect.

The genuine pleasure with which Beneš welcomed the Soviet entry into the war did not mean that he cast aside all his apprehensions regarding the Soviet Union. He was glad, of course, that the Soviet Union finally occupied its proper status as an ally of the West and of

Czechoslovakia because he could not see how else the war against Nazi Germany could be won in a manner that would restore his country to its pre-Munich boundaries. At the same time, however, he was not unaware that Soviet participation in the war carried with it the danger of increased Soviet and communist influence in Czechoslovakia and the rest of East Central Europe. As early as April 26, 1941, in informing the Czech underground of the forthcoming German attack on the Soviet Union, he cautioned:

> "We shall continue as we have done up to now: we shall go with the Allies and of course with Russia with which we shall simply renew our state of alliance that we had before Munich. It therefore does not mean that any internal political change will be made; that is, there will not be any special shift toward the communists. If they join us in the struggle, good; if they do the fighting on their own, all right. Our state and national policy toward Russia will be such as it was after my trip to Moscow and after signing the pact of alliance with the Soviets [in 1935]; that is, friendly and loyal, but ours, Czechoslovak. One must not forget that we would never defeat Germany without the help of England and America; and neither of them likes Russia. Therefore, even on this occasion—*soberness and calm!*[19]

Anxious to deprive Czechoslovak communists of anything they could exploit in their anticipated postwar bid for power, Beneš concluded after the Soviet entry into the war that it was time for Emil Hácha, the president of the Protectorate Bohemia-Moravia, and his government to resign. On June 24, 1941, two days after the German invasion of the Soviet Union, he sent, through his collaborators in the Czech underground, an urgent message explaining the situation to Hácha and Gen. Alois Eliáš, the premier of the Protectorate Cabinet:

> The war is entering a new and decisive phase. What is happening now will have considerable influence on our internal politics and will decide our future development ... In the interest of the national honor, in the interest of the postwar unity and in order to prevent quarrels among ourselves after the war and to avoid giving communism the pretext and reason to attain power on the basis of justifiable accusations that we have aided Hitler, you have to re-examine your policies and make a definite decision ... I consider it necessary that you help provoke a situation that will cause the abdication of the president. This will also mean the departure of the cabinet. Whatever happens, the time has arrived for this change. The war will no longer be lost. You at home can save almost nothing, but to us here it will prove beneficial and for the future it will

mean again saving the unity of the nation in the direst moment of our history . . . Any assisting of the Nazi regime, making some new appeals or declaring yourselves directly or indirectly for the Reich, is no longer tolerable. If you begin to do this after the events of these days . . . we would be compelled to begin propaganda *against you*, make attacks against the government, the president, the Protectorate, and this would be fatal. I expect that Radio Moscow would undertake this course of action very soon and thus three centers would arise: Prague, London, and Moscow. At no price would I want to be compelled to do this. We must keep our shield unstained for the future as a united nation. Our cooperation up to now will once become a beautiful page in our history. Consider this and let me have your answer immediately. I want to decide the future course of action in cooperation with you.[20]

Many other messages followed, all along the same line, urging Hácha and his cabinet to resign. Some were answered with vague promises that the advice would be heeded at the right moment. Once Hácha even informed Beneš that he would actually resign. But nothing happened, and even the martyrdom and the execution of General Eliáš (who was arrested by the Gestapo in September 1941 for being in contact with Beneš) did not convince Hácha to listen to Beneš's desperate pleas. After Eliáš's arrest Hácha did instruct his office to prepare a letter of resignation, written in German and addressed to Hitler, citing his advanced age as the main reason.[21] But the letter remained undelivered. Instead, Hácha assured Reinhard Heydrich, von Neurath's replacement as *Reichsprotektor* of Bohemia-Moravia, of his loyal cooperation.[22]

Beneš's efforts to prevail on Hácha and his government to resign remained fruitless, and the communists were left with another handy target in their endeavor to blame the country's misfortune on the "treachery of the Czechoslovak bourgeoisie." Indeed, the problem of Hácha arose in the talks Beneš had with Gottwald and his three top associates during his visit to Moscow in December 1943. Not only did they condemn Hácha in the sharpest terms, but they made it clear to Beneš that they disapproved of his contacts with the *Staatspräsident* and the Protectorate government. They even suspected that Beneš had made a secret deal with Hácha and, as Beneš put it in his *Memoirs*, "cross-examined" him about it.[23] On the other hand, when Beneš talked about Hácha with Stalin, he was surprised to find the marshal much more accommodating than Gottwald and his associates. Stalin himself initiated the topic by asking Beneš: "And what about Hácha? What kind of a man is he?" Beneš explained that Hácha justified remaining in office by claiming that his continued presence prevented the worst elements from taking over, but that he had gradually become a pliable tool of the Nazis and would have to be punished after the war. "I have asked him a number of times to resign," Beneš concluded his brief summation, "but he is still sitting there, helping the Germans and compromising us by holding on to his office." Beneš fully expected Stalin to express dissatisfaction with Hácha's behavior. But Stalin only waved his hand, as if brushing away Beneš's criticism of Hácha, and declared: "If he can still be useful in some way, don't ask him to resign."[24]

As soon as the German-Soviet war commenced, the attitude of the Soviet Union toward Beneš's government changed. Our envoy's humiliating ejection from Moscow in December 1939 was forgotten as was the Soviet recognition of "independent" Slovakia. On July 4, 1941, less than two weeks after the German invasion of the Soviet Union, Ambassador Maisky telephoned and told me that he had an important message for the president. We anticipated what the message was, and we were not mistaken. "The Soviet government instructed me to give you the following message," Maisky informed Beneš when they met at the Soviet Embassy on July 8, 1941.

> (1) The political program of the Soviet Union includes an independent Czechoslovakia with a national government. (2) It is self-evident that the Soviet government will not interfere in the internal affairs of Czechoslovakia and that its internal regime and structure will be decided by the Czechoslovak people alone. (3) If the Czechoslovak government wishes to send an envoy to the Soviet Union, the Soviet government will be pleased to receive him. The Soviet government will gladly help organize Czechoslovak military units in the Soviet Union. In that case they think it will be possible to establish a special Czechoslovak national committee that will help organize the army. The only condition is that these units be subordinated to the High Command of the Red Army in operative and technical matters. Otherwise they will have a Czechoslovak commander as well as Czechoslovak officers.[25]

The president gladly accepted. Only the idea that a special committee should organize our army in the Soviet Union did not appeal to him, for he sensed the danger that this arrangement might create a communist-controlled "shadow government" in Moscow. He immediately told Maisky that the only official representative in Moscow must be our minister there and that military matters could be arranged only through a high Czechoslovak officer. In arranging for the restoration of Soviet-Czechoslovak diplomatic relations, however, Beneš committed a serious error. When the Soviet ambassador mentioned the exchange of diplomatic representatives, Beneš asked him whether our former minister to the Soviet Union, Zdeněk Fierlinger, could return to his post in Moscow. "Since we insist on the principle of juridical continuity and on establishing our relations with Soviet Russia as they existed before Munich," Beneš explained, "we would like you to again accept Minister Fierlinger." Maisky, not at all surprisingly, told Beneš that Fierlinger would be welcome in Moscow. Thus, for the sake of buttressing his cherished thesis of juridical continuity, Beneš sent to Moscow as his official spokesman an uncritical admirer of all things Soviet who was a representative more of Soviet interests than of those of his own country. Subsequently, Beneš came to regret his decision bitterly and was often quite desperate about Fierlinger's actions. Yet for fear of Soviet displeasure, he refused to recall Fierlinger even when his own cabinet requested this. Thus, he unwittingly gave the Czechoslovak communists in Moscow the opportunity to promote Fierlinger, formally a Social Democrat but already a communist, as their candidate for the premiership of the first government of liberated Czechoslovakia. Fierlinger eventually became one of the gravediggers of Czechoslovak democracy.

The arrangements made between Beneš and Maisky on July 8 were consummated ten days later by a formal agreement providing for the exchange of ministers, the formation within the USSR of Czechoslovak military units under a commander to be appointed by the Czechoslovak government in agreement with the Soviet government, and a mutual commitment of aid and support "in every way in the present war against Hitlerite Germany."[26] Shortly thereafter Fierlinger left for Moscow, carrying with him personal letters from Beneš to Stalin, Kalinin, Molotov, and Litvinov. After expressing to Stalin his admiration "for the great effort and enormous successes of the Soviet Union in the fight against German Hitlerite fascism" and his gratification over the agreement of July 18, 1941, the president wrote:

> I would like to stress . . . that from the year 1935, in spite of all that has happened in the world, I have never in any way changed my political line toward the Soviet Union. I have expected that the Soviet Union would take part in this new war in one form or another, and I have therefore consistently and systematically prepared myself for the moment when both our countries would again be able to renew the policy that I regard to

be natural and obvious for them as well as necessary for their present and future interests and, of course, preeminently corresponding to all feelings and requirements of the peoples of both our countries.

On this reality I want also to base our relations and our cooperation. By this I express the desire of a tremendous majority of the people of our country. I shall continue to pursue this line during the present wartime cooperation and especially during preparations for the future peace and even after its conclusion. For I believe that, even after victory has been won, the interests of our countries will not conflict and that in the future organization of Europe the foundations of our mutual relations, established in 1935 and renewed on July 18, 1941, will be one of the most important factors for preserving peace in Eastern and Central Europe.

I know that our political aims will meet with understanding in Moscow, and I only wish that we might bring this war to a victorious conclusion in the shortest possible time and then we could all dedicate ourselves successfully to the common task of reconstruction of a new, better Europe and a new, better social and economic postwar order.[27]

Although the Soviet governments's prompt normalization of relations and, in particular, its resolve not to interfere in Czechoslovakia's internal affairs pleased Beneš, he by no means concluded that there would not be problems. In a message sent to his collaborators in the Czech underground on July 12, 1941, four days after Maisky transmitted to him the Soviet assurance of noninterference, he said: "The Soviet declaration concerning our internal affairs can be taken seriously. The Soviets *as a state* will actually proceed in this manner. Of course, the Comintern and the communist party will conduct their politics as before."[28]

As mentioned earlier, since spring 1939, Beneš had contemplated a visit to Moscow at the appropriate time. While the Soviet Union was flirting with Nazi Germany in 1939–1941, any such undertaking was unthinkable. But when the German attack converted the Soviet Union into an ally of the West and Czechoslovakia, the unthinkable became thinkable and, indeed, in Beneš's view, highly desirable and virtually imperative. His collaborators and followers back in Czechoslovakia also thought so. In fact, some messages Beneš received from Czechoslovakia even before the German invasion of the Soviet Union urged him to go to Moscow. For instance, one typical message asked: "Has Dr. Beneš already been to Moscow? If not, why not? Does he think that the West will have enough trump cards in their hand?" This was, it should be emphasized, a message sent by *noncommunists* at a time when Stalin was zealously appeasing Hitler. This and similar messages were simply products of the desperation that manifested itself in Czechoslovakia after the French collapse when people saw Soviet entry into the war as the only hope for salvation, a hope they clung to with the desperation of a drowning man.

With the outbreak of the German-Soviet war, there appeared to be no visible impediment to a trip to Moscow. It was, however, less clear to Beneš whether the appropriate time for a visit had arrived. The Soviet Union was fighting for its survival. The Soviet capital was in grave danger, and many government agencies as well as foreign diplomatic missions had moved to Kuybishev on the Volga River. The Soviet rulers were totally absorbed in conducting the war and obtaining Western aid. The shape of relations between the Soviet Union and Great Britain and the United States had not yet been finalized. A visit to Stalin under such circumstances, Beneš knew, would be ill-timed. Thus he did not begin seriously considering a visit until April-May 1942. Noting that Great Britain and the Soviet Union were about to sign a long-term treaty of alliance, he concluded that the time would soon be ripe for negotiating a similar Czechoslovak-Soviet agreement and crowning its conclusion with an official visit to the Kremlin. About this time, he first revealed his intention both to the British and Soviet envoys and to Fierlinger. "I am constantly thinking of going to Russia at an opportune moment," read a telegram sent to Fierlinger on May 5, 1942.

> The Anglo-Russian agreement, the details of which we have given you, will probably soon be concluded . . . After its signing, other Central European questions will become actual: the question of our confederation with Poland, Danubian matters, and the entire German problem. I regard it as necessary to talk matters over with Russia in time. I would utilize this journey for that purpose. I have informed Bogomolov of this. At the same time I should like to inform the Soviets of the way I conceive the transition to postwar conditions in our country.[29]

It was somewhat ironic that it was not Stalin but Roosevelt who was primarily instrumental, though only unwittingly, in influencing Beneš's determination that the "opportune moment" had arrived. As mentioned in the preceding chapter, Beneš wanted his official visits to the United States and to the Soviet Union to follow closely, with the journey to the United States to take place first. When, in December 1942, he received Roosevelt's invitation to pay him a visit, he decided at once that he would proceed to Moscow shortly after returning from the United States and began his political preparations without delay.[30] Since he wanted to couple his visit to Moscow with the conclusion of a new long-term

Soviet-Czechoslovak treaty of alliance, his first step was to ascertain Soviet interest in such a treaty. In a talk with Bogomolov on March 19, 1942, he explained at some length to the Soviet envoy the sort of agreement he envisioned. In particular, he listed three fundamental principles for the treaty:

> (1) It would be a renewal of the previous Soviet-Czechoslovak treaty of mutual assistance, which would simply be adapted to meet present circumstances;
> (2) It would be analogous to the treaty Czechoslovakia would like to have with Poland so that the ground would be prepared for an eventual tripartite Soviet-Czechoslovak-Polish alliance and, in fact, for future Slav policy;
> (3) It would be done within the framework of the Anglo-Soviet treaty of 1942 or at least would follow the same principles so that it could not be interpreted as Soviet imperialism.[31]

Asked to determine Moscow's attitude, Bogomolov expressed his conviction that the Soviet Union would surely want to conclude an alliance with Czechoslovakia. But he doubted that it was wise to connect it in any way with the Anglo-Soviet treaty because, as he put it, in so doing "we would be obliged to asked British permission and would thus be deprived of our contractual freedom."[32]

Moscow's reply did not take long. On April 23, 1943, Bogomolov brought the following answer:

> a. Moscow thinks that the president's question was an inquiry [un sondage] and at the same time a proposal. With regard to the sondage, Moscow replies that it is willing to sign a pact of mutual aid with the Czechoslovak republic before the end of the war. If this was the president's proposal, Moscow accepts it.
> b. Moscow is willing to sign a pact with the Czechoslovak republic in the spirit of, and in the same sense as, that of the Anglo-Soviet pact. Moscow proposes that the president prepare the text of the treaty and present it for mutual discussion. The matter does not have to be ready tomorrow; we are to take adequate time and prepare it quietly.
> c. Regarding the tripartite pact in the sense in which the president spoke of it, the Soviet government, in principle, expresses agreement with the president's proposal. But, of course, given the present relations between Poland and the Soviet Union, it is not yet possible to do anything definitively. It is essential to gain time.[33]

Moscow's reply came as a pleasant surprise, for in view of the negative

Soviet attitude toward the Polish government, Beneš feared that the Soviets would not want to enter into a definitive political arrangement with his government either. "I have reached the conclusion," he wrote to Fierlinger on February 10, 1942, "that the Soviets will not want to agree with us on anything definitive before the end of the war."[34] His satisfaction with Moscow's positive reply was echoed in a telegram informing Fierlinger of the good news Bogomolov had brought him on April 23, 1942:

> I consider it a decisive and definitive agreement for our future. It clarifies our relations with Russia, both internationally and internally. It can calm all our people and allay their anxiety in every respect. It provides proof to all that the Soviet Union will also respect our internal affairs; and it is a guarantee to the Soviet Union and to our socialists and communists that the ČSR [the Czechoslovak republic] and the USSR will maintain lasting friendly relations and that Czechoslovakia will not join any Central European anti-Soviet adventure. It also reveals [our] absolute loyalty and goodwill to Poland in the future, where great changes are sure to occur.[35]

When Beneš left for the United States two weeks later, he was firmly convinced that nothing stood in the way of his forthcoming visit to Moscow and the signing of the Soviet-Czechoslovak treaty on that occasion.[36] This conviction was reinforced by Roosevelt's wholehearted agreement with Beneš's policy toward the Soviet Union and by what Beneš believed to be U.S. approval of his intention to visit Stalin and to enter into a treaty with the Soviet Union.

Therefore it came as a shock to Beneš when, after his return from the United States, Eden informed him on June 24, 1943, that the British were opposed to a treaty with the Soviet Union at this time since it would make the position of the Poles more difficult and hence worsen Soviet-British relations. When Beneš, pressed by Bogomolov and Fierlinger to proceed with the project despite British opposition and himself dissatisfied with the British attitude, called on Eden at the House of Commons on July 1, 1943, to discuss the matter, the British foreign secretary pulled out protocol on Anglo-Soviet negotiations conducted during Molotov's visit to London in 1942. From the protocol it was clear that Molotov and Eden had agreed that Great Britain and the Soviet Union would not conclude treaties with other countries regarding frontiers and other postwar matters until after the war. Eden also showed the president the text of a telegram sent by the British ambassador in Moscow, Sir Archibald Clark Kerr, stating that Molotov had promised the British ambassador that the Soviet Union would refrain from entering into such treaties.

Eden's evidence convinced Beneš that the Soviets had indeed assumed such an obligation. However, this did not make him any happier. He was angry with both the British and the Russians for not informing him of this mutual undertaking. "It is a sort of an oriental trick on the part of the Russians," he complained. "They knew that they had promised not to conclude such treaties. But when the obligation became a political burden for them, they tried to use us to get rid of it. They do not care one bit that they have placed us in a difficult position. All that matters to them is to achieve what they want. It is typical of them; and Fierlinger joyfully dances to their tune, believing that this is the best policy."

While sharply critical of the Soviets' devious attempt to take advantage of him, Beneš also held the British responsible. Although aware of his intention to conclude an alliance with the Russians, they did not bother to inform him of the agreement barring such treaties. "I cannot understand it," Beneš complained. "Had I known about it beforehand, I could have proceeded differently and the problem would not have arisen. Besides, the English are very shortsighted if they seek to prevent us from concluding the treaty *now*. It is a fundamental mistake to think that we might be safer against the Soviet Union without a treaty than with a treaty. To have a clear and timely agreement guaranteeing our independence and promising noninterference in our internal affairs is better than having none at all."[37]

Beneš informed Bogomolov on June 25, 1943, of the unexpected obstacle, and on July 7, 1943, the Soviet envoy brought him the Soviet version. He conceded that Britain and the Soviet Union had discussed the matter of refraining from such agreements with small nations. But, he claimed, no agreement had been reached, and therefore, Moscow was free to conclude the proposed treaty of alliance with Czechoslovakia. However, Bogomolov added, if the president had doubts whether it would be possible or convenient to sign the treaty, it would perhaps be better to defer his journey to Moscow. Faced with this none too subtle attempt to exonerate Moscow and lay the blame on him, the president countered by saying that "if this was Moscow's opinion," he fully agreed and would defer the trip. After discussing the matter for a while "as if we wished to shift responsibility from one to the other," Beneš finally told the Soviet envoy:

> Let us speak quite frankly and clearly. Last year I promised that I would

visit Russia. It was to be a political journey as well as a manifestation, just as had been my visit to the United States. It was to show our people at home and the whole world how friendly the relationship was between us. I feel bound to keep the promise . . . and, therefore, I will not and cannot do anything that would mean that I promised to make a political journey and did not keep my word. Therefore *I* cannot propose that the journey be canceled. It must be made clear that *I* do not revoke the trip and that it was not *my* fault that it did not take place. Due to the developments of the last month, this journey has changed its character and has become a journey for the purpose of signing a treaty. When the British raised objections against the signing of the treaty, the situation became so complicated that the question arose whether the journey could be undertaken. Thus, a situation developed that neither you nor I have instigated. It is therefore necessary to proceed accordingly. One cannot place the responsibility for this situation on your side or ours. You wish that the journey be undertaken; so do I. You wish that the treaty be signed; so do I. But a third party, Britain, requests that the treaty not be signed at the present time, and therefore the situation is: (1) You are of the opinion that after all that has happened, a journey without signing the treaty would not be appropriate. (2) On the other hand, I have doubts whether it would be possible or appropriate to sign the treaty now, during this journey. It means that we should both realize that for reasons that were not caused by us and for which we cannot be held responsible, we have mutually (*d'un commun accord*) decided for the time being to defer the journey.

According to Beneš's account of the conversation: "After a period of uncertainty whether it was in accord with what he [Bogomolov] had told me previously, he accepted this proposal. He then emphasized that it was a delicate situation. For those in Moscow, he said, it is easy to say that I ought to come and sign. For them, it is easy, but for us it is difficult. He understands that we are still in many respects dependent on England, but Moscow is not. Several times he repeated: '*Certes, la situation est délicate*'—in French and in Russian."

From his long talk with Bogomolov, Beneš gained the definite impression that the negotiations between England and the Soviet Union were quite clear, that both knew what they wanted, and that the Soviet reply confirmed Eden's belief that the Soviet commitment was firm, whereas Moscow evidently considered its reply evasive. In handling the thorny issue, Moscow maneuvered, in Beneš's opinion, "so as to get the journey postponed without conceding that Britain was right and that Moscow did not behave correctly toward us when it did not tell us about its commitment."[38]

Beneš's impression that the primary fault lay with the Soviet Union was further strengthened when, on July 29, 1943, Bogomolov admitted that Maisky had indeed communicated to Eden the Soviet government's consent to the British desire that neither Britain nor the USSR conclude treaties with small countries during the war. However, since Eden had not sent any proposal regarding it as Maisky had allegedly asked him to do, the Soviet Union considered itself freed from any such obligation. Moreover, Bogomolov claimed, the negotiations dealt only with treaties concerning postwar boundaries, not with treaties about mutual aid.

Beneš was perturbed by this unexpected development. He wished to remain friends with both Britain and the Soviet Union. His supreme hope—and his policy—was to contribute as much as he could toward a betterment of East-West relations. Instead, Czechoslovakia had now become an object of discord. The Soviets had attempted to misuse him in order to shake off a burdensome obligation. Although the president was eager to have the best possible relations with the Soviet Union, he was not ready to achieve this at the price of British friendship. Despite Bogomolov's suggestion that he should avail himself of his prerogative as head of a sovereign state and disregard British objections, Beneš remained adamant and decided to postpone his journey until the British and the Soviets had settled their dispute.[39]

This did not mean, however, that Beneš adopted a passive wait-and-see attitude. On the contrary, he kept striving to overcome British opposition to the treaty, an opposition that he considered unwise and harmful for both Czechoslovakia and Britain, and eventually even for Poland. As had been the case when Beneš pushed for British repudiation of Munich, the hapless Nichols once again became the primary target of Beneš's pressure. In a long talk with the British envoy on August 5, 1943, Beneš took the British to task for preventing him from reaching a timely understanding with the Soviets. He complained that they were thereby making his endeavors to consolidate Czechoslovakia internally more difficult. "Do you want to put us into the position vis-à-vis the Soviet Union in which Poland finds itself?" he asked Nichols somewhat unfairly. He cautioned Nichols that this intolerable situation could not be prolonged, that the British must help him find a solution, and soon: "The end of this month is the latest date on which I could go to Russia. Therefore, the matter must be settled before that time."[40] Judging from Beneš's account of the talk, it was a rather one-sided affair, with Beneš lecturing Nichols and the British envoy listening, apologizing, and assuring the president that the whole matter was under consideration and that "it will be surely arranged." (Beneš quoted this phrase in English in the Czech text of his account.)

Meanwhile, Beneš prepared a draft of the proposed treaty, which the Soviets accepted with two additions: (1) a provision that none of the contracting parties would be allowed to join a coalition of powers aimed directly or indirectly against the other party; and (2) a provision for mutual consultation in case of a threat of attack. The whole question became a matter of public discussion, and sharp criticisms of the British attitude began appearing in the British press. Nichols himself continued to be hopeful that a mutually acceptable solution would be found, and Lockhart even told Beneš that if he did not yield, the British would give in and his point of view would prevail. Thus, when a conference at Moscow of the foreign ministers of the Soviet Union, Great Britain, and the United States was scheduled for October 1943 and the question of the Czechoslovak-Soviet treaty was, on Beneš's request, placed on its agenda, Beneš was convinced that he would soon be on his way to Moscow.

Hence, it is hardly surprising that the president was shocked when Masaryk telephoned him on October 19, 1943, that Sir Alexander Cadogan, under-secretary of state in the British Foreign Office, had just officially informed him that Eden had left for the Moscow conference with the intention that no Soviet-Czechoslovak treaty be signed before the end of the war.[41] Moreover, on the same day the Soviet chargé d'affaires, P. Orlov, called on the president and suggested that the text of the treaty be published even if the treaty were not signed. It appeared that Moscow already knew of the negative British attitude and had possibly given up.

Yet one week later, on October 26, 1943, Orlov informed Beneš that the British no longer objected to the signing of the treaty. "So we shall pack after all," the president remarked with a contented smile when Orlov left.

> I knew that the British would see reason in the end. But after Cadogan's categorical declaration, I did not expect it so soon. I wonder what happened to cause the British point of view to undergo such a sharp metamorphosis within one week. It must have been some kind of a compromise, and the British must have used their consent as a payoff for some Soviet concessions, maybe on the Polish question. If this is so, perhaps we helped in this way to improve the position of the Poles.[42]

Beneš subsequently raised the question of the reason for the British change of mind in a conversation with Molotov during his visit to Moscow. As the Soviet foreign commissar told Beneš, he had sent the text of the proposed treaty to Eden in advance of its consideration at the conference. When the subject of the treaty came up in the talks, Molotov briefly explained the whole matter and asked for Eden's and Cordell Hull's opinions. Eden answered in a few sentences that had he known the text of the treaty previously, everything would have been different. He ended by expressing full agreement with the treaty, and Hull concurred. "I expected a major discussion, but there was none," Molotov concluded.[43] Although Beneš had not given the British the actual text of the treaty, he did inform them fully about its contents and Eden must have known quite well what the proposed text contained. Hence, ignorance of the treaty's provisions could hardly have been the real reason for the sudden and rather unexpected British volte-face. Whatever the reason, Beneš's patient insistence paid off, and he could proceed to Moscow and sign the treaty with the British and U.S. approval, just as he wanted.

Writing about the treaty and the Moscow conference in his *Memoirs*, Beneš stated: "I . . . declared that I would go to Moscow in any case after the meeting of the three Ministers and would agree to the signing of the treaty between us and the Soviet Union and also put it into operation."[44] I was somewhat surprised on reading this passage, for it did not accord with Beneš's comments to us at the time. Rather, his attitude then was that he definitely would not sign the treaty unless the British agreed. When sending Fierlinger directives about the Moscow conference, he stated quite clearly, though in a somewhat cumbersome style:

> In case England and Russia persevere in their respective positions and no agreement is reached, or in case Russia holds to its standpoint that it is the matter for only the two of us, that it is none of England's business, and that they will not parley about it with England, it is necessary that you know quite clearly *that in such a case I cannot go to Russia and cannot sign the treaty*. It would be a direct and sharp conflict, not only between England and Russia, but between Czechoslovakia and England with all the consequences thereof. We are not in a situation in which we could afford to do this.[45]

We left England for Moscow at 1:00 A.M. on November 23, 1943. Since we had to fly by way of North Africa and the Middle East to avoid the Luftwaffe, our trip was scheduled to take four days, including a day of rest at Cairo. But bad weather over the Soviet Union—and probably also Stalin's preoccupation with the Teheran Big-Three conference— kept us grounded at the Royal Air Force base at Habbanyiah in Iraq until December 3. Moreover, low clouds over Moscow prevented our plane from landing in Moscow for several more days. We finally left for Moscow on December 7, 1943, on a train Stalin sent to Baku for us. Because of a poor track, we did not reach Moscow until December 11.

Thus, Beneš had the opportunity to begin official talks with the Soviets even before his arrival in Moscow. While stranded in the middle of the Iraq desert near Baghdad, he had five long talks with Soviet Deputy Foreign Commissar Alexander Korneichuk, whom Stalin sent to Habbanyiah to serve as Beneš's official escort to Moscow. Stalin could not have picked a better man for the job. Unlike the typical tight-lipped Soviet diplomat, Korneichuk had a most pleasing personality and very affable manners. A Ukrainian, a born extrovert, a writer and inveterate storyteller, he never stopped smiling. He had a fine sense of humor and was a clever debater who did not hesitate to volunteer his opinions even about delicate questions and possessed the knack of giving his interlocutor the impression that he meant what he said.

In his Habbanyiah talks with Korneichuk and in their sequel during the four long days on the train from Baku to Moscow, Beneš covered all the principal items he intended to discuss with Stalin and Molotov. "I explained to him our policy and my ideas," wrote Beneš in his summary of the talks, "and at his request I handed over to him a list of all the questions we had discussed, in some cases with the solution I was suggesting."[46] Indeed, there was hardly any question concerning Czechoslovak-Soviet relations or international politics that was not considered in their conversations, which ranged over such topics as postwar Czechoslovak-Soviet cooperation, especially in the economic and military fields; Czechoslovakia's postwar boundaries and Beneš's request that the Soviet Union help Czechoslovakia reoccupy the territories torn away as a result of Munich and its aftermath; Soviet support for the transfer of Sudeten Germans to the Reich; the thorny issue of Poland; severe punishment of traitors and war criminals; the postwar status of Germany and Hungary and the formulation of a joint Soviet-Czechoslovak stand on this important issue; Beneš's recommendations that Austria remain independent, Yugoslavia be united as one country, Transylvania be returned to Romania, and France again be recognized as a great power and brought back into full cooperation in the postwar order of Europe; and the question of the Slav cooperation.

Since these topics were raised again in Beneš's talks with Stalin and Molotov, any further elaboration at this point is unnecessary. The main purpose of the Beneš-Korneichuk conversations was to expedite matters by providing the latter's Kremlin superiors with advance notice of what the president intended to discuss with them. But it may be of some interest to mention a few details. In talking about the transfer of the Sudeten Germans, Beneš pulled out a map and began to show Korneichuk the areas he would be willing to surrender in order to facilitate the transfer of the Sudeten Germans. But Korneichuk's reaction was that we simply ought to chase the Germans out without giving up any territory. On the contrary, he thought that we should annex parts of Germany.[47] When the discussion shifted to the punishment of war criminals, Beneš expressed the desire that the Soviet government itself demand strict punishment of those Slovaks who had joined Germany in declaring war on the Soviet Union, for he felt that such a demand would make their punishment politically easier for him. As Beneš told us afterward, he thought that this would help us get rid of "all those parasites who had enriched themselves in Slovakia from this war" and would want to save themselves after the war.[48] The issue of Ruthenia also came up. While telling Korneichuk that he expected the province to be returned to Czechoslovakia, he suggested that culturally it should attach itself to the Ukraine. This was, of course, a pleasant surprise for Korneichuk, whose views were strongly colored by Ukrainian nationalism.

But the two topics discussed at the greatest length were Slav cooperation and Poland. (For the gist of the Beneš-Korneichuk talks concerning Poland, see Chapter Four.) Their exchange of views regarding Slav cooperation deserves somewhat fuller coverage. After stressing his own positive stand on the matter, Beneš raised three straightforward questions to which he wanted frank answers:

> 1. Can I take it for granted that the Soviet Union, once it has accepted the Slav question as one of the main problems of its policy, will not abandon it? That is to say, will the Slav question remain a permanent part of Soviet policy?
>
> 2. Is the opinion favoring Slav cooperation held not only by certain groups of people, such as professors, scientists, and the like, but also by the communist party? Will not the communist party abandon it again later for some ideological reasons? Can one be assured that it will be retained as a lasting consideration in the formulation of the aims of Soviet policy?
>
> 3. Does the Soviet Union accept the Slav policy in its democratic conception; that is, as a close cooperation among all Slav nations on the

basis of equality, as a people's idea having nothing in common with the old conception of pan-Slavism, which was viewed at all times by other Slav nations, particularly the Poles, as another form of imperialism and expansion?

Korneichuk responded with a long exposition of his personal views, leaving, however, no doubt that this was what he believed to be the Soviet official stand. He spoke with contempt of the "old ideology of leftist trends and deviations that were often abstractly international, had nothing in common with the traditions of the Russian and Ukrainian peoples, and had by now been abandoned." Although conceding that among the Soviet communists were a few specimens of "the old extremist Bolshevistic type" who "were nearer to the old conception of the Slav idea," he assured Beneš that Stalin and his collaborators did not share these views. He reminisced that some years before he had raised the Slav question at a meeting in the Kremlin and Stalin, who "understood that the Slav democratic people's policy fitted into the realistic and permanent interests of the USSR," had received it favorably. He pleaded repeatedly and enthusiastically for brotherly cooperation among the Slav nations based on full equality and independence, a cooperation that "did not mean spreading of a new pan-Russianism, which the Soviet Union had definitely rejected," and that "had nothing in common with the old tsarist imperialism." This type of cooperation, Korneichuk concluded, "must become the very foundation of Soviet policy."

Korneichuk's apparent open-mindedness and sincerity, coupled with his refreshingly undogmatic attitudes, strongly impressed Beneš; so much so that he came to believe that this shrewd Kremlin emissary was "our good friend."[49] Moreover, from Korneichuk's comments, Beneš concluded that his forthcoming discussions with Stalin and Molotov would proceed smoothly and that, as he stated in his *Memoirs*, they "would agree well together in Moscow on every point."[50]

When Beneš arrived in Moscow on December 11, he was in a buoyant mood, certain of the complete and speedy success of his mission. He was received with highest honors. The Kursk Station in Moscow, lavishly decorated with Czechoslovak and Soviet flags, was full of Soviet dignitaries from Molotov and Voroshilov down. Even the aging Litvinov was taken out of cold storage, as was the former ambassador to Britain, Ivan Maisky, since it was rightly believed that Beneš had good personal relations with them. The guard of honor was mustered for a rumbling review. The air was chilly, but the atmosphere was cordial.

The main event of the day was a Kremlin banquet. There Beneš met Joseph Stalin for the first time in eight years.[51] Many men who met and talked with Stalin in the era of the Grand Alliance have testified that Stalin could be downright winsome when he wanted to weaken the caution of his victim. He used this magic successfully with President Roosevelt and Prime Minister Churchill, and he was superb in his encounter with Beneš. With an old man's short steps, he trotted toward us as we waited in the reception hall in the Kremlin, a jovial smile lighting up his wrinkled face, his eyes humorously half-shut, and commenced immediately with his customary *shutki* (jokes). There was indeed nothing about him that betrayed the "man of steel," the dictator who could ruthlessly liquidate his collaborators as well as his enemies, who let millions die from hunger rather than yield in his policy of forcible collectivization, and who threw additional millions into jail and labor camps. At that meeting, with his charming, roguish smile above his graying mustache, he looked like a good-natured Dutch uncle.

This impression was further strengthened by the way he acted and negotiated. In dealing with Beneš in 1943, this top Bolshevik did not sound like a man dedicated to any rigid political dogma. He seemed to act in a thoroughly practical, matter-of-fact way like a down-to-earth realist, as if he were concerned solely with defeating the Germans, liquidating fascism, and preventing the recurrence of German aggression. He showed no inclination toward diplomatic artifice. His approach to even the most delicate problems was direct, even abrupt. His was a rather unorthodox and undiplomatic approach, but it left a strong impression of frankness.

Beneš transacted his state business in two working sessions with Molotov on December 14 and 16, and one session with Stalin and Molotov on December 18. Apart from that, Beneš had an opportunity to talk with Stalin and Molotov at the two official banquets given in his honor on December 11 and 22. He also had a long impromptu conversation with Stalin (mentioned earlier) about Poland on December 12 at the Bolshoi Theater. Beneš met Stalin again on the occasion of the signing of the Czechoslovak-Soviet Treaty of Friendship, Mutual Assistance, and Postwar Cooperation on December 12 and again when the instruments of ratification were formally exchanged in the Kremlin on December 22, 1943. But no business discussions occurred during these two brief encounters.

Although Beneš dealt at some length with his 1943 visit to the Soviet Union in his *Memoirs*, he did not give a full account of his working sessions with Stalin and Molotov. Instead, he merely included part of his report from Moscow to his government in London "about the Moscow negotiations as a whole."[52] Smutný prepared a fairly detailed account of Beneš's two conversations with Molotov (as well as the Stalin-Beneš discussion at the Bolshoi Theater), which are preserved in his papers.[53] No detailed account is available about the Beneš-Stalin meeting of December 18, which Smutný did not attend. Nor does Fierlinger, who participated in Beneš's sessions with Stalin and Molotov, say much about the 1943 Moscow negotiations in his book *Ve službách ČSR*, published in Prague in 1948.[54] I myself did not take part in Beneš's negotiations with Molotov or his meeting with Stalin on December 18, but I noted down at the time what the president told me about them. On the basis of these materials, it is possible to reconstruct a fairly accurate account of that fateful exchange of views in December 1943.

As Beneš had done in preparing for his talks with Roosevelt, he brought to the Moscow negotiations a list of items he wished to discuss and went through them one after the other. The gist of the talks is as follows.

Germany. Stressing that he wished Czechoslovakia's and the Soviet Union's international policies to be coordinated, Beneš wanted to know Soviet intentions regarding Germany as accurately as possible. When he raised the question in his first talk with Molotov, the Soviet foreign commissar appeared rather hesitant about revealing Soviet plans. Finally he admitted that "in principle" they anticipated the Reich's dismemberment after the war, although they had not yet decided the number of parts. But in their second talk, held two days later, Molotov returned to the German issue in a manner that sounded almost like an apology for his earlier evasiveness. Reaffirming once again the Soviet Union's determination to dismember Germany, he told Beneš that they could not reveal their real intentions concerning Germany because they would only help Hitler. "Seydlitz is making excellent propaganda for us. We even intercepted an order of a German general in which he felt it necessary to assure his troops that it was not the real General Seydlitz who was speaking, for he would never do a thing like this. We shall even use the German communists in the same way."[55]

Hungary. Besides informing Molotov that Czechoslovakia intended to reoccupy the areas lost to Hungary in 1938–1939 and expressing the hope that feudalism would be destroyed in Hungary after the war, Beneš urged the Soviets to participate in the Allied occupation of Hungary. "I think it to be important that you take part in it, not only the English and the Americans," he advised Molotov at their first meeting.[56] If the English occupied Hungary alone, Beneš argued, the Hungarian aristocrats would do what they did after World War I. They would invite them for hunting weekends and use the opportunity to impress them with lies and gain their support. Aware of the assiduous pro-Hungarian propaganda waged in Britain and the United States and the way in which some Hungarian exiles in these countries attempted to influence Western policy in Hungary's favor and against Czechoslovakia, Beneš felt very strongly that only Soviet participation would thwart such endeavors. In particular, he was afraid that since neither Britain nor the United States had committed itself to the restoration of Czechoslovakia's pre-Munich boundaries, he might encounter difficulties in that respect should Hungary be occupied only by Anglo-American forces.

The punishment of war criminals. Afraid that the West might be too lenient toward war criminals, Beneš in both his talks with Molotov commended the Soviet Union for its resolute stand in this matter. His primary concern was, of course, the Sudeten Germans. "The punishment of our Germans—that is a big question for us," he told Molotov, stressing the Sudeten Germans' responsibility for Munich, the Nazi occupation, and "all that happened" and estimating that as many as 90 percent of them were guilty.

Beneš also used the occasion to bring up, as he had already done in his talks with Korneichuk, what he himself labeled "a somewhat delicate question"; namely, that the Soviet government "demand in a friendly fashion" the punishment of those Slovaks responsible for declaring war on the Soviet Union and guilty of collaborating with the Germans. Beneš's desire to secure the just punishment of the leading Slovak war criminals and collaborators without unduly exacerbating Czech-Slovak relations prompted this appeal. He knew that, since there was a higher proportion of collaborators among the Slovaks than among the Czechs, the outcry might rise in Slovakia that the Czechs were persecuting and punishing the Slovaks. He felt that it would help if the Soviet government insisted on punishment. That is also why the draft of the protocol about his exchange of views with Stalin and Molotov, which Beneš wanted (but did not get) published, contained a passage stating that although the government of the Soviet Union was aware of the substantial differences in the degree of guilt of Germany and Slovakia, it expected that the Slovak people would "strictly punish those who had brought them into the murderous struggle against their Slav brethern."[57]

The transfer of the Sudeten Germans and the Hungarians. Even before he reached Moscow, Beneš was confident that the Soviet Union fully supported his plan to transfer a substantial number of Sudeten Germans to the Reich. After all, that was the gist of Moscow's answer to Beneš's inquiry that was sent to him through Bogomolov on June 5, 1943, while the president was visiting the United States. That was also the impression he gained from his Habbanyiah talks with Korneichuk. But Beneš wanted Stalin and Molotov to reconfirm the Soviet stand. Hence, he used the first opportunity he had, the welcoming banquet in the Kremlin on December 11, 1943, to raise the issue of the transfer briefly with Stalin, who expressed his approval. He then discussed the matter in full during his two working sessions with Molotov on December 14 and 16. After summarizing the reasons he deemed the transfer of the Sudeten Germans so vitally important for his country, Beneš handed to Molotov a memorandum detailing his thoughts on implementing the transfer. (He had prepared the memo before leaving for Moscow and then had it translated in Moscow from Czech into Russian.)[58]

According to the memorandum, the transfer plan was "part of an extensive political, economic, and social five-year plan for the entire reconstruction of the new republic." The bulk of the transfer was to be completed in two years, but "the worst categories," such as employees of the Gestapo, SS, police, and members of the Henlein party, were to be shipped to Germany within two months after the liberation of the country (unless, of course, they were held for punishment). Czechoslovakia would become "a national state in which members of national minorities would have full individual civil rights, but would not be recognized by law as special national and political entities." The official languages of the republic would be Czech, Slovak, and Ukrainian. The nationality of at least 67 percent of the residents of every town or village would be Czech, Slovak, or Ukrainian. The Germans allowed to remain in Czechoslovakia would, if possible, have elementary schools with German as the language of instruction. The Hungarians were to be treated similarly.

Although Beneš did not mention in his memorandum the number of Germans affected by the transfer, in his oral explanation he mentioned that he would like to eject "at least two million." Moreover, as he had done in his talks with Korneichuk, the president expressed his willingness to facilitate the transfer of the largest possible number of Sudeten Germans by ceding some border areas to Germany. "If it is necessary, I am prepared to make compromises," he told Molotov. "I have to consider the English and the Americans from whom I expect difficulties, and I think that they would be more willing if we explained to them that we did not want just to export the Germans, but also to cede a piece of territory with them."[59] Beneš then pulled out a map and showed Molotov the border areas he was prepared to cede to Germany in exchange for certain small slices of German territory to straighten the boundaries and improve them from the strategic viewpoint, making the whole transaction look like an exchange of territory rather than a unilateral cession.

Indeed, Beneš was not at all anxious to gain any additional German territory. When discussing the question of postwar boundaries between Germany and Poland with Molotov, Beneš pleaded with the Soviet foreign commissar to let Poland have more of Germany's territory along the Czechoslovak border so that Czechoslovakia's frontier with Poland would become longer and that with Germany shorter. At the same time, however, he stressed that he did not want any Germany territory for Czechoslovakia, even though the London Poles had urged him to claim it. "When we talked about it [with the Poles], they urged that we, too, enlarge our territory at Germany's expense in that region," Beneš told Molotov. "But we do not want this, for it would mean an increase in the number of the Germans we want to transfer out of our land." Again, in his meeting with Stalin on December 18, Beneš displayed similar reluctance. Toward the close of the meeting the Soviet dictator showed him a map of Europe on which he had already marked the future eastern frontiers of Germany. The territory of East Prussian Königsberg was marked off for the Soviet Union, and the Oder line was the boundary between Germany and Poland. When Beneš remarked that the Poles thought that their territory should extend to the river Neisse, Stalin took his pencil and readily assigned that area to the Poles. He then handed the pencil to Beneš and invited him to mark the portion of Germany Beneš wanted for Czechoslovakia.[60] But Beneš merely repeated that he desired only to straighten the boundary line somewhat and as an example he pointed to the Glatz region. Hardly concealing his astonishment and disappointment at Beneš's moderation, Stalin assigned the region to Czechoslovakia. (Eventually, however, the Glatz region was given to Poland.)

Both in his memorandum and in his oral presentation, Beneš sought to link the transfer of the Sudeten Germans with the issue of German reparations in a manner that made even Molotov, whose sense of humor was only slightly above that of a grizzly bear, smile. Rather than asking for reparations from Germany, Beneš proposed that Czechoslovakia take over the property left behind by the expelled Sudeten Germans. They would be issued receipts indicating the value of the expropriated property, which they could then present to the Reich's authorities and collect compensation from Germany under the title of war reparations due to Czechoslovakia.

Beneš's endeavor to facilitate the transfer of undesirable Germans and Hungarians was also the primary reason behind his desire that Czechoslovakia participate in the military occupation of Germany and Hungary. In this way, he thought, a sizable portion of transferees could simply be moved to areas assigned to Czechoslovak occupation. Thus, he inserted in one memorandum the clause that "Czechoslovakia wished to participate in the occupation of Germany and Hungary side by side with the great powers should it be decided that the military occupation would be one of long duration and the small states were asked to participate in it."

Economic cooperation. Beneš also brought a memorandum on economic cooperation, which he handed to Molotov during their second conversation on December 16.[61] After stating that a great part of Czechoslovakia's postwar foreign trade would be with the East, especially the Soviet Union, the memorandum called for the adaptation of "the Czechoslovak production plan to the state plan of the USSR," which "would take into consideration in a suitable manner all the fundamental needs of Czechoslovakia regarding not only the necessary raw materials but also the disposal of finished products." While stressing that the "necessary regard" would have to be paid to "Czechoslovakia's essential economic relations with other countries," it gave vent to the belief that the envisioned adaptation would lead to "the most purposeful cooperation with the USSR in the principal branches and ensure full employment for Czechoslovak industry for a long period." It recommended that the Soviet and Czechoslovak armament industries be adapted to the requirements of the Czechoslovak and Soviet armies, which would have "in principle, the same war equipment, according to plans prepared by their respective general staffs"; that a joint plan be devised for the rapid construction of railway, road, and air transportation facilities between the two countries; and that "technical experiences and all the improvements obtained in the different spheres of production be exchanged" and close cooperation in industrial, technical, and scientific research be arranged. Finally, it suggested that "at a suitable time" appropriate commissions be formed to work out in detail this plan for economic cooperations and to prepare a survey of the most essential products and raw materials so that economic cooperation could begin immediately after the liberation of Czechoslovakia.

Since everything Beneš wanted to say on this subject was included in the memorandum and the memorandum was intended for experts, little was said about it in the conversation. Nonetheless, Molotov clearly and strongly approved of the envisaged reorientation of Czechoslovak trade toward the East and termed the lopsided Czechoslovak economic orientation toward the West "a very serious matter."[62]

Military cooperation. Another memorandum dealt with Czechoslovak-Soviet military cooperation, including such matters as standardization of weaponry, coordination of armament production, exchange of military technology, construction of suitable airports, and other aspects of joint Czechoslovak-Soviet planning in the realm of defense.[63] In transmitting the memorandum to Molotov during their working session on December 16, Beneš stressed his desire to make the Czechoslovak army, then fighting on the eastern front, as large as possible so that a second brigade could join the one already in action. He also expressed the wish that a Czechoslovak air force unit be set up on Soviet soil and promised to send Czechoslovak pilots from Britain. Finally, he asked for weapons and ammunition for the Czechoslovak underground: "We know that we could not fight at the very beginning. So at least we want to fight toward the end, before the war is over, so that our entire nation will feel itself to be at war and in full military cooperation with Russia. That is why we want you to help us with armaments, because in the end there will be a revolution and partisan warfare in Czechoslovakia."[64]

In speaking to Stalin on December 18, Beneš raised the issue of the entry of the Red Army into Czechoslovakia. Specifically, he requested that Czechoslovak army units march into Czechoslovakia together with those of the Red Army and that liberated Czechoslovak territories be handed over to the Czechoslovak civil administration immediately. Stalin agreed and said that he would give orders accordingly.

The issue of sabotage. To Beneš's regret and dismay, his remark about partisan warfare provided Molotov with a welcome opportunity to express disappointment with what the Soviet government perceived as an inadequate level of sabotage in Czechoslovakia. "The Poles carry out one act of sabotage after another," Molotov pointed out in an unmistakable tone of reproach. "They wreck bridges and trains. Even after we broke off diplomatic relations with them, they continued supplying us with lists of all the acts of sabotage carried out by their resistance movement in Poland. Yet we do not hear about any sabotage in Czechoslovakia." The president, somewhat taken aback by Molotov's criticism, did his best to counter it. He pointed to Czechoslovakia's distance from the front, the density of its population, and the difference in Czechoslovakia's terrain, which did not lend itself to the kinds of sabotage possible in Poland. He averred that numerous acts of sabotage were taking place, but that they were more in the nature of "so-called scientific sabotage," a continuous commission or omission of acts that, though not so conspicuous or spectacular, were nonetheless substantially damaging the German war machine. He explained that to facilitate sabotage, he had asked the British, as well as the Soviets, to bombard factories inside Czechoslovakia, but to no avail. Molotov listened patiently to Beneš's apologetic presentation but obviously remained unconvinced. The topic cropped up once more in Beneš's conversation with Stalin on December 18: "Don't you have vast forests in Czechoslovakia?" the marshal wanted to know, bewailing the virtual absence of partisan activities in Czechoslovakia. To remedy this, he offered to place at Beneš's disposal a transmitter near Smolensk or Orsha (after the Soviet army retook it from the Germans), to provide planes to parachute agents behind German lines, and to do anything that might intensify the Czechoslovak resistance.

Czechoslovakia's internal affairs. In line with his precept of "laying all his cards on the table," Beneš also thought it appropriate to inform Soviet leaders of his views on the arrangement of internal affairs in postwar Czechoslovakia. There were three main reasons for this decision. First, he believed that it would document his loyalty and openness vis-à-vis the Soviet Union. Second, he saw in it a good way to correct whatever misleading or distorted information Soviet leaders might have been supplied by their own agents or by Czechoslovak communists who had found refuge in the USSR. And third, he imagined that after hearing of his plans to steer Czechoslovakia along socialist lines, Stalin and Molotov would be more inclined to aid Czechoslovakia in the postwar settlement with its enemies. Hence, in talking about the transfer of the Sudeten Germans, Beneš referred to it as "the beginning of a big social revolution"[65] since enterprises expropriated from the Germans would not be handed over to private hands but would be nationalized, as would large enterprises owned by Czechs or Slovaks.

In explaining these proposals, Beneš did not expect the Soviet leaders to adopt any stand, let alone advise him what he ought to do. Still, he could not help being impressed that apart from a few minor questions, both Stalin and Molotov continually stressed that although they could not refuse to listen, these were strictly internal matters that were none of their business. "There was not a single occasion during our negotiations here," wrote Beneš from Moscow to Jan Masaryk, "where our partners would not emphasize, wherever possible, that our internal affairs did not concern them and that they would not interfere in them."[66]

Ruthenia (Subcarpathian Ukraine). As Beneš was explaining his plans for postwar Czechoslovakia, mention was made of Ruthenia. Responding to Molotov's question concerning the postwar status of Slovakia, Beneš showed the Soviet foreign commissar on a map the four provinces of which the new decentralized Czechoslovakia was to consist, including Subcarpathian Ukraine. He again expressed his desire that after the war Subcarpathian Ukraine be affiliated culturally and linguistically with the Soviet Ukraine. However, not only did he leave no doubt in Molotov's mind that he expected the province to be returned to Czechoslovakia, but he also inserted a clause to that effect in a memorandum transmitted to the Soviet leaders (through Korneichuk): "*Czechoslovakia will be recognized internationally as the Czechoslovak national state,* that is, a state of Czechs and Slovaks to which there will be attached Subcarpathian Ukraine with a special autonomous status."[67] Beneš included an identical clause in the draft of the protocol he expected to be published.[68] Moreover, when the future of Subcarpathian Ukraine came up during Beneš's conversation with Stalin, the marshal told Beneš with a tone of finality in his voice: "Subcarpathian Ukraine will be returned to Czechoslovakia. We have recognized the pre-Munich frontiers of Czechoslovakia, and that settles it once and for all."

Third countries. Beneš and the Soviet leaders, especially Molotov, exchanged opinions about a number of countries other than Germany,

Hungary, and Poland. With the exception of France's postwar role, they had no difficulty reaching a consensus. The Soviets vetoed any Austro-Hungarian or Austro-Bavarian union and urged Austrian independence. Molotov fully approved the president's contention that despite Romania's participation in the war on Germany's side, the Romanians had behaved better than the Hungarians and that Transylvania should be returned to them. They agreed that Serbo-Croatian dissensions notwithstanding, Yugoslavia should not be allowed to disintegrate. When their talk shifted to Italy, Beneš commended Count Carlo Sforza, Italy's new foreign minister, told Molotov of Sforza's difficulties with the British and the Americans, and transmitted Sforza's message that he desired to conclude an agreement with the Soviet Union.

The one disagreement concerned France. As in his conversations with Roosevelt and Korneichuk, Beneš pleaded for the speediest possible restoration of France to the status of a great power and its full participation in the armistice negotiations and the postwar reorganization of Europe. He urged equitable treatment for France to prevent any bitterness that would hinder the creation of a new European order. But Molotov remained unswayed by Beneš's pleading. He accused the "entire ruling stratum" of France of helping Hitler, called it "politically rotten" and a nation of weaklings, and argued that the French must be punished for their actions.

The Treaty of Alliance. Even though the signing of the Czechoslovak-Soviet Treaty of Friendship, Mutual Assistance, and Postwar Cooperation was the ostensible reason for Beneš's visit, it was not mentioned in his negotiations with the Soviet leaders since its text had been settled months before. One day after our arrival in Moscow, on December 12, 1943, Molotov and Fierlinger signed the treaty in a brief ceremony in Molotov's study in the Kremlin in the presence of Beneš, Stalin, Kalinin, Voroshilov, and a host of other dignitaries. The president and Stalin made short speeches, and all of us toasted the Soviet-Czechoslovak friendship with Soviet-made champagne. Stalin seemed in high spirits, and when Beneš concluded his speech (delivered in Russian), the marshal patted him on the shoulder and jokingly remarked: "The pronunciation was better than yesterday."

The only hitch occurred when the Soviet government proposed a last-minute change in the treaty's text. Beneš originally proposed an initial term of five years, and his draft of the treaty stipulated that the exchange of the instruments of ratification, which was to take place "in

Moscow as soon as possible," was to be followed by an "additional approval" by the Czechoslovak parliament after the war. The Soviet version extended the term to twenty years and left out any mention of the subsequent approval by the Czechoslovak parliament. As Beneš stated in his *Memoirs*, he did not want to prolong the discussion and accepted Moscow's version.[69] The ratification instruments were exchanged on the eve of our departure on December 22, 1943.[70]

Beneš had no objection to the lengthened term of the treaty. But he would have definitely preferred to provide for an additional ratification by the postwar Czechoslovak parliament. He felt that this would have been a more democratic procedure, which would also have been in accordance with the 1920 Czechoslovak constitution, which called for an affirmation by parliament of treaties "entailing personal, especially military, burdens."

In essence, it was a treaty of alliance against future aggression by Germany (and countries allied with Germany) similar to that concluded between Great Britain and the Soviet Union one year earlier. Like the Anglo-Soviet treaty, it contained pledges not to interfere in internal affairs, and "not to conclude any alliance and not to take part in any coalition directed against the other High Contracting Party," a promise to develop economic relations "upon the broadest possible scale and to afford each other all possible economic assistance after the war," and an undertaking of mutual support in the war against Germany and the states "associated with it in acts of aggression in Europe."

There were, however, some notable differences from the Anglo-Soviet treaty of 1942. The military aid clause of the Anglo-Soviet treaty was to remain in force only until the adoption of "proposals for common action to preserve peace and resist aggression in the postwar period"; the Czechoslovak-Soviet treaty contained no such limitation. The former pledged mutual aid against attack; the latter used the considerably broader phrase "in case one of them should, in the postwar period, become involved in hostilities." The Anglo-Soviet treaty limited the alliance to a *casus foederis* arising out of acts perpetrated by "Germany or any of the states associated with her in acts of aggression in Europe," which clearly referred only to Germany and its *wartime* European allies. On the other hand, the corresponding clause in the Czechoslovak-Soviet treaty referred to Germany and "any of the states that may unite with it directly or in any other form in such a war," which clearly included any country whether allied with Germany in the Second World War or not.

The broadened scope of the Czechoslovak-Soviet treaty was desired both by Beneš and the Soviets, save for one important aspect. Much like the Anglo-Soviet treaty, Beneš's first draft of the Czechoslovak-Soviet treaty contained the provision that its military aid clause should remain in force only until the high contracting parties, by mutual agreement, recognized that it was superseded by the adoption of "proposals for common action and collective security to preserve peace and resist aggression in the postwar period." This provision had to be dropped at Soviet request; and so was the reference (made in the preamble to the treaty) to the desire to collaborate with the United Nations "at the peace settlement and during the ensuing period of reconstruction on the basis of the principles enunciated in the declaration made August 14, 1941, by the President of the United States of America and the Prime Minister of Great Britain, to which the government of the Union of Soviet Socialist Republics and the government of the Czechoslovak Republic have adhered."[71]

In December 1943, given the prevailing circumstances and Beneš's beliefs regarding East-West relations, Beneš saw nothing wrong in the broader scope of the Czechoslovak-Soviet alliance. He could not have anticipated that four years later Stalin would invoke the treaty to prevent Czechoslovak participation in the Marshall Plan discussions in Paris, arguing that the plan was a coalition aimed against the USSR.

The main purpose of Beneš's visit to Moscow was to gain Soviet support for Czechoslovakia's cause. But he also wanted to hold talks, which he deemed very important, with the top leaders of Czechoslovakia's communist party, who had found wartime refuge in Moscow, reach an understanding with them, and thus create a mutually acceptable basis for their participation in Czechoslovakia's postwar reconstruction. Beneš was fully aware of the risks involved. He anticipated that the communists would utilize the surge of radicalism that was bound to spread through the countries that had succumbed to the Nazis. He could already see that, proletarian internationalism notwithstanding, the communists were encouraging Slovak nationalism in an effort to gain political leverage and enhance their appeal in Slovakia. Above all, he realized how much the prestige and the popularity of the Soviet Union as the heroic victor over the Nazis and the liberator of the countries subjugated by them would aid the communists. Beneš was convinced that only full-fledged communist participation in the governance of Czechoslovakia would save the republic from bitter political strife and possibly civil war. He thought that it would be better to have communists in the government rather than in the opposition and that sharing responsibility for governing the country would tone down their radicalism.

Beneš had six long working sessions with the veteran quadrumvirate of Czechoslovak communist leaders, Klement Gottwald, Rudolf Slánský, Jan Šverma, and Václav Kopecký.[72] Anxious to involve Gottwald and his comrades fully in his government in exile, Beneš offered them two seats in his cabinet. But they declined. Although they assured Beneš that they recognized his government as the legitimate representative of Czechoslovakia, pointing out also that their comrades in London sat on the State Council (an advisory body of exiled Czechoslovak politicians in London), they did not want to share responsibility for the London government's sins of commission or omission. In particular, as Gottwald wrote to his comrades in London about the talks with Beneš, they sharply criticized Beneš's government for its alleged passivity and its failure to "organize on the territory of the republic an active struggle against the occupation forces" and to issue "a clear official declaration that would emphasize armed struggle and the formation of armed groups and partisan detachments."[73]

Their main reason, however, for refusing Beneš's offer was that they opposed a return of the London government to liberated Czechoslovakia "even in a state of demission," as Gottwald put it. Rather, they wanted a new government that would include, in addition to some members of the London government, a large contingent of communist ministers and representatives of the resistance movement at home. Although they refrained from demanding the premiership for themselves, they insisted that the new premier must be "a member of the left" so as to reflect the decisive postwar shift to the left they anticipated.[74] Since the communists would probably be the strongest leftist party in the government, read Gottwald's letter (couched in the third person plural), "in accordance with the old parliamentary tradition, they are entitled to the premiership. However, without giving it up for the future, they do not stake their claim to it for the time being." Gottwald and his comrades also indicated that they expected to be given government positions that corresponded to the party's anticipated strength and allowed them to play "an effective role." They did not tell Beneš the specific cabinet posts they had in mind, but Gottwald's letter listed the Ministry of the Interior (which was to be in charge of national police and the maintenance of public order) and the Ministry of Defense.

Stressing the importance of national unity in the difficult task of postwar reconstruction, they urged, and Beneš agreed to, the creation of a national front that would comprise all political parties and whose leading nucleus would be a bloc consisting of communists, Social Democrats, and Czech Socialists. Among the parties Gottwald and company wanted included was the Agrarian party, although subsequently they changed their minds and opted for that party's prohibition. Nor did they want to refer to this bloc of three socialist parties as a "bloc of the left." Rather, in an obvious endeavor to broaden its appeal, they preferred a designation like the National Bloc of the Working People of the Towns and Countryside. In the same vein, Gottwald and his associates pleaded for unity in the postwar reorganization of the labor and cooperative movements and other groupings. But when Beneš, who was anxious to prevent the proliferation of political parties that had plagued prewar Czechoslovakia and favored a three-party system (left wing, right wing, and center), suggested a merger of communists, Social Democrats, and Czech Socialists into a single socialist party, communist fervor for unity suddenly cooled. Although the communists were not opposed "in principle," they maintained that such an action could be taken only after the return to Czechoslovakia and only "in a democratic fashion and with full participation of the entire membership of the parties concerned," stated Gottwald in his letter.

Much of Beneš's discussion with the Moscow communists concerned the provisional administration to be set up in liberated Czechoslovakia. The communists argued that since the entire apparatus of public administration in Czechoslovakia was compromised by its cooperation with the Nazis (however involuntary), it had to be replaced by new administrative organs—people's committees at the local, district, and provincial levels. Inhabitants of the cities and villages concerned were to elect the local people's committees. Representatives of the local committees would choose the members of the district committees, which in turn would choose the provincial committees. Representatives of the provincial committees would then elect members of the provisional National Assembly that was to assume the functions of the pre-Munich parliament.

Beneš could not help noticing that these bodies closely resembled the soviets of Lenin's days, and he was anything but enthusiastic about the proposal. Although critical of the overcentralization of local government in prewar Czechoslovakia and supportive of increased authority for local elective organs, he feared that a drastic change at the time of the

German collapse would lead to chaos and mismanagement. Nor did the thought escape him that the scheme would work to the communists' advantage, allowing them to utilize the chaotic situation to secure the most important local government positions for themselves. Nevertheless, he felt that he had no choice but to concur, for he knew that the idea would be popular and that the existing apparatus was too tainted with the stigma of collaboration to function properly once the Nazis had been expelled. He pleaded, however, for careful consideration of the matter to minimize the problems of transition. "My final comment was," he wrote in his *Memoirs*, "that the most important consideration would be *to prevent legal and administrative choas and to replace the previous legal order quickly with a new post-revolutionary legal order.*"[75] When, after his return to London, the president signed the decree establishing the people's committees, he deliberately explained in a letter to the premier, Jan Šrámek, that in his conception, the people's committees would exercise their authority through existing official organs—namely, the appointive provincial district, and municipal administrations.

Another topic discussed at some length was whether the Slovaks were to be considered and recognized as a separate Slav nation united with the Czech nation as a single country or whether they were merely a component of one single Czechoslovak nation. Much like the Slovak autonomists, the communists promoted the former view and wanted Beneš and his government to issue an official proclamation recognizing the Slovaks as a separate nation within one Czechoslovak republic. But the president, who was adamant in his conviction that the Czechs and the Slovaks were two ethnic groups forming the Czechoslovak nation, refused. As he told the communist leaders, he felt that the Czechs and the Slovaks themselves should settle the matter after the liberation.

The issue of Slovak nationhood and the question of Beneš's behavior at the time of Munich were the only two items on which Beneš and the Moscow communists remained irreconcilably opposed, and neither side displayed any inclination to compromise. Otherwise, the president seemed well pleased with his talk with Gottwald and his colleagues. "I am very satisfied with my talks with the communists," he told Smutný and myself at their conclusion. "They are more positively inclined and calmer that I expected. They know what they want; they have their own plan. We talked about everything quite openly, and they had the courage to tell me face to face what they thought and where they disagreed with me. It is not as it is in London where even those who are close to me tell me nothing face to face but then go to the nearest bar and criticize me behind my back."[76] In his report to Jan Masaryk, Beneš averred that there was *"general agreement between us about what should be done in the immediate future, at the time of transition at home after the fall of Germany, and about the procedure for establishing a single national front immediately after the revolution."*[77] He reported in a similar vein to the Czech underground:

> I dealt in great detail with the representatives of our communists in Moscow, and I am, of course, in continuous contact and collaboration with our communists here in London. All are loyal to the republic, go along with the president and the government, and cooperate patriotically. As soon as it will be possible after Germany's collapse to nominate a new government in agreement with our people at home, the communists will join it. We are at one even with the communists that the number of the parties at home will be reduced to three, the left, the center, and the conservatives, and that the National Front will be preserved after the war for a number of years, and this, of course, without all the fascists and the Czech and Slovak culprits.[78]

In December 1943 (and for several months thereafter) Beneš firmly believed that relations between Czechoslovakia and the Soviet Union, as well as between him and the Czechoslovak communists, were excellent and that no matter what happened elsewhere, his country would emerge from the holocaust of the war and the Nazi occupation as the bastion of democracy in East Central Europe, as it was called so often and by so many in prewar days. I still remember Beneš's elation when he returned to our Moscow *osobniak* after his long final conversation with Stalin and Molotov on December 18, 1943. "We came to a complete agreement— about everything!" he exclaimed jubilantly the moment he stepped through the doorway.[79] He gave vent to his sincere belief in Soviet good intentions in a speech to his countrymen broadcast from Moscow in which he underscored the Soviet Union's "full respect" for Czechoslovakia's sovereignty and its solemn treaty commitment of noninterference in internal affairs.[80] He spoke in the same vein with Winston Churchill when, on our way back to London, he visited the British prime minister at Marrakesh. And he reiterated the same faith in Soviet assurances in the confidential report he sent to his collaborators in Czechoslovakia after his return to London:

> The Moscow negotiations, the signing of the treaty, and the talks with all the leading Soviet representatives have given me complete satisfaction. The Russians will support us in all principal questions regarding the

security of the republic, and as far as it concerns them, they maintain an absolutely positive attitude regarding our international affairs. This also covers the full recognition of the independent pre-Munich republic, that is, our pre-Munich frontiers; the realization of a common Czechoslovak-Soviet frontier in Ruthenia; the carrying out of the transfer of the guilty minority population from the republic on the largest possible scale; full respect for our sovereignty; and noninterference in our internal affairs.

Having stressed that the Soviet Union did not stipulate any conditions for cooperation with Czechoslovakia, Beneš assured his collaborators that the Soviets had only one interest:

that the republic carry out as quickly as possible in unity and peace all necessary constitutional, administrative, economic, and social reforms that postwar conditions will require and again become the first and best organized and most prosperous state of Central Europe. How these reforms will go will depend exclusively on the will of the majority of our people and on European conditions in general. It is not a question of communizing the state, but of progressively reforming economic and social conditions.[81]

7

The End of Illusions

The eight months following Beneš's triumphant return to London were the happiest period in his life since the darkness had begun descending on his country in 1938. The Munich humiliation was erased, the Third Reich was about to collapse, and fascist Italy already lay prostrate. Beneš's arrangements with Stalin safeguarded Czechoslovakia against any future German threat, and the solemn Soviet commitment of noninterference in Czechoslovakia's internal affairs seemed to eliminate any danger of forcible communization. According to a Czechoslovak-Soviet agreement in May 1944, the Soviet authorities were to hand over the administration of liberated Czechoslovak territory to a delegate of Beneš's government. The cooperation between East and West, of such crucial importance to Beneš, seemed to be a reality. Even the thorny Polish issue appeared to be on the verge of resolution.

Beneš and all of us around him were genuinely elated when it was announced on April 8, 1944, that the Soviet army had reached the Carpathian Mountains, the northern border of eastern Czechoslovakia. "Fires of victory burn on the summits of our Carpathian Mountains, all bells began to ring, welcoming those who are the first to bring liberty, justice, and human dignity to the tormented people of Czechoslovakia," read the lyrical declaration with which Beneš's government greeted that memorable event.[1] As late as July 16, 1944, the president's confidence in

Czechoslovak-Soviet and East-West relations allowed him to assure the Czech underground that "the Soviets will not interfere in our internal affairs" and "we shall decide by ourselves how we will want to arrange our new life and order."[2]

But one month later, Beneš's imperturbable faith in Soviet loyalty and good intentions toward Czechoslovakia sustained its first jolt when the Soviets began secret negotiations with puppet Slovakia's minister of war, Gen. Ferdinand Čatloš, a man high on the Czechoslovak list of quislings and war criminals. (In a conversation with Molotov during his 1943 visit to Moscow, Beneš had named Čatloš as one of those who "must hang.")[3]

In the summer of 1944, General Čatloš and some of his associates felt that it was time to think about saving their own skins. Since at the time the Red Army was poised on a wide front along the northern boundary of Slovakia, they thought that their best chance to escape punishment would be to establish contact with the Soviets, offer them military cooperation, and place themselves fully at the Soviets' disposal for whatever plans, both military and political, Stalin might have. They knew that should the Czechoslovak republic be re-established and Beneš's government assume control, they could not escape retribution for their crimes. They also knew that many Slovak communists believed that Stalin would convert Slovakia into a constituent republic of the USSR. Hence, they thought that the best chance of salvation lay in offering Stalin their services for this nefarious deal. Having surrendered their country to the Nazis in 1939, they now intended to sell it to the Soviets.

On August 4, 1944, Čatloš's emissaries, accompanied by Karol Šmidke, the leading Slovak communist, and Lt. Col. Mikuláš Ferjenčik, a representative of the Slovak democrats, flew to the Soviet advance base at Vinnitsa, from where they were taken to Moscow. The treacherous nature of their mission was made amply clear by two paragraphs in Čatloš's memo for the Soviet authorities:

> 1. Slovak military dictatorship would find understanding and support in all strata of the population . . . The Slovak declaration of war on the USSR and the Allies would be canceled and simultaneously war would be declared on Hungary, which would make the new regime at once popular. Overnight, German military and civilian measures in Slovakia would be eliminated and possibilities for big Soviet operations created. *The prerequisite for this is, however, that the Slovak army would retain its character as an independent state army while becoming part of the armies of the USSR and cooperating with Czechoslovak units on the basis of mutual independence. Otherwise mutual controversies and serious conflicts would arise.*

2. The secret organization of Slovak Bolsheviks would take care of mutual contact with the Soviets, although for the time being, in the interest of the natural course of events and of gaining all the people, it would not do so openly. Anyhow, the *state-political consequences would ensue after the end of the war so that the Slovak political matters might be solved in accordance with the interests of the USSR.* As regards the Soviet-Czechoslovak agreements hitherto concluded, the Slovaks ought to be given the right to take an independent standpoint. Therefore, Slovak-Soviet contact ought to be direct.[4]

On learning of the departure of the Slovak delegation from our collaborators in Slovakia, who were in daily radio contact with us, Beneš expected that the Soviets would apprise him of Čatloš's overture and inform him of their intentions. After all, a matter so pregnant with grave consequences for the delicate and potentially explosive issue of Czech-Slovak relations required consultation with Beneš. But not only did the Soviet authorities fail to notify Beneš, but they did all they could to prevent Ferjenčik from contacting Czechoslovakia's official representatives in Moscow. Except for Šmidke, who was actually a Soviet agent,[5] no member of the delegation was ever left unescorted. On August 17, however, at the theater, Ferjenčik spotted two members of the Czechoslovak military mission in Moscow, who gave him the mission's address. He subsequently managed to elude his Soviet escort, contacted Col. Heliodor Pika, the chief of the mission, and gave Pika a copy of Čatloš's memo.[6]

The Soviet behavior in the Čatloš affair worried the president. He had nothing against the Soviets' receiving Čatloš's emissaries. But he resented the Soviet failure to inform him, seeing it as an undeserved mark of disloyalty. "Incredible, inconceivable," he muttered while reading and rereading Colonel Pika's report on the matter. "So this is our reward for having so often stood up for the Russians! This would not work. This must be stopped." He wrote a resolute instruction to Fierlinger directing him to discuss the matter with the Soviet government:

We count with certainty that the Soviet government, acting in the spirit of our common policy and on the basis of our alliance and the agreement of May of this year, will not undertake anything that might be in contradiction to those treaties. The Czechoslovak government will by no means change its line in this respect, will fulfill the treaties to all consequences, and will ask similar fulfillment from the other side. It will not take part in any such parley with the quislings . . . Any negotiations about collaboration with the Slovak military units may be undertaken only in accord with us, or after our approval and recommendation. That means that any such negotiations must be made only through us . . . Any other procedure would needs be considered here in the West as a proof that our policy with the Soviets has failed.[7]

The impact of Beneš's firm protest in Moscow cannot be determined. On September 5, 1944, however, Soviet Ambassador Lebedev informed the president that the negotiations with Čatloš and his people had been abandoned. Blushing slightly, he excused the Soviet failure to apprise Beneš by explaining that "the negotiations were conducted by the communist party. The Soviet government had nothing to do with it."[8]

Despite Lebedev's explanation, Beneš was pleased with the outcome of the Čatloš affair. But he was shortly served another example of the unreliability of Stalin's pledges and assurances. At the end of August 1944 an uprising involving some two divisions of Slovak troops was staged in mountainous Central Slovakia in the rear of German armies. The rebellion was organized in agreement with Beneš and on the assumption that prompt and effective Soviet aid would be forthcoming. After all, during Beneš's 1943 visit to Moscow, Stalin himself had expressed dissatisfaction with the low level of anti-German activity in occupied Czechoslovakia and urged that it be stepped up, promising all-out Soviet aid.[9] Beneš had every reason to believe that the Soviets would do all they could to help the Slovak rebels. So confident was he that the Soviets would fulfill Stalin's promises that he wrote to his collaborators in the Czechoslovak underground on July 16, 1944: "We are negotiating with the Soviets in order to prepare deliveries of weapons to Slovakia and the Czech lands. Count on it with certainty that at the given moment you shall get the weapons."[10] Also, he and the Slovaks hoped that the Soviet army, which was only some fifty to sixty miles away, would take advantage of the uprising, push across the Carpathian Mountains, and cooperate with the Slovak patriots.

However, when the "given moment" came, the Soviet response was disappointing. Throughout the ten weeks of the Slovak uprising, the Soviet armies, already poised on the northern boundary of Slovakia, made no serious attempt to mount an offensive to relieve German pressure on the beleaguered Slovaks, who sorely lacked heavy weapons capable of stopping German tanks and armored cars. Nor were the Soviets in any hurry to supply the rebels with badly needed weapons and other forms of military support, such as air raids against the advancing German columns. On September 6, 1944, one week after the outbreak of the uprising, two Soviet staff officers landed at the rebel-held airfield of Tri Duby in order, as they said, to reconnoiter the situation and make arrangements for assistance. They left and still no help came. In desperation the rebel command wired Beneš on September 8, 1944: "The Germans have superiority in the air and in tanks. If one squadron of fighter planes and one battalion of paratroopers do not arrive within 24 hours, the general situation will be very bad. Please radio what is the matter with the promised assistance."[11]

Gravely dismayed by Soviet procrastination, Beneš directed Fierlinger and Pika to urge the Soviets to hasten the promised aid. The Slovak National Council, which was at the head of the uprising, also sent an urgent SOS to Moscow. Responding at last, the Soviets began air drops of weapons and ammunition and agreed to send to Slovakia the Czechoslovak paratroop brigade and Czechoslovak air force wing that had been organized on Soviet soil. But the aid was so modest and so slow that its impact was negligible, and the uprising finally collapsed. The transfer of the Czechoslovak paratroopers took so long that the planes bringing the last group had to unload under direct bombardment by the heavy German cannonade that preceded the general German offensive against the rebels.[12] General Rudolf Viest, who had been sent from London to take command of the Slovak troops, reported that the Slovaks had no minethrowers, no barbed wire, few anti-tank weapons, and only six tanks. "Koniev [the Soviet marshal commanding the Russian troops on the Czechoslovak border] gave nothing of what he had promised," read the somber conclusion of Viest's report.[13]

Bitterly disappointed by the Soviets' benign neglect of the hard-pressed Slovaks, Beneš turned to the Americans and the British. Since the Anglo-American forces had already conquered southern Italy and established air bases there, he thought the U.S. air force could drop weapons and bombard the German convoys and columns converging on the rebels. Indeed, to the president's great satisfaction, the Allied command in Italy was willing to help, and on September 17, 1944, the U.S. Office of Strategic Services dispatched a liaison officer to the rebels to arrange for weapons deliveries from southern Italy.[14] Also, on September 17 and October 7, 1944, U.S. planes delivered 24 tons of weapons and ammunition to the Slovaks (taking back with them several American airmen who had escaped from German prison camps and found refuge in liberated Slovak territory).[15] But the deliveries suddenly stopped. When Beneš's military aides in London urged their continuation, they were informed that Washington had vetoed further aid. When the aides asked the reason for this sudden change of mind, they were told that since Slovakia lay within the sphere of Soviet operations, no such aid missions could be undertaken without Soviet approval, which obviously had been refused. They received a similar reply from the British, who said that they could not provide any assistance because the Soviets had not replied to the request for approval.[16]

All this came as a surprise to Beneš, for this was the first time that he learned, albeit indirectly, that the United States, Great Britain, and the Soviet Union had reached agreement regarding their respective zones of operations and had evidently assigned Slovakia, and probably all of Czechoslovakia, to the Soviet zone. He now understood the lack of British interest in an agreement on the rights and duties of British forces in Czechoslovakia similar to those they had concluded with Belgium, the Netherlands, and Norway. Beneš had offered the British such an agreement in February 1944 when he began negotiating a similar arrangement with the Soviets. So certain was he then that the British would concur that he wired Fierlinger on February 19, 1944: "We have also begun discussing the matter [of the entry of British troops into Czechoslovakia] with the British government, and we shall conclude an agreement with them as Belgium, the Netherlands, and Norway have done. You will be informed in good time. It would be good if these negotiations [with the British and the Soviets] could proceed simultaneously and in accord."[17] However, without mentioning zones of operations, the British declined, claiming that in view of the military situation it was unlikely that the Western armies would get to Czechoslovakia before Germany's capitulation.

Beneš became quite concerned about Czechoslovakia's assignment to the Soviet zone, for he knew that a zone of operations, even though meant only as a temporary wartime arrangement designed to avoid undesirable overlap and confusion in military operations, might all too easily be converted into a zone of influence and be viewed by the country operating therein as permanent and exclusive. He felt that Western assent to the inclusion of Czechoslovakia in the Soviet zone, however logical from the military standpoint, would further complicate his endeavors to maintain his country on a balanced course midway between the East and the West.

However, the worst breach of faith perpetrated by Stalin on Beneš in 1944–1945 was the Soviet rape of Ruthenia, especially the devious manner in which it was committed.

Since Czechoslovakia's dismemberment in 1938–1939, Beneš had doubted that he could or should reclaim Ruthenia. The province was alloted to Czechoslovakia after the First World War more by chance or default than by any planned and preconceived action. Neither Tomáš Masaryk nor Beneš, when visualizing the future frontiers of their renascent country, envisioned Ruthenia as part of it. The problem arose when Austria-Hungary disintegrated and the non-Magyar ethnic groups residing in territory belonging to Hungary's St. Stephen's crown established their own independent states or joined neighboring countries. Had imperial or liberal Russia survived the war or had the Ukrainian bid for independence been successful, Ruthenia, far too small and far too backward to be viable as an independent country, would undoubtedly have been incorporated into the Ukraine since the Ruthenians were ethnically and linguistically most closely related to the Ukrainians. But the Bolshevik takeover made such a solution impractical in 1918, and Ruthenia was assigned to Czechoslovakia as an autonomous province.

Beneš, in line with his thesis of juridical continuity, maintained that Ruthenia had never ceased to be a legal part of Czechoslovakia and that it could not be left to Hungary, which had seized the province in 1939. However, since from the beginning of the war Beneš had reckoned on eventual Soviet participation on the Allied side, he speculated that the Soviet Union, as a future covictor, might claim Ruthenia on ethnic grounds as it had done in the case of the eastern, largely Ukrainian-inhabited parts of Poland. Morever, it was obvious that Ruthenia would be liberated by the Red Army and come under the control of the Soviet Union, which might surrender to the temptation to convert a temporary occupation into a permanent unification of Ruthenians with their ethnic cousins across the border.

Beneš's post-1939 attitude toward this delicate issue can be summarized as follows: He disliked the idea of giving up a province that had experienced impressive political, economic, social, and educational progress during the twenty years of its association with Czechoslovakia. On the other hand, he did not want to alienate the Soviets. He felt that he must remain on good terms with them, for otherwise the communists might deliberately create chaos and confusion in Czechoslovakia at the end of the war and might exploit it to transform the country into a communist dictatorship. If the price of good relations with the Soviets was Ruthenia, he was prepared to sacrifice it. Hence, before committing himself, he was anxious to ascertain Soviet intentions regarding Ruthenia's future.

Beneš began his exploratory forays as early as September 19, 1939, when in a conversation with Maisky, he told the Soviet ambassador: "The question of Subcarpathian Ruthenia will be solved between us later and we surely will agree!"[18] Although Maisky refrained from commenting, he must have concluded that Beneš was prepared to let the Soviet Union have the province if it wanted it. Indeed, as the president subsequently learned during his second wartime visit to Moscow in March 1945, Maisky had so written to his superiors in his report on the conversation.

In 1939 Beneš did not expect that the Soviets would give him any clear indication of their designs regarding Ruthenia. He simply wanted to inform them that unlike the Poles, who were unwilling to concede the Ukrainian-inhabited parts of Poland to the Soviet Union, he was flexible and would not allow Ruthenia to become an international controversy between Czechoslovakia and the Soviet Union. But when the Soviet Union became Czechoslovakia's ally following the German invasion, he felt that the time had come to ascertain the Soviet stand. On August 28, 1941, he spoke with Maisky about Czechoslovakia's territorial questions. In a memo on the conversation, the president wrote:

> Maisky knows that we adhere to the principle of juridical continuity, that Munich does not exist as far as we are concerned, and that in substance we want to re-establish our country as it had been before Munich. That means: the Czech lands, containing also the Sudeten German regions; Slovakia; and Ruthenia. We do not exclude small changes, but in substance the republic will consist of the same parts as before. According to what we hear from Moscow broadcasts, you seem to be following the same policy and have the same line. According to our view, the Subcarpathian Ukraine will again belong to us as will Slovakia, of course; the Sudeten German districts must also be returned to us.
>
> Maisky asked why we wanted these [Sudeten] areas and if their possession would not prove disadvantageous for us. I told him to look at the post-Munich frontiers on the map, and further that we needed them economically and strategically—because we do not know what will happen to Germany, etc. He asked whether we also would insist on this in the event that Germany would be different after this war, for example, revolutionary and socialist. I replied most decidedly yes . . . The result of our discussion, with which he concurred, was as follows: Ruthenia cannot be retained by the Hungarians; the Poles cannot have it; that province can belong only to Czechoslovakia or Russia.[19]

As can be seen from Beneš memo, Maisky did not commit himself.

Nonetheless, the Soviet decision to ignore a virtual offer of Ruthenia merely for the asking convinced the president that the Soviet Union did not want it. Also, unlike the British, the Soviet government assured Beneš several times that it recognized Czechoslovakia in its pre-Munich boundaries, which, as Beneš understood it, also included Ruthenia. When during an official visit to London in June 1942 Molotov met with Beneš, the Soviet foreign commissar confirmed, as the president wrote in his memo on their talk, "that the USSR was for our pre-Munich boundaries, since it could not approve and accept anything that was connected with Munich and its consequences."[20] Moreover, the Soviet action in allowing the Ruthenians who had been taken prisoners while serving in the Hungarian army fighting on the eastern front to join the Czechoslovak army on Soviet soil seemed to Beneš to be additional, compelling evidence that the Soviets considered Ruthenia an integral part of Czechoslovakia.

So sure was Beneš of Soviet respect for the territorial integrity of pre-Munich Czechoslovakia that he wrote to his collaborators in Slovakia on March 3, 1943:

> All threats of bolshevism and bolshevist Russia are ridiculous gossip. We have a firm agreement with Russia regarding our independence and the integrity of our territory. Russia simply recognizes our pre-Munich republic and will help us renew it in its former shape. Talk about the inclusion of our republic in the Soviet Union is ridiculous because not even the Soviet Union desires it, and it knows that it would not be in its interest since it would bring it into undesirable controversies that Russia does not want, especially with Western Europe ... The union of Slovakia and Ruthenia with the Czech lands is an accomplished fact that no power in the world will prevent.[21]

During Beneš's 1943 visit to the Soviet Union there was no suggestion that the Soviets might claim Ruthenia. As noted in the preceding chapter, one of Beneš's memos for Molotov stated in no uncertain terms that the Subcarpathian Ukraine would again be part of Czechoslovakia. When Beneš mentioned the subject in his conversation with Stalin in December 1943, the marshal told him that the province would definitely be returned to Czechoslovakia.

Therefore, one can well imagine the president's shock when he learned that Soviet radio had broadcast a message (presumably sent to Stalin from Užhorod, the capital of Ruthenia, on November 7, 1944) that spoke of the "eternal dream" of the Subcarpathian Ukrainians "to live as one family with the Ukrainian people."[22] He was further aggravated by a simultaneous report from our people in Ruthenia that the Soviet command had begun drafting Ruthenians into the Red Army. At a luncheon with Lebedev on November 13, Beneš expressed his amazement at such behavior and asked the Soviet ambassador to transmit to Moscow Beneš's urgent request that the enrollment of Ruthenians be stopped. Lebedev seemed genuinely surprised by Beneš's comments, said that he knew nothing of the matter, and promised to contact Moscow at once. But Moscow's reply, which Lebedev brought the next day, was an icy no: "Molotov asks you not to insist on the dismissal of the Subcarpathian Ukrainian volunteers from the Red Army and not to oppose further enrollments into Soviet military units."[23] In cold anger, Beneš stubbornly stuck to his point:

> We must insist on this matter. All that is done in the Subcarpathian Ukraine by your army commanders is in contradiction to our laws. First, I have to request that all propaganda for the enrollment of our citizens into the Red Army be stopped at once. Nor is it permissible to publish Soviet appeals asking the Subcarpathian Ukrainians to join the Soviet military units. They are Czechoslovaks, and consequently their place is in the Czechoslovak army. In 1942 your government released for service in the Czechoslovak army in Russia all the Subcarpathian Ukrainian prisoners of war. Now you seem to reverse your policy completely.
>
> As regards those Subcarpathian Ukrainians who have already joined the Red Army, we have no intention of disavowing the local Soviet commanders. Nor do we desire to allow public controversies to arise. That would be harmful. Our law does not absolutely prohibit Czechoslovak citizens from serving in foreign armies, and a number of our people are, in fact, serving in the Allied armies in the West. But they all had to secure individual permission to do so from the president of the republic. Otherwise, they would be considered deserters. This procedure might be applied to those who have already joined the Red Army, and thus the matter might be solved. But what we most decidedly must oppose is a mass enrollment of our citizens into your army. Not only would it make it impossible for us to organize our own army, but it would have also serious political consequences. I therefore have to ask you to present the matter in Moscow once again and have it settled along the lines that I have just described.[24]

Lebedev, already scheduled to travel to Moscow on November 15, 1944, promised to "take the matter up personally" there. The president hoped that the ambassador, who appeared anything but happy about the whole affair, would impress on his superiors the need for a reasonable solution along the lines Beneš had suggested. But Lebedev did not return to his post in London. We never saw him again, and Beneš never learned the results of the ambassador's discussions in Moscow. Judging from the continued flow of alarming reports from Ruthenia, however, the Soviets had decided to take advantage of the Red Army's occupation of Ruthenia to annex the province. Not only did Beneš receive several telegrams asking for the incorporation of Ruthenian villages into the Ukraine, but Ukrainian radio broadcast the telegrams as well.

At the same time, people loyal to the president and to Czechoslovakia informed us how such telegrams were obtained. Communist agents, accompanied by military guards, called on a village mayor, presented him with a ready-made petition asking that his village be "reunited with the Ukrainian brothers on the other side of the Carpathians," and demanded that he sign it. Similar pressure was applied to make Ruthenians volunteer for service with the Red Army. Soviet recruiters simply rounded up men of military age and sent them under armed escort to a Red Army depot. The Czechoslovak government delegate, František Němec, to whom the administration of liberated Czechoslovak areas was to be handed over under the terms of the Czechoslovak-Soviet agreement of May 1944, was left completely at the mercy of local gangs acting with the benevolent acquiescence of Soviet agents. A self-styled National Council of the Subcarpathian Ukraine even gave the Czechoslovak government delegate an ultimatum to leave the province within three days.[25] Moreover, one day an armed gang invaded the delegation's office and confiscated several bags of bank notes that the delegation had brought for official purposes, while Soviet guards did nothing. When Němec protested these and other misdeeds, the Soviet commander shrugged his shoulders, stating that the Soviet army could hardly be expected to interfere with an expression of the "legitimate will of the people."

Still, the President kept on fighting. On November 24, 1944, he instructed Fierlinger:

> 1. Czechoslovakia holds fast and will continue to hold fast to the legal basis of our treaty. That refers to this case as well as any other during the whole time of the occupation of our territory by the Red Army. Naturally, it refers also to Slovakia. If we departed from the basis of law and treaty in one question, we would be lost in all the others. Therefore, adhere to our original attitude and act accordingly. I am asking Minister Němec to do the same.

2. I gave Lebedev the promise that I shall attempt to settle the matter so that no controversies and international discussions might arise. I shall keep it and do not wish to cause incidents and make interventions. But this presupposes that it must be stopped in Ruthenia. We must insist on our rights, calmly, objectively, but unwaveringly.

3. Does anybody in the Red Army or in political circles think that a similar procedure would be repeated in Slovakia? Please try to find out discreetly.

4. Today I received requests from two municipalities in Ruthenia to be allowed to join the Ukraine. I shall not answer similar requests, and do not let our authorities answer them either. All that will be discussed at the peace conference between us. Meanwhile the [Soviet] commitments regarding our pre-Munich frontiers continue to exist. I am only surprised that the Soviet censorship allows such telegrams to be sent "from the Ukrainian front." The British have them and shall, of course, use them when it will suit them. We shall not, however, discuss these matters in public.[26]

In spite of everything, Beneš refused to believe that the Kremlin had cheated him. "I can't understand why they are doing this," he muttered one gloomy day in December 1944 when, as was sometimes his habit, he verbalized his thoughts while pacing nervously across his spacious Aston Abotts study.

If they wanted Ruthenia, they could have told me. I never wanted to keep it if the price would be Russian hostility. Whenever I spoke with them about Ruthenia, I always intentionally avoided claiming it for us. I only insisted that it could not remain Hungarian, that it could belong only to Czechoslovakia or the Soviet Union. Only when I was sure that they had no intention of claiming it for themselves, did I begin to count with Ruthenia in my policy. No, I do not understand it at all. Why should they want to grab it in this way when they could have had it through direct negotiations with us? No, there can be no other explanation than that the Ukrainian nationalists are forcing the situation and are doing it over Moscow's head. Yes, that is the only logical explanation. When we were in Moscow last year, I noticed that Stalin was a little afraid of the danger connected with the growing Ukrainian nationalism.[27]

The president used the same rationalization in his telegram instructing the Czechoslovak government delegate how to proceed in the difficult situation he confronted:

1. Come what may, we shall adhere to the treaty and will demand in

Moscow that it also be fulfilled. We shall not relinquish anything and shall not abandon our rights.

2. Where we shall be prevented from asserting and exercising our rights, as is now happening to you, we shall state that fact, will become observers, and will passively await future developments. It would be a mistake on our part to use force. On the one hand we do not possess sufficient executive power, and on the other they would exploit such an act as a pretext against us and would misuse it.

3. We shall not relinquish our position but will remain correctly at our post and fulfill our duty to the last.[28]

Yet, by that time, the decision that Ruthenia be surrendered to the Soviet Union had already been made in Moscow. The first hint reached Beneš on December 19, 1944, when Fierlinger reported a comment of the Soviet deputy commissar for foreign affairs, Valerian Zorin (who later became Soviet ambassador to Czechoslovakia and thereafter re-appeared in Czechoslovakia during the February 1948 communist coup): "As we have promised you and as it is stipulated in the Soviet-Czechoslovak Treaty, we are not authorized and we do not wish to interfere in your internal affairs. Therefore it is difficult for us to help you in solving your problem in the Subcarpathian Ukraine."[29]

Beneš literally shuddered when he read Zorin's statement: "Their agents force our people to sign petitions for reunion with the Ukraine, and Soviet commanders organize compulsory enrollment of our citizens into the Red Army. Yet when we protest, they say they are sorry but cannot interfere in our internal affairs!"[30]

Ten days later a telegram arrived reporting a meeting between Němec and Fierlinger and Molotov and Vyshinsky in Moscow. Molotov presented his apologies for certain "incidents" that had happened in the Subcarpathian Ukraine and explained them as the result of "general fatigue." But he stressed that the Soviet Union respected the undoubted desire of the Subcarpathian Ukrainians to join the Ukraine: "One cannot expect that the Soviet Union would oppose a spontaneous expression of the free will of a people feeling close affinity with the Ukrainian nation."[31]

It was then that Beneš finally realized that Ruthenia was lost. He might have said no, of course, but he was convinced that it would not help and might even worsen the situation. He knew that should Stalin wish to do so, the Soviets could easily invoke "the will of the people" in Slovakia in much the same manner as in Ruthenia. He knew that some Slovak communists were toying with the idea of a Soviet Slovak republic.

He looked at a map of the war fronts and saw that the Anglo-American forces were still west of the Rhine while the Red Army had already penetrated deep into Czechoslovakia. He felt that he had no choice but to bow to what had already become an accomplished fact. However, he instructed Fierlinger to inform the Soviet government of two stipulations: (1) that the formal cession of the province to the Soviet Union be postponed until such time as it could be approved by Czechoslovakia's parliament; and (2) that in return for his promise to surrender the province without causing any international trouble, the Soviet government assure him that it would not follow the same procedure in Slovakia.

At this point Stalin sent Beneš a personal letter:

Dear President Beneš:

Today I have learned from Comrade Gottwald that the Czechoslovak government is worried in regard to happenings in the Subcarpathian Ukraine, thinking that the Soviet government intends unilaterally to solve the question of the Subcarpathian Ukraine despite the agreement existing between our two countries.

I must tell you that if you have formed such an opinion, it is founded on a misunderstanding.

The Soviet government has not forbidden and could not have forbidden the population of the Subcarpathian Ukraine to express their national will. This is all the more understandable as you yourself told me in Moscow that you were prepared to cede the Subcarpathian Ukraine to the Soviet Union. As you will certainly remember, at that time I did not give my consent to it.

However, the fact that the Soviet Union has not forbidden the Subcarpathian Ukrainians to express their will does not mean that the Soviet government has the intention of breaking the agreement between our countries and unilaterally solving the question of the Subcarpathian Ukraine. Such an opinion would be offensive to the Soviet government.

As the question of the Subcarpathian Ukraine was raised by the population of the Subcarpathian Ukraine itself, it will, of course, be necessary to solve it. But this question can only be solved by an agreement between Czechoslovakia and the Soviet Union either before the end of the war with Germany or after the end of the war, according to how both governments will deem it suitable.

I beg you to believe that the Soviet government has no intention whatsoever of harming the interests of the republic of Czechoslovakia or its prestige. On the contrary, the Soviet government is fully resolved to give the Czechoslovak republic all the assistance for its liberation and reconstruction.

Yours respectfully,
J. Stalin
January 23, 1945[32]

Chargé d'Affaires Chichayev handed the letter to the president on January 25, 1945. Although it finally and irrevocably sealed the loss of Ruthenia, it did somewhat alleviate Beneš's worries. To understand this, one must realize the circumstances under which the letter arrived. Ruthenia was lost; nothing could change that. It was obvious that Czechoslovakia would be liberated by and come under the full physical control of the Red Army and the NKVD. As Beneš knew, no effective Western aid could be expected should trouble develop between Czechoslovakia and the Soviet Union. The sad fate of neighboring Poland was a bad omen and a frightening example of what would await him and his government should they choose to defy the Soviet Union and trust in Western support. He saw no option but to hold fast to whatever remained of Soviet goodwill. This must be borne in mind in order to understand the tone and the purpose of Beneš's reply to Stalin:

January 28, 1945
London

Dear Mr. Chairman of the Council of People's Commissars:

I have received your personal message of January 23, and I thank you for it most sincerely. I thank you, in particular, for expressing your point of view so clearly and in such a definite form and for giving me thus the opportunity to formulate my point of view just as clearly. It responds to the sincere and friendly relations between our two countries and peoples.

I confirm that in *some* of our circles uneasiness has indeed been caused by the events in the Subcarpathian Ukraine. It was the result of events that were *of a purely local nature* and due to the participation *of purely local factors*. In addition to this there were some announcements broadcast by the Kiev radio which were misused by the international press and by opponents of the Soviet Union and Czechoslovakia.

Nevertheless, I assure you most emphatically, Mr. Chairman, that neither I personally nor the Czechoslovak government has for one moment believed that the Soviet government desired to solve the question of the Subcarpathian Ukraine unilaterally or that it had the intention of violating the agreement between our two countries. I am thoroughly acquainted with the principles of the policy of the Soviet Union and I know that such an action on their part is definitely excluded. I beg you fully to believe these words of mine.

Further, I fully agree with you that this question should be resolved solely by agreement between Czechoslovakia and the Soviet Union and according to "how both governments will deem it suitable," as you formulate it yourself in your message. We would desire that this should take place after the conclusion of the war against Germany, i.e., after the restoration of our pre-Munich frontiers with Germany and Poland had been ensured and when I am in a position to discuss this matter with our people in Praha [Prague]. I would add to this two remarks:

1. I have not changed my standpoint in respect to this question since the time I discussed it for the first time with your ambassador in London, I. Maisky, in September 1939 and I will not change it in the future. In this sense I will also present my standpoint in Praha.

2. From our side this question will not be made the object of discussions or interventions with other Powers and we wish to attend the Peace Conference having already fully settled this question in complete friendship with you. As I and the government view this matter, this question will never be the cause for any controversy between us.

At the end of your message you inform me that the Soviet government has no intention whatsoever to harm the interests of the Czechoslovak Republic, but on the contrary is fully prepared to render it every assistance in its liberation and reconstruction. I am truly thankful to you for those words. I would like to emphasize that the Soviet Union is already bringing those words to realization through the immense and admirable actions of the Red Army during many past months and by the political support which it has always so readily given us on various important occasions as, for example, lastly during negotiations with Hungary. The Czechoslovak people are fully aware of this. Permit me, Mr. Chairman, to stress on this occasion that there is no other country and people that appreciate it more than the Czechoslovak people and there is no other country that fosters such sincere feelings of real friendship towards the Soviet Union than does the Republic of Czechoslovakia.

Yours respectfully,
Dr. Edvard Beneš[33]

In agreeing to surrender Ruthenia without causing difficulties, Beneš expected the Soviets to reciprocate by refraining from duplicating their Ruthenian stance in Slovakia. Unfortunately, his expectation proved only partially correct. There was no drafting of Slovaks into the Soviet army, and Soviet agents made no attempt to initiate in Slovakia any spontaneous movement in favor of its separation from Czech lands. On the contrary, they refused to support those Slovak communists who wanted to convert Slovakia into a Soviet republic in the erroneous belief that this was the Soviet intention.[34] Although vetoing any action intended to disrupt the reunion of the Czechs and the Slovaks, Soviet military commanders and NKVD agents promoted the efforts of Slovak and Czech communists to facilitate Czechoslovakia's communization.

In particular, Soviet agents were instrumental in helping local communists secure a dominant position in most of the people's committees that replaced the previous local government organs discredited by cooperation (albeit mostly coerced) with the Germans. Protected by the Red Army and profiting from the chaos of the first days of liberation, local communists would hurriedly convene a citizens' meeting and make it "elect," usually by acclamation, a list of candidates who were mostly communists or fellow travelers. Above all, they arranged for the posts of chief of police and his main assistants to be filled by persons whom they could rely on to follow communist directives. They were successful mainly because, by the time such meetings were held, the population had already been exposed to misdeeds on the part of Soviet soldiers and knew that anyone who challenged the communists risked arrest or deportation on trumped-up charges of being pro-Nazi or anti-people.

By seizing control of most of the people's committees, the communists gained tremendous political leverage. In the absence of an effective central government during the initial months of the liberation, the communist-controlled people's committees emerged as incontestable masters in their respective areas, able to harass their opponents at will, confiscate the property of anyone accused, rightly or wrongly, of collaboration, and incarcerate people on the basis of unsubstantiated or false accusations. Moreover, since the members of each level of people's committees elected the members of the next higher level, control of the local committees virtually assured the communists and their fellow travelers an overwhelming position of power throughout all echelons of Czechoslovakia's representative bodies.

Another successful *coup de force* of the communists was the liquidation of the Slovak Social Democratic party. Taking advantage of the prevailing chaos, disorientation, and fear, they convened a meeting of some Slovak Social Democrats and prevailed on them to agree "unanimously" to the "unification" of the two parties as the Communist Party of Slovakia. The conditions under which the merger was pushed through are well illustrated by the warning of Jan Ursiny, the top politician of the Slovak Democratic party, to Horvath, a prominent functionary of the

Slovak Social Democratic party, that Horvath risked assassination because of his opposition to the merger.[35] The true nature of the unification was confirmed by a resolution adopted by the unification congress that condemned the "reformists" (as the communists usually referred to the Social Democrats) and declared "Marxist-Leninist teaching" as the "basis" of the new party.[36] When some Slovak Social Democrats who disagreed with the communist takeover of their party established an independent Social Democratic organization in Košice, the largest city in eastern Slovakia, the Soviet commander ordered the organization dissolved. Nor did the communists permit the re-establishment in Slovakia of the Czechoslovak Socialist party, which had been suppressed there in 1938–1939. As a former Czechoslovak Socialist member of parliament reported to Beneš in October 1944, the communists argued that the Czechoslovak Socialist party in Slovakia had merged in 1939 with the Slovak People's party and that even the president opposed its re-establishment.[37]

Furthermore, the Soviet policy of considering all enterprises, stores, warehouses, and stockpiles controlled by the Germans as legitimate Soviet war booty facilitated communist machinations. Since the Germans, who in the course of the war converted Czechoslovakia into a major industrial base for military purposes, had taken over most of Czechoslovakia's major production facilities and economic assets, Soviet military commanders routinely claimed and seized all such facilities and assets as prizes of war. In this manner they also came into possession of all paper mills and stockpiles of paper and newsprint; anyone needing paper, especially for publication purposes, had to apply to Soviet military authorities. Consequently, the communists were invariably able to obtain all the paper they needed to publicize their cause, but their opponents were discriminated against and had to search desperately for paper that Soviet "booty hunters" might have overlooked.

Thus, Beneš's response to Molotov's remark, reported to him by Fierlinger on December 29, 1944, that "it would be good if he and his government were closer" is understandable.[38] Molotov originally suggested the Galician city of Lwow as Beneš's new headquarters but acquiesced to Fierlinger's proposal of the Slovak city of Košice. The president immediately wired Fierlinger to transmit to the Soviet government his wholehearted approval:

> Please inform the Soviet government that the transfer of myself and the government to the liberated territory is, in my opinion, the only solution

that can resolve definitively our present political and military difficulties. That is why I welcome and accept this indirect Soviet invitation, and I shall at once make preparations for the transfer. I add that I was waiting for just such an invitation. I deem it to be more appropriate, with regard to the West, that we move straight to our territory (Košice) and not to Lwow or some other Soviet city, except if it were only for a very short time.[39]

The president's main hope was that his and his government's presence in liberated Czechoslovak territory would revitalize the democratic forces and make them oppose the endeavors of local communists and their Soviet mentors more vigorously and more successfully. "I shall leave for home the very first day it will be possible," he told me. "I shall not delay one single moment. If our authority does not take over in Slovakia, another authority will assume control. That is inevitable."[40] As shown in Chapter Nine, the president's expectations were only partially fulfilled, to a small extent because of his own miscalculations, but overwhelmingly because of factors beyond his control.

8

Homeward Bound

Considering all that happened between Beneš and the Soviets in late 1944 and early 1945 and the ominous events throughout Soviet-liberated Eastern Europe, one can easily imagine Beneš's feelings as he left on March 11, 1945, for his second wartime visit to the Kremlin (from which he was then to proceed to Košice, the largest city in the liberated part of Slovakia). Typical of his mood at that time is the following paragraph from his personal account of the farewell luncheon with Winston Churchill on February 24, 1945, at Chequers: "Before lunch we were alone for a while. Churchill began by saying: 'I heard that you have some fears of what the Soviets and the Red Army might do to your country.' I confirmed that I had certain worries, not fears. I did all that was possible: I concluded a treaty with Moscow, I pursued democratic domestic policy—I could do no more. I hope it will be possible to keep matters under control."[1]

So intense was the president's anxiety about the communist menace to his country that he felt a compelling need to discuss it repeatedly with me in those hectic days preceding the Moscow leg of our journey to the liberated portion of Czechoslovakia. The noticeable decrease in his customary optimism surprised some of those who came to bid him farewell or receive his final instructions or wishes before his departure. One of Beneš's loyal collaborators, Ladislav Feierabend, who had served as Beneš's finance minister, reported that the president was "skeptical concerning the international situation," "not optimistic with regard to the situation at home," and "so pessimistic that he expected a new world war within the next twenty years if things continued to develop as they had thus far."[2]

Nor was Beneš's mood unaffected by the apparent stroke he suffered on the eve of his scheduled departure. He recovered quickly enough to be able to leave for Moscow a few days later and even to pay, against his physician's advice, a visit to the pyramids during our stopover at Cairo. But it undermined his vigor and energy precisely at a time when it was needed most.

Should Beneš and his government have gone to Moscow in March 1945 or would it have been better for Czechoslovakia had they remained in London and gone directly from London to liberated Czechoslovakia later on? The first view was held by Beneš's Slovak and Czech right-wing opponents and critics, who habitually found fault with his actions. But Feierabend held a similar view. When he called on the president (who wanted him to proceed to the United States to obtain a loan for Czechoslovakia's reconstruction) on March 9, 1945, two days after the president's collapse, Feierabend urged Beneš to remain in London: "You now have a serious health reason with which you can justify changing your decision [to go], and no one can see political motives in it. Mr. President, do not go to Moscow!"[3]

Although Feierabend did not explain the reasons for this last-minute effort to change the president's mind, they can be inferred from his general political outlook. He evidently believed that Beneš would be under less pressure from the communists and communist influence would be less pronounced if the new government, which was to include communists and representatives of the resistance movement at home, were formed and its program for Czechoslovakia's postwar reconstruction were adopted in London rather than in Moscow.

However, even if Gottwald and his comrades had come to London, it is unlikely that they would have settled for fewer cabinet posts or ministries of lesser importance than those they got in Moscow or have agreed to a program substantially different from the so-called Košice program that was approved in Moscow. The communists' decisive trump cards in the spring of 1945 were the full-fledged backing of the Soviet Union, whose armed forces and police controlled the liberated areas of Czechoslovakia, and the all-too-obvious unwillingness or inability of the West to counteract Soviet conduct in Eastern Europe. These would have remained basic facts even if Beneš and his government had stayed in London; and they would have remained the same, if not worse, had Beneš been able (which he was not, without Soviet approval and help) to proceed directly to liberated Czechoslovak territory without stopping in Moscow. Moreover, had Beneš opted to remain in London, he would probably have had to stay there until the end of the war in Europe in May 1945, and this would have meant that Czechoslovakia's beleaguered democratic forces would have had to do without their most important leader for several more months and the communists would have found the pursuit of their goals even easier.

Under the circumstances, Beneš's decision to go to Moscow in March 1945 was absolutely correct. Indeed, his desire to preserve as much as possible Czechoslovakia's independence and democracy made it imperative.

Before leaving Britain, the president added another codicil to his will. The original portion of the testament was written on May 5, 1943, on the eve of Beneš's journey to the United States, his first crossing of the Atlantic by plane, which accounts for his decision to make a will at that particular time.

The 1943 holograph (in Czech) reads in full:

Aston Abbotts, 5/5/43

Should anything happen to me on my way to the United States, I leave this message for the prime minister and for the minister of foreign affairs:

1. I advise that the question of my successor in the presidency be settled in accordance with our constitution until the war is over.[4]
2. If it were decided to settle the problem by choosing another man, I recommend that Jan Masaryk be appointed.
3. I advise that no change be made in the government and that its present composition and distribution of functions remain the same until the end of the war.
4. I advise and beg that until the end of the war all follow the political line hitherto followed by me and that they maintain concord and unity.
5. I am satisfied that I succeeded in undoing the year 1938, and I believe in the further future of our people and state.

Remain faithful to the line of [Tomáš G.] Masaryk and myself, and all will be well.

Dr. Edvard Beneš[5]

Before his departure for Moscow in November 1943, Beneš added the first codicil to the will:

Aston Abbots, 6/11/43

I add to the arrangements of 5/5/43 the following:

1. For my journey to the Soviet Union the same holds good as for my journey to the United States.
2. Should personal arrangements be taken for the nomination of a new president, I advise that their provisional character be expressly declared.
3. I recommend that after the conclusion of the treaty with the Soviet Union, the cabinet be completed by the inclusion of two communists as its members.
4. All the rest remains valid.

Dr. E. B.

Finally, in March 1945, he added yet another codicil:

Aston Abbots, 6/3/45

1. The same is valid for my journey to Russia and to Slovakia in March 1945 as was for the two previous journeys.
2. I advise that until final liberation is achieved, the procedure as indicated for both previous journeys be adopted and that after the liberation of Prague the [Czechoslovak] nation follow the way of democracy in accordance with conditions at home. It is sufficiently mature therefor.

Dr. E. B.

On learning, after the war, of the contents of the president's testament, I was surprised to find that he had recommended Jan Masaryk as his successor because Beneš did not consider Masaryk qualified for such a high and responsible office. Undoubtedly this assertion will astonish those who knew or thought they knew Jan.

Despite his apparent joviality and good humor, Jan was an unhappy man. His jokes, his splendid esprit, his exuberance, his disarming smile, all that made him such a perfect companion, were facade hiding an unbalanced and occasionally even desperate man. The real Jan was, in fact, a melancholy creature. His childlike smile would often abruptly disappear and be replaced by absentminded gloominess as soon as the door shut behind guests. Outwardly he appeared the most sociable person imaginable. Yet there were occasions when he would disappear, to lock himself in, disconnect his phone, and deny entry even to his most intimate friends, just to remain alone, either in his London apartment near Victoria Station or in some other hideout, dressed in pyjamas, cooking his own food, and not allowing anyone to contact him. Such occasions arose in particular on special dates, such as Christmas and his father's birthday.[6]

What caused this split personality, one for society and the public, and another in private? First, Masaryk's stout, almost clumsy body was a shell for a sensitive and fragile soul and a malleable mind. Often he would swear Mr. X or Mr. Y would never be given this or that function because he was wholly unfit to perform it and appointing him would be "a crime against the state," as he used to say. Yet the next day X or Y would triumphantly brandish his nomination to the job before the disbelieving eyes of Masaryk's collaborators. The explanation was always the same: the man had sought out Masaryk, woefully beseeching him, saying that his wife or child was ill, he was in debt, or some other touching story, and that the appointment would save him.

Masaryk's softness of heart and malleability were closely linked with another salient feature of his character—his inconsistency. Jan Masaryk did base his decisions on some guiding principles. But somehow he never worked these principles into an elaborate and consistent conception. As Smutný noted in his diary, Masaryk had "moments of ingenious ideas alongside moments of supremely idiotic ones."[7] He was capable of saying one thing one day and just the opposite the next, and of being sincere both times. An intelligent man who insisted on his point with sufficient energy, persistence, and cleverness, could usually mold Masaryk's opinion, at least temporarily, to his liking.

Moreover, Jan lacked organizational and administrative skills and a proper sense of responsibility. Unlike his father or Beneš, he was not a systematic thinker or worker. He was impulsive, often rash and erratic, and always restless. He made a brilliant goodwill ambassador; no one matched him in that respect. To appear, make an excellent and witty speech in any of the many languages he spoke so well, to have a tête-à-tête with journalists and politicians, and then off again to another place, to meet other people, to sparkle elsewhere—that was what he liked best. But to sit down, to listen patiently to other people's arguments (particularly protracted ones), to argue, to do the everyday, laborious work that any democratic statesman must do to succeed, to administer his department, to take the necessary time to make a wise decision—that was not for him. Smutný's comment that Jan Masaryk "lacked the capability of patient negotiation and systematic discourse" is correct.[8]

One typical incident will illustrate Masaryk's character. As often happened when a meeting of the Czechoslovak cabinet in exile appeared unbearably long to him, one day he asked Premier Šrámek to excuse him for the rest of the session because "he had a lunch with Anthony Eden." No one would hold him back from such an important political engagement, of course, and so, regretfully, Šrámek let him go. Next week, when the cabinet reassembled, Šrámek, who had a good sense of humor, asked Masaryk: "Well, since last time Mr. Foreign Minister Masaryk [Šrámek was always extremely formal], having been invited to meet His Excellency the British Foreign Secretary, deserted us just before lunch, we may perhaps ask him to tell us what was discussed during that important political luncheon."

After Masaryk fulfilled Šrámek's request, the premier cleared his throat and in a quizzical tone said: "We thank Mr. Minister for Foreign Affairs for his excellent statement and for having so successfully brought forward our point of view before the British foreign secretary. Since none of the gentlemen present has any question, may I ask Mr. Minister for Foreign Affairs whether what he has just told us was discussed during the luncheon that he had with Mr. Eden at the time of our last cabinet meeting?"

"Yes, that's right," Masaryk replied, turning somewhat uneasily in his chair.

"Was it discussed *during* the lunch, or was it perhaps discussed only while Mr. Foreign Minister was drinking coffee with Mr. Eden *after lunch?*"

"No, during the lunch," Masaryk insisted with visible hesitation.

"All right," the premier concluded, again clearing his throat. "I thank Mr. Minister for Foreign Affairs for his clear and important statement. Let us pass on to the next item on our agenda."

On the day of the supposed luncheon with Eden, Šrámek's secretary happened to see Jan Masaryk sitting in a French restaurant somewhere in Soho and, with an expression of supreme contentment and in lonely seclusion, enjoying a steak.

Jan Masaryk was aware of his shortcomings. He felt unequal to the tremendous burden that fate put on his shoulders. Hence, he tried to avoid responsibility and the administrative chores that bored him by being absent as often as possible from his ministry, by taking advantage of every opportunity to travel, mainly to the United States. But even when he was in London, he left the entire burden of administrative duties and day-to-day political work to Hubert Ripka, who, as state secretary in the Ministry of Foreign Affairs, was Masaryk's first deputy. Morever, Beneš handled the main direction of foreign policy. Thus, although a truly brilliant ambassador at large, Masaryk made an inadequate foreign minister. His awareness of his own shortcomings was a permanent and painful strain for his sensitive and profoundly honest mind. "People are expecting wonders from me," he told me once in a moment of depression, "and look at me, Tábordo" (his nickname for me). He made one of his indescribable mimicries, stretching out his hands and legs, twisting his body, sticking his tongue out from a wide-opened, grimacing mouth, to stress, with his usual gross exaggeration, how inadequate he felt in comparison to his great father.

Before the war few people knew him well in Czechoslovakia, and those who did never took him seriously. During the war, the Czechoslovak people looked toward him as Beneš's right-hand man and successor. He knew how popular he had become in Czechoslovakia thanks to his regular BBC broadcasts to his countrymen for whom he always managed to find exactly the right words to console them in their suffering, to lift their spirits, and to sustain their hopes and aspirations. Being Tomáš Masaryk's son became a veritable plight for him. He loved his father as few sons ever did and venerated him above everyone. He knew that the millions of people in Czechoslovakia who loved and revered his father would measure the son by the same yardstick, and he was fully aware that he could not fulfill their expectations. He inherited, it is true, some of the genius of his father, but definitely not those qualities that make a man a great statesman and a great thinker. He somehow felt that he was failing his father, and that was the ever recurrent source of his dismay and frustration.

Nor was that all. Jan Masaryk was also plagued by a fixed idea that his family, including himself, would come to grief. He took it extremely hard, in particular, when within a short time during the war both his nephews suddenly died. I recall him sitting one day in an armchair in the corner of my study at Aston Abbots in a state of complete dejection and thinking aloud: "So the whole Masaryk family is doomed, me included. Take my word, Tábordo, one day I shall end in a lunatic asylum just like Alice" (referring to his sister who spent some time during the war in a sanatorium in the United States). He seemed deadly serious, as if he really believed and feared this. On various occasions he reverted to the subject. He quite often imagined that he was a victim of some mortal illness, in particular cancer. On September 6, 1942, Oskar Klinger, Beneš's personal physician, told Smutný, "Masaryk calls me now every other day. He is terribly afraid concerning his health. On the president's wish I am also checking the state of his mental health."[9]

The failure of Jan Masaryk's marriage also contributed, I think, to his unbalanced state of mind. He had remained a bachelor ever since, and his general attitude toward women was cynical. He used to tell me stories about being approached by women. For instance, on returning to his hotel in New York during a trip to the United States, he found a young, undressed female admirer waiting for him. It took him some time to persuade the girl that he was not in a position to give her what she wanted.

I never believed more than a tenth of these stories, and neither did those who knew him well, for he was always prone to gross exaggeration. Although on good terms with many statesmen and politicians in both Britain and the United States, he always tried to make everybody, including the president, believe that these relations were more intimate than they actually were. "I'll ring up Winston [Churchill] at once and tell him that he cannot do this to us." Or "I have just received a telegram from Winston that it is OK." In these or similar words, he used to express himself in front of me and others, although I knew that his intimacy with Churchill was not as close as he wanted us to believe.

The president was well acquainted with these foibles and was at times almost exasperated about them. "The solution of our postwar domestic problems will depend perhaps more than anything else on the way in which international problems will be resolved," he said to me as we were driving home after a visit to Oxford in February 1943. "That is why the task of the foreign minister will be so vitally important. But do I have a man who could do it? Masaryk? Besides being a bad administrator, he has no consistency, not enough endurance, or self-discipline. In short, he is not the man who would be able to handle that heavy job. I think that Ripka may be better fitted for it, although I know that he has a tendency to be too personal at times."[10]

Why, then, did Beneš recommend Masaryk as his successor? Why did he at one time consider him for the premiership of a reconstituted Czechoslovak government, even though he finally had to give that job to Fierlinger?

The reason is simple. There seemed to be no better choice under the circumstances. Despite all his shortcomings (which were not known by the general public), Jan Masaryk at least bore a great name, a name cherished by virtually all Czechoslovaks, a name that meant a definite program of progressive, social, and humanitarian democracy. At the state funeral of Tomáš Masaryk, Beneš solemnly promised on behalf of the Czechoslovak people: "President-Liberator, we shall remain faithful to your legacy." Could there be anything more symbolic than, on Beneš's death, having Tomáš Masaryk's son take his place? Moreover, Jan Masaryk was tremendously popular with the Czechoslovak people. He was also a man without party ties, and his appointment would not evoke party jealousies. He was known in the West as a genuine democrat, and his selection would have signaled that Czechoslovakia was continuing to strive for a fair balance between the East and the West. There was, indeed, no other man who could serve these purposes better than Jan Masaryk.

Moreover, the wish to repay a debt of gratitude to Tomáš Masaryk also played a role, though certainly a minor one, in Beneš's decision to recommend Jan Masaryk as his successor. Tomáš Masaryk made Beneš. He had been his teacher, helper, and friend. The elder Masaryk trusted Beneš completely and protected him from those who were always working to eliminate him. Masaryk recommended Beneš as his successor in the presidency when he resigned in 1935. Beneš was grateful and wanted to do all he could for Tomáš Masaryk's son.

When Beneš arrived in Moscow on March 17, 1945, he was received with the same high honors as in 1943. Again, Molotov welcomed Beneš with his usual stony smile. We were assigned the same *osobniak* on Ostrovskiego street. There were the same types of official banquets and theatrical performances at the Bolshoi. But the outward similarity of the two visits made the contrast between the easygoing and friendly get-together of 1943 and the tenseness we all felt in going through the same motions in 1945 even stronger, although the tension subsided considerably toward the end of our visit.

The negotiations with the Soviets began with the visit of the president, Prime Minister Šrámek, and Ambassador Fierlinger to Stalin and Molotov on March 19, 1945.[11] The session dealt mainly with military matters. Beneš again tried to secure Soviet equipment for the Czechoslovak army, despite his previous disappointment with Soviet performance in this respect, for he knew that a reliable Czechoslovak army would be important in the unstable times that were bound to follow the liberation. Stalin promised aid as readily as he had in 1943 and declared that equipment for ten divisions was available. (This proved to be one of the few promises that Stalin did fulfill.) The rest of their conversation was a general review of the overall international situation, in much the same spirit as in 1943. As Beneš told us after returning to our *osobniak*, Stalin was very optimistic about the war and was convinced that it would be over in a few months.

The most important discussions Beneš had with Soviet leaders in 1945 were two sessions with Molotov on March 21 and 23. Indeed, this was symptomatic of the altered circumstances between the two visits. In 1943 Beneš negotiated directly with Stalin, holding only preliminary talks or arranging details with Molotov. In 1945 it looked as if Stalin, having already obtained what he wanted, did not want to waste his time on someone who had already become much less important to him. Beneš himself remarked that this time, unlike in 1943, he had "few direct contacts with the leading Russians."[12]

The two main topics covered in the 1945 Beneš-Molotov meetings were the determination of legitimate Soviet war booty in Czechoslovakia and the fate of the Subcarpathian Ukraine.[13]

As mentioned in the preceding chapter, when the Red Army entered Czechoslovakia, it began seizing all German-administered or controlled industrial plants and supplies of raw materials, claiming them as legitimate war booty. This was the second pillaging of Czechoslovakia's industrial wealth in seven years. As soon as Beneš was informed of this behavior, he instructed Fierlinger to persuade the Soviets to change this policy, but Fierlinger was unsuccessful. So Beneš had to attend to this, as was the case with so many other difficult matters. In the first meeting with Molotov, the president insisted as strongly as he could that the practice be abandoned.[14] Although Molotov insisted that the Red Army was entitled to confiscate enterprises that had been built in Czechoslovakia by the Germans during the war and served military purposes, he did promise that they "would think of a new formula." Indeed on the eve of our departure from Moscow, a new protocol was signed that stated, in substance, that only those enterprises that the Germans had transferred to Czechoslovakia or built there since their occupation of the country would fall under the category of war booty.

The two statesmen reviewed several other issues of mutual concern that had also been discussed during Beneš's earlier visit, such as the restoration of the pre-Munich boundaries of Czechoslovakia, the transfer of the Sudeten Germans and Hungarians, and Czechoslovakia's and the Soviet Union's relations with Poland.[15] The president found Molotov especially generous in disposing of German real estate. Like Stalin in

1943, the Soviet foreign commissar invited Beneš to indicate the parts of German territory he wanted. And he was just as disappointed as Stalin had been when Beneš did not want any. "We do not want the Germans in; we want them out," Beneš said. He explained once again his idea of transferring the Sudeten Germans, reminding the Soviet foreign commissar of the 1943 Soviet promise of active support for the plan. Yet the earlier Soviet eagerness to help seemed to have cooled somewhat. Molotov did not commit himself and only expressed his "understanding" of the problem.[16]

Despite Molotov's ambivalence on the transfer issue, Beneš was well satisfied with his March 21 talk with Molotov. He thought that everything was settled, eliminating the need for further working sessions with Soviet leaders. However, on March 23 Molotov's secretary telephoned to arrange for another Beneš-Molotov meeting, this one to deal specifically with the January 1945 correspondence between Stalin and Beneš concerning the Subcarpathian Ukraine. The president was puzzled and somewhat dismayed by this unexpected summons. In his letter to Stalin he had made it clear that he was prepared to let the Soviets have the province but had expressed the desire to settle the matter formally only after his return to Prague. Had the Soviets changed their mind? Did they perhaps want him to consummate the deal now? After all, that was what Gottwald and his comrades kept pressing the president to do,[17] and perhaps they had succeeded in persuading the Soviet leaders.

As it turned out, all that Molotov wanted was to get Beneš to sign a paper confirming his willingness to cede the Subcarpathian Ukraine to the Soviet Union. Someone in the Kremlin evidently became suspicious that Beneš's commitment in his letter to Stalin was not as specific and as explicit as the Soviets wanted it. When Beneš entered Molotov's study, the Soviet foreign commissar already had before him a complete dossier containing reports of all the talks that Beneš had had with Soviet statesmen and diplomats since 1939 (when he had first raised the issue of Ruthenia with Ambassador Maisky in London). Clearly this was intended to serve as an inducement should Beneš prove reluctant to comply with Soviet insistence that he confirm in writing his willingness to surrender the province. Needless to say, the president, who had no ulterior motives in this respect, readily complied. Well aware of persistent rumors that the Soviets might claim a portion of eastern Slovakia as part of the Subcarpathian Ukraine, he had Molotov reconfirm that the new boundary between the Soviet Ukraine (enlarged by the addition of the Subcarpathian Ukraine) and Czechoslovakia was the prewar boundary of Slovakia. The president was pleased by Molotov's apologetic statement reiterating the earlier Soviet thesis that they had to claim the Subcarpathian Ukraine in order to satisfy the Ukrainians, and despite everything, he still seemed to believe it.[18]

Although by no means put to rest, Beneš's worries about Soviet designs concerning Czechoslovakia were alleviated by several other occurrences during his sojourn in the Soviet capital. Stalin and Molotov continued to speak of Roosevelt and Churchill with great respect and had high praise for Western aid to the Soviet Union. At an official banquet in Beneš's honor at Moscow's Spiridinovka on March 20, 1944, Molotov cordially referred to the cooperation of the Big Three, Stalin, Roosevelt, and Churchill, and proposed a toast to its future continuation. At the farewell dinner in the Kremlin on March 28, 1945, Stalin himself made two short speeches (see Chapter One),[19] which reminded us of the good days of 1943. In the first speech the Marshal made an unusual remark. In front of top communist officials he publicly apologized for the misconduct of the Red Army in Czechoslovakia:

> You drank toasts to the audacious, glorious, heroic Red Army, and everyone honors the Red Army in this manner when speaking of their battles. But it is not an army of angels. Like every army, the Red Army has also committed acts of wantonness. It is, however, necessary to comprehend this. We have already mobilized more than twelve million people. Those people have actually accomplished great and heroic deeds, but it is necessary to realize that they came from Stalingrad to the vicinity of Berlin. The war is not finished yet, and some of them assume that they can still be killed. Therefore, one cannot be surprised that after all that they have seen and lived through, they commit errors and cause disorder. Everyone speaks of the Red soldier as a hero, and so he feels himself a hero. He therefore thinks that, being a hero, he must be forgiven as a hero. One must have understanding and view him indulgently. I know that many misunderstandings will still occur and that the Red Army will still commit many acts of wantonness on your territory. You know, in this army are many people, and just those who are uneducated consider themselves heroes and are misusing this honor. In order not to disturb our mutual friendship, it is essential to comprehend that the army is not composed of angels. Grasp this and forgive them.

In his second speech, Stalin turned to the subject of neo-Slavism:

> I am raising my glass to drink a toast to all neo-Slavs. I especially emphasize this—to *new* Slavs—to differentiate it [neo-Slavism] from the

old conception of Slavism that Aksakov, the pioneer of tsaristic Slavism, preached. As is known, the substance of that form of Slavism was to unite all Slavs under the tsarist regime. It would have meant that every Slav nation would have had to accept the Russian state constitution and would have had to adapt its entire state life to the Russian system, irrespective of its individuality and characteristics. We Bolsheviks, or you can say communists, have another idea of Slavism. We wish that all will be allied irrespective of whether small or large, *but every nation will preserve its independence and arrange its life according to its ideology and tradition, be they good or bad.* It rests with each state individually to determine how it arranges it.

I hate the Germans. The Slavs footed the bill for the First World War, and the Second World War is also being solved at their expense. In the First World War the English and the French fought the Germans, but the Slavs paid dearly for that. And finally the Germans were put on their feet again to form the so-called European balance of power. Also, in the present world war everything is being solved at the Slavs' expense. The French have opened the door for the Germans; the Germans have occupied a part of France and a part remained unoccupied; and Belgium and Holland have also failed. [Stalin accompanied these words with a disdainful gesture of his hands.] England is an island and could therefore hold out. And who suffered again? Germans threw themselves at the Slavs, and Czechs, Slovaks, Ukrainians, Russians, and Yugoslavs paid dearly for it. Only the Bulgarians thought that if they remained neutral, they could escape the storm. But it proved neither honorable nor profitable. But this time we will break the Germans so that never again will attacks against the Slavs be repeated. We are attempting to make them harmless.

The Soviet Union wants nothing other than to gain allies who will always be prepared to resist the German danger. The Soviet Union will not interfere in the internal affairs of its allies. I know that even among you are some who doubt it. *Perhaps even you are a little dubious* [Stalin turned toward Beneš], *but I give the assurance that we will never interfere in the internal affairs of our allies.* Such is Lenin's neo-Slavism, which we, Bolshevik communists, are following. There can be no talk of a "hegemony of the Soviet union."

Stalin's remarks to Beneš during an intimate tête-à-tête after dinner also impressed the president. As Beneš told us afterwards, when their conversation shifted to the formation of the new Czechoslovak government (agreed upon during our sojourn in Moscow), Stalin expressed misgivings about the excessive number of cabinet posts assigned to the communists and the choice of Fierlinger as the new Prime Minister.

"You should have chosen someone else, Šrámek maybe," he told Beneš, explaining that the West would now blame the Soviets for these appointments. He was rather critical of the Czechoslovak communists, whom he characterized as "simple people without erudition." Referring to the suggestion in his speech that even Beneš was a little dubious about Soviet assurances, he said: "Do not believe anybody, not even myself . . . Our people had been preaching so much about the bolshevization of Europe that you were bound to be mistrustful."[20]

Beneš was not, of course, so naive as to accept this literally, certainly not after his sad experiences with the Soviets in 1944–1945. He knew that he had to assume that Stalin's underlings had informed him of the contents of the negotiations over the formation of the new Czechoslovak government. Had Stalin really wanted communist representation to be smaller and someone other than Fierlinger as the new premier, he could have instructed Gottwald accordingly and it would have been done. Nonetheless, Beneš viewed Stalin's telling him such things (as if taking him into his confidence) as a promising sign. He considered it an indication that Stalin still wanted to utilize Czechoslovakia to show the West how smooth and mutually correct Soviet relations with friendly East European countries could be. That had always been the basis of Beneš's expectation that Stalin would be reasonable and stop short of forcing Czechoslovakia into the communist straitjacket. In talking to us at our *osobniak* about the Soviet treatment of him, he characterized their behavior as "surprisingly friendly" and attributed this to Soviet gratification that Czechoslovakia was the first country whose president and entire government were brought to Moscow.[21]

Important though his talks with Stalin and Molotov were, they were not the principal reason Beneš went to Moscow in 1945. The primary purpose of his journey was to form a new cabinet that would then proceed to the liberated part of Czechoslovakia. During his 1943 visit, Beneš had several long discussions with the quadrumvirate of Czech communist leaders in exile in Moscow—Gottwald, Slánský, Šverma, and Kopecký. At that time the communist leaders declined to join his cabinet in London and insisted that a new cabinet be formed when the time came to go home. They urged that this cabinet be headed by a man of the left and communist representation be commensurate with the anticipated strength of their party.

When in 1945 the time came to return to Czechoslovakia, all sides— Beneš, the communists, and the other parties—agreed that a new cabinet should be formed in Moscow of representatives of the four major parties that had been reconstituted in exile (the Czech Communist party, the Social Democratic party, the Czechoslovak Socialist party, and the nonsocialist People's party) and representatives of the two parties that were established in liberated Slovakia (the Communist party of Slovakia and the nonsocialist Democratic party). Gottwald and his associates completely dominated the negotiations, however. When the delegates of the other parties arrived in Moscow, Gottwald handed them a mimeographed 32-page outline, "Program of the Government of the National Front of Czechs and Slovaks." The Czechoslovak Socialist party and the People's party strongly opposed some points in this communist program, but only minor changes were made. The first session of the new cabinet at its provisional headquarters at Košice subsequently proclaimed the program.

Gottwald and his comrades had also prepared a list of the new cabinet, with posts tentatively distributed among the parties. They designated their fellow traveler, the "Social Democrat" Fierlinger, for the premiership and selected for themselves and their Slovak party comrades the most important ministries, in particular those that had the most influence in domestic affairs. After some tough bargaining they got all they wanted, except the Ministry of Justice, which they had to yield to the Czechoslovak Socialist party. The result was that the key position of power and coercion, the Ministry of the Interior, which controlled the whole apparatus of internal administration and the police, fell to the communists. So did the ministries of Information and Education, placing in communist hands a powerful weapon of thought control, and the Ministry of Agriculture, which could gain them credit among the peasants through distribution of land confiscated from the Sudeten Germans. They obtained another important position of power, the Ministry of Defense, for one of their fellow travelers, Gen. Ludvík Svoboda, a man whom, as commander of the Czechoslovak brigade in Russia, they had built from an unimportant lieutenant colonel into an almost legendary hero. And they got their man, the Slovak communist Vladimír Clementis, appointed as deputy foreign minister to watch Foreign Minister Jan Masaryk. Finally, the heads of the Czech and Slovak communist parties, Gottwald and Široký, became deputy premiers.[22] Thus, Beneš took back to Czechoslovakia a cabinet in which communists or their fellow travelers held the most important positions.

Why did Beneš consent to this? The answer lies in the situation in Czechoslovakia as well as in the state of relations between the Soviet

Union and the Western forces. The Red Army and the ubiquitous NKVD were deep inside Czechoslovakia, and with their backing, local communists were ruthlessly liquidating their democratic opponents. The same process was occurring throughout Eastern Europe. Western diplomatic protests and reminders of Soviet promises made at Teheran and Yalta could not change the situation, and the behavior of Britain and the United States in 1945 clearly indicated that they intended to do nothing more than protest. Moreover, the communists, by committing themselves to support Slovak autonomist demands, managed to obtain the backing of Slovak Democrats in their bid for key cabinet positions. This was an especially sad disappointment for the president, who had counted on the Slovak Democrats as a counterweight to the Slovak communists. "In the end they will pay dearly for playing the communist game," he complained in a bitter and prophetic comment. "They think that they are very clever in joining hands with the communists in a kind of opportunistic brotherhood for mutual support. But after the communists have finished exploiting them, they will move against them ruthlessly. Can't they see that the communists are playing up Slovak autonomy only in a bid to gain absolute power that, once attained, they will use to destroy the very thing that they are promising now?"[23]

Moreover, Gottwald and his associates, in staking their claim to key positions in the new government, could and did invoke a precedent. In pre-Munich Czechoslovakia, the leaders of the largest party (then the Agrarian party), always held the posts of premier, minister of the interior, and minister of defense. Since they had every reason to expect that theirs would be the strongest postwar party, the communists argued, they were merely respecting the parliamentary tradition established in prewar days. In fact, they quickly flaunted their own self-restraint in letting a Social Democrat assume the premiership rather than claiming it for their own party. The communists knew, of course, that they would thus automatically secure the support of the Social Democrats, who could not very well oppose the selection of one of their party members. At the same time, they could rest assured that Fierlinger, who was notorious for his pro-Sovietism and his deference to Gottwald and who now owed his undreamed of promotion to the communists, would be their obedient tool and that Gottwald would thus be head of the cabinet in everything but name.

Although Beneš clearly saw through all this, he could do nothing.[24] He felt that the only correct course for him as a constitutional president was to stay "above the parties," to treat the communist party as he treated the other parties, and to abide by the time-honored political practices of the prewar democratic era. "If I want the communists to follow democratic procedures, I must respect them myself," was his wistful comment. He hoped that if the communists became partners in the governance of Czechoslovakia and shared government responsibility and authority in a degree commensurate with their strength, their temptation to resort to nondemocratic methods and to violence would be lessened. They might even grow accustomed to the system and the proper ways of behavior in a socialist democracy such as Beneš had in mind. Should his hope fail to materialize, he thought that by treating the communists fairly and by giving them no legitimate reason to complain or misbehave, he would prove their hypocrisy and thereby undermine their position among many of their supporters, who would then realize they had been misled by communist promises and assurances. Besides, had he denied the communists a chance to participate in his new government, or had the communists felt compelled to decline such an offer because they considered it inadequate, Beneš rightly feared that it would have led to civil war in one form or another—with the overwhelming odds in favor of the communists.

Finally, the president's freedom of action was inevitably affected by his haste. He knew that the earliest possible return to Czechoslovakia was essential to bolster the low morale of Czechoslovakia's democratic forces. But if he refused to accept the communist-sponsored proposal for the composition of the new cabinet, the negotiations would have dragged on. Each day that his sojourn in Moscow was prolonged meant that much more opportunity for the communists operating under the aegis of the advancing Red Army and enjoying generous support from the NKVD. Under the circumstances Beneš could afford neither the formation of a cabinet without communists nor a deadlock that would have unduly delayed his departure for Czechoslovakia.

9

From Triumph to Disaster

On March 31, 1945, Beneš set out on the last leg of his journey home, his mood much improved. He still believed that Stalin would find it more beneficial for the Soviet Union not to jeopardize its relations with the United States and Great Britain by treating Czechoslovakia as he was treating Poland and Romania. He was unhappy with the composition of the new cabinet but remained confident that he could correct it later. His good mood suited the overall atmosphere at the railway station. The ambience seemed more relaxed and the tenseness we had felt on our arrival all but dissipated. Even Molotov looked much less antipathetic than when he had met us on March 17.

After a three-day ride across the Soviet Ukraine with stops at Kiev and Lwow, our train crossed the Soviet-Czechoslovak border on April 3. Six and one-half years of exile came to an end, and the president was home again. Pending the liberation of the rest of Czechoslovakia, he established provisional headquarters at Košice, where we remained until May 8, 1945. The five weeks he spent at Košice, were not, however, the happy homecoming he and all of us had hoped for. The president was glad to be on Czechoslovak soil again. But his pleasure was marred by an unceasing flow of saddening reports about the misdeeds of Soviet soldiers and agents and local communists and their fellow travelers—tragic stories of pillage and rape, forcible communization of local administration, arrest and deportation of those who dared oppose communist abuses, and innumerable other lawless acts committed daily against the defenseless population. We had known in London of many of these acts from clandestine radio reports from our collaborators in Czechoslovakia. (They had to be sent clandestinely because Soviet army commanders forbade direct radio communications between London and the liberated parts of Czechoslovakia.) But only after our arrival did we hear from eyewitnesses who found their way to Košice of their experiences at the hands of those they had been ready to welcome as liberators and friends.

One can thus well understand the president's joy at learning that on April 17, 1945, General Patton's army corps crossed from Bavaria into Czechoslovakia. "Thank God, thank God," he said when I told him that Patton was at long last on Czechoslovak soil. Unable to control his excitement, he began to pace. Judging from the expression in his eyes, he was already visualizing the beneficial political consequences of this event. Then he hurried into the adjoining room to share the good news with his wife. "Haničko, Haničko, the Americans have entered Czechoslovakia," I heard him say to Madame Beneš in a voice filled with emotion. "Patton is across the border!" In a few moments he was back instructing me to send Patton a telegram of congratulations and welcome.[1]

Beneš had every reason to be enthusiastic about the U.S. army's penetration into Czechoslovakia. Considering the speed of Patton's advance and the Germans' all too obvious preference for being captured by the Americans rather than the Russians, nothing seemed to stand in the way of an American liberation not only of Prague, but also of Bohemia and probably a sizable portion of Moravia. Had that happened, the country's capital and the most populous part of Czechoslovakia would have remained free of Soviet control, its population spared Soviet occupation, and the communists denied the tremendous advantage conferred by the presence and active support of the Red Army and the NKVD. Unfortunately, Beneš's joyful anticipation was premature. Patton was ordered, on Soviet insistence, to halt his eastward drive before he could liberate Prague, thus allowing all of Czechoslovakia, save for a narrow slice of western Bohemia, to fall under exclusive Soviet control.[2]

On May 8, 1945, the president left Košice for his ultimate destination, Prague's Hradčany Castle, fully aware of the grave damage his cause had sustained due to the Anglo-American failure to push deeper into

Czechoslovakia. Denied the benefit of a countervailing Western presence, Beneš realized more than ever before that the preservation of democracy in his country depended most of all on the attitude, the wisdom, and, above all, the willpower of the Czechoslovak people. He felt sure that the overwhelming majority favored the kind of humanitarian democracy, combining political freedoms with social justice and a good measure of socialism in the economic sphere, outlined in his *Democracy Today and Tomorrow*. But would they have the courage to fight for it? Would they have enough determination and perseverance to overcome the great initial advantages of the communists?

Beneš's desire to stiffen the morale of the people was one reason behind his decision to travel to Prague by car through Banska Bystrica (the chief city of the Slovak uprising of 1944), Bratislava (Slovakia's capital), Brno (Moravia's capital) and from there by train to Prague. He thought that by passing through a great many towns and villages and coming into contact with huge numbers of ordinary people from many walks of life, he could gauge their reactions and feelings. Beneš knew, of course, that the Czechoslovak people would welcome him enthusiastically. All the reports we had received in London spoke of Beneš's tremendous popularity and of the complete faith in him among all segments of the population, including his onetime adversaries. But the president's reception all along the route of our small motorcade surpassed our greatest expectations. A description, based on my diary, of the events in a small Moravian town near the Slovak border can serve to illustrate a scene that recurred throughout our entire journey.[3]

The whole populace of the town and surrounding villages was jammed into the town square and the nearby streets. An old woman leaning heavily on her stick with one hand frantically waved a small Czechoslovak flag with the other. Next to her little children three to five years old patiently waited. Everyone was in his Sunday best, and many were dressed in national costumes and in Sokol (the patriotic gymnastic organization) uniforms, which they must have kept hidden throughout the Nazi occupation. Flags, flowers, and portraits of Tomáš Masaryk and Edvard Beneš were displayed in all the windows, far outnumbering pictures of Stalin and red stars.

As soon as the onlookers noticed the first car of our convoy, a hurricane of enthusiasm broke out: "Long live President Beneš, long live President Beneš." And again and again. Our convoy stopped. It would have had to stop even if we had not intended to. The gaily colored crowd of thousands made an impenetrable ring around us. A man stepped forward and welcomed President and Madame Beneš. Tears ran down his cheeks as he finished his brief speech. The president, unable to speak, his throat contracted with emotion, managed to mumble his thanks. Madame Beneš's eyes were shining with tears. A uniformed policeman opposite us sobbed openly. Next to him, a young partisan cried unabashedly, his chin trembling like an old man's. Several women struggled desperately through the crowd, just to touch the president's sleeve and kiss his hand. A middle-aged woman whose husband was murdered in one of the Nazi torture chambers thanked Beneš for what he had done, forgetting for a while her own grief: "How glad we are that you have come back, how glad . . ."—she could not finish for her tears. A mother who had just managed to wipe away her tears on Madame Beneš's shoulder called frantically after her little daughter, lost somewhere in the crowd: "Jirunko, Jirunko, come and caress the hand of Madame Beneš." A boy and a girl in national costumes got through and handed the president the traditional bread and salt, the Slavic symbol of hospitality.

Finally, we resumed our places in the cars, the tight embrace of the masses opened up, and we slowly moved forward. As if touched by a magic wand, the deep emotion erupted again. We looked back. Above the heads of the huge crowds we saw the burned-out roofs, shattered walls, and broken windows, a strange backdrop for the colorful mass of waving hands and flags.

Not even the Soviet guards who accompanied our convoy to "ensure Dr. Beneš's personal safety" remained immune from the enthusiasm. At first they were uneasy. When those huge masses of people began to gather around the president in the first villages on our route, I noticed that they promptly readied their submachine guns for any eventuality. Evidently, allowing the common folk to approach a leader in such an uncontrollable crowd was quite a novel spectacle for them. But as the scene repeated itself day after day and nothing happened, they got used to it and ended up shouting hurrahs in Beneš's honor in unison with the people, leaving their submachine guns hanging over their shoulders.

The enthusiastic spontaneity of the greeting in every town and village, not only in the Czech lands but also in Slovakia, was unwelcome news for Gottwald and his associates. They knew that the biggest obstacle to their drive for power was Beneš himself. "The communists see in Dr. Beneš too strong a personality, and they would wish to have a weak president," read a report on the Czechoslovak communist leaders in Moscow that Col. Heliodor Pika, our military attaché in Moscow, sent us in 1943, that is, at a time when Beneš was still deemed *persona grata* by the Kremlin. "That is why even now [they think that] Beneš must by all means be pushed into the background, and the authority of a united workers' party must be increased."⁴ The communists' feelings were reflected quite pointedly in a caustic remark made by Gustav Husák, then a member of the Slovak Communist party delegation to the 1945 Moscow negotiations on the formation of a new Czechoslovak government. "Dr. Beneš? We may have to protect him with barbed wire against the [Slovak] people," Husák extemporized during one of the sessions, while criticizing Beneš's refusal to mandate that the Slovaks be considered a separate Slav nation rather than a component of one single Czechoslovak nation.

Although Beneš's triumphant reception was highly disagreeable to communist leaders, it was a powerful and badly needed tonic for the president and his followers. It seemed to vindicate Beneš's trust in the democratic maturity of the Czechoslovak people expressed in the March 1945 codicil to his political testament. Clearly, the overwhelming majority of Czechs and Slovaks sided with him rather than with Gottwald, and he could count on their support in the difficult times ahead. "The battle will be hard," the president told me when I reported to work at Hradčany Castle on the day following our return to Prague. "But I have no doubt about our victory. With such people as ours democracy cannot be beaten. It will take some time before all is well again, and we shall have many difficulties before all danger is averted. But if those in the West hold firm and keep strong, then I have no fears. Then we shall be able to hold the balance, and I think that the Munich lesson taught the West that appeasement and sacrificing others does not pay in the end."⁵

Preventing the communists from achieving their ultimate goal of monopolizing power became the president's main preoccupation, the supreme task to which he devoted his remaining energy. Basically his strategy was eightfold.

To bolster popular morale. The overwhelming welcome accorded Beneš on his homecoming did not blind the president to the sad fact that the long years of Nazi terror had undermined the people's civic courage, demoralized them, and made them less resistant to communist intimidation. He realized that they most needed credible assurance that despite the advantages the communists gained from the Soviet liberation, democracy would prevail. In talking about democracy's prospects, the president invariably tried to sound as optimistic as possible in an effort to convince his interlocutors that the situation was not as bad as it seemed, to allay their fears, and to infuse them with renewed hope. He kept making similar optimistic prognoses even after the situation worsened in the fall of 1947 and Gottwald and his associates began their final offensive against Czechoslovakia's democracy. As late as November 1947, he expressed himself in the same optimistic vein to the U.S. ambassador, Laurence Steinhardt, and assured him that the communists would not succeed.

The president also sought to strengthen the people's morale and to engourage them to fight evil influences in public life and defend democracy by numerous talks, addresses, and messages to various groups and organizations, such as the Sokols, the Legionnaires, Liberated Political Prisoners, and volunteer, youth, and student associations. Especially noteworthy was a dramatic November 1947 message to the Czechoslovak Legionnaires in which he solemnly accepted the Legionnaire's vow to safeguard and, if need be, defend Czechoslovakia's liberty and told them that he would hold them to their vow and was counting on them.[6] With his tacit approval, Prokop Drtina, his close associate and the minister of justice, ordered the prosecution of several policemen who had placed loyalty to the communist party and their boss, the communist minister of the interior, above respect for the law and citizens' rights. He approved wholeheartedly of Drtina's bold action, for he knew that nothing would boost the democrats' courage more than seeing communist policemen tried for abuses of authority.

To treat the communist party like other political parties. He had already been following this precept during the Moscow negotiations over the Czechoslovak government. He hoped that if he treated the communists fairly, they might gradually become accustomed to playing by democratic rules. Moreover, he was well aware that hard-line communists constituted only a comparatively small fraction of the inflated postwar ranks of the party and that a large number of party members had no inclination to go to extremes, especially if they saw their party treated fairly.

To make the communists share governmental responsibility in proportion to their strength. Beneš knew that many unpopular decisions would have to be made in the difficult postwar years, and he wanted all parties to assume their fair share of responsibility for the successes and the failures.[7] For this reason, he welcomed Fierlinger's replacement as premier by the communist leader Klement Gotttwald after the 1946 elections.

To prevent the communists from gaining a parliamentary majority. Beneš feared that should the communists obtain a parliamentary majority, they would never give their democratic opponents a chance to regain the majority in another free election. He did not expect the communists to win an absolute majority by themselves. What he feared, especially after the parliamentary elections of 1946, was that Social Democratic supporters of a close alliance with the communists might somehow induce that party to ally itself with the communists and help them secure the coveted majority in the National Assembly. Since the communists obtained 38 percent of the votes and 114 seats and the Social Democrats 12.8 percent of the votes and 37 seats in the 1946 elections, such a combination would have given the communists control of Czechoslovakia's legislature and thereby also of the Council of Ministers, which needed a parliamentary majority behind it to function.

Hence, Beneš concentrated from the outset on preventing this calamity. When I returned to Prague from my diplomatic post in Sweden (to deliver a series of lectures at Charles University) in the spring of 1947, the president discussed the matter with me. "The Social Democrats are holding the key to the situation," he told me. "The whole fate of the republic depends on their behavior in the coming months. If they stick together with the other democratic parties, if they can resist communist allurements and do not succumb to Fierlinger's intrigues, I am confident that we can master the situation." Since I was a member of the Social Democratic party and had served on its Central Executive Committee during the war, he entrusted me with the mission of speaking to those leading Social Democrats who could be trusted and urging them to stand firm against communist machinations.

In his endeavor to strengthen the Social Democrats and make them more immune to the blandishments of the communists, Beneš toyed with the idea of persuading Jan Masaryk to run on the Social Democratic ticket in the elections scheduled to take place in 1948.[8] Knowing that of all the noncommunist parties, the Social Democrats had the best chance of wooing blue-collar workers away from the communists, he felt that Jan Masaryk's tremendous popularity could help them accomplish this. Although Masaryk disliked partisan politics, he seemed willing. When the leaders of the Czechoslovak Socialist party learned about the idea, however, they began to worry that many socialist-minded voters who had cast their votes for the Czechoslovak Socialist party in the 1946 elections, seeing in it the staunchest opponent of communism, would switch to the Social Democrats if Jan Masaryk were on that party's ballot. Arguing that the Czechoslovak Socialist party would lose votes to a party infested with procommunist elements, they persuaded the president to abandon the scheme.

To engage in an "elastic" defense by yielding, if necessary, to communist pressure in social and economic matters but defending the basic postulates of political freedom. As noted in Chapter One, Beneš was a non-Marxian socialist who favored a mixed economic system in which key industries, such as mines, steel, and armaments as well as transportation and banks, would be nationalized but private and cooperative enterprises would continue in other sectors. He realized, however, that the communists would insist on a far more extensive collectivization of industry and commerce than he deemed economically sound. At the same time, he anticipated that they would seek, and were likely to find, support for their radical stand among broad segments of the Czechoslovak people, especially blue-collar workers, who in their initial revolutionary zeal would not foresee the dangers of such ultraradical measures. Therefore, the president was prepared to yield in the economic and social sphere even though he was convinced of the harmfulness of such ventures. He hoped that in so doing, he would improve his chances to hold firm on political liberties. A message he sent his collaborators in the Czechoslovak underground on May 15, 1942, illustrated his thinking:

> Everyone must understand that the revolution will be socially and economically radical. It will be necessary to *combine well the national and social revolution,* to obtain all possible national advantages, to undo all that happened since Munich. At the same time it will be necessary from the very first moment to win over the broad masses of the people for constructive work by adopting a radical social program in such a manner that the communists could participate from the start with the others in the work of reconstruction. The aim of this program is to prevent any attempt to force a unilateral internal revolution and civil war upon our people at a moment when the very existence of the state and the nation will be in danger... I believe that our national and state interests after the war will demand such a radical policy, which will mean a substantial change in our former social structure... For the realization of these plans a good relationship with Russia now and at the moment of the revolution, as well as good relations with Great Britain and the United States, will be an

inevitable requisite. Russia will be standing next to our frontiers and from Great Britain and the United States we shall require foodstuffs and raw materials. It will be necessary to select in everything the correct compromise between these three factors, being guided primarily by our domestic requirements. Even after this war we must remain ourselves, Czechoslovaks.[9]

Adhering to such a compromise, which he considered a purely Czechoslovak solution, proved more difficult than he expected. Anxious to avoid a confrontation with the communists and the communist-controlled organized labor movement, particularly while the Soviet army was still on Czechoslovak soil, Beneš yielded to communist demands and in October 1945 signed the nationalization decrees as they were laid before him. At the same time he publicly warned against any hasty decisions in these matters.

To utilize the prestige, popularity, moral authority, and confidence he enjoyed among all segments of the population. I discussed this particular issue with the president many times during the war, especially in its final phase when the communist challenge was becoming ever more menacing. I argued that after the war, especially in the chaos and confusion of the period following the liberation, the country would need a strong leader who would be fully involved in the conduct of state affairs and would not hesitate to use drastic and quasi-autocratic measures to prevent the communists from usurping the governance of the country. The president agreed that he would have to take "a much more active part in government than in normal times."

Unfortunately, as shown below, Beneš never managed to reassert this kind of strong, no-nonsense leadership. He made no determined effort to do so and instead allowed Gottwald and his comrades to wrest the leadership from his hands. The first test came soon. On June 8, 1945, Gottwald sent the president a decree on the confiscation of agricultural land owned by Sudeten Germans, Hungarians, and Czech and Slovak collaborators. Gottwald had not previously cleared the decree with the president, and no explanation accompanied it. Yet he asked me to have the president sign the decree without delay and sent cameramen to film the ceremony.

That is not the way a premier should treat his head of state. Moreover, I found several legal flaws in the phrasing of the decree. So I urged the president not to sign the decree, and he complied with my suggestion. Yet less than two weeks later, on June 21, he conceded and signed it, although he still disagreed with its wording. This was the first confrontation between Beneš and Gottwald after the president's return to

Prague—and the president gave in. Although the subject matter was not of any crucial political importance, Beneš's capitulation was, nonetheless, a dangerous precedent. I felt that Beneš should not have signed the decree until after its flaws had been corrected. He would have been fully within his rights since the president and not the Council of Ministers had the authority to legislate by decree until the National Assembly had been reconstituted.

To keep the avenues to the West open. The president's chief concern was that the Western powers might conclude that Czechoslovakia had already been engulfed in the Soviet orbit and consequently would write it off. Although Beneš could no longer adhere to his favorite 50-50 ratio in his policy between East and West, he wanted to retain as many ties with the West as possible. Most of all he wanted a U.S. loan, not only because it was needed financially , but also because it would document continued American interest in Czechoslovakia's well-being and would thus offset the lopsided communist propaganda that the Soviet Union was Czechoslovakia's only reliable friend.

However, Beneš's endeavors to obtain economic aid were frustrated by rising U.S. animosity toward Czechoslovakia's nationalization program, which affected a number of American-owned enterprises, and by Czechoslovakia's pro-Soviet voting record at international conferences. When U.S. Secretary of State James Byrnes witnessed two communist members of the Czechoslovak delegation to the 1945 Paris peace conference applauding a Soviet attack on the United States, he brusquely annulled a $50 million American credit to Czechoslovakia and was instrumental in inducing the Export-Import Bank to suspend negotiations over a $150 million loan.[10] Although the president and his associates strove to explain to the Americans the reasons that made it imperative for Czechoslovakia not to vote or speak against the Soviet Union at international forums,[11] the negative U.S. attitude toward Czechoslovakia continued. In late 1946, disregarding the pleas of Czechoslovak and other Central European delegates, the United States brought about the termination of the United Nations Relief and Rehabilitation Administration, which had been so helpful in supplying the suffering population of Central Europe with food and other necessities of life. Even after a poor harvest in 1947 in Czechoslovakia and a Soviet commitment of grain deliveries, the U.S. embassy in Prague persisted in recommending that the United States adopt a policy of "no food and no loans" toward Czechoslovakia.[12]

Nor was Beneš successful in yet another of his postwar attempts at "openings to the West"; namely, an alliance treaty with France. Despite France's betrayal in September 1938, Beneš was anxious to renew the

Franco-Czechoslovak alliance, not so much for its military as for its symbolic value. "For us it would be a window to the West," he told Ripka. "The more the Soviet circle closes in on us, the more important it is to tighten the ties that unite us with France and the Anglo-Saxon countries."[13] To underscore the treaty's significance, it was agreed that after the treaty had been signed, Beneš would pay an official visit to France. The draft of the proposed treaty was sent to Paris in June 1946, but the French did not act on it until May 1947, when they returned it with amendments limiting, among other things, the obligation of mutual assistance to a threat from Germany alone. (The original Czechoslovak draft provided for assistance against any country that joined Germany in an act of aggression.) Although the Czechoslovak government was displeased with the French amendments, it was the eleven-month delay (rather than the amendments) that proved fatal for the entire project. During those eleven months, relations between the Soviet Union and the Western powers decayed so sharply that Czechoslovak communists, who had initially supported the alliance, turned against it. In a desperate gesture to salvage the project, the president prepared a memo for Stalin in which he tried to allay any suspicions the Soviet dictator may have had. But it was to no avail.[14]

To reduce Soviet interference in Czechoslovakia's domestic affairs. To achieve this all-important objective, which Beneš rightly considered a prerequisite for the preservation of Czechoslovak democracy, he believed that he had to avoid any act that provided the Soviets with a pretext for interfering. He invariably instructed Jan Masaryk and other Czechoslovak delegates to international conferences to follow the Soviet lead in voting. As mentioned above, Beneš decided not to publish his report on Munich because it would have contradicted the Soviet contention that the Soviet Union was prepared to fight Germany on Czechoslovakia's behalf even if France was not. In his wartime *Memoirs* and his public statements he carefully gave the Soviets all possible credit, usually even more than they deserved. He kept reassuring the Kremlin of his loyalty and gratitude while meticulously refraining from any public criticism, even though he strongly resented Soviet behavior toward Czechoslovakia. Beneš was even willing to accept for himself and Czechoslovakia a virtual vassalage status if that was the Soviet overlord's price for allowing his country a reasonable measure of internal democracy.

Despite the setbacks the president sustained in his struggle to preserve democracy, his strategy was working—or so it seemed. Popular morale was improving; civic courage, so badly shaken in the initial months of the liberation, was on the upswing; and opposition to communism was stiffening. Czechoslovakia's airwaves were still under rigid communist control, and hardly anything the communists found objectionable was allowed on Czechoslovak radio transmissions. But noncommunist newspapers and periodicals managed to reclaim a substantial measure of freedom, which they did not hesitate to use to criticize communist malpractices and abuses (although anything that might offend the Soviet Union itself was carefully avoided). Communist strength at all levels of local government began to weaken, and the communist party was forced to give up the Ministry of Education, thus losing a prime position for the indoctrination of Czechoslovakia's youth.

I found a high degree of optimism in the democratic camp when I returned to Czechoslovakia in the spring of 1947. Everyone I met during my three-month stay, from high-ranking politicians to ordinary people, was convinced that the worst was over and the situation under control. The president himself seemed confident that democracy would prevail, but he felt that much depended on the Americans and the British. "I am struggling for time," he told me in June 1947. "We cannot be saved unless the Russian advance is checked by a tremendous show of power on the part of the West. Once the Russians see that any further step would mean a general war, they will stop, but not one moment earlier. The Russians will do everything possible to enlarge and strengthen their grip on Germany and the whole of Central and Eastern Europe in the coming months, before they are definitely checked. If we can manage to hold out until next summer or fall, the highest point of danger will have passed by then."[15]

Neither Stalin's ruthless veto in July 1947 of Czechoslovak participation in the Marshall Plan (after the Czechoslovak Council of Ministers, including its communist members, unanimously accepted the U.S. invitation)[16] nor the creation of the Cominform in September 1947 shattered Beneš's belief that Czechoslovakia would remain a democratic nation. In fact, his belief was reinforced by several major setbacks for communists in the fall of 1947 and January 1948. In November 1947 the congress of the Czechoslovak Social Democratic party ousted Zdeněk Fierlinger, its foremost procommunist, from the party chairmanship,[17] nullified the 1945 communist-engineered incorporation of the Slovak Social Democratic party into the Slovak Communist party and reasserted the party's independence. These actions dashed communist hopes of achieving a peaceful transition to communism by winning a majority in the next parliamentary elections. In university elections held the same month, communist candidates were soundly beaten, obtaining a mere 20 percent of the vote. Worse still, a poll conducted in January 1948 by the Institute of Public Opinion Research, which operated under the aegis of the communist-controlled Ministry of Information, revealed that in the parliamentary election to be held later that year, the communist vote might decrease by as much as 25 percent over the 1946 elections.

These signs were the basis of Beneš's conclusion that the cause of democracy was advancing and communist prospects were deteriorating. In a talk with Steinhardt in November 1947, he felt confident enough to assure the U.S. ambassador that "the turning point had been reached" and the communists would not prevail. As late as January 12, 1948, a mere six weeks before the communist takeover, he told Josef Korbel, then ambassador to Yugoslavia, that the communists had "thought of a coup in September 1947," but had "abandoned the idea" and "the danger of a Communist coup had passed."[18] Strangely enough, Beneš remained optimistic even during the first days of the February crisis. When Gottwald came to him on February 17 with a trumped-up complaint that the Czechoslovak Socialists wanted the president to name a new cabinet consisting solely of civil servants, Beneš interpreted Gottwald's step as a manifestation of weakness and insecurity and was convinced that a compromise solution could be reached.[19] He shared his evaluation of Gottwald's behavior with the ministers of the Czechoslovak Socialist party, Petr Zenkl and Hubert Ripka, who saw him the next day: "It seems to me that the communists are not sure about their thing, that they are afraid . . . They have come to me because they want me to protect them. This is the first victory due to your firmness."[20]

Beneš's optimistic assessment of the situation in the first days of the February crisis accounts, at least in part, for his rather passive behavior. According to Smutný, both Beneš and the leaders of the democratic parties initially thought it possible to resolve the conflict by a compromise reached through the usual interparty negotiations.[21] The president concentrated on pleading with those concerned to show restraint and to refrain from resorting to methods incompatible with traditional parliamentary devices. However commendable from the democratic standpoint, this course of action created an impression of weakness and indecision that encouraged the communists to push even harder, disheartened the president's followers, and made fence-sitters gravitate toward what they began to consider the winning side.

Since the February 1948 crisis itself has already been studied in great detail, by both outside observers and participants,[22] it will suffice for the purposes of this volume to sum up briefly the substance and the course of the crisis. What brought the crisis, which had been building for many months, to a climax in February 1948 was the determination of the noncommunist parties to stop the communization of the police. Headed by a high-ranking communist, Václav Nosek, the Ministry of the Interior had since 1945 gradually filled the ranks of the police with communists and procommunists and replaced noncommunist police officers in key positions with communists, especially in Prague. When, on February 13, 1948, the ministry removed eight noncommunist district police chiefs in Prague, the noncommunist ministers, who formed the majority on the Council of Ministers, pushed through a resolution instructing the communist minister of the interior to desist from any further transfers of police officers and to reinstate the eight police chiefs. When it became clear that Gottwald, who as chairman of the council was obligated to see that the directive was carried out, had no intention of doing so, the ministers of three democratic parties, the Czechoslovak Socialist party, the People's party, and the Slovak Democratic party, tendered their resignations. They expected that the president would not accept their resignations but would ask them to stay in office on an interim basis pending resolution of the conflict. They assumed that Gottwald would not back down, necessitating the dissolution of the National Assembly and new elections, in which it was predicted that the communist vote would decline by 20 to 25 percent over the 1946 elections.

The communists, however, promptly unleashed a furious counteroffensive. They held mass rallies and demonstrations, called strikes, and organized "action committees" in all government agencies, economic enterprises, and other establishments. Hordes of armed "workers' militia" patrolled the streets of Prague and intimidated the party's opponents. Communists occupied government buildings and the headquarters of noncommunist parties and applied relentless pressure on Beneš to accept the democratic ministers' resignations and appoint a new cabinet consisting of communists and a few turncoats hand picked by Gottwald to "represent" the other "regenerated" parties.

This strategy paid off. After resisting Gottwald's persistent demands that he follow "the will of the people," Beneš submitted after five days and on February 25 signed what he knew was the death warrant of Czechoslovak democracy. Why did he do it? How could a man so devoted to freedom hand over his country to the communists?

Beneš's ill health and subsequent death in September 1948 prevented him from preparing an exhaustive account of his behavior in the

February crisis. But he did discuss the crisis with several persons who left records of these conversations. The most important are the testimonies of Jaromír Smutný, the head of the President's Office; Dr. Oskar Klinger, Beneš's personal physician; Hubert Ripka, minister of foreign trade; and Amelie Posse-Brázdová, the Swedish writer and close friend of President and Madame Beneš, who sent me, through the Swedish diplomatic pouch, a report about her talk with the president two weeks before his death.[23]

As in 1938, Beneš appeared in 1947–1948 to be resolved not to yield and to quash any communist coup d'etat with armed force if necessary. In June 1947, he told me that should the communists try to seize power by violence, he was determined to fight them to the bitter end and that he would call on the Sokols, the Legionnaires, and even the army. "I shall make no compromise that would destroy democracy in this country," he concluded. "The communists could seize power only over my dead body."[24] Talking to Korbel on January 12, 1948, he said: "I shall not move from my place, and I shall defend our democracy till my last breath."[25] In a conversation with the ministers of the Czechoslovak Socialist party, Zenkl and Ripka, on February 18, 1948, he assured them that he would not yield and that they could count on him. He even exhorted them to stand firm.[26] Beneš expressed himself similarly when talking to others.[27] As late as February 23, 1948, he declared in the presence of Madame Beneš, Smutný, and Klinger: "I would rather die than yield to terror and betray [Tomáš] Masaryk's ideals."[28] Earlier the same day he had directed Gen. Ludvík Svoboda, the minister of defense, to issue an order stating that the army supported the president as commander in chief and that it would defend democracy and the constitution.[29]

Why, then, did he accept the resignation of the twelve democratic ministers after assuring them repeatedly that he would not do so?[30] Why did he appoint and swear in Gottwald's new government after insisting that he would not approve any new government that had not been agreed on by the leaders of all the parties?[31] Why did he not order the army to restore order when communist gangs began occupying public buildings and the headquarters of the democratic parties, thus destroying any prospect for the hoped-for parliamentary solution of the crisis?

The decisive reason for Beneš's surrender was his conviction that any forcible attempt to suppress the communist coup would lead to Soviet military intervention. The sudden arrival in Prague of Stalin's emissary, Soviet Deputy Foreign Minister Valerian Zorin, on the eve of the

February crisis and his behavior indicated to Beneš that the Soviets had decided to support Gottwald.[32] Despite the confinement of Czechoslovakia's foreign minister, Jan Masaryk, in his apartment in the Czernin Palace due to influenza, Zorin insisted on seeing him and telling him that the international situation had deteriorated and the cooperation of the people's democracies with the Soviet Union must be increased. This could hardly happen in Czechoslovakia, Zorin continued, if various reactionary elements inside and outside the government were allowed to pursue aims inimical to Soviet-Czechoslovak friendship. "There are certain members of the government," Zorin said quite bluntly, "whom the Soviet Union cannot trust. Gottwald knows them, and he has prepared a list of ministers who should be excluded from the new government." And, Zorin added, tongue in cheek: "We know that you personally sympathize with the USSR, and we want you to stay in the new government. But the present government must be changed, and we shall give Gottwald all our support in that endeavor."[33] In the same vein, Stalin's emissary sought to influence the Social Democratic Minister Václav Majer, and a secretary of the Soviet embassy in Prague worked on Bohumil Laušman, chairman of the Social Democratic party.[34] In a February 23 discussion with the leaders of the Czechoslovak Socialist party, the subject of the communist-circulated rumors that the Red Army was massing along Czechoslovakia's borders, ready to intervene, arose. The president opined that such an intervention could not be excluded. "In that case—what to do?" he asked, becoming more and more worried as he repeated the agonizing question. Neither he nor his interlocutors had a satisfactory answer.[35] When the three top generals of the Czechoslovak army, Ludvík Svoboda, Bohumil Boček, and Karel Klapálek, came to him on February 25 and asked for his orders, Beneš thanked them for their gesture but made it clear that he could not consider using the army to resolve the situation. "It would mean that you would have to arrest Gottwald, and this the Russians would not tolerate."[36] (According to Posse-Brázdová, Gottwald told Beneš that the Russians were standing fully prepared along the borders, ready to invade should the communists ask for help.)[37]

Neither could the president be altogether certain that any such order would be carried out. Although the troops and most of the officer corps were loyal to the president and the cause of democracy, the higher command echelons were infiltrated by communists, and there were many fencesitters ready to join the winning side. Svoboda, though not yet a party member, owed his spectacular rise from an obscure lieutenant colonel to army general and minister of defense to the communists. In complying with Beneš's February 23 directive to issue an order stressing the army's loyalty to the president and to democracy, Generals Svoboda and Boček diluted the order's intended thrust by adding an ambivalent passage stating that the army would "always remain faithful to the people," defend the accomplishments of the revolution, and remain loyal to the Soviet Union.[38] The phrases were similar to those used by the communists throughout the February crisis. Furthermore, Svoboda, Boček, and Klapálek made it a point to attend the meeting convened by the communists to form the Central Action Committee of the new communist-controlled National Front. Svoboda's speech at the meeting, in which he lashed out at those who did not want to cooperate and called for their elimination, could only be understood as the three generals' support for Gottwald's cause.[39] At a public meeting in Prague on February 23, 1948, in honor of a visiting Soviet general, Boček delivered a talk stressing the vital importance of the Czechoslovak-Soviet alliance "in a world where the antipopular and imperialist forces were fighting against the forces of freedom, progress, and new democracy" and called for a resolute stand "against all tendencies concealing the desire to bring about a reactionary change in our domestic politics."[40]

Another factor that played a major role in inducing Beneš to yield to communist demands was the virtual paralysis of Gottwald's democratic opponents. In his plans for coping with the communist challenge, the president counted heavily on the massive, active support of the overwhelming majority of Czechoslovaks who had remained loyal to him and to democracy. In particular, he pinned great hopes on the Legionnaires and the Sokols, with their hundreds of thousands of well-disciplined members. In the months preceding the February putsch the president kept telling his friends and associates that he would call on the Legionnaires and the Sokols should the communists attempt to seize power. As mentioned above, he told me the same thing in June 1947. But when the need for resolute democratic counteraction arose after the communists began staging their mass demonstrations, nothing happened. Not only did the Sokols, the Legionnaires, the Scouts, and the democratic parties fail to organize counterdemonstrations and mass rallies in support of the democratic cause, but they even let communist ruffians seize their offices and headquarters.

Perhaps nothing illustrates the woeful unpreparedness of the democratic camp more poignantly than the outlandish business-as-usual attitude of the leaders of the democratic parties while the communists were stepping up their offensive. Instead of organizing massive counter-demonstrations of their followers and urging them to stand up to the communists, the ministers of the People's party, Monsignore František Hála and Adolf Procházka, and the party's secretary general, Dr. Adolf Klímek, attended the Women's Congress of their party; the chairman of the Czechoslovak Socialist party, Petr Zenkl, left for Moravia to accept honorary citizenship in one of the Moravian cities; Vladimír Krajina, the secretary general of the party, was on a speaking tour in Moravia; and his colleague, Hubert Ripka, went on a routine visit to his constituents.[41] The newspapers of the democratic parties advised their followers to stay calm and not to allow themselves to be provoked.[42] Incredible as it sounds, the leaders of the noncommunist parties even authorized party members to participate in the nationwide one-hour strike decreed on February 24 by the communist-controlled congress of worker-delegates, even though they knew that the purpose of the strike was to induce the president to comply with Gottwald's demands. The Sokols proved to be no better. When Smutný asked the organization's representatives who came to see him on February 24 of their plans, they told him that they could do nothing because their chairman had left for the Tatra Mountains of Slovakia to attend the opening of the Sokol ski championships.[43]

Beneš did not expect, of course, that counteractions by democratic forces would overpower the communists. But he hoped that they would stymie Gottwald's quest for absolute control and force him to compromise. When, save for a brief demonstration of several thousand Prague university students on February 25, 1948, the democratic forces remained passive in the face of the communist menace it was a bitter disappointment for the president. This inaction certainly contributed to his ultimate acquiescence. Talking on August 18, 1948, with Posse-Brázdová about the failure of the Sokols, the democratic parties, and others to stage the hoped-for counterdemonstrations, Beneš complained:

> They are accusing me of disappointing them. But I am accusing them of disappointing me at the decisive moment. Without the help that they promised I was helpless. When Gottwald filled the Old Town Square with armed, blood-thirsty militia, I expected a counterrally of others on St. Wenceslaus Square. I knew that the Sokols had enough weapons to arm even the others. But I could not imagine that they were so lacking in organization and determination when it was so needed. I believed that the demonstration of unarmed students would be the signal for a general uprising. When, however, nobody made a move, I could not allow Gott-

wald's hordes, who were spoiling for a fight, to perpetrate a wholesale massacre on the defenseless Prague population. There was no limit to what they threatened to do in that respect.[44]

Describing Beneš's feelings, Smutný spoke of "the bitterness of an abandoned man whom his friends placed in a difficult situation and left him there."[45]

Beneš's fear of a bloodbath and harsh reprisals against his collaborators unless he accepted Gottwald's new cabinet of communists and fellow travelers also appears to have influenced his decision to concede. Indeed, in pressuring the president to yield, Gottwald boasted of communist preparations to crush any resistance and the strength of the workers' militia and cautioned him that "terrible bloodshed" would ensue if fighting broke out in the streets. When, on February 25, 1948, he brought the president the list of the new cabinet for Beneš's signature, Gottwald had with him another list containing the names of several hundred democratic politicians earmarked for "elimination" should the president persist in his refusal to sign. Before making his final decision, the president, broken, helpless, and in utter despair, turned to his wife: "Haničko, what can I do, what can I do?"

"Would you help someone if you did not sign?" she replied gently, desiring to relieve as much of his unbearable strain as possible. The president then returned to the room where Gottwald waited impatiently and, with death in his soul, signed the fateful list.[46] According to Beneš's handwritten notes, he told Gottwald when the latter paid him a visit at Sezimovo Ústí on March 7, 1948, that he signed the list to prevent bloodshed.[47]

Although Beneš was quite right in blaming his followers for their passivity in face of the communist menace, he himself was not without blame, for he was remiss in providing the forceful leadership that was so desperately needed. As noted earlier, the president was aware of this need and seemed inclined to meet it. But he did not. Instead of placing himself squarely at the head of the democratic camp, firmly controlling it, and coordinating its strategy, he resumed the traditional prewar presidential role of a nonpartisan head of state who was available merely as an honest broker or impartial moderator prepared to help resolve interparty disputes.[48] Anxious as he was to show Gottwald and his associates that he would treat them fairly and correctly, he developed a tendency to overlook their misbehavior, sought to avoid confrontations with them, and stayed more aloof from the democratic parties than he should have.

This behavior was, of course, an integral part of Beneš's strategy. Undoubtedly, it was the proper course of action (and, indeed, the only one possible) under the circumstances prevailing in 1945. But it was proper only as long as the communists were willing to operate within the framework of parliamentary rules. By 1946–1947 it was amply clear, however, that they were unwilling, and the president should have adjusted his strategy accordingly. In particular, he should have done all he could to end the progressive communization of the country's police apparatus carried out with blatant arrogance by the communist minister of the interior.

An excellent opportunity to act occurred when a new government was appointed following the parliamentary elections of April 1946 in which the noncommunist parties obtained a clear majority of 62 percent. By then there was already no doubt about communist intentions, and it was, therefore, vitally important to prevent them from converting the police into a private army. Beneš should have declined to appoint anyone but a staunch nonparty man as the new minister of the interior. I believed then, and I still believe today, that Jan Masaryk would have been a brilliant choice. For reasons explained earlier, Masaryk was not well qualified for such an office. But his tremendous popularity and strict nonpartisanship would have discouraged even communist opposition, and Beneš's wholehearted support would have guaranteed his appointment. Since Masaryk was totally devoted to Beneš and always followed his instructions, the president would have become his own minister of the interior. Moreover, all the noncommunist parties were disgusted with the communist machinations with regard to the police. Since they had a clear majority in the National Assembly, Masaryk's appointment would have conformed to established parliamentary procedures and to Beneš's strategy of treating the communist party like the other parties.

I subsequently raised this particular question with the president in June 1947. "But what could I have done," he told me, "when the parties agreed on the distribution of seats in the new government? The fault is that I never get any chance to 'solve a party controversy.' The [democratic] parties always make a compromise without referring the matter to me, that is, they always bow to communist pressure. As president I cannot then say: 'Gentlemen, I do not approve of what you have already agreed on.' "[49] I did not agree. Beneš failed to participate actively enough in interparty disputes. The democratic parties would have made no compromises harmful to their own cause had they known that the president supported them and stood *on their side* rather than on a pedestal of studied impartiality whenever a major controversy developed with the communists. But at the time Beneš was tired, and I kept these thoughts to myself.

Later, Beneš's attitude toward the communists began to stiffen. Although he never mentioned communism or the communist party by name, the tenor and thrust of his public pronouncements became increasingly anticommunist in the latter part of 1947.[50] In his *Memoirs*, published in the fall of 1947, he embarrassed Gottwald by exposing the hostile attitude adopted by the Czechoslovak communists toward him and the Czechoslovak liberation movement after the conclusion of the Nazi-Soviet Nonaggression Pact in August 1939 and by including in the volume a resolution of the underground leaders of the Czechoslovak Communist party of December 15, 1940, that denounced him as "an extremely dangerous agent of the Anglo-American capital."[51] On the eve of the February crisis, Beneš even departed briefly from his oft-stated principle of remaining above the parties. When the Czechoslovak Socialist ministers consulted with him on February 18, 1948, regarding Gottwald's refusal to implement the resolution of the Council of Ministers concerning the police, the president urged them to stand firm: "You would commit an irreparable mistake if you retreated. The cause would be lost for you."[52] Yet when he received the ministers again a few days later, he reverted to his above-the-parties stance: "It is up to you to defend yourselves," he told them. "As far as I am concerned, I must remain *au dessus de la mêlée*."[53] Nor did Beneš adopt the shrewd suggestion made by Blažej Vilím, secretary general of the Czechoslovak Social Democratic party, on February 21, 1948, that he steal the initiative from the communists by convening a meeting of the chairmen of all political parties to solve the crisis.[54]

Some of Beneš's passivity in the face of the rising communist menace and his reluctance to act more forcefully stemmed from his mistaken belief that he would be able to resolve the conflict through normal parliamentary means. His tendency to look for hopeful signs even in hopeless situations misled him in yet another way: it made him believe that communism would assume a much more moderate form in Czechoslovakia than in the Soviet Union. He knew that a communist takeover would mean the end of democracy, the dismissal of the opponents of communism from office, and their replacement by communists or fellow travelers. But he hoped that there would be no bloodletting, no monster trials, no massive reprisals. One of the reasons (though a minor one) he surrendered "peacefully" was his desire to prevent bloodshed and to minimize the harshness of the transition. "I assure you that I shall not, and do not want to, cause you any difficulties," the president told Gottwald when the latter brought him the list of the new cabinet members on February 26, 1948. "I shall make it possible for you that everything concerning the crisis be taken care of quickly so that we might return to calm, normal conditions."[55] The president also abandoned his initial intention to resign from the presidency immediately because he hoped that his continued incumbency would induce the new masters to behave less repressively.[56]

The president's hope that communism in Czechoslovakia would be considerably less oppressive than its counterpart in the Soviet Union, that it would be, so to speak, more civilized, was based in no small degree on Beneš's opinion of Gottwald. Despite Gottwald's prewar record of unblemished Soviet-style orthodoxy, Beneš believed that he did not want to reshape Czechoslovakia in strict conformity with the Soviet model but would follow a less radical, less drastic "Czechoslovak way to socialism."[57] Although aware of Gottwald's imperative need to remain on good terms with the Kremlin, Beneš credited him with a good deal of common sense and hoped that he would avoid extremism and seek solutions better suited to Czechoslovakia than the crude Soviet devices would be. Gottwald's initial vote in favor of Czechoslovakia's participation in the Marshall Plan talks in July 1947 seemed to Beneš yet another proof of Gottwald's practicality. Moreover, the president knew that Gottwald had been none too happy with the Soviets' poor-relation treatment of himself and his comrades during their wartime sojourn in Moscow, especially in the period preceding the Nazi invasion of the Soviet Union. Nor had their prolonged stay in the motherland of Marxism-Leninism convinced them that the Soviet way of life was desirable for their own country. Beneš somehow gained the impression that Gottwald's word could be trusted. In contrasting Gottwald with his predecessor in the premiership, Zdeněk Fierlinger, Beneš told me: "It is tough to bargain with Gottwald. But when we reach an agreement, I know that he will do what he has promised."[58] Eventually, Gottwald disappointed him. But between 1945 and 1947, and even during the February 1948 crisis, Beneš clung to his belief that Gottwald would deliver on his promises and that his regime, though dictatorial, would be tolerable. Had Gottwald been able to act independently, he would probably have been relatively moderate and would have justified, at least in part, Beneš's expectations. Since, however, he and his party owed their victory to Stalin's backing, they became Stalin's stooges and in the end followed the Soviet dictator's orders regardless of their own opinions.

Finally, in exploring the reasons for Beneš's comparative passivity after his return to Czechoslovakia and for his eventual surrender to the communists in 1948, one must consider his state of health. Throughout his exile in England, Beneš's health appeared good. He neither smoked nor drank (except for an occasional sip of wine); he exercised regularly, (though, I think, not enough) by taking brisk walks; he indulged in short after-lunch naps nearly every day. The rare cases of indisposition were due mainly to colds, temporary intestinal disorders, and slight attacks of dizziness and headache caused, I was told, by a mild form of Ménière's disease.[59] Characteristic of his physical vigor and agility was his habit of running up stairs two or three at a time to reach the bathroom located on the floor above his London office. (Another reason for this was that he was invariably behind schedule in appointments.) He felt well enough to forgo taking his personal physician with him when we went to the United States in 1943, although Klinger did accompany him on his trips to the Soviet Union in 1943 and 1945.

However, the day before our scheduled departure for Moscow on the morning of March 8, 1945, Beneš suddenly lost consciousness. That night he fainted once more, and our departure had to be postponed. A cardiologist summoned to examine him evidently found nothing basically wrong, blaming the whole thing, as Dr. Klinger told me, on "fatigue." I suspect that we may not have been told the whole truth. Although the president recovered quickly and we were able to leave for Moscow on March 11, 1945, from then on he was no longer as vigorous as he had been. On the night of July 9–10, 1947, he suffered a serious stroke from which he never fully recovered and which was eventually followed by another that took his life in September 1948.[60]

Thus, the president was indeed gravely ill when, after the creation of the Cominform in 1947, the confrontation between communist and democratic forces in Czechoslovakia built toward its climax in 1947–1948. But in what way, if any, did his illness affect his behavior and his decisions? According to Smutný:

> There is no doubt that the extraordinarily serious illness from which Dr. B. was suffering months before the February events could not remain without influence on his political activity and on his attitude toward the various actions of the other political factors. Had B. been as healthy in 1948 as he had been, for instance, in 1946, he would hardly have watched passively how conditions were evolving in the second half of 1947, he

would hardly have permitted the government crisis to occur in February 1948 in the form in which it did occur. The impact of his illness thus stretched far beyond the time of the critical days of February. It manifested itself by a steadily diminishing active involvement in the relations brought about by other factors.

Yet, while holding the president's illness accountable for his passivity, Smutný did not think that it played a major role in his decision to yield to the communists in 1948:

> The decisions that Dr. B. reached at the time of the crisis resulted from considerations whose clarity is safely attested by all those who came into contact with the president at that time. The reduced physical resilience and willpower of the sick man did influence his behavior at the time of the crisis, but not to the extent that one could seek in it a basic explanation.[61]

I fully subscribe to this view. In an article published in *Foreign Affairs* in July 1958, I expressed my firm belief that the president's decision to give in to communist demands in February 1948 "was a decision made carefully and in full realization of its tragic significance" and could by no means be explained by his illness, which "did not impair his mental capacities, his power of reasoning and making responsible judgments." "I am certain," I added, "that his decision in February 1948 would have been exactly the same had he been in the prime of health."[62]

10

The Prisoner of Sezimovo Ústí

Utterly broken, Beneš left Hradčany Castle on February 27, 1948, never to return. His presidential flag, with its motto "Truth Prevails," was taken down, never to be flown again. For the third time in his life, he went into exile, this one the saddest of all. Unlike in 1915 and in 1938, this was an exile in the midst of his own people. This time he did not feel strong enough to go abroad to resume the struggle to regain liberty for his nation. He knew he was mortally wounded, both in spirit and in body. Rudyard Kipling's famous poem "If," which he always placed on a small stand on his desk and which inspired him at the time of Munich and throughout the difficult years of the war, seemed to lose its power of inspiration. To "watch the things he gave his life to, broken, and stoop and build 'em with worn-out tools," "to lose and start again at his beginnings and never breathe a word about the loss," exceeded his powers. He felt he could no longer "hold on when there was nothing in him."

For the first months of his stay at his country home at Sezimovo Ústí, he refused to consider my urgent suggestion that he leave the country and lead our liberation movement. "I am incapable of anything. I would only be a burden and a liability," read his first message, and this testifies more than anything else to his state of mind. When Gottwald called on him at Sezimovo Ústí on March 7, 1948, Beneš told him that he would not go into exile or participate in any action aimed against the Soviet Union or against his own country.[1] He repeated these promises in a conversation with the premier on May 4.[2] His defeat, the humiliation of the past few months, and his illness made him unsure of himself. The man who was known for always having a plan had none. At first he was not even certain whether organizing a liberation movement was desirable. Only later did he finally express his approval of such a movement and agree to go into exile abroad.

This difficulty in determining the proper course of action was also reflected in his handling (or, I should say, mishandling) of his resignation from the presidency. At first he was firmly resolved to step down immediately. As early as May 1942, he had written: "If conditions at the time of Germany's defeat will show that my views are superseded by events and that the USSR has other international conceptions and wants and can, under the influence of the Comintern, carry out its special plans in our country, or if our people request that their president's political tendency be more to the right or more to the left, then most certainly it will not be I but others who will negotiate and fulfill it."[3] The situation he envisioned then did not occur at the end of the war, but it did materialize in February 1948. Even before he officially notified Gottwald on February 25, 1948, of his decision to accept the new cabinet, the president informed the chairman of the National Assembly, Josef David, of his intention to resign.[4] He reconfirmed this decision in forceful terms in his reply to the representatives of the Czechoslovak armed forces, led by General Svoboda, who came to see him on February 27 and begged him to remain in office.[5] Nor did he allow the presidential flag to be hoisted at Sezimovo Ústí as was the established custom whenever the president stayed at his country home.[6]

However, when Smutný brought Beneš the draft of the letter of resignation on March 1, 1948 (which the president had instructed Smutný to prepare before he left Prague), Beneš had already changed his mind and decided to leave the matter in abeyance for the time being. Gottwald easily persuaded the president to remain in office when he visited him on March 7, 1948, and induced him to allow the presidential flag to be flown at Sezimovo Ústí.

The reasoning that prompted Beneš to abandon his initial, and seemingly definitive, intention to resign can be safely deduced from the president's notes on his conversation with the premier on March 7. "*I am waiting* to see what will come next . . . I am displeased to see that you [Gottwald] are throwing out so many people; what you will do in this respect will be decisive for me . . . I shall work for an accord so as to prevent a complete schism in the nation. *Or I shall go* . . . I have no illusions, but I am looking for *people of goodwill*."[7] These fragmentary annotations in Beneš's own handwriting and his underscorings show beyond doubt that Beneš's main (and most probably the only) reason for changing his mind was his desire to do whatever he could (or his belief that he could do something) to lessen the severity of the communist repression and to save as many of his collaborators as he could. He knew that Gottwald and his colleagues wanted him to remain in office, for they thought that this would lend more credence to their thesis that the events of February 1948 were not a putsch, or coup d'état, but a proper and lawful resolution of a political crisis in line with established parliamentary procedures. The continued presence in office of a man so devoted to democracy and social justice could only mean that he approved the new government. Beneš hoped that his presence would have a moderating impact and that reprisals against the opponents of communism would be less drastic than if he resigned.

Beneš soon realized that his hopes were in vain. Despite Gottwald's assurances, repression increased. People were harassed, dismissed, and arrested for political reasons; purges of undesirable faculty and students were staged at universities and colleges. The president's protests and reminders of promises given him were fruitless. The very reason for remaining in office turned out to be invalid. After some second thoughts, the president concluded that his decision had been politically wrong and had allowed the communists to exploit his name for nefarious purposes.[8]

In late April, the president finally decided to correct his mistake and resign. Along with his unhappiness about the communists' broken promises, the major factor behind his decision was his determination not to sign the new, communist-prepared constitution, which he found an ambiguous document long on generalities and short on true guarantees of civil rights. Gottwald was very anxious to have Beneš sign the constitution, for that could have been cited as further evidence of Beneš's approval of the regime and would thus underpin the communist legend of the peaceful transition to socialism. In a long conversation with the president on May 4, Gottwald endeavored to persuade Beneš to remain in office, or at least to settle for a six-month leave of absence for reasons of health.[9] Although Beneš would not budge from his intention to resign, he did accommodate Gottwald once again. The premier threatened that if Beneš abdicated before the elections or stated that he was resigning for political reasons, the communists would not refrain from "commentary."[10] "You are throwing us a glove," Gottwald warned, "and we would have to pick it up."[11] Anxious to avoid a confrontation, Beneš agreed to delay his departure until after the elections and to change the text of his letter of resignation to make it look as though the major consideration was his health.

In the original draft of the letter, Beneš stated that "his conscience, his democratic conviction, and his perception of human and civil rights prevented him from giving his full approval" to some articles in the new constitution and that rather than refusing to sign it, he "decided to return the Presidential Office to the Constituent National Assembly."[12] In the final version of the letter, delivered to Gottwald on June 7, 1948, the president made only a veiled reference to the real reasons for his resignation, stating that he and Gottwald had discussed the decision "in connection with the problems of the overall political situation."[13] He further obliged Gottwald by referring to "the physicians' recommendation that he consider his present state of health."

Those of us who had begun organizing a new movement for the liberation of Czechoslovakia from the communist yoke were pleased that the president had severed his last formal link to Gottwald's regime. Indeed, it was becoming ever more difficult and ever more embarrassing to explain to our Western supporters why Beneš was still in office. Knowing the state of his health, I was afraid that he might suffer a fatal stroke before stepping down, thus enabling the communists to perpetuate the myth that Beneš had sided "with the people" in February 1948. I was somewhat disappointed with the meek phrasing of the letter of resignation, and I became even more disappointed after learning of the original version of the letter and of his capitulation to Gottwald even in this last act of his presidency.

From Smutný's memo on that crucial Beneš-Gottwald conversation at Sezimovo Ústí on May 4, it appears that Beneš wanted to part with Gottwald in a decent, loyal, and friendly manner. He did not want to depart in conflict with the premier, he told Gottwald. He wanted to avoid adverse international publicity or anything that would harm his beloved Czechoslovakia. He hoped that despite their differences of opinion, they would part on good terms and that friendly relations between them would be possible in the future. He did not want his resignation to be turned against the communists, and he even assured Gottwald that he would remain at his disposal if needed.[14]

His behavior is difficult to understand. He had every moral, political, and even constitutional right to phrase his resignation as he pleased. It was an act with which, as he told Gottwald, he was ending his whole life, and that ending was painful.[15] It was virtually his last chance to dissociate himself forcefully and clearly for his own people and all the world to see and understand from a regime that he hated and a system that contradicted his lifelong beliefs and struggles. Yet the mere threat that the communists "would have to pick up the glove" sufficed to prevent him from utilizing this opportunity. What did he or his people stand to lose had he sent in his letter of resignation in its original version? Certainly neither Gottwald's friendship nor communist gratitude and restraint nor more consideration on the part of Moscow (the last was evidently what he meant when he told Gottwald that he would do nothing to harm his country). Given his experiences since 1945 with Stalin and Gottwald and his comrades and the humiliations inflicted on him in February 1948 and thereafter, how could he have continued to believe this?[16]

As a matter of fact, I doubt that he did. Rather I think that his bowing to Gottwald in the last act of his presidency was due to other factors, such as his lifetime habits of trying to smooth the sharp edges of conflicts; papering over dissensions; searching for compromises, formulas, and terms vague enough to accommodate everyone and offend no one; avoiding, so to speak, calling a spade a spade. Other possible factors were his weakened willpower because of his illness and the political etiquette he was accustomed to.

His regard for routine etiquette seems also to have prompted Beneš to send Gottwald a congratulatory telegram when the premier was elected to succeed him as president. I was shocked when I read that congratulatory message. I never imagined that Beneš would send his good wishes to a man who had cheated him, lied to him, humiliated him, and played such a role in destroying his and Tomáš Masaryk's legacy. In a message I sent him shortly afterward, I criticized his actions. He explained that he deemed it necessary to send such a telegram (couched in "conventionally lukewarm terms," as he pointed out) to someone who had been his premier. But, he added, he regretted doing it.[17]

In the first months after the communist coup, Beneš's attitude toward the attempts to organize a liberation movement abroad was somewhat negative. He was pleased that most of his high-level collaborators who faced the danger of communist reprisals had found refuge in the West, and he did what he could to help them do so.[18] But he felt that unlike the situation in 1938, the state of affairs in 1948 was not conducive to such action. In 1939 the country had been overrun by a foreign enemy, dismembered, eliminated as a state, and faced the danger of obliteration. But in 1948 Czechoslovakia continued to exist as the country of the Czechs and the Slovaks, retained its statehood, and did not confront the danger of national extinction.[19] When the president assured Gottwald on March 7 and May 4, 1948, that he would not go into exile or participate in any action against his own country, the communists, or the Soviet Union,[20] he meant it.

Later his attitude changed. By the time Posse-Brázdová got through to him on August 19, 1948, with my report about the activities of Czechoslovak exiles in the West and my urgent plea that he come and lead us, he was willing to try. These second thoughts were due mainly to his growing indignation over the ever more repressive and ever more totalitarian behavior of the new regime. "For a long time I believed that Gottwald at least did not lie to me," he told Posse-Brázdová, "but now I see that all of them, without exception, do it. It is a common matter with all communists, especially the Russian ones. My greatest mistake was that I refused to believe to the very last that even Stalin lied to me, cold-bloodedly and cynically, both in 1935 and later, and that his assurances to me and to Masaryk were an intentional deceit."[21] But a contributing factor was the near total isolation in which he had to live at Sezimovo Ústí, especially after his resignation from the presidency.

It was a cruel stroke of irony that the place he and Madame Beneš loved so much became in the end a virtual prison. I still recall quite vividly the frequent conversations between President and Madame Beneš during our exile in Great Britain about their cherished country home. They seemed to visualize details of the garden, the rooms, the furnishings and impatiently anticipated the time when they would again be able to stroll through the lovely garden on the slopes of the Lužnice River and sit peacefully on the veranda enjoying the enticing bucolic scenery and breathing the fresh, invigorating country air of southern Bohemia.

But when they retreated to Sezimovo Ústí after the communist coup, they soon found that under the changed circumstances, life was quite different from their dreams in exile in England. Communist gunmen, including spies and informers whose task was to check and report anybody coming and going, gradually replaced the old guards. Even Beneš's brother Vojta was stopped and checked. After the president's resignation, the Beneš's were virtually without visitors, save for occasional calls by Smutný (who, to my surprise and disbelief, remained the chief of the Presidential Office even after Gottwald replaced Beneš as president) and Václav Sýkora, my successor as Beneš's secretary. When Beneš listened to Czech-language broadcasts of the Voice of America or the BBC on the second floor, Madame Beneš saw to it that the radio on the first floor was switched to the local station to prevent the communist guards surrounding the place from learning that Beneš was listening to "enemy" broadcasts from abroad. She also insisted that no written messages or documents from abroad, including those I managed to get to him, be kept in the house for fear of a communist inspection (which, however, never took place).

Beneš's isolation from the outside world, coupled with the grave illness that drastically curtailed his ability to work, resulted in depression. An energetic, industrious man, he had been accustomed to talking to people all the time, to debating, to preparing memos, and to writing books in his spare time. He was not being overly dramatic when he told Gottwald in their conversation of May 4 that in resigning, he was "actually leaving his whole life,"[22] for politics was virtually his whole life and the only work he enjoyed. Having no hobbies to fall back on in his retirement and his state of health, and having no one to talk to but Madame Beneš, the expresident had too much time to brood, to examine and re-examine his behavior during the February crisis.[23] His gnawing doubts about the correctness of his decision to yield were compounded by the Stalin-Tito split. In Tito he saw a man who had successfully opposed Stalin. Although the Yugoslav situation was vastly different from that of Czechoslovakia in February 1948, Tito's success could not but make Beneš wonder whether a stronger stand on his part might not have paid off.

Under the circumstances it is hardly surprising that Beneš and Madame Beneš, who saw how badly their isolation affected her husband, decided to leave Sezimovo Ústí in the fall and move to an apartment on Loretta Place, close to the Czernin Palace, the main headquarters of Czechoslovakia's Ministry for Foreign Affairs, and only some two blocks from Hradčany Castle. As Posse-Brázdová wrote me on August 19, 1948, after a long talk with the Benešes, the ex-president "wanted to be 'closer to events,' and both said that they could no longer stand that absolute remoteness and isolation, which was in reality nothing but a prison."[24]

When Posse-Brázdová arrived at Sezimovo Ústí on August 19, Beneš's mood was just right to make him receptive to what I had been attempting all along to persuade him to do. He had already decided to leave the stifling isolation of his country home. His disillusionment with Gottwald, Stalin, and the communists had reached a nadir. Moreover, Madame Beneš was very anxious to obtain the best medical help for her ailing husband. As shown by the messages he asked Posse-Brázdová to transmit to me, his attitude toward the liberation movement abroad had changed:

> Tell them that I give them my blessings and that only the thought of their work gives me a certain consolation in these difficult times. Tell them that there are now so many reasonable and experienced Czechs outside the country that it is impossible that they would not unite in a broad common line of policy, despite the differences of the parties. This is especially important in order to influence the governments and statesmen of countries where they live and work. They must try to open these statesmen's eyes to the fact that once again Czechoslovakia has become a European matter, that there will be no permanent peace as long as this country is not free. Tell them that there is logically, psychologically, and historically no possibility for that state of affairs to become definitive. It is all built on a false foundation, it is a colossus with feet of clay, which must soon crumble.[25]

Those of us involved in the new liberation struggle wanted Beneš to leave Czechoslovakia and lead us, at least nominally, in that struggle. In several messages I sent to him following the communist takeover, I urged him to leave even if he felt unable to become actively involved in the struggle. I described to him the difficulties that we would encounter unless we had an uncontested authority, a recognized leader. I wrote him bluntly about the great damage our cause had sustained when he yielded to Gottwald's ultimatum in February 1948, allowing the communists to claim that they had attained power legally. I did not conceal from him that, whatever his reasons, his continued tenure as president made a bad impression abroad. I told him that even if he could not have prevented the communist coup, he should not have approved and sworn in the new government but rather left the country and presented its case before the United Nations.

At first there was no response. Beneš seemed to have given up. According to reports I received from his entourage, some days he just sat apathetically in his armchair or lay in bed, dejected, his mind wandering somewhere far away, not even listening to the news. "It is a volatile situation in which one day gives great hopes, but the following days take them away," read a report I received in July 1948.[26] Although the report was not encouraging, it did not seem altogether hopeless. In fact, it made me think that a change of atmosphere would provide Beneš with the best chance of getting better by allowing him to escape the morbid political climate of his oppressed country and to breathe the invigorating air of freedom again. He was one of those people who needed such air to survive.

I summed up all imaginable arguments for his leaving the country in yet another letter. Posse-Brázdová succeeded in transmitting the message first to Madame Beneš and then to Beneš himself when she visited them at Sezimovo Ústí on August 19, 1948. This time both Beneš and Madame Beneš concurred and agreed that Beneš would first try to obtain the government's permission to go to Switzerland for treatment by a renowned cardiovascular specialist. Beneš became quite enthusiastic about the project. It seemed to give a new perspective to what was left of his life. "If and as soon as I cross the border," he told Posse-Brázdová, "I would feel better and more hopeful. Why, I feel that even now, despite my having been such a miserable wreck this morning. Maybe that wonderful doctor in Switzerland would know what to do about these clogged-up arteries of mine so that I would not just have to sit around as a sort of a helpless yes-man, but could gradually help a little—as Masaryk used to do quite often after his abdication . . . Perhaps it might be, perhaps it is possible. I promise that I shall try—if only I shall live."[27]

We believed that obtaining permission to seek medical treatment abroad was not impossible. The communists feared that they might be blamed if Beneš died, and they seemed inclined to do anything to prove themselves guiltless in that respect. At one point, the new regime had considered sending Beneš to the Soviet Union for medical treatment, but then dismissed the idea, since it might look as though Beneš had been deported to the Soviet Union.

The possibility of an illegal exit was also considered, although I personally had grave doubts about any such venture. When Blažej Vilím, who had found refuge in England following the communist coup, visited me in Stockholm on May 10, 1948, he mentioned that such a plan was being contemplated, but I told him that the president was not yet in any mood to leave the country.[28] Again, Jan Papánek, head of the Czechoslovak delegation to the United Nations until the communist coup, informed me on August 20 that a Mr. Valušek, an American of Czech origin, had asked President Truman on August 12 whether something might be done to get Beneš out. "Could be, could be," Truman said. "We are interested in that possibility. Maybe something could be done."[29] Posse-Brázdová's son Slavo also came up with a proposition to get Beneš and his family out of Czechoslovakia by means of a clandestine landing and takeoff.[30]

As Posse-Brázdová mentions in her book, I myself had serious misgivings about the feasibility of any such plan, even if Beneš were willing to risk it (which Posse-Brázdová claims he was if he could not leave legally).[31] According to my information, the area surrounding Sezimovo Ústí was so strongly guarded as to make an escape attempt a highly venturesome operation. Moreover, given Beneš's state of health and the nature of his illness, I was afraid that the tension bound to be connected with such an exploit would be too much for him.

I was overjoyed when I received, on August 22, 1948, Posse-Brázdová's report that Beneš had agreed to leave Czechoslovakia and join us in our struggle abroad. Nor did I become concerned on August 30, 1948, when I heard on the radio that Beneš's illness had taken a sudden turn for the worse. "Do not become alarmed if there are bulletins about the worsening of his health—*that is a part of the plan*," Posse-Brázdová wrote me in a postscript, dated August 20, 1948, to her report.[32] I thought that this was just a ploy to persuade the regime to let Beneš go by pretending that he was worse off than he actually was.

Unfortunately, that was not the case. As I learned subsequently, Beneš got worse on August 20, 1948, and could hardly speak. He improved markedly over the weekend, which gave new hopes, and Beneš was able to speak again, almost without difficulty. When he was alone with Dr. Prusík, whom he trusted, he began to talk feverishly about how he had been forced to accept the resignation of the democratic ministers, what the communists were threatening him with, how most people he relied on had failed him. He tried to explain that even after the communist seizure of power, he had agreed to deliver a speech at the commemoration of the 600th anniversary of Charles University (held in April 1948) in order to speak out one last time about the freedom of thought and scientific research. "Being a professor and not a communist, you surely understand how important it was," he told Prusík.[33]

It was as if, feeling the approach of death, he was making one last attempt to justify his actions. Even in his last thoughts he was denied the serenity that he so deserved. The loss of consciousness that followed shortly thereafter and marked the beginning of the final coma was a release for his frail body and his tortured mind. "If I die," he said shortly before passing away, "if I die, it will not be my fault. The guilt will lie with those who have so inhumanly tortured me."[34]

11

Beneš: An Assessment

What, then, is the overall assessment of Beneš's behavior in that fateful decade of 1938–1948? Was he guilty, and if so, of what? Could he have averted the disasters that befell his country, or at least improved its situation had he behaved differently?

The main criticism of the president's behavior during the crisis of 1938 has been that he should have fought rather than bow to Hitler's demands and the Anglo-French ultimatum. The communists argued, and still argue to this day, that had Beneš decided to fight, the Soviet Union would have joined Czechoslovakia and together they would have won the war against Germany even if France did not honor its treaty obligation. Others have claimed that had Beneš rejected the Anglo-French ultimatum and gone to war against Germany, France and Great Britain would have changed their minds and come to Czechoslovakia's rescue. When several Czechoslovak generals called on the president on September 29, 1938, to plead with him to fight, they were convinced that "the big Western powers would be compelled to follow."[1] So was a group of deputies from the Czechoslovak National Assembly whom Beneš received later that day.[2] Writing in 1977, Korbel expressed the belief that "the valor of Czechoslovakia" could have been "a catalyst to unite the frightened and diffused elements of the West."[3] Such was also the belief of some Western opponents of Neville Chamberlain's appeasement policy, such as Winston Churchill. "After consultation with many others, Churchill is conjuring us not to surrender our vital fortifications for another 48 hours," reported Jan Masaryk (then Czechoslovakia's envoy to Great Britain), on October 1, 1938. "He is convinced that a great reaction is growing here against the betrayal committed on us."[4] "Do fight and those who vacillate will fight with you," telegraphed Bertolt Brecht on September 20, 1938.

Another criticism, which originated mostly from Czechoslovakia's political right wing, was that, instead of relying on alliances with France and the Soviet Union, Beneš should have striven to reach some accommodation with Nazi Germany.

Finally, Beneš is taken to task by some of his critics for concluding the 1935 treaty of alliance with the Soviet Union. These critics claim that far from being beneficial, Czechoslovakia's alliance with a hated communist dictatorship undermined its position in the West by causing "fear and abhorrence" among "many leading and influential person- alities in Western Democracies"[5] and played into the hands of Nazi propaganda, which portrayed Czechoslovakia as a "carrier for Soviet aircraft," a spearhead of communism, and a "Soviet corridor" in Central Europe.[6] One critic even claims that "the main reason for the Western hostile attitude toward Beneš was not their fear of Germany per se but their dislike of Beneš's close association with Soviet Russia."[7]

None of these criticisms appears to be valid. As borne out by the materials assembled in this study, especially in Chapter Three, the Soviet Union was neither able nor willing to give Czechoslovakia the promised "immediate and effective aid." Nor was it willing to become embroiled, on behalf of Czechoslovakia, in a war with Germany with- out French participation. Nothing supports the thesis that had Czecho- slovakia gone to war in September-October 1938, France and Great Britain would have suddenly woken up and come to Czechoslovakia's aid. Rather, all available evidence points in the opposite direction. What Churchill called the betrayal of Czechoslovakia was subsequently approved by an overwhelming majority in both the French and British parliaments. Chamberlain was acclaimed a hero on his return from Munich, and was so popular that the Conservative Central Office urged him to capitalize on it by going to the country in a general election on the Munich issue.[8] Chamberlain and Daladier not only managed to remain in office but continued to appease Hitler until the very outbreak of the war and, at least as far as Daladier is concerned, even after Hitler's destruction of Poland. All those assumptions of an impending change of mind in Britain and France seem more the result of wishful thinking and moral indignation than a sober estimate of the realities in September-October 1938. Beneš was right in concluding that the British and French apostles of appeasement not only would not have aided his country but would have blamed Czechoslovakia's destruction on Beneš's stubborn refusal to grant the Sudeten Germans their just right of national self-determination.[9]

Nor is there a shred of evidence to support the contention that Czechoslovakia might have escaped the fate that befell it in 1938–1939 had Beneš struck a deal with Hitler. The route of accommodating Hitler that Poland took by concluding a nonaggression pact with Nazi Germany in 1934 and helping Germany dismember Czechoslovakia in 1938 did not prevent Hitler from liquidating that country in 1939. Besides, it is wrong to imply that Beneš was unwilling to reach a *reasonable* understanding with Germany. As he described at some length in his *Memoirs*,[10] in November and December 1936 he twice received Hitler's emissaries, Count F. J. Trauttmannsdorf and Albrecht Haushofer, who brought him the Führer's offer to conclude an agreement along the lines of the German-Polish Nonaggression Pact. He even sent to Berlin a draft of a Czechoslovak-German agreement stressing the peaceful settlement of disputes, noninterference in internal affairs, and good neighborly relations.[11] But he never got any reply, for he made it clear to Hitler's emissaries that while he was anxious to establish good relations with Germany, he would not give up the alliances with France and the Soviet Union.[12] Furthermore, save for transferring the Sudetenland to the Third Reich, the president was prepared in 1938 to grant the Sudeten Germans all they wanted. As a last resort he was willing to let Hitler have certain Sudeten areas that were outside the periphery of Czechoslovakia's fortifications.[13] Beneš went as far as he could in seeking a decent modus vivendi with both the Third Reich and the Sudeten Germans. But no person of sound mind could have expected him to abandon the entire alliance system on which Czechoslovakia's security was built for a promissory note guaranteed by someone so untrustworthy as the author of *Mein Kampf*.

The assertion that Czechoslovakia would have been better off without an alliance with the Soviet Union is just as farfetched. Certainly, the alliance was exploited by Nazi propagandists and certain reactionary circles in the West. But it is preposterous to suggest that this was a factor in the West's abandonment of Czechoslovakia. Can anyone believe that France and Great Britain would have refrained from forcing Czechoslovakia to accommodate Hitler in 1938, let alone gone to war against Nazi Germany on Czechoslovakia's behalf, had there been no Czechoslovak-Soviet alliance? France itself had concluded an alliance with the Soviet Union, an alliance that was unconditional, whereas the Soviet-Czechoslovak alliance made Soviet aid to Czechoslovakia contingent on simultaneous French assistance.

There is, however, one criticism of Beneš's behavior in 1938 that is difficult to refute, for its acceptance or rejection depends solely on a highly subjective credo; namely, personal beliefs about a leader's and a nation's moral duty in situations such as Beneš's and Czechoslovakia's in 1938. Does a nation have a moral obligation to defend itself even if it faces certain defeat and threat of national obliteration? Does a leader have the duty to order his nation to go to war even if he is convinced, as Beneš was in 1938, that there is no chance of winning and that his nation risks extinction? Does, as one of Beneš's critics maintains, "the valiant ethos of the nation demand from its leaders the ethical, not the practical solution," that is, the rejection of Munich-like diktats regardless of consequences?[14] Beneš did not think so, and being the man he was, he could not have been expected to "lead the nation to a slaughterhouse" and jeopardize its survival for a gesture of futile heroism, for the sake of "national honor" or "valiant ethos." I think that he was right and, thanks to his decision to yield in 1938, the Czechoslovak people fared better than they would have had he opted for war.

The main target of the critics of Beneš's attitude, policies, and actions during the Second World War has been his behavior toward Stalin and the Soviet Union.[15] The gist of their criticism is that Beneš was grossly mistaken in trusting Stalin's word and in believing that the Soviet dictator was reasonable and that his desire to maintain good relations with Great Britain and the United States would restrain him from forcibly communizing as much of Europe as he could. Beneš was instrumental in persuading Western leaders, such as Roosevelt and Churchill, that the Soviet Union could and should be trusted. His abandonment of the Czechoslovak-Polish confederation after the Soviet veto was an error,[16] as was the concluding of the 1943 Treaty of Friendship, Mutual Assistance, and Postwar Cooperation with the Soviet Union. Nor should he have accepted the Soviet invitation to return to Czechoslovakia through the Soviet Union in 1945 since this strengthened the communists' political leverage and bargaining position. In his dealings with the Soviet leaders, he was too deferential, too anxious to please, too accommodating. He was so fearful that he could not resist Soviet wishes and demands that were clearly contrary to Czechoslovakia's interests. Some of his harshest accusers even assert that he was eager to convert his country to "a willing front-row Soviet-Russian satellite," that he handed "the keys of Central Europe over to bolshevism," that he was "highly satisfied with Czechoslovakia's being placed in the Soviet Zone of military operations," that he recommended that the Soviet Union occupy Poland, and that he actually invited the Soviets to interfere in Czechoslovakia's internal affairs.[17]

Although these last accusations are false or grossly distorted, some criticisms of Beneš's conduct during the Second World War appear to be valid. He himself confessed that trusting Stalin and Gottwald was his "greatest mistake."[18] He may indeed have reinforced Roosevelt's and Churchill's faith in Stalin's trustworthiness. At times he was overly accommodating toward the Soviets.

On the other hand, it is absurd to criticize Beneš for visiting Moscow in 1943 and 1945 and concluding a treaty with the Soviet Union. Would Czechoslovakia have avoided engulfment in the Soviet orbit had he not gone to Moscow and concluded the alliance? Would a refusal on Beneš's part to return to Czechoslovakia by way of the Soviet Union and a decision to remain in London in 1945 have been politically more advantageous for his country? A retrospective analysis of Beneš's visits to Moscow, undertaken in December 1949 by a group of exiled Czechoslovak politicians and diplomats, answered in the negative: "The Czechoslovak government could not wait in London because it could not achieve anything better there than in Moscow and back home in Czechoslovakia."[19] Judging from events in the countries of East Central Europe, the answer to both questions is no. In fact, because of Beneš's wartime activities, Czechoslovakia was the only country liberated from the East to which its exiled head of state returned and restored a good measure of democracy. Far from worsening Czechoslovakia's position, Beneš's conduct gave it a second chance (even though it was subsequently wasted). Similarly, it is unfair to condemn Beneš for his unwillingness to persist in his efforts to bring about a Czechoslovak-Polish confederation after the Soviet Union took strong exception to it. Beneš endeavored to overcome the Soviet objections. But he could hardly side with Poland against the Soviet Union when he needed Soviet support so badly in his fight to regain Czechoslovakia's lost territories and to prevent the recurrence of another Munich by transferring the Sudeten Germans.

Despite his critics' assertions and his eventual failure, Beneš's struggle to promote the mutual understanding and continued cooperation between the Soviet Union and the Western democracies that he deemed the *unum necessarium* for peace and stability in Europe and the world is laudable. Every responsible statesman during the Second World War believed that the Soviet Union had to be given the option of trading its previous status of international villain engaged in subversion for a newly won position of respected and influential great power enjoying unprecedented international prestige and sharing world leadership with the United States.[20] Nor are Beneš's critics right in portraying the president as eager to become a confidant of the Kremlin and to make his country a protectorate of the Soviet Union. He wanted the best possible relations with Soviet leaders. However, despite his bitter experience in 1938–1939, he strove to involve the Western powers in East Central Europe to offset and counter Soviet influence. It was not his fault that his efforts remained fruitless and his cherished hope of a 50–50 ratio in Soviet and Western influence in Czechoslovakia failed to materialize.

Although for the most part the criticisms of the president's behavior at the time of Munich and during the Second World War are wrong and unconvincing, his critics' case is stronger when they deal with his postwar conduct. A number of these criticisms appear to be valid.[21] Indeed, as shown in Chapters Nine and Ten, I myself have been critical of some aspects of Beneš's modus operandi in postwar Czechoslovakia. Beneš's relative inaction when Gottwald and his associates wrested the leadership of the country out of his hands was a fateful mistake. He erred when, anxious to convince communist leaders of his fairness and impartiality, he adopted a studied *au dessus de la mêlée* stance, for it weakened his ties with the democratic parties, denied them his guidance and advice, and played into communist hands. So did his desire to avoid a showdown with the communists, which only encouraged Gottwald to push even harder and helped convince him that the president would capitulate once appropriate pressure was applied. It was also instrumental in convincing more and more people that the communists would emerge victorious and that they should not risk supporting a lost cause. Moreover, together with his tendency to make overly optimistic assessments, Beneš's desire to avoid confrontations with the communists made him neglect the few good opportunities to take resolute steps that might have halted the ongoing communization of his country. Most importantly, he should have ordered the Army to protect government buildings and to maintain order at the beginning of the February crisis; in this way, he would have been in a stronger position to seek a parliamentary solution.[22] Finally, when his inability to prevent the communist takeover in February 1948 became apparent, he should have resigned rather than stay in office and thus lend some credibility to the communist claim that he approved the new regime.[23]

On the other hand, there have been two serious criticisms of Beneš's conduct that are rather questionable or at least controversial. Some of his critics doubt the likelihood of a Soviet military intervention in Czechoslovakia in February 1948, thus invalidating the most important reason advanced to mollify or excuse surrender. One critic sees in this contention merely an "*ex post facto* rationalization on the part of those who lost the struggle," while another, a former member of the Czechoslovak parliament and a loyal supporter of the president, opines in a massive volume on the February 1948 crisis that "the Soviet Union would not have sent the Red Army into Czechoslovakia because America had the monopoly of atomic bombs."[24] Since Beneš ruled out armed force, Stalin's response to a successful suppression of the coup by the Czechoslovak army remains a matter of speculation. As far as the president is concerned, it is definitely wrong to view the Soviet threat as a mere ex post facto rationalization. All available evidence indicates that in February 1948 the president believed that Stalin could not afford to let the Czechoslovak communists be defeated and that, as a last resort, he would have intervened militarily.[25] As mentioned earlier, it was only after Tito's successful resistance to Stalin's overlordship that Beneš began to wonder whether his fear of Soviet military intervention had been exaggerated. Nor is it credible to suggest that the Soviets would not have intervened because of the U.S. monopoly of atomic weapons. This suggestion rests on an untenable assumption; namely, that the United States would have used atomic weapons to defend Czechoslovakia. The U.S. atomic superiority dissuaded Stalin neither from communizing the other countries of East Central Europe nor from creating the 1948 power confrontation in West Berlin nor from triggering and supporting the 1950 invasion of South Korea. If President Truman refrained from resorting, or even threatening to resort to, atomic weapons to counter Soviet actions in West Berlin and Korea, would he have used atomic weapons to save Czechoslovakia, which was by then virtually written off by the West as a Soviet satellite?

"It was clear that Western powers would not lift one finger, just as they did not when democratic regimes fell in Romania, Poland, and Hungary," wrote Peroutka in 1950.[26] According to Zenkl, Steinhardt told him on the eve of the crisis that the United States was in no position to aid Czechoslovakia's democrats other than by expressions of sympathy and moral support.[27] Indeed, as is clearly documented by a U.S. State Department memo prepared by H. Freeman Matthews, then director of the department's Office of European Affairs, all that the United States was prepared to do was to "establish as a matter of public record the character and extent of Soviet responsibility" and to grant asylum to Czechoslovak refugees.[28]

Equally questionable is the assertion, made mainly by some Czecho-slovak critics of the president's behavior, that the nation would have responded to a call from him to rise and fight and the communists would have been defeated.[29] Such assertions seem more a product of the critics' own soul-searching and wounded patriotism than a sober and realistic appraisal of the situation in postwar Czechoslovakia. Unfortunately, the disasters that have befallen the Czechs and the Slovaks during recent centuries have injected into their national character an overdose of caution and a reluctance to assume personal risks. The average Czech and Slovak, confronted with what he believes to be superior power, prefers to preserve his strength for a better opportunity rather than to make a gesture of bold defiance. The Munich betrayal, the twilight post-Munich existence leading up to Hitler's coup de grace of March 15, 1939, and the long ordeal of Nazi oppression had badly damaged the Czechoslovak people's morale. Even under the most propitious circumstances, it would have taken some time to re-establish their self-confidence and spirit. When, instead of finding the freedom from fear they had longed for, they were subjected to the communist variety of intimidation and lawlessness, their civic courage slipped to an all-time low.

Under the circumstances, the response to a call to arms would have been disappointing. Undoubtedly clashes between the communists and their opponents would have occurred, but only a small fraction of anticommunists would have participated.[30] Communist die-hards, backed by the communist-controlled police and workers' militia, would have had little difficulty in gaining the upper hand and meting out harsh punishment to their adversaries. Most noncommunists would have opted for the apparent safety of their homes rather than risk fighting in the streets, smugly hoping that the gravely sick man in

Hradčany Castle would somehow produce a miracle and save them from the communists. Thus, a call for a general uprising would have led not to a victory but to futile bloodshed. The president was well aware of the reluctance of his supporters to fight, which was one reason that the idea never entered his mind. He did, however, expect his followers to stage peaceful mass rallies in support of democracy in the hope that a massive display of pro-democratic popular will might induce Gottwald to lessen his demands. Posse-Brázdová quotes Beneš as saying that he sent an SOS to party leaders, the Sokols, and even to those generals he thought were reliable.[31] But I am sure that the president was referring to his repeated calls in late 1947 for people to rally in support and defense of democracy.

Although most criticisms of Beneš's behavior between 1938–1948 are unconvincing and some are patently unfair, he did commit mistakes, especially in the fateful postwar years. In passing judgment on his policies and actions, however, one should keep in mind that the fate that befell his hapless country would have struck it irrespective of the president's actions. Once the West chose, despite Beneš's strenuous efforts to the contrary, not to go beyond mere verbal protests against first the Nazi and then the Soviet quest to control Czechoslovakia, the country's fate was all but sealed. As aptly stated by Peroutka, "there is perhaps in this world no [workable] conception of foreign policy for a small country in an era of big usurpers."[32]

Both in 1938 and in 1948 Beneš was left with only two options, both of them evil. In 1938 it was: either fight Nazi Germany alone and witness the destruction of Czechoslovakia as a nation and the slaughter of hundreds of thousands of Czechs and Slovaks or surrender the border regions to Nazi Germany, preserve his mutilated nation, and recover what had been lost after Germany's defeat in a general war that, as Beneš firmly believed, Hitler was bound to provoke.[33] In 1948, it was: either use armed force to suppress the communist coup, which would have led, in Beneš's opinion, to civil war, bloodshed, and Soviet military intervention followed by the establishment of a harsh communist regime and wholesale persecution of Gottwald's opponents, or give in to communist demands, which meant the end of democracy in Czechoslovakia but, as Beneš hoped, would prevent a bloodbath and would result in the establishment of a comparatively moderate communist rule.

In opting for what he deemed the lesser of two evils, Beneš was guided primarily by his concern for preserving the physical substance of his nation. He acted in conformity with a maxim that he expressed in these terms: "A statesman must consider such matters *sub specie aeternitatis*, as [Tomáš] Masaryk used to say. We are a small nation. One cannot be concerned solely with the happiness of just one generation. One must think of the generations of the future, and of how to assure them the chance to be born and to live in the land of their forefathers."

Notes

CHAPTER 1

1. Robert Bruce Lockhart, *Retreat from Glory* (London: Putnam, 1934), p. 77.

2. On June 24, 1944, Beneš remarked to Jaromír Smutný, the chief of the President's Office, that "with the Russians one has to deal always decently but firmly; to know what one wants; to respect the situation in which they find themselves after their long isolation; but it is always possible to come to an agreement with them when one does not yield" (Smutný papers, Columbia University Archives, Box 10.2.1.5).

3. The Czech original of Beneš's letter to Stalin, in the author's archive.

4. See also Smutný papers, Box 10.2.1.6.

5. See Edward Taborsky, "Beneš and the Soviets," *Foreign Affairs* 27, no. 2 (January 1949): 305–6.

6. Smutný papers, Box 10.2.1.6.

7. Libuše Otáhalová and Milada Červinková, cds., *Dokumenty z historie československé politiky, 1939–1943* (Prague: Academia, 1966), Document no. 69, 1: 91–92.

8. Beneš, *Paměti* (Prague: Orbis, 1947), p. 364.

9. See, for example, ibid., pp. 391, 423, 425, 430.

10. Quoting a report sent to me by the late Countess Amelie Posse-Brázdová, the Swedish writer and longtime friend of the Benešes, about a conversation with Beneš on August 19, 1948. See also Amelie Posse, *När Järn ridå föll över Prag* (Stockholm: Natur och Kultur, 1968), p. 150.

11. Beneš, *Czechoslovak Policy for Victory and Peace* (London: Lincolns-Praeger, 1942), p. 28.

12. An earlier biographer summarized Beneš's views on this subject as follows: "It is great naiveté to believe that a few conversations in corridors or

salons . . . might have a real influence on the course of the world or foreign politics" (Louis Eisenmann, *Un Grand Européen, Edouard Beneš* [Paris: Paul Hartman, 1934], p. 93).

13. Beneš, *Democracy Today and Tomorrow* (London: Macmillan, 1940), p. 203.

14. Beneš, *Demokracie dnes a zítra* (London: Čechoslovák, 1944), 2: 184 ff. For a fuller discussion of Beneš's ideas about the progressive political, economic, and social rapprochement of Western democracy and the Soviet system, see František Hník, *Edvard Beneš, filosof demokracie* (Prague: Melantrich, 1946), especially pp. 118 ff.

15. See Edward Taborsky, "The Triumph and Disaster of Eduard Beneš," *Foreign Affairs* 36, no. 4 (July 1958): 679. Beneš expressed himself similarly in interviews he granted Compton Mackenzie; see Mackenzie's *Dr Beneš* (London: G. Harrap and Co., 1946), pp. 296, 310; and Beneš, *Paměti*, pp. 418–19.

16. General Čatloš's memo sent to Moscow, in the author's archive.

17. Typescript of Mackenzie's conversation, in the author's archive.

18. From the author's archive. See also Taborsky, "Beneš and the Soviets," p. 312.

19. From the author's archive. See also František Němec and Vladimír Moudrý, *The Soviet Seizure of Ruthenia* (Toronto: William B. Anderson, 1955), pp. 143–45 and 322 ff.

20. Dated January 23, 1945, and delivered by the Soviet chargé d'affaires, Chichayev, on January 26, 1945; in the author's archive.

21. Smutný papers, Box 10.2.1.5.

22. Beneš, *Problémy nové Evropy a zahraniční politika československá* (Prague: Melantrich, 1924).

23. Jan Ciechanowski, *Defeat in Victory* (Garden City, N.Y.: Doubleday, 1947), p. 172.

24. Beneš, *Paměti*, p. 415.

25. Smutný papers, Box 10.2.1.5.

26. Mackenzie, *Dr Beneš*, p. 295.

27. See Beneš, *Mnichovské dny* (Prague: Svoboda, 1968), pp. 245-48; and Georges Bonnet, *Défense de la paix: De Washington au Quai d'Orsay* (Geneva: Constant Bourguin, 1946), pp. 237–39. Bonnet mentions September 15 as the date of the Beneš–de Lacroix talk.

28. Mackenzie, *Dr Beneš*, p. 273.

29. Jaroslav Papoušek, *Eduard Beneš* (Prague: Svaz národního osvobození, 1934), p. 173. See also Alois Hajn, *Dr. Edvard Beneš a jeho životní dílo* (Prague: The author, 1935), p. 55.

30. Edward Hitchcock, *Beneš, the Man and the Statesman* (London: Hamish Hamilton, 1940), p. 314.

31. Mackenzie, *Dr Beneš*, p. 263.

32. British Foreign Office Files, N. 3240/160/38, FO 371/19461 (hereafter cited as BFO).

33. Ibid., R. 3066/2594/12, FO 371/21134; R. 7381/1799/12, FO 371/20378; and R. 7442/1162/12, FO 371/20377.

34. See also František Moravec, *Špión, jemuž nevěřili* (Toronto: Sixty-Eight Publishers, 1977), p. 231; and Clement Attlee, *As It Happened* (London: William Heinemann, 1954), pp. 90 and 93.

35. Steinhardt's telegram no. 1564, dated November 24, 1947, recounting a conversation of November 20, 1947; Records of the U.S. Department of State, National Archives, Washington, D.C., 860F.00/11–2447 (hereafter cited as USDS).

36. Beneš, *Paměti*, p. 424; Mackenzie, *Dr Beneš*, pp. 276, 302–3; and Hník, *Edvard Beneš*, p. 51.

37. Quoting Beneš's written account of the conversation; also reprinted in Otáhalová and Červinková, *Dokumenty*, 2: 750.

38. "Draft of Conversations Between President Beneš and Mr. Compton Mackenzie," p. 17; in the author's archive. The paper Beneš alluded to was *Právo lidu*, the daily of the Czech Social Democratic party.

39. Beneš, *Democracy Today and Tomorrow*, p. 64.

40. Beneš, *Demokracie dnes a zítra*, 2: 182–83, 191; italics in the original.

41. Mackenzie, *Dr Beneš*, p. 282.

42. Beneš, *Demokracie dnes a zítra*, 2: 192.

43. Edward Taborsky, *Communism in Czechoslovakia, 1948–1960* (Princeton, N.J.: Princeton University Press, 1961), pp. 355–56; and *Plánované hospodářství v Československu* (Prague: Orbis, 1948).

44. Mackenzie, *Dr Beneš*, pp. 284, 269.

45. Ibid., p. 313. Beneš told Mackenzie that he had spent "four very interesting days" in Azerbaijan (p. 314), but this was an error. On our way to Moscow, we landed at Baku at 2:00 P.M., on Tuesday, December 7, 1943, and left at 5:30 P.M. by train. We did indeed spend four interesting days on the train from Moscow to Baku, but we arrived in Baku at 8:00 P.M. on Monday, December 27, and left by plane for Teheran at 11:00 A.M. on Tuesday, December 28, 1943.

46. Beneš, *Paměti*, pp. 394, 420; see also Mackenzie, *Dr Beneš*, p. 308.

47. Beneš, *Democracy Today and Tomorrow*, pp. 214–15; italics in the original.

48. Beneš, *Úvahy o slovanství* (London: Lincoln & Praeger, n.d.), pp. 11, 58.

49. Beneš, *Paměti*, p. 396; see also idem, *Úvahy*, p. 217; and Mackenzie, *Dr Beneš*, p. 309.

50. Beneš, *Úvahy*, p. 7.

51. Smutný papers, Box 10.2.1.5.

52. Reprinted in Mackenzie, *Dr Beneš*, p. 309; see also Beneš, *Paměti*, p. 396.

53. Mackenzie, *Dr Beneš*, p. 309; and Beneš, *Paměti*, p. 396.

54. Beneš, *Úvahy*, pp. 194, 206–7, 195, and 197.

55. From the author's archive.

56. For an early reference to this habit, see Zdeněk Fierlinger, "Několik vzpomínek na válečnou Paříž," in *Padesát let Edvarda Beneše* (Prague: Československá obec legionářská, 1934), p. 197; see also Lockhart's memo of February 10, 1940, and Leeper's comments, BFO C 2321/2/12, FO 371/24287.

57. Otáhalová and Červinková, *Dokumenty*, Document no. 288, 1: 349.

58. Beneš's pre-eminence among Czechoslovak political exiles was always recognized by U.S. and British statesmen, such as Roosevelt, Churchill, Eden, and even Chamberlain. Although some of the characterizations of Beneš drawn by a few British and U.S. diplomats during the era of appeasement were quite critical, those written after the outbreak of the war had borne out the correctness of Beneš's predictions clearly viewed him as the most outstanding Czechoslovak statesman. See, for example, BFO C 13304/7/12, FO 22899; and BFO-17895/7/12, FO 371/22899.

59. Otáhalová and Červinková, *Dokumenty*, Document no. 69, 1: 91.

60. See also ibid., Document no. 324, 1: 394. Other criticisms of his ministers may be found in Documents nos. 188 (1: 229), 199 (1: 214), and 223 (1: 284–85). See also "Londýnská emigrace Benešovýma očima," *Predvoj*, no. 39 (September 30, 1965): 10–11, which recounts Beneš's talks with the Czechoslovak communists in Moscow in 1943 in which he was allegedly highly critical of some Czechoslovak émigré politicians in London.

61. I was therefore much surprised that the political testaments Beneš wrote before his trips to the United States and the Soviet Union in 1943 recommended Masaryk as his successor.

62. Otáhalová and Červinková, *Dokumenty*, Documents nos. 324 (1: 394), 286 (1: 344), and 317 (1: 388).

63. BFO C 13304/7/12, FO 22899; BFO C 17805/7/12, FO 371/22899; and BFO C 13304/7/12, FO 371/22899.

64. Otáhalová and Červinková, *Dokumenty*, Document no. 199, 1: 245.

65. Ibid., Document no. 310, 1: 379.

66. Beneš, *Paměti*, p. 414; italics and exclamation marks are the president's.

67. "Draft of Conversations," p. 168. In the published book the original version was modified slightly to read: ". . . considered for a certain time a kind of saint" (Mackenzie, *Dr Beneš*, p. 377).

68. BFO C 2331/2/12, FO 371/24287.

69. Otáhalová and Červinková, *Dokumenty*, Document no. 69, 1: 91.

70. Ibid.

71. BFO C 2331/2/12, FO 371/24287.

72. Ibid.

73. Otáhalová and Červinková, *Dokumenty*, Document no. 289, 1: 349.

74. Ibid., 2: 753–54.

75. The manuscript of Drtina's memoirs was smuggled out of Czechoslovakia. The quotation was supplied by Jaroslav Drábek, who served as chief prosecutor before the communist takeover.

76. It was, of course, Smutný who refused to let Drtina see the president. However, as I know (and as Drtina also knew) from our previous experience, Smutný must have subsequently informed the president, who, if he so desired, could have directed Smutný to ask Drtina back.

77. Entry in the author's diary, October 22, 1943. Although Beneš was

anxious to conclude the treaty, he felt strongly that the signing should be delayed until the Soviets and the British had settled their differences.

78. Ibid., January 31, 1945. See also Smutný's note dated June 24, 1944: "I am sure," Smutný reported Beneš as saying, "that if a communist were our envoy in Moscow, he would have more regard for our interests than Fierlinger" (Smutný papers, Box 10.2.1.5).

79. It is ironic that Beneš finally took action against Fierlinger only after the communist coup (when Beneš was virtually a prisoner at his country home). Beneš adamantly refused to follow Gottwald's recommendation that Fierlinger replace the deceased Jan Masaryk as foreign minister, thus thwarting Fierlinger's lifelong ambition. (See Smutný papers, Box 30.8.1.13.)

80. Entry in the author's diary, June 18, 1944.

81. Smutný papers, Box 10.2.12; see also Hubert Ripka, *Le Coup de Prague* (Paris: Librairie Plon, 1949), p. 268.

82. See, for example, Smutný papers, Box 10.2.1.3.

83. Ibid., Box 10.2.1.2. Beneš reportedly said this in the presence of Madame Beneš and Dr. Klinger, his personal physician.

CHAPTER 2

1. See Beneš, *Paměti* (Prague: Orbis, 1947), p. 78; and Compton Mackenzie, *Dr Beneš* (London: G. Harrap and Co., 1946), pp. 317–18.

2. From the author's archive.

3. An entry in the author's diary for December 28, 1940, notes that Beneš was working on this report; see also Libuše Otáhalová and Milada Červinková, eds., *Dokumenty z historie československé politiky, 1939–1943* (Prague: Academia, 1966), Document no. 124, 1: 172–73.

4. Entry in the author's diary, September 30, 1943; see also the entry in Smutný's papers of September 28, 1943, noting that Beneš handed Smutný a copy for his perusal and comment (Otáhalová and Červinková, *Dokumenty*, Document no. 310, 1: 379).

5. Beneš, *Mnichovské dny* (Prague: Svoboda, 1968), p. 507.

6. Beneš, *Paměti*, p. 70.

7. See the epilogue in Beneš's *Mnichovské dny*, pp. 508–16.

8. See, for example, Boris Čelovský, *Das Münchener Abkommen von 1938* (Stuttgart: Deutscher Verlag, 1958); Hubert Ripka, *Munich: Before and After* (London: Gollancz, 1939); John W. Wheeler-Bennett, *Munich: Prologue to Tragedy* (London: Macmillan, 1948); and Keith Eubank, *Munich* (Norman: Oklahoma University Press, 1963).

9. See Georges Bonnet, *Défense de la paix: De Washington au Quai d'Orsay* (Geneva: Constant Bourguin, 1946), pp. 246–49; and Beneš, *Mnichovské dny*, pp. 283–89.

10. Beneš, *Mnichovské dny*, pp. 245–48. and Eubank, *Munich*, p. 140.

11. Mackenzie, *Dr Beneš*, p. 319; see also Beneš, *Paměti*, p. 87.

12. See the discussion in J. W. Bruegel, *Czechoslovakia Before Munich* (Cambridge, Eng.: Cambridge University Press, 1973), pp. 270 ff, in which the author proves that Chamberlain "imagined a guarantee which did not guarantee anything and did not commit anyone"; see also Wheeler-Bennett, *Munich*, pp. 319–20.

13. Beneš, *Paměti*, p. 97.

14. *London Times*, October 1, 1938; see also Wheeler-Bennett, *Munich*, p. 180.

15. See Eubank, *Munich*, p. 229.

16. For details, see ibid., p. 234.

17. Wheeler-Bennett, *Munich*, p. 297.

18. Chamberlain's speech at Birmingham, March 17, 1939.

19. For a fuller discussion, see Edward Taborsky, *The Czechoslovak Cause* (London: H.F. and G. Witherby, 1944), pp. 49 ff. Criticizing the action in a speech in the House of Commons on May 26, 1939, Churchill referred to it as "a public disaster, namely, the transference of this £6,000,000 of Czech money into the hands of those who have overthrown and destroyed the Czech Republic" (Hansard, p. 2772). See also Otáhalová and Červinková, *Dokumenty*, Document no. 252, 1: 300 ff.

20. Eubank, *Munich*, p. 270.

21. See Taborsky, *Czechoslovak Cause*, p. 61–63.

22. Such had been the case of Ethiopia after its annexation by fascist Italy. Britain at first refused to recognize the conquest; then it recognized the Italian government as the de facto government of Ethiopia; finally came recognition de jure.

23. For the text of the letter, see FO 371/22898/183–4.

24. Ibid.; reprinted in Julius Firt, "Cestou k únoru: Počátky byly v Londýně Záznamy-II," *Svědectví* 12, no. 46 (1973): 213.

25. Notebook of Halder, August 14, 1939, DG. Series D, Vii, pp. 5551–556. For a good discussion of the British efforts to bring about a "second Munich conference," see Eubank, *Munich*, pp. 268 ff.

26. Robert B. Lockhart, "The Second Exile of Edward Beneš," *Slavonic and East European Review* 28, no. 70 (November 1949): 40.

27. BFO C 13246/12, FO 371/21588.

28. BFO C 9152/7/12, FO 371/22898; Beneš, *Paměti*, p. 123; and Lockhart, "Second Exile."

29. Beneš's account, in the author's archive; this account formed the basis for the lengthy discussion of the event in Beneš's *Memoirs* (*Paměti*, pp. 123–28).

30. From the author's archive. The memo was dated New York, April 20, 1939.

31. See comments of Cadogan, Roberts, and Troutbeck in BFO C 12826/7/12, FO 371/22892.

32. See Taborsky, *Czechoslovak Cause*, pp. 70 ff. The reason for choosing the formula authorizing the National Committee to represent the "Czechoslovak peoples" rather than Czechoslovakia as a state was the British desire to avoid any

commitment to the "resurrection of old Czechoslovakia" (see Sir Orme Sargent's letter of September 26, 1939, to the British minister in Budapest, Foreign Office File, vol. 22899).

33. See records of Beneš's talks with Cadogan on November 11 and 13, 1939, in Otáhalová and Červinková, *Dokumenty*, Documents nos. 36 and 37, 1: 65–66; and BFO C 18322/7/12, FO 371/22900.

34. Otáhalová and Červinková, *Dokumenty*, Document no. 37, 1: 65–66.

35. Osuský's letter to Beneš, dated October 23, 1939, in Otáhalová and Červinková, *Dokumenty*, Document no. 21, 1: 51–55. See also a letter to Beneš from Outrata and Ripka brought by Smutný from Paris on September 22, 1939, reporting Osuský's statement to them that any direct participation by Beneš was not acceptable to the French government "in any form" because it would render French negotiations with Italy and other countries more difficult and impede the "conception of a new reorganization in Central Europe" (ibid., Document no. 3, 1: 20–21; see also Document no. 2, 1: 18–20; Document no. 10, 1: 38–40; Document no. 13, 1: 41–42; Document no. 146, 1: 195; Beneš, *Paměti*, pp. 137 ff; and Jan Křen, *V emigraci: Západní zahraniční odboj, 1939–1940* [Prague: Naše vojsko, 1969], pp. 214 ff).

36. Unlike Daladier, Chamberlain acknowledged receipt of Beneš's telegram of September 9, 1939, with a kind telegram of his own.

37. Owing to the collapse of France in May-June 1940, the issue of French recognition became moot. For the documents on recognition, see BFO C 7647/12, FO 371/24289.

38. For a further discussion, see Taborsky, *Czechoslovak Cause*, pp. 89–91.

39. For some of the difficulties connected with "provisionality," see Otáhalová and Červinková, *Dokumenty*, Document 113, 1: 141.

40. See Lord Halifax's letter to Beneš of July 18, 1940; reprinted in Beneš, *Memoirs* (London: George Allen & Unwin, 1954), pp. 109–10.

41. Ibid., p. 106. Also, "Political and Juridical Relationship of the Czechoslovak Republic to Great Britain," prepared by Beneš to support his claim of juridical continuity (in the author's archive).

42. Beneš, *Memoirs*, pp. 108–9.

43. When Beneš openly began his fight for the liberation of Czechoslovakia on March 16, 1939, the day after Hitler's destruction of the post-Munich rump of Czechoslovakia, by sending telegrams of protest to Chamberlain, Daladier, Litvinov, and the president of the Council of the League of Nations, he signed the telegrams as "former" president of Czechoslovakia. Not until later did he realize that this could be construed as an admission that he considered his October 1938 resignation as legal. Hence, he began referring to himself as "second" president—a description that was broad enough to accommodate his thesis that he had never validly resigned from the presidency and to allow those who could not agree with this thesis to contend that it merely stated the historical fact that Beneš had been the second president of the Czechoslovak republic.

44. See Lord Halifax's letter of July 18, 1940, in reply to Beneš's letter of July 9, 1940.

45. Eden's letter to Masaryk of July 18, 1941.

46. Entry in the author's diary, April 20, 1941.

47. Ibid., April 23, 1941. For a facsimile of Churchill's and Eden's comments, see *Svědectví* 12, no. 46 (1973), following p. 224.

48. Entry in the author's diary, July 2, 1941. The Soviet recognition took effect at noon on July 18, 1941; the British action after 4:00 P.M. of the same day.

49. For Eden's letter, see Otáhalová and Červinková, *Dokumenty*, Document no. 203, 1: 247.

50. See Beneš, *Paměti*, pp. 244 and 303.

51. Beneš's memo on his conversation with Molotov (from the author's archive).

52. Entry in the author's diary, July 18, 1941.

53. Beneš suspected Malkin; see also Otáhalová and Červinková, *Dokumenty*, Documents nos. 209, 1: 254, and 211, 1: 255–56.

54. See ibid., Document no. 211, 1: 255–56; and entry in the author's diary, July 30, 1941.

55. Otáhalová and Červinková, *Dokumenty*, Document no. 211, 1: 255–56.

56. Ibid., Document no. 210, 1: 255; and entry in the author's diary, July 25, 1941.

57. For the text of the note, signed by the Czechoslovak secretary of state in the Foreign Ministry, see *Tři roky světové války* (London: Čechoslovák, n.d.), pp. 156 ff.

58. The author's list of Beneš's appointments for that period shows that he met five times with Eden and twelve times with Nichols. Moreover, in the same seven-month period, he also had as many as 37 meetings with Lockhart. Although the primary intent of these meetings with Lockhart was to pass on information received from underground sources in Czechoslovakia, Beneš was not averse to using them to persuade the British to accede to his wishes regarding boundaries and juridical continuity.

59. Beneš, *Paměti*, p. 301.

60. See Beneš's memo on a conversation with Nichols on May 1, 1942 (from the author's archive); see also an entry in the author's diary, May 1, 1942.

61. Entries in the author's diary, February 9, 1942, and May 1, 1942.

62. Ibid., January 22, 1942.

63. From the author's archive.

64. When de Gaulle's committee renamed itself the provisional government of France in May 1944 and was promptly recognized as such by the Beneš government, the French repudiation of the Munich agreement was reconfirmed in a new declaration signed on August 22, 1944 (see Beneš, *Paměti*, pp. 236–37).

65. See Otáhalová and Červinková, *Dokumenty*, Documents no. 240 and 242, 1: 288–90; and Beneš, *Paměti*, p. 231.

66. For the text, see *Documents on International Affairs* (London: Royal Institute of International Affairs, 1943), 2: 365; see also Mackenzie, *Dr Beneš*, p. 221.

67. See Beneš, *Paměti*, p. 257.

68. Beneš, *Mnichovské dny*, pp. 332 and 336.

69. Ibid., p. 336. Typically, Beneš's adverse feelings were not reflected in his reply to Roosevelt. Rather, he stressed Czechoslovak gratitude for Roosevelt's message, which he said would contribute to a just solution of the conflict (ibid., p. 335).

70. Ibid., p. 336; and Beneš, *Paměti*, pp. 255–57.

71. Beneš, *Paměti*, p. 95.

72. For the text of Sumner Welles's statement of March 17, 1939, see *Czechoslovak Yearbook of International Law* (London: Čechoslovák, 1942), p. 228; and *Czechoslovak Sources and Documents*, no. 2 (New York: Czechoslovak Information Service, 1943), p. 20.

73. For the text, see Beneš, *Memoirs*, p. 68; and *Czechoslovak Sources and Documents*, p. 38. Chamberlain answered with a brief telegram referring to his Birmingham speech of March 17, 1939; Litvinov sent a copy of the Soviet note protesting the German action to the Czechoslovak minister in Moscow; and Daladier did not bother to acknowledge receipt of Beneš's telegram.

74. *Czechoslovak Sources and Documents*, pp. 39–40.

75. USDS 860F.00/774.

76. The British government followed Beneš's activities in the United States closely and had misgivings about them; see BFO C 6071/7/12, FO 371/22898; BFO C 6789/7/12, FO 371/22898; and BFO C 4964/3955/18, FO 371/2308.

77. Beneš, *Paměti*, p. 258.

78. For example, in April 1939 the Hungarian foreign minister, Count Csaky, sharply protested Beneš's activities in the United States; see USDS 860F.01/217; BFO C 6227/7/12, FO 371/22898; and USDS 860F.00/941. For Polish objections, see USDS 860.C.01/508.

79. Edward Hitchcock, *Beneš, the Man and the Statesman* (London: Hamish Hamilton, 1940), p. 325.

80. For an exhaustive account of the talks, see Beneš, *Paměti*, pp. 115–20.

81. Ibid., p. 116.

82. Ibid., pp. 120 and 128.

83. Ibid., pp. 121 and 116.

84. From the author's archive.

85. From the author's archive.

86. Following the French and British recognition of the Czechoslovak National Committee in autumn, 1939, Beneš instructed the Czechoslovak envoy in Washington, V. Hurban, to ascertain the prospects of similar action by the United States. But when Hurban was informed that the United States "could not well, as a neutral, recognize as the Government of Czechoslovakia a Committee formed outside the country and which had no constitutional continuity with previous governments," Beneš dropped the matter. See statement made to Hurban by Moffat, the chief of the European Division of the Department of State, on February 14, 1940 (USDS 860F.01/314; and Beneš, *Paměti*, p. 260).

87. From the author's archive.

88. Quoting a conversation between the first secretary of the Czechoslovak legation in Washington with the acting chief of the State Department's Division of European Affairs, Atherton (USDS 860F.01–374).

89. From the author's archive. Beneš also prepared a massive memorandum in support of his quest for U.S. recognition, which Hurban delivered to Cordell Hull on March 14, 1941 (USDS 860F.01/367).

90. Beneš, *Paměti*, p. 261.

91. USDS 860F.01/377 and 860F.01/370.

92. For the full text, see U.S., Department of State, *Foreign Relations of the United States*, 1941, 2: 29–31; and Beneš, *Paměti*, pp. 262–66.

93. For the text of the letter, see U.S., Department of State, *Foreign Relations of the United States*, 1941, 2: 33.

94. For the text of the notification, see Beneš, *Memoirs*, p. 178; and USDS 860F/400b.

95. "President's Secret Folder, A.J.D. Biddle, Jr.," Franklin Delano Roosevelt Library, cited in Georg V. Rimek, "Presidency of Edvard Beneš," Ph.D. dissertation, University of Ottawa, 1975, p. 523.

CHAPTER 3

1. V. F. Klochko et al., eds., *New Documents on the History of Munich* (Prague: Orbis, 1958), Document no. 36, pp. 86–88. Beneš in his *Mnichovské dny* (Prague: Svoboda, 1968) phrases the two questions somewhat differently, but the substance is the same.

2. Klochko, *New Documents*, Document no. 38, p. 90.

3. Beneš, *Mnichovské dny*, pp. 316–17.

4. Ibid., p. 317.

5. Ibid.

6. See Litvinov's speeches at Geneva, September 21 and 23, in Klochko, *New Documents*, Documents no. 46, 51, pp. 104–5 and 114–16.

7. Beneš, *Mnichovské dny*, p. 318.

8. See also Georges Bonnet, *Défense de la paix: De Washington au Quai d'Orsay* (Geneva: Constant Bourguin, 1946), pp. 197–200, 303; and Ivan Pfaff, "Jak tomu opravdu bylo so sovětskou pomocí v mnichovské krizi, II," *Svědectví* 15, no. 57 (1978): 54.

9. For Beneš's attempt to seek a reconciliation with Poland in those crucial days, see Beneš, *Mnichovské dny*, p. 303 ff.

10. Pfaff, "Mnichovské krizi, I," *Svědectví* 14, no. 56 (1978): 584.

11. See Arnošt Heidrich, "Zahraničně-politické příčiny našich tragedií v letech 1938 a 1948," a lecture delivered in Czech in Washington, D.C., in 1949; in the author's archive. The lecture was subsequently published in English as "International Political Causes of the Czechoslovak Tragedies of 1938 and

1948," mimeo. (Washington, D.C.: Czechoslovak Society of Arts and Sciences in America, 1962), 2: 1–27. Heidrich was a high-level official of the Czechoslovak Ministry for Foreign Affairs whom Beneš frequently used for confidential talks. On September 15, 1938, the Czechoslovak legation in Bucharest was given renewed assurances by the Romanian government that it would tolerate over-flights by Soviet planes. Georges Bonnet also recounted that both the Poles and the Romanians were opposed to the transit of Soviet troops across their countries. (*Défense de la paix*, pp. 126, 133–34, 201–2). See also Keith Eubank, *Munich* (Norman: Oklahoma University Press, 1963), pp. 108–9; *Documents on German Foreign Policy* (Washington, D.C.: Government Printing Office, 1962), C.iv, nos. 339, 353, 362, 385, 405; and Pfaff, "Mnichovské krizi, I," pp. 575–85. On the other hand Ripka mentions in *Munich: Before and After* (London: Gol lancz, 1939) that "in conversations which M. Litvinov had at Geneva with M. Com-nen, the Rumanian Foreign Minister, every arrangement was made for the pas-sage of Soviet troops over Rumanian territory on their way to Czechoslovakia" (pp. 338–39). But Ripka, who does not substantiate this assertion, is wrong. Beneš, who ought to know, said in *Mnichovské dny* that "even Romania refused to let [Soviet] aid through its territory" (p. 322).

12. Klochko, *New Documents*, Document no. 46, pp. 104–5. Italics added.

13. Beneš, *Mnichovské dny*, p. 322. See also Beneš's letter to Ladislav Rašín of November 1938 in which he expressed the fear that the Soviet Union might have helped only with planes, in which case Czechoslovakia's fate would have been the same as that of Republican Spain (*Šest let exilu a druhé světové války* [Prague, 1946], pp. 28–30).

14. See also Jaromír Smutný, "Edvard Beneš a čs odboj za druhé světové války," *Svědectví* 6, no. 21 (1963): 50–60.

15. Beneš, *Úvahy o slovanství* (London: Lincolns-Praeger, n.d.), p. 180. "Neither the West nor Russia was prepared for the war [in 1938]. I knew it," he told Smutný in July 1941 (Libuše Otáhalová and Milada Červinková, eds., *Documenty z historie československé politiky, 1939–1943* [Prague: Academia, 1966], Document no. 195, 1: 236–39).

16. Beneš, *Úvahy*, p. 80; and *Mnichovské dny*, p. 321.

17. Beneš, *Úvahy*, p. 180.

18. Otáhalová and Červinková, *Dokumenty*, Document no. 195, 1: 238.

19. Klochko, *New Documents*, Document no. 51, pp. 114–16.

20. Eubank, *Munich*, p. 110; see also Pfaff, "Mnichovské krizi."

21. Heidrich's lecture; see also Josef Korbel, *The Communist Subversion of Czechoslovakia, 1938–1948* (Princeton, N.J.: Princeton University Press, 1959), pp. 32–33.

22. Weizsäcker to Trautman, May 30, *Documents on German Foreign Policy*, series D.I., p. 864; Eubank, *Munich*, p. 111; see also Pfaff, "Mnichovské krizi, II," pp. 53, 55, 57.

23. E. L. Woodward and Rohan Butler, eds., *Documents on British Foreign Policy, 1919–1939, Third Series* (London: His Majesty's Stationery Office, 1949), Document no. 194, 1: 265.

24. Schulenburg to Woermann, August 22, 23, and 26, 1938, *Documents on German Foreign Policy*, series D.II, pp. 601–2, 604–5, 629–31; Eubank, *Munich*, p. 111.

25. Kirk's telegram 271 of August 29, 1938, USDS, 760F.62/614.

26. Heidrich's lecture.

27. From the author's archive.

28. Beneš, *Mnichovské dny*, pp. 263–64, 268, 316, 324. Italics in original.

29. Otáhalová and Červinková, *Dokumenty*, Document no. 325, 1: 397–401. See also Edward Taborsky, "President Edvard Beneš and the Crises of 1938 and 1948," *East Central Europe (L'Europe du Centre-Est)* 5, no. 2 (1978): 203 ff.

30. Herben's report is published as Annex 1 in Ladislav Feierabend, *Beneš mezi Washingtonem a Moskvou* (Washington, D.C.: The author, 1966), pp. 133–35.

31. Alexandrovsky's telegram to the People's Commissariat for Foreign Affairs, in Klochko, *New Documents*, Documents no. 57, 60, pp. 126–27 and 130–31. Beneš did not refer to this in *Munich Days*.

32. Klochko, *New Documents*, Documents no. 58, 60, pp. 128 and 130–31.

33. For samples of communist criticism of Beneš's behavior during the Munich crises, see Vladimir G. Poliakov, *Angliia i miunkhenskii sgovor* (Moscow: Izdatelstvo Akademii nauk SSSR, 1960); J. S. Hájek, *Mnichov* (Prague, 1958); Václav Král, *O Masarykově a Benešově kontrarevoluční protisovětské politice* (Prague, 1953) idem, "Československo a Mnichov," *Československý časopis historický* 7, no. 1 (1959); Alexandrovsky's letter of September 29, 1938, to the People's Commissariat for Foreign Affairs (Klochko, *New Documents*, Document no. 56, pp. 124–25), in which he characterizes Beneš as "regarding assistance from the USSR to defend Czechoslovakia against an attack by Hitler as an extremely suicidal measure for the Czechoslovak bourgeoisie"; *Diplomaticheskii slovar'*, 2: 198; *History of Soviet Foreign Policy, 1917–1945* (Moscow: Progress Publishers, 1969), p. 350; "K politice Sovětského svazu na obranu Československa v roce 1938," *Dějepis ve škole*, no. 1 (September 1970): 6–10; "Zrada buržoazie," *Rudé právo*, March 31, 1973, p. 3; and *Guilty Men of Czechoslovakia* (a pamphlet circulated in England during the era of the Nazi-Soviet honeymoon, 1939–1941).

34. See Litvinov's speeches at Geneva on September 21 and 23, 1938, in Klochko, *New Documents*, Documents no. 46, 51, pp. 104–5 and 114–16. As noted above, Alexandrovsky's statement to Beneš on September 21, 1938, which did not appear to make Soviet aid contingent on French participation, was ignored by Soviet sources.

35. Cited in V. Sipols and M. Pankrashova, "Preparation of the Munich Deal," *International Affairs* (Moscow), 1973, no. 7 (July): 76. Gottwald's assertion is also referred to in *Diplomaticheskii slovar'*, 2: 198; the official *History of Soviet Foreign Policy*, pp. 347–48;I. Zemskov's review of *New Documents* in *International Affairs* (Moscow), 1958, no. 10 (October): 70; and *Československo- sovětské vztahy jako faktor mezinárodní politiky, 1917–1970* (Prague: Academia, 1975), p. 129. See also Barry M. Cohen, "Moscow at Munich: Did the Soviet Union Offer Uni-

lateral Aid to Czechoslovakia?" *East European Quarterly* 12, no. 3 (September 1978): 341–48.

36. Poliakov, *Angliia i miunkhenskii sgovor*, p. 234; and Ivan Maisky, *Wer half Hitler* (Moscow, n.d.), p. 70. See also Cohen, "Moscow at Munich," pp. 342–44.

37. Klochko, *New Documents*, Document no. 37, p. 89, dated September 20, 1938. Italics added.

38. See also William Wallace, "New Documents on the History of Munich," *International Affairs* (London), 35, no. 4 (October 1959): 447–54.

39. Cited in Max Beloff, *The Foreign Policy of Soviet Russia*, vol. 2, *1936–1941* (London: Oxford University Press, 1949), p. 158.

40. Otáhalová and Červinková, *Dokumenty*, Document no. 195, 1: 236–39.

41. See, for example, the long resolution adopted on December 15, 1940, by the underground leaders of the Czechoslovak Communist party (cited in Beneš, *Paměti* [Prague: Orbis, 1947], pp. 160 ff.

42. Ibid., p. 274.

43. See also Smutný papers, Box 10.2.11.

44. See, for example, *Chtěli jsme bojovat: Dokumenty o boji KSČ a lidu na obranu Československa, 1938*, 2 vols. (Prague: Státní nakladatelství politické literatury, 1963); to Král, *O Masarykově a Benešově*; Rudolf Beckman, *O diplomatickém pozadí Mnichova* (Prague: Státní nakladatelství politické literatury, 1954); and Hájek, *Mnichov*. See also Edward Taborsky, *Communism in Czechoslovakia, 1948–1960* (Princeton, N.J.: Princeton University Press, 1961).

45. Míla Lvová, "Mnichovská křižovatka," *Svět práce*, no. 38 (September 24, 1969): 4.

46. See, for example, "Zrada buržoazie," *Rudé právo*, March 31, 1973.

47. Ibid.

48. Compton Mackenzie, *Dr Beneš* (London: G. Harrap and Co., 1946), p. 322. Beneš described his attitude in similar words in *Paměti*, p. 294.

49. For Beneš's criticism of Bonnet's behavior, see *Mnichovské dny*, pp. 283–91.

50. Beneš, *Paměti*, pp. 338–42. Thus, Josef Korbel is wrong when he refers to Beneš's "bitterness" toward France in his *Twentieth Century Czechoslovakia* (New York: Columbia University Press, 1977), p. 148; as is František Moravec in *Špión, jemuž nevěřili* (Toronto: Sixty-Eight Publishers, 1977), p. 275.

51. For details, see Hubert Ripka, *Le Coup de Prague* (Paris: Librairie Plon, 1949), pp. 66 ff.

52. Beneš, *Úvahy*, p. 8.

53. See, for example, Smutný's memo dated August 22, 1943, in Otáhalová and Červinková, *Dokumenty*, Document no. 298, 1: 362.

54. Mackenzie, *Dr Beneš*, p. 334.

55. Otáhalová and Červinková, *Dokumenty*, Document 295, 1: 359, dated August 7, 1943. Smutný remarked in another entry in his diary, dated August 22, 1943, that Beneš's "realization that Munich was his *personal* defeat, *personal* humiliation, a defeat of his *personal* policy will never disappear" (italics in

original). Although this may have been true in 1938–1939, I think that it was not a correct interpretation of Beneš's views in 1942–1943.

CHAPTER 4

1. Libuše Otáhalová and Milada Červinková, eds., *Dokumenty z historie československé politiky, 1939–1943* (Prague: Academia, 1966), Document no. 76, 1: 96–99.

2. From the author's archive. This volume of Beneš's *Memoirs* was never published.

3. See Beneš, *Paměti* (Prague: Orbis, 1947), pp. 10 ff.

4. Ibid., p. 35.

5. The letter was written in French. For the Czech version, see Beneš, *Mnichovské dny* (Prague: Svoboda, 1968), pp. 304–5.

6. Germany. Auswärtiges Amt. *Dokumente zur Vorgeschichte des Krieges* (Berlin: Reichsdruckerei, 1939), no. 2, p. 193.

7. *Polish White Book*, p. 64.

8. Edward Taborsky, *Pravda zvítězila* (Prague: Družstevní nakladatelství, 1947), 1: 265.

9. Ibid., 274–75. The document is in the author's archive.

10. From the author's archive. For Raczynski's report of the conversation, see Polish General Staff, VI Department, Papers, 1940–1945 (microfilms of the originals in the Sikorski Institute in London are deposited at the Hoover Institution, Stanford), Document no. 106/Br. The Polish desire to incorporate Lithuania is stated several times in the papers. See also Piotr S. Wandycz, *Czechoslovak-Polish Confederation and the Great Powers, 1940–1943* (Bloomington: Indiana University Publications, 1956), p. 61 and especially pp. 86–87 for mention of Lithuania as a possible member of the planned federation in Sikorski's memo to Sumner Welles, which Sikorski gave Welles during a visit to the United States in December 1942. See also Otáhalová and Červinková, *Dokumenty*, Document no. 258, 1: 309.

11. See Chapter 2.

12. Italics in original.

13. Document in the author's archive. See also Edward Taborsky, "A Polish-Czechoslovak Confederation: A Story of the First Soviet Veto," *Journal of Central European Affairs* 9, no. 4 (January 1950): 379 ff.

14. Italics in original.

15. For the text, see *Czechoslovak Yearbook of International Law* (London, 1942), pp. 235–36. See also Edward Taborsky, *The Czechoslovak Cause* (London: H. F. and G. Witherby, 1944), pp. 137 ff.

16. From the author's archive.

17. Beneš prepared an account summarizing the gist of their conversation immediately after the Polish premier left. He refers to it in his *Paměti*, pp. 225-26

and more fully in the unpublished chapter on Polish-Czechoslovak relations mentioned earlier.

18. Ibid., p. 226.

19. From the unpublished chapter on Polish-Czechoslovak relations. He added this sentence in longhand to the draft I had prepared for him.

20. From a copy of the Polish original in the author's archive.

21. From the author's archive. Italics in original.

22. From a copy of the Polish original in the author's archive.

23. From a copy of the Czech original, dated October 27, 1941, in the author's archive. Italics in original.

24. From a copy in the author's archive. Italics in original.

25. Beneš's memo of the conversation, from the author's archive.

26. For the English text, see Wandycz, *Czechoslovak-Polish Confederation*, pp. 133–35. See also Taborsky, *Czechoslovak Cause*, pp. 139–41.

27. Beneš, "The Organization of Postwar Europe," *Foreign Affairs*, 20, no. 2 (January 1942): 5.

28. See *Toward a Lasting Peace* (London, 1942), p. 6.

29. From the author's archive.

30. Ibid.

31. Ibid.

32. Ibid.

33. Ibid.

34. Ibid.

35. Some Polish circles were advocating a monarchy like the British system over a republican form of government. See "Zasady Aktw Konstytucyjnogo Zwiazku Polski i Czechoslowacji," in Polish General Staff, VI Department, Papers, 83b. This was, of course, wholly unacceptable to Beneš.

36. From the author's archive.

37. Ibid.

38. Jan Ciechanowski, *Defeat in Victory* (Garden City, N.Y.: Doubleday, 1947), p. 172.

39. From the author's archive.

40. Ibid.

41. Ibid.

42. Ibid. Italics in original.

43. Ibid. Italics in original.

44. Smutný papers, Box 10.2.1.5.

45. See also Smutný papers, Box 10.2.1.5; and Beneš, *Paměti*, pp. 263 ff.

46. Smutný papers, Box 10.2.1.5; see also Vojtěch Mastný, "Benešovy rozhovory se Stalinem a Molotovem," *Svědectví* 12, no. 47 (1947): 467 ff.

47. Entry in the author's diary, January 4, 1944; see also Beneš, *Paměti*, pp. 265–66.

48. From the author's archive.

49. Entry in the author's diary, June 2, 1944.

50. On the Polish-Soviet talks, see also Edward Rozek, *Allied Wartime Diplomacy: A Pattern in Poland* (New York: Wiley, 1958), p. 219; Stanislaw Mikolajczyk, *The Rape of Poland: Pattern of Soviet Aggression* (New York: Whittlesey House, 1948), pp. 64–65; and *Documents on Polish-Soviet Relations, 1939–1945* (London: General Sikorski Historical Institute, 1967), pp. 129–30.

51. From the author's archive.

52. Ibid.

53. Ibid.

54. Ibid.

55. Ibid.

56. Ibid.

57. Ibid.

58. Ibid.

CHAPTER 5

1. Beneš, *Memoirs of Dr. Eduard Beneš* (London: George Allen & Unwin, 1954), p. 180.

2. Libůse Otáhalová and Milada Červinková, eds., *Dokumenty z historie československé politiky, 1939–1943* (Prague: Academia, 1966), Document no. 271, 1: 325–27.

3. From the author's archive.

4. Ibid.

5. Ibid.

6. Ibid.

7. Otáhalová and Červinková, *Dokumenty*, Document no. 198, 1: 241.

8. Beneš, *Memoirs*, p. 229.

9. From the author's archive.

10. See Otáhalová and Červinková, *Dokumenty*, Document no. 270, 1: 324–25.

11. Compton Mackenzie, *Dr Beneš* (London: G. Harrap and Co., 1946), pp. 320–3.

12. For the text of the memo, see Beneš, *Memoirs*, pp. 335 ff.

13. This account of Beneš's talks with Roosevelt is based on Beneš's notes, the reports he sent back to London from Washington, his 54-page description of his visit to the United States delivered at a special session of the Czechoslovak Council of Ministers in London on June 17, 1943, and—last but not least—on what he told me when he returned to Blair House after each of his meetings with Roosevelt.

14. Beneš, *Memoirs*, p. 184.

15. Beneš later wrote: "I think that broadly speaking, he [Roosevelt] appre-

ciated my arguments, but for the time being his attitude continued to be reserved" (*Memoirs*, p. 184).

16. Transcript of Beneš's speech, from the author's archive.

17. Entry in the author's diary, May 13, 1943. Italics in original.

18. Telegram dated May 13, 1943; reprinted in Beneš, *Memoirs*, p. 193.

19. Beneš, *Memoirs*, p. 196.

20. See also ibid., p. 187.

21. Entry in the author's diary, April 4, 1943.

22. To make it easier for the Russians to answer affirmatively, Beneš told Bogomolov that his "plan for partial transference" of the Germans "concerned primarily the German bourgeoisie and the intellectuals" and that "it would be justified by their guilt for 1938 and during the present war" (from Beneš's written account of his talk with Bogomolov, in the author's archive).

23. Beneš, *Memoirs*, p. 195. Italics in original.

24. Ibid.

25. Ibid., p. 194.

26. Entry in the author's diary, June 1, 1943.

27. Ibid., June 8, 1943.

28. Ibid., May 18, 1943.

29. Beneš, *Memoirs*, pp. 194, 182, 187.

30. Entry in the author's diary, May 13, 1943.

31. Ibid., June 7, 1943.

32. A revealing example of Beneš's influence on Western views regarding the Soviet Union is provided by the minutes of the Combined Chiefs of Staff at Quebec on August 30, 1943. Sir Alan Brooke, chief of the Imperial General Staff, is mentioned as having abandoned, after a talk with Beneš, his earlier belief that Russia might seize the opportunity of the war to further international communism (cited in Georg V. Rimek, "Presidency of Edvard Beneš," Ph.D. dissertation, University of Ottawa, 1975).

33. Ladislav Feierabend, *Beneš mezi Washingtonem a Moskvou* (Washington, D.C.: The author, 1966), p. 36.

34. Ibid., pp. 133–35.

35. Document FW 760F.61/99, National Archives, Washington, D.C. See also J. Bouček, "President Beneš's Rocky Road to Moscow in 1943," paper delivered at the Eighth Congress of the Czechoslovak Society of Arts and Sciences in America, Georgetown University, Washington, D.C., August 12–15, 1976.

36. Document FW 760F.61/108, National Archives, Washington, D.C.; and Bouček, "President Beneš's Rocky Road."

37. Beneš, *Memoirs*, p. 195.

38. See ibid., pp. 193, 196.

39. Biddle's message to the State Department, dated June 16, 1943, USDS 760F.61/99.

40. See also an entry in Smutný's diary stating that Roosevelt "did indeed talk

as if he were charging Beneš with a certain mission" on the occasion of Beneš's visit to Moscow (Otáhalová and Červinková, *Dokumenty*, Document no. 298, 1: 361).

CHAPTER 6

1. *Izvestiia*, December 21, 1943.

2. Beneš, *Memoirs of Dr. Eduard Beneš* (London: George Allen & Unwin, 1954), p. 262. Italics in original. See also Beneš's description of his 1943 trip in Compton Mackenzie, *Dr Beneš* (London: G. Harrap and Co., 1946), pp. 307 ff.

3. From the author's archive; see also Eduard Táborský, *Pravda zvítězila* (Prague: Družstevní nalkadatelství, 1947), p. 290. Italics in original.

4. Táborský, *Pravda zvítězila*, p. 326.

5. Ibid., p. 398.

6. See also František Moravec, *Špión, jemuž nevěřili* (Toronto: Sixty-Eight Publishers, 1977), p. 279.

7. Táborský, *Pravda zvítězila*, p. 300–301.

8. Ibid., p. 354.

9. Ibid., p. 426.

10. Beneš, *Memoirs*, p. 145.

11. Ibid.

12. Ibid., p. 152.

13. Ibid., p. 154.

14. Ibid.

15. Ibid., p. 151.

16. Libuše Otáhalová and Milada Červinková, eds., *Dokumenty z historie československé politiky, 1939–1943* (Prague: Academia, 1966), Document no. 191, 1: 232, dated June 21, 1941.

17. He so informed his collaborators in the Czech underground in a message sent on April 26, 1941; in the author's archive.

18. Otáhalová and Červinková, *Dokumenty*, Document no. 193, 1: 234–35.

19. From the author's archive. Italics in original.

20. Ibid.; see also Otáhalová and Červinková, *Dokumenty*, Document no. 447, 2: 614.

21. Otáhalová and Červinková, *Dokumenty*, Document no. 453, appendix A, 2: 625.

22. Ibid., appendix C, 2: 627.

23. Beneš, *Memoirs*, p. 272.

24. Entry in the author's diary, December 18, 1943.

25. From the author's archive.

26. For the English text of the agreement, see *Czechoslovak Yearbook of International Law* (London: Čechoslovák, 1942), p. 236; and Beneš, *Memoirs*, p. 157.

27. From the author's archive.

28. Ibid. Italics in the original.

29. Ibid.

30. "I wanted to leave for Moscow already in the summer of 1943 immediately after my return to England from the United States," he said in his *Memoirs* (p. 243). On May 4, 1943, Beneš wired Fierlinger that he would want to proceed to Moscow in the last week of June and return to London around July 15 (Zdenek Fierlinger, *Ve službách ČSR* [Prague: Svoboda, 1948], 2: 119).

31. From the author's archive.

32. Beneš's account of the conversation; from the author's archive.

33. Ibid.

34. Ibid.

35. Ibid.

36. In May 1943 Fierlinger told the British ambassador to Moscow, Archibald Clark Kerr, that Beneš intended to visit Moscow and conclude a treaty of alliance that would enable Poland to join later. Kerr was, according to Fierlinger, enthusiastic about it and declared that the president's policy was correct (Fierlinger, *Ve službách ČSR*, p. 130).

37. Entry in the author's diary, July 1, 1943. Beneš also criticized the Soviets' behavior in a telegram to Fierlinger on July 6, 1943, and told him that he would not visit Moscow until the matter had been cleared up.

38. This discussion is based on Beneš's account of his talk with Bogomolov; in the author's archive. Italics in original. See also Fierlinger, *Ve službách ČSR*, pp. 141–42.

39. See also Julius Firt, "Cestou k únoru," *Svědectví* 12, no. 46 (1973): 241.

40. From the author's archive.

41. Entry in the author's diary, October 19, 1943; see also Fierlinger, *Ve službách ČSR*, p. 167.

42. Entry in the author's diary, October 26, 1943.

43. Smutný papers, Box 10.2.1.5; see also Fierlinger, *Ve službách ČSR*, pp. 170–71.

44. Beneš, *Memoirs*, p. 245.

45. From the author's archive. Italics in original. See also Fierlinger, *Ve službách ČSR*, pp. 138, 142.

46. From the author's archive. After each talk with Korneichuk (conducted in Russian and Ukrainian), Beneš prepared an extensive longhand account in Czech, which, since we had no typist with us, I typed for him in the office of the air base.

47. Smutný papers, Box 10.2.1.5.

48. Ibid.

49. Beneš, *Memoirs*, p. 260; and Mackenzie, *Dr Beneš*, p. 307.

50. Beneš, *Memoirs*, p. 260.

51. They met for the first time in 1935 on the occasion of the signing of the alliance treaty between Czechoslovakia and the Soviet Union.

52. Beneš, *Memoirs*, pp. 261–65.

53. These accounts were published in English by Vojtěch Mastný, "The Beneš-Stalin-Molotov Conversations in December 1943," *Jahrbücher für Geschichte-Osteuropas* 20, no. 3 (1972), pp. 367–402; and in Czech in Mastný, "Benešovy rozhovory se Stalinem a Molotovem," *Svědectví* 12, no. 47 (1974): 467–98.

54. Fierlinger, *Ve službách ČSR*, pp. 190–94. "For understandable reasons, I have listed only the most important things," Fierlinger remarked cryptically in concluding his brief narrative.

55. Walter von Seydlitz was the captured German general whom the Soviets persuaded to head a German committee in Moscow and to make anti-Hitler speeches over Radio Moscow.

56. Smutný papers, Box 10.2.1.6; and Mastný, "Benešovy rozhovory," p. 497.

57. Mastný, "Benešovy rozhovory," p. 497.

58. A copy of the memo is preserved in the author's archive.

59. Mastný, "Benešovy rozhovory," p. 497.

60. See also Fierlinger, *Ve službách ČSR*, p. 193.

61. A copy of the memo is preserved in the author's archive.

62. Mastný, "Benešovy rozhovory," p. 489.

63. Beneš also discussed these matters briefly with Marshal Zhukov in a half-hour meeting on the morning of December 18, 1943.

64. Mastný, "Benešovy rozhovory," p. 489.

65. Ibid., p. 485.

66. Beneš, *Memoirs*, p. 262–63.

67. From the author's archive. Italics in original.

68. Mastný, "Benešovy rozhovory," p. 498.

69. Beneš, *Memoirs*, p. 287. Although Beneš did say that his draft "provided that the treaty should be ratified by our parliament at home in Prague after the end of the war," the draft called for the exchange of the instruments of ratification in Moscow "as soon as possible." (Draft, dated June 23, 1943; in the author's archive).

70. Beneš's statement that the ratification occurred "one day after the signature" (Mackenzie, *Dr Beneš*, p. 308) is erroneous. Further, according to Fierlinger, Beneš's proposed treaty included the provision that "the treaty be ratified as soon as possible and the exchange of the ratification documents be done in Moscow"; and that the Czechoslovak government would present the treaty to the Czechoslovak parliament for "additional ratification" (*Ve službách ČSR*, p. 154).

71. The draft in the author's archive.

72. In his *Memoirs* (p. 268), Beneš speaks of four such meetings, but there were actually six: two on December 13, the first in the morning and the second in the late afternoon, and one each on December 14, 15, 16, and 18. For the communist version of the talks, see M. Klimeš et al., eds., *Cesta ke květnu* (Prague: Československá Akademie věd, 1965); see also Bohuslav Lašto-

vička, *V Londýně za války* (Prague: Státní nakladatelství politické literatury, 1960), pp. 311 ff.

73. From the author's archive.

74. See also Beneš, *Memoirs*, p. 272.

75. Ibid., p. 271. Italics in original.

76. See Smutný papers, Box 10.2.1.5.

77. Beneš, *Memoirs*, p. 263. Italics in original.

78. From the author's archive.

79. Entry in the author's diary, December 18, 1943.

80. For the Czech text of the broadcast, see *Šest let exilu a druhé světové války* (Prague, 1946), pp. 223–30. For excerpts in English, see Beneš, *Memoirs*, p. 288–90.

81. From the author's archive.

CHAPTER 7

1. From the author's archive.

2. Ibid.

3. Smutný papers, Box 10.2.1.5; see also Vojtěch Mastný, "Benešovy rozhovory se Stalinem a Molotovem," *Svědectví* 12, no. 47 (1974): 490.

4. From the author's archive. Italics in original.

5. Martin Kvetko et al., eds. *Zborník o slovenskom národnom povstání* (Toronto: Stálá konference slovenských demokratických exulantov, 1976), p. 189.

6. Ibid., pp. 190–91.

7. From the author's archive.

8. Entry in the author's diary, September 5, 1944.

9. Similar assurances that the Soviet Union would provide "maximum support" both for the organization of Czechoslovak military units and for anti-German operations on the home front were given to Fierlinger. See Zdenek Fierlinger, *Ve službách ČSR* (Prague: Svoboda, 1948), 2: 160.

10. From the author's archive.

11. Ibid.

12. Kvetko, *Zborník*, p. 236.

13. From the author's archive.

14. Kvetko, *Zborník*, p. 237; for the Czechoslovak request for U.S. aid to the Slovaks, see U.S., Department of State, *Foreign Relations of the United States*, 3 (1944): 521–22.

15. Kvetko, *Zborník*, p. 237.

16. Ibid., p. 241. Fierlinger also confirmed this. In September 1944, he reported that he received a "somewhat evasive answer" when he raised the question of British aid for the Slovak fighters (*Ve službách ČSR*, 2: 353).

17. From the author's archive.

18. Beneš, *Memoirs of Dr Eduard Beneš* (London: George Allen & Unwin, 1954), p. 139; see also Jan Křen, *V emigraci* (Prague: Naše vojsko, 1969), p. 505.

19. From the author's archive.

20. Ibid.

21. Ibid.

22. Ibid.

23. Ibid.

24. Ibid.

25. See František Němec and Vladimír Moudrý, *The Soviet Seizure of Ruthenia* (Toronto: William B. Anderson, 1955), pp. 120, 263.

26. From the author's archive.

27. Entry in the author's diary, December 9, 1944.

28. From the author's archive.

29. Ibid. See also Němec and Moudrý, *Soviet Seizure of Ruthenia*, pp. 133, 295.

30. Entry in the author's diary, December 19, 1944.

31. From the author's archive. See also Němec and Moudrý, *Soviet Seizure of Ruthenia*, pp. 144, 317.

32. From the author's archive. See also Edward Taborsky, "Beneš and Stalin: Moscow, 1943 and 1945," *Journal of Central European Affairs* 13, no. 2 (July 1953): 173–74, for a translation of the original Russian version.

33. From the author's archive. See also Taborsky, "Beneš and Stalin," pp. 174–75. Italics in original.

34. See Drtina's report from Slovakia, dated October 13, 1944, in the author's archive.

35. Ibid.

36. From the author's archive.

37. Entry in the author's diary, October 19, 1944.

38. From the author's archive.

39. Ibid.

40. Entry in the author's diary, January 11, 1945.

CHAPTER 8

1. From the author's archive; see also Libuše Otáhalová and Milada Červinková, *Dokumenty z historie československé politiky, 1939–1943* (Prague: Academia, 1966), appendix, 2: 750.

2. Ladislav Feierabend, *Soumrak československé demokracie* (Washington, D.C.: The author, 1967), p. 144, reminiscing about a visit to Aston Abbots on March 6, 1945.

3. Ibid., p. 146.

4. Beneš was referring to Article 60 of the Czechoslovak constitution, which allowed the cabinet to assume the functions of the head of state temporarily and invest the premier with specific duties.

5. On another sheet attached to the testament, the president bequeathed all his property in England, the United States, and Czechoslovakia to his wife.

6. Beneš told Smutný that Masaryk chose to live in a relatively small bachelor's apartment so as to have a good excuse not to entertain (Otáhalová and Červinková, *Dokumenty*, Document no. 310, 1: 378–80, dated September 28, 1943.

7. Ibid., Document 316, 1: 383–87.

8. Ibid.

9. Ibid., Document no. 241, 1: 289. Medical tests, however, showed nothing wrong.

10. Entry in the author's diary, February 27, 1943.

11. After arriving in Moscow, Beneš paid the customary courtesy visit to Kalinin, who, as chairman of the Presidium of the Supreme Soviet, was the closest equivalent to a head of state, but no business was transacted during that visit.

12. Smutný papers, Box 10.2.1.5.

13. A summary of the two Beneš-Molotov meetings can also be found in Zdenek Fierlinger, *Ve službách ČSR* (Prague: Svoboda, 1948), 2: 594–601.

14. Others attending the meeting were Masaryk and Fierlinger for the Czechoslovak side and Vyshinsky and Zorin for the Soviet side.

15. Smutný papers, Box 10.2.1.5.

16. Entry in the author's diary, March 21, 1945. According to Fierlinger, Molotov said that the Soviet government had already expressed its agreement in 1943 and the principle of the transfer was clear to it and "Moscow was willing to go all the way in this respect" (*Ve službách ČSR*, p. 595).

17. See also František Němec and Vladimír Moudrý, *The Soviet Seizure of Ruthenia* (Toronto: William B. Anderson, 1955), p. 145.

18. Smutný papers, Box 10.2.1.5.

19. The texts of the speeches were taken down by one of the Czechoslovak participants; copies in the author's archive.

20. Smutný papers, Box 10.2.1.5; see also Fierlinger, *Ve službách ČSR*, p. 601.

21. See also Smutný papers, Box 10.2.1.5.

22. For a complete listing, see Josef Josten, *Oh My Country* (London: Latimer House, 1949), p. 43.

23. Entry in the author's diary, March 23, 1945.

24. "I am not at all pleased that Fierlinger became premier," Beneš told Gottwald (Smutný papers, Box 10.2.1.5).

CHAPTER 9

1. Entry in the author's diary, April 17, 1945.

2. Communist worries about the possibility of an American liberation of Prague and western Czechoslovakia were subsequently described in Václav

Kopecký, *ČSR a KČS* (Prague: Státní nakladatelství politické literatury, 1960), p. 384.

3. Entry in the author's diary, May 12, 1945.

4. From the author's archive.

5. Ibid.

6. The message was published in the Legionnaires' daily paper, *Národní osvobození*, on November 12, 1947. For a fuller discussion of this aspect of Beneš's activity in 1945–1947, see Georg V. Rimek, "Presidency of Edvard Beneš," Ph.D. dissertation, University of Ottawa, 1975, pp. 671 ff.

7. See Josef Korbel, *Twentieth Century Czechoslovakia* (New York: Columbia University Press, 1977), p. 208.

8. This was confirmed in a conversation I had with Julius Firt, a prominent member of the Czechoslovak Socialist party who went into exile after the communist coup, in New York on January 19, 1949; an account of the conversation is in the author's archive.

9. From the author's archive.

10. James F. Byrnes, *Speaking Frankly* (New York: Harper and Brothers, 1947), p. 143; see also Korbel, *Twentieth Century Czechoslovakia*, p. 242; for the postwar animosity of the U.S. State Department, see its *Foreign Relations of the United States* 4 (1945), pp. 420 ff.

11. See, for example, a conversation between Beneš and Ambassador Steinhardt on December 23, 1946, USDS 860F.00/12–2346.

12. See the telegram of December 5, 1947, sent by Chargé d'affaires John Bruins, USDS 860F.6131/12–547.

13. Hubert Ripka, *Le Coup de Prague* (Paris: Librairie Plon, 1949), p. 185.

14. The story of the project is fully recounted in ibid, pp. 66 ff; see also Korbel, *Twentieth Century Czechoslovakia*, pp. 243–44.

15. The author's account of the conversation, in the author's archive.

16. For details of this episode, see Ripka, *Le Coup de Prague*, pp. 49 ff.

17. Fearing his forthcoming ouster and suspecting that the president was behind it, Fierlinger wrote Beneš on October 29, 1947, a plaintive letter in which he asserted that he had "always been absolutely loyal" to Beneš and asked the president to reconsider. The letter was attached to another in French from Madame Fierlinger to Madame Beneš. (Smutný papers, Box 10.2.13.)

18. Korbel, *Twentieth Century Czechoslovakia*, p. 246; see also Ota Hora, *Svědectví o puči* (Toronto: Sixty-Eight Publishers, 1978), p. 305.

19. See Jaromír Smutný, "Únorový převrat 1948," mimeo. (London: Ústav dr. Edvarda Beneše, 1953, 1955), 1: 18, 2: 45.

20. Ripka, *Le Coup de Prague*, p. 223.

21. Smutný, "Únorový převrat 1948," 2: 45.

22. See, for example, Smutný, "Únorový převrat 1948"; "Průběh československé krize v únoru 1948," a day-by-day record of the crisis prepared by Czechoslovak politicians who found refuge in the West; Ripka, *Le Coup de Prague*; Josef Korbel, *The Communist Subversion of Czechoslovakia, 1938–1948*

(Princeton, N.J.: Princeton University Press, 1959); Josef Josten, *Oh My Country* (London: Latimer House, 1949); Otto Friedman, *The Break-up of Czech Democracy* (London: Gollancz, 1950); Hora, *Svědectví*; and Vratislav Bušek, *Poučení z únorového převratu* (New York: CS Publishing Co., 1954).

23. This report was posthumously published in Sweden in 1968: Amelie Posse, *När Järn ridå föll över Prag* (Stockholm: Natur och Kultur, 1968). I also obtained valuable firsthand information from another person, who wishes to remain anonymous.

24. Edward Taborsky, "The Triumph and Disaster of Eduard Beneš," *Foreign Affairs* 36, no. 4 (July 1958): 683–84.

25. Korbel, *Twentieth Century Czechoslovakia*, p. 246.

26. Ripka, *Le Coup de Prague*, p. 225; see also "Průběh."

27. Smutný papers, Box 10.2.13.

28. Ibid., Box 10.2.1.2; see also "Průběh."

29. Smutný papers, Box 10.2.1.2.

30. As late as February 24, 1948, Beneš told the leaders of the Slovak Democratic party that he would not accept the resignation of the democratic ministers and that he would appoint a new government only after consultations with all political parties (Smutný, "Únorový převrat 1948," 4: 32). He gave similar assurances to the leaders of the Czechoslovak Socialist party and the People's party (ibid., p. 140). See also Vladimír Krajina, "Byl president Beneš skutečně vinen?" *České slovo* 1977, no. 5 (May): 5.

31. He repeated this remark to the leaders of the Social Democratic party on February 21, 1948, and to the leaders of the Slovak Democratic party on February 24, 1948 (Smutný, "Únorový převrat 1948," 2: 49, 4: 132, 134).

32. Ripka, *Le Coup de Prague*, pp. 328–29; see also Karel Kaplan, "Úvahy o nevyhnutelnosti února," *Svědectví*, 14, no. 55 (1978): 363; and Edward Taborsky, "President Edvard Beneš and the Crises of 1938 and 1948," *East-Central Europe (L'Europe du Centre-Est))* 5, no. 2 (1978): 208–13.

33. As related by Klinger, in the author's archive; see also Bušek, *Poučení*, p. 80.

34. Smutný papers, Box 10.2.1.7. On February 20, 1948, Zorin told the chef de cabinet of the Czechoslovak Ministry of Transportation that the Soviet Union supported "the resolute action of the CPCZ [the Communist Party of Czecho-slovakia]" ("Průběh"). See also Korbel, *Communist Subversion of Czechoslovakia*, pp. 222–23; Bušek, *Poučení*, pp. 80, 103; and Julius Firt, Záznamy-I," *Svědectví* 10, no. 40 (1971): 526–27.

35. Ripka, *Le Coup de Prague*, pp. 273–74; see also Smutný papers, Box 10.2.1.3.

36. Klinger's report.

37. Letter dated August 19, 1948; in the author's archive. See also Posse, *När Järn*, p. 151; and Bušek, *Poučení*, pp. 94–97.

38. Ripka, *Le Coup de Prague*, p. 298; Smutný papers, Box 10.2.1.2; "Průběh"; and Bušek, *Poučení*, pp. 105–6.

39. Ripka, *Le Coup de Prague*, pp. 298–99. According to Mirko Sedlák (a deputy of the Social Democratic party), Gen. Antonín Hasal, the chief of the military

section of the President's Office, told him that Beneš gave an order that four regiments of the communist police be disarmed. But General Svoboda told Gottwald, who prevented it. (Based on my talks with Sedlák in Stockholm on September 7, 1948.) On the unreliability of the army, see Korbel, *Communist Subversion*, p. 225; and Ferdinand Peroutka, *Byl Eduard Beneš vinen?* (Paris: Masarykův demokratický svaz, 1950), p. 27; and Hora, *Svědectví*, pp. 444–45.

40. Ripka, *Le Coup de Prague*, p. 285.

41. Smutný, "Únorový převrat, 1948," 2: 53–54; and Kaplan, "Úvahy," p. 362.

42. Smutný, "Únorový převrat, 1948," 2: 29; see also Paul E. Zinner, "Marxism in Action: The Seizure of Power in Czechoslovakia," *Foreign Affairs*, 28, no. 4 (July 1950): 644–58.

43. Smutný, "Únorový převrat 1948," 4: 152; and Hora, *Svědectví*, p. 458.

44. Letter in the author's archive; see also Posse, *När Järn*, p. 151.

45. Smutný papers, Box 30.8.1.13.

46. Klinger's report; see also Bušek, *Poučení*, p. 92.

47. Smutný, "Únorový převrat 1948," 5: 56; see also Smutný papers, Box 30.8.1.5; "Průběh"; and Hora, *Svědectví*, p. 480.

48. See also Zinner, "Marxism in Action," pp. 136, 214.

49. The author's written account of the conversation, in the author's archive.

50. See, for instance, Beneš's letter to the Legionnaires (*Národní osvobození*, November 12, 1947); his address to a delegation of Catholic bishops led by Archbishop Josef Beran (ibid., November 21, 1947); his talk to students (ibid., November 28, 1947); his radio message to Czechoslovak youth (ibid., October 28, 1947); and his 1947 Christmas message (ibid., December 25, 1947). Quoted in Rimek, "Presidency of Edvard Beneš," pp. 683 ff.

51. Beneš, *Paměti* (Prague: Orbis, 1947), p. 212–14.

52. Ripka, *Le Coup de Prague*, p. 225; Smutný, "Únorový převrat 1948," 2: 18.

53. Ripka, *Le Coup de Prague*, p. 268.

54. Smutný, "Únovorý převrat 1948," 2: 50.

55. Stenographic report of Beneš's conversation, in ibid., 4: 156–60.

56. Ibid., 5: 15.

57. According to Eugene Loebl and Dušan Pokorný, Gottwald was a defender of the political concept of a specific way to socialism, and his references to the "Czechoslovak way to socialism" were not "mere words" (*Die Revolution rehabilitiert ihre Kinder* [Vienna: Europa Verlag, 1968], pp. 22, 214). Douglas Hyde, a disillusioned British communist, reports that Gottwald got into trouble with Stalin for advocating democratic methods of achieving communism in Czechoslovakia (*I Believed* [London: Heinemann, 1951], p. 234).

58. Edward Taborsky, *Communism in Czechoslovakia, 1948–1960* (Princeton, N.J.: Princeton University Press, 1961), p. 100.

59. See also Smutný papers, Box 39.8.1.13. On the other hand, Beneš did not suffer from diabetes, as some have thought. On this question, see Stanley B. Winters, "Document. The Health of Edvard Beneš: An Unpublished Letter from 1948," *East-Central Europe* 4, no. 1 (1977): 60–66.

60. See also Ripka, *Le Coup de Prague*, p. 92; and Ladislav Feierabend, *Pod vládou národní fronty* (Washington, D.C.: The author, 1966), pp. 217–19, citing a statement about Beneš's stroke made by Arnošt Heidrich.

61. Smutný papers, Box 29.8.1.13. Petr Zenkl confirmed this in a conversation in Washington, D.C., in January 1949, when he told me that Beneš's illness had not affected the president's thinking and judgment.

62. Taborsky, "Triumph and Disaster," p. 684.

CHAPTER 10

1. Based on Beneš's memo about the conversation; see Jaromír Smutný, "Únorový převrat 1948," mimeo. (London: Ústav dr. Edvarda Beneše, 1957), 5: 56; and Smutný papers, Box 30.8.1.13.

2. Smutný, "Únorový převrat 1948," 5: 35.

3. Telegram to Fierlinger, dated May 20, 1942; in the author's archive.

4. Smutný, "Únorový převrat 1948," 4: 165. When Beneš received the ministers of the Czechoslovak Socialist party on February 23, 1948, he told them that he would abdicate if he were unable to reach an agreement with the communists (Hubert Ripka, *Le Coup de Prague* [Paris: Librairie Plon, 1949], p. 271).

5. Smutný, "Únorový převrat 1948," 4: 170–71.

6. Ibid., 5: 9.

7. Ibid., 5: 56.

8. Ibid., 5: 17. According to Smutný, in some talks with him, Beneš "deemed sometimes that his decision [to remain in office] was not correct." He also told Gottwald this in their conversation on May 4, 1948. (Ibid., 5: 36; and Smutný papers, Box 30.8.1.13.)

9. Smutný, "Únorový převrat 1948," 5: 31; and Smutný papers, Box 30.8.1.13.

10. See Smutný's memo about the conversation in "Únorový převrat 1948," 5: 31 ff.

11. Ibid., 5: 41; see also Smutný papers, Box 30.8.1.13.

12. Smutný, "Únorový převrat 1948," 5: 58–59.

13. Ibid., 5: 1.

14. Ibid.

15. Ibid.

16. In his conversation with Gottwald, Beneš referred several times to the humiliation that he had to suffer in February, a humiliation forced on him by "the street." "I resent it deeply, feel it as a humiliation of the president of the republic, and I cannot forget it," he told Gottwald. (Ibid.)

17. From the author's archive; see also Amelie Posse, *När Järn ridå föll över Prag* (Stockholm: Natur och Kultur, 1968), p. 152.

18. Such was the case, for example, of Vladimír Krajina, secretary general of

the Czechoslovak Socialist party, who was arrested on February 26, 1948, but was then released. He credited his release to Beneš's personal intervention. ("Byl president Beneš skutečně vinen?" *České slovo* 1977, no. 5 (May): 5.

19. Letter dated July 29, 1948; in the author's archive.

20. Smutný, "Únorový převrat 1948," 5: 12, 35.

21. From the author's archive; see also Posse, *När Järn*, p. 150.

22. Smutný, "Únorový převrat 1948," 5: 39.

23. He had always said that he would occupy himself by writing books when he retired. But due to his illness, he could not do much writing, except for revising his manuscript of *Mnichovské dny*.

24. From the author's archive; see also Posse, *När Järn*, p. 154.

25. From the author's archive; see also Posse, *När Järn*, p. 152.

26. From the author's archive.

27. Ibid.; see also Posse, *När Järn*, p. 156.

28. The account of the conversation, in the author's archive.

29. From the author's archive.

30. See Posse, *När Järn*, p. 158 ff.

31. Ibid., pp. 159–60.

32. Ibid., p. 157; also in the author's archive.

33. From the author's archive; see also Posse, *När Järn*, p. 164.

34. From the author's archive; see also Posse, *När Järn*, p. 165.

CHAPTER 11

1. Edvard Beneš, *Mnichovské dny* (Prague: Svoboda, 1968), p. 341.

2. Václav Král, *Politické strany a Mnichov* (Prague: Svobodné slovo, 1961), pp. 160–64; and Josef Korbel, *Twentieth Century Czechoslovakia* (New York: Columbia University Press, 1977), pp. 140–43.

3. Korbel, *Twentieth Century Czechoslovakia*, p. 147.

4. From the author's archive. See also Míla Lvová, *Mnichov a Edvard Beneš* (Prague: Svoboda, 1968), p. 192. Churchill evidently continued to believe this even after the war (*The Second World War, vol. 1, The Gathering Storm* [Boston: Houghton Mifflin, 1948], p. 302).

5. Georg V. Rimek, "Presidency of Edvard Beneš," Ph.D. dissertation, University of Ottawa, 1975, p. 368.

6. See Josef Kalvoda, *Czechoslovakia's Role in Soviet Strategy* (Washington, D.C.: University Press of America, 1978), p. 161.

7. Rimek, "Presidency of Edvard Beneš," p. 383.

8. See John W. Wheeler-Bennett, *Munich: Prologue to Tragedy* (London: Macmillan, 1948), p. 181.

9. See Beneš, *Mnichovské dny*, pp. 318–19.

10. See Beneš, *Paměti* (Prague: Orbis, 1947), pp. 24 ff.

11. Ibid., pp. 31–33; see also Gerhard L. Weinberg, "Secret Hitler-Beneš Negotiations in 1936–1937," *Journal of Central European Affairs* 19, no. 4 (January 1960): 366–74.

12. Beneš, *Paměti*, pp. 30–33.

13. I was then secretary to Czechoslovakia's foreign minister and Beneš's right-hand man, Kamil Krofta, and I remember that on September 29, 1938, Krofta showed us on a map of Czechoslovakia the areas that Beneš was willing to surrender.

14. Korbel, *Twentieth Century Czechoslovakia*, p. 148.

15. For a representative sampling of such criticism, see Kalvoda, *Czechoslovakia's Role*; Korbel, *Twentieth Century Czechoslovakia*; Ladislav Feierabend, *Ve vládě v exilu* (Washington, D.C.: The author, 1966); idem, *Beneš mezi Washingtonem a Moskvou* (Washington, D.C.: The author, 1966); Paul E. Zinner, "Marxism in Action: The Seizure of Power in Czechoslovakia," *Foreign Affairs* 28, no. 4 (July 1950): 644–58; Vojtěch Mastný, "Benešovy rozhovory se Stalinem a Molotovem," *Svědectví* 12, no. 47 (1974): 467–98; František Moravec, *Špión, jemuž nevěřili* (Toronto: Sixty-Eight Publishers, 1977); F. A. Voigt (editor), "Constants in Russian Foreign Policy," *Nineteenth Century and After* 134, no. 802 (1943): 246; and Jan Ciechanowski, *Defeat in Victory* (Garden City, N.Y.: Doubleday, 1947), p. 172.

16. Kalvoda, *Czechoslovakia's Role*, p. 148.

17. Ciechanowski, *Defeat in Victory*, p. 172; Kalvoda, *Czechoslovakia's Role*, pp. 161, 159; Mastný, "Benešovy rozhovory," pp. 472, 475.

18. Amelie Posse, *När Järn ridå föll över Prag* (Stockholm: Natur och Kultur, 1968), p. 150.

19. Unpublished minutes of the session held in London on December 6, 1949; in the author's archive.

20. In perusing the papers of Štefan Osuský deposited in the Hoover Institution, I was quite surprised to find that Beneš's archrival and stern critic between 1938 and 1945 shared Beneš's belief in the desirability and feasibility of cooperation between the Soviet Union and the West (see especially Boxes 27–30).

21. For a sampling, see Korbel, *Twentieth Century Czechoslovakia*; Zinner, "Marxism in Action"; Kalvoda, *Czechoslovakia's Role*; Mastný, "Benešovy rozhovory"; Rimek, "Presidency of Edvard Beneš"; Ota Hora, *Svědectví o puči* (Toronto: Sixty-Eight Publishers, 1978); and Ferdinand Peroutka, *Byl Eduard Beneš vinen?* (Paris: Masarykův demokratický svaz, 1950).

22. When a communist action committee barred Prokop Drtina from entering his office at the Ministry of Justice on February 23, 1948, Drtina telephoned the head of the political section of the President's Office and asked him to transmit this dramatic message to the president:

> Mr. President, what has been happening in the city since this morning is no longer a political crisis, it is a revolution, a putsch. The Ministry of Justice is occupied by the political police of the Ministry of the Interior. Dr.

Marianko [a high officer of the Ministry of Justice] has been arrested and so have the commander, the chief physician, and other high officers from the Pankrác Penitentiary. The main post office is seized, and I was refused entrance into the building of the Ministry of Justice. As minister of justice, I declare that act unconstitutional and request the president of the republic as supreme guardian of the law and the constitution to intervene and remedy the situation. Otherwise even he could not escape responsibility for this crime. [From the author's archive.]

23. Peroutka (*Byl Eduard Beneš vinen?*, p. 29) considers Beneš's remaining in office after the communist coup as his most serious mistake.

24. Zinner, "Marxism in Action," p. 229; and Hora, *Svědectví*, p. 524.

25. See Hubert Ripka, *Le Coup de Prague* (Paris: Librairie Plon, 1949), pp. 273–74; Smutný papers, Box 10.2.1.7; Peroutka, *Byl Eduard Beneš vinen?* p. 27; Posse, *När Järn*, p. 151; Steinhardt's report to the U.S. secretary of state, dated March 3, 1948, cited in Walter Ullman, *The United States in Prague, 1945–1948* (Boulder, Colo.: East European quarterly, 1978), p. 159; Karel Kaplan, "Úvahy o nevyhnutelnosti února," *Svědectví* 14, no. 55 (1978): 363; William Griffith, "Myth and Realities of Czechoslovak History," *East Europe* 11, no. 3 (1962): 41; Vratislav Bušek, *Poučení z únorového převratu* (New York: CS Publishing Co., 1954), p. 97; and Julius Firt, "Záznamy-I," *Svědectví* 10, no. 40 (1971): 529, 531.

26. Peroutka, *Byl Eduard Beneš vinen?* p. 31.

27. Morton A. Kaplan, *The Communist Coup in Czechoslovakia* (Princeton, N.J.: Center for International Studies, 1960), p. 36; and Bušek, *Poučení*, p. 122.

28. Cited in Ullman, *The United States*, pp. 133–34.

29. See, for example, Hora, *Svědectví*, pp. 511, 524.

30. As noted in the Smutný papers (Box 10.2.1.3), Václav Majer, the Social Democratic minister, was among those who did not believe that there were forces in Czechoslovakia in 1948 that would have been willing and able go into battle against the mobilized street mobs and armed workers' militia.

31. Posse, *När Järn*, p. 151.

32. Peroutka, *Byl Eduard Beneš vinen?* p. 11.

33. See also Beneš's explanation of his behavior in 1938 in a letter to Rašín written in November 1938 (*Šest let exilu druhé světové války* [Prague, 1946], p. 28). According to Ernst Eisenlohr, Nazi Germany's envoy to Czechoslovakia, Hitler wanted to utilize a war with an isolated Czechoslovakia to destroy the Czech people physically (see Julius Firt, *Knihy a osudy* [Cologne: Index, 1972], p. 235).

Bibliography

UNPUBLISHED MATERIALS

Bouček, Jaroslav. "President Beneš's Rocky Road to Moscow in 1943." Paper delivered at the Eighth Congress of the Czechoslovak Society of Arts and Sciences in America, Georgetown University, Washington, D.C., August 12–15, 1976.

Draft of Conversations Between President Beneš and Compton Mackenzie, 1944–1945. In the author's archive.

Great Britain. Cabinet Papers, 1935–1945. London, Public Record Office.

———. Foreign Office, General Correspondence, 1935–1940. London, Public Record Office.

Heidrich, Arnošt. "Zahraničně-politické příčiny našich tragedií v letech 1938 a 1948." Lecture delivered in Washington, D.C., 1949. Subsequently published in English as "International Political Causes of the Czechoslovak Tragedies of 1938 and 1948." Mimeographed. Washington, D.C.: Czechoslovak Society of Arts and Sciences in America, 1962.

Osuský, Štefan (Czechoslovak envoy to France, 1918–1939). Papers. Stanford, Hoover Institution Archives.

Polish General Staff. VI Department. Papers, 1940–1945. London, General Sikorski Institute (microfilms available at the Hoover Institution, Stanford).

"Průběh československé krize v únoru 1948." Frankfurt, 1949 (a day-by-day record of the February 1948 crisis prepared by a meeting of Czechoslovak politicians who had found refuge in the West). In the author's archive.

Rimek, Georg V. "Presidency of Edvard Beneš." Ph.D. dissertation, University of Ottawa, 1975.

Smutný, Jaromír (head of the President's Office, 1939–1948). Papers. New York, Columbia University Archives.

Taborsky, Edward, Archives, 1938–1948.

————. "Pravda zvítězila" (vols. 2–3 of wartime diary; see Books section of this bibliography for vol. 1).

U.S. Department of State. General Records, Record Group 59: Czechoslovakia. Washington, D.C., National Archives.

PUBLISHED DOCUMENTARY MATERIALS

Beneš, Edvard. *Czechoslovak Policy for Victory and Peace.* London, Lincolns-Praeger, 1942.

Československo-sovětské vztahy v době velké vlastenecké války, 1941–1945: Dokumenty a materiály. Prague: Státní nakladatelstvi politické literatury, 1960.

Chtěli jsme bojovat: Dokumenty o boji KSČ a lidu na obranu Československa, 1938. 2 vols. Prague: Státní nakladatelství politické literatury, 1963.

Czechoslovak Yearbook of International Law. London: Čechoslovák, 1942.

Documents on German Foreign Policy, 1918–1945. Washington, D.C.: Government Printing Office, 1949–1966.

Documents on International Affairs, 1934–1950. London: Royal Institute of International Affairs, 1935–1954.

Dokumenty československé zahraniční politiky, 1945–1960. Prague: Ústav pro mezinárodní politiku a ekonomii, 1960.

France. Ministère des Affaires Etrangères. *Documents diplomatiques français, 1932–1939.* Paris: Imprimerie nationale, 1963–1968.

Germany. Auswärtiges Amt. *Dokumente zur Vorgeschichte des Krieges.* Berlin: Reichsdruckerei, 1939.

Klimeš, M., et al., eds. *Cesta ke květnu: Dokumenty o vzniku a vývoji lidové demokracie v Československu do února 1948.* Prague: Československá Akademie věd, 1965.

Klochko, V. F., et al., eds. *New Documents on the History of Munich.* Prague: Orbis, 1958.

Král, Václav, ed. *Cestou k únoru: Dokumenty.* Prague: Svobodné slovo, 1963.

Mnichov v dokumentech. 2 vols. Prague: Státní nakladatelství politické literatury, 1958.

Otáhalová, Libuše, and Červinková, Milada, eds. *Dokumenty z historie československé politiky, 1939–1943.* 2 vols. Prague: Academia, 1966.

Šest let exilu a druhé světové války. Prague, 1946.

Toward a Lasting Peace. London, 1942.

Tři roky světové války: Projevy a dokumenty z r. 1938–1942. London: Čechoslovák, n.d.

U.S. Department of State. *Foreign Relations of the United States: Diplomatic Papers.* Washington, D.C.: Government Printing Office, annual publication.

Woodward, E. L., and Butler, Rohan, eds. *Documents on British Foreign Policy, 1919–1939, Third Series,* 9 vols. London: His Majesty's Stationery Office, 1949.

BOOKS

Attlee, Clement R. *As It Happened*. London: William Heinemann, 1954.

Beckman, Rudolf. *O diplomatickém pozadí Mnichova: Kapitoly o britské mnichovské politice*. Prague: Státní nakladatelství politické literatury, 1954.

Beloff, Max. *The Foreign Policy of Soviet Russia, 1929–1941*. 2 vols. London: Oxford University Press, 1947, 1949.

Beneš, Edvard. *Demokracie dnes a zítra*. 2 vols. London: Čechoslovák, 1944.

———. *Democracy Today and Tomorrow*. London: Macmillan, 1940.

———. *Mnichovské dny*. Prague: Svoboda, 1968.

———. *Memoirs of Dr Evuard Beneš: From Munich to New War and New Victory*. Translated by Godfrey Lias. London: George Allen & Unwin, 1954 (English translation of the following item).

———. *Paměti: Od Mnichova k nové válce a novému vítězství*. Prague: Orbis, 1947.

———. *Problémy nové Evropy a zahraniční politika československá*. Prague: Melantrich, 1924.

———. *Úvahy o slovanství*. London: Lincolns-Praeger, n.d.

Bonnet, Georges. *Défense de la paix: De Washington au Quai d'Orsay*. Geneva: Constant Bourguin, 1946.

Bruegel, J. W. *Czechoslovakia Before Munich*. Cambridge, Eng.: Cambridge University Press, 1973.

Bušek, Vratislav. *Poučení z únorového převratu*. New York: CS Publishing Co., 1954.

Byrnes, James F. *Speaking Frankly*. New York: Harper and Brothers, 1947.

Čelovský, Boris. *Das Münchener Abkommen von 1938*. Stuttgart: Deutscher Verlag, 1958.

Československo-sovětské vztahy jako faktor mezinárodní politiky, 1917–1970. Prague: Academia, 1975.

Churchill, Winston. *The Second World War, vol. 1, The Gathering Storm*. Boston: Houghton Mifflin, 1948.

Ciechanowski, Jan. *Defeat in Victory*. Garden City, N.Y.: Doubleday, 1947.

Crabitès, P. *Beneš, Statesman of Central Europe*. London: G. Routledge & Sons, 1935.

Diplomaticheskii slovar.' Moscow, 1950.

Eisenmann, Louis. *Un Grand Européen, Edouard Beneš*. Paris: Paul Hartman, 1934.

Eubank, Keith. *Munich*. Norman: Oklahoma University Press, 1963.

Feierabend, Ladislav. *Beneš mezi Washingtonem a Moskvou*. Washington, D.C.: The author, 1966.

———. *Pod vládou národní fronty*. Washington, D.C.: The author, 1966.

———. *Soumrak československé demokracie*. Washington, D.C.: The author, 1967.

———. *Ve vládě v exilu*. 2 vols. Washington, D.C.: The author, 1965, 1966.

Fierlinger, Zdeněk. *Ve službách ČSR*. 2 vols. Prague: Dělnické nakladatelství, 1947, and Svoboda, 1948.

Firt, Julius. *Knihy a osudy.* Cologne: Index, 1972.

Friedmann, Otto. *The Break-up of Czech Democracy.* London: Gollancz, 1950.

Hájek, J. S. *Mnichov.* Prague, 1958.

Hajn, Alois. *Dr. Edvard Beneš a jeho životní dílo.* Prague: The author, 1935.

History of Soviet Foreign Policy, 1917–1945. Moscow: Progress Publishers, 1969.

Hitchcock, Edward. *Beneš, the Man and the Statesman.* London: Hamish Hamilton, 1940.

Hník, František. *Edvard Beneš, filosof demokracie.* Prague: Melantrich, 1946.

Hora, Ota. *Svědectví o puči.* Toronto: Sixty-Eight Publishers, 1978.

Hyde, Douglas. *I Believed.* London: Heinemann, 1951.

Josten, Josef. *Oh My Country.* London: Latimer House, 1949.

Kaplan, Morton A. *The Communist Coup in Czechoslovakia.* Princeton, N.J.: Center for International Studies, 1960.

Kalvoda, Josef. *Czechoslovakia's Role in Soviet Strategy.* Washington, D.C.: University Press of America, 1978.

Kopecký, Václav. *ČSR a KČS.* Prague: Státní nakladatelství politické literatury, 1960.

Korbel, Josef. *The Communist Subversion of Czechoslovakia, 1938–1948.* Princeton, N.J.: Princeton University Press, 1959.

———. *Twentieth Century Czechoslovakia: The Meaning of Its History.* New York: Columbia University Press, 1977.

Král, Václav. *O Masarykově a Benešově kontrarevoluční protisovětské politice.* Prague, 1953.

———. *Politické strany a Mnichov.* Prague: Svobodné slovo, 1961.

Křen, Jan. *Do emigrace.* Prague: Naše vojsko, 1963.

———. *V emigraci: Západní zahraniční odboj, 1939–1940.* Prague: Naše vojsko, 1969.

Kvetko, Martin, et al., eds. *Zborník o slovenskom národnom povstání.* Toronto: Stálá konference slovenských demokratických exulantov, 1976.

Laštovička, Bohuslav. *V Londýně za války.* Prague: Státní nakladatelství politické literatury, 1960.

Lockhart, Robert Bruce. *Comes the Reckoning.* London: Putnam, 1947.

———. *Retreat from Glory.* London: Putnam, 1934.

Loebl, Eugene, and Pokorný, Dušan. *Die Revolution rehabilitiert ihre Kinder.* Vienna: Europa Verlag, 1968.

Lvová, Míla. *Mnichov a Edvard Beneš.* Prague: Svoboda, 1968.

Mackenzie, Compton. *Dr Beneš.* London: G. Harrap and Co., 1946.

Mamatey, Victor, and Luža, Radomír, eds. *A History of the Czechoslovak Republic, 1918–1948.* Princeton, N.J.: Princeton University Press, 1973.

Mikolajczyk, Stanislaw. *The Rape of Poland: Pattern of Soviet Aggression.* New York: Whittlesey House, 1948.

Moravec, František. *Master of Spies.* London: Bodley Head, 1975 (English version of the following).

————. *Špión, jemuž nevěřili.* Toronto: Sixty-Eight Publishers, 1977.

Němec, František, and Moudrý, Vladimír. *The Soviet Seizure of Ruthenia.* Toronto: William B. Anderson, 1955.

Padesát let Edvarda Beneše. Prague: Československá obec legionářská, 1934.

Papoušek, Jaroslav. *Eduard Beneš.* Prague: Svaz národního osvobození, 1934.

Peroutka, Ferdinand. *Byl Eduard Beneš vinen?* Paris: Masarykův demokratický svaz, 1950.

Plánované hospodářství v Československu. Prague: Orbis, 1948.

Poliakov, Vladimir G. *Angliia i miunkhenskii sgovor.* Moscow: Izdatelstvo Akademii nauk SSSR, 1960.

Posse, Amelie. *När Järn ridå föll över Prag.* Stockholm: Natur och Kultur, 1968.

Ripka, Hubert. *Le Coup de Prague: Une révolution préfabriquée.* Paris: Librairie Plon, 1949.

————. *Munich: Before and After.* London: Gollancz, 1939.

Rozek, Edward. *Allied Wartime Diplomacy: A Pattern in Poland.* New York: Wiley, 1958.

Smutný, Jaromír. "Únorový převrat 1948." 5 vols. Mimeographed. London: Ústav dr. Edvarda Beneše, 1953–1957.

Taborsky, Edward. *Communism in Czechoslovakia, 1948–1960.* Princeton, N.J.: Princeton University Press, 1961.

————, *The Czechoslovak Cause.* London: H.F. and G. Witherby, 1944.

————. *Pravda zvítězila.* Prague: Družstevní nakladatelství, 1947.

————. *Presidentův sekretář vypovídá.* Zurich: Konfrontation, 1978.

Ullman, Walter. *The United States in Prague, 1945–1948.* Boulder, Colo.: East European Quarterly, 1978.

Veselý-Štainer, Karel. *Cestou národního odboje: Bojový vývoj odbojového hnutí v letech 1938–45.* Prague: Sfinx, 1947.

Wandycz, Piotr S. *Czechoslovak-Polish Confederation and the Great Powers, 1940–1943.* Bloomington: Indiana University Publications, 1956.

Wheeler-Bennett, John W. *Munich: Prologue to Tragedy.* London: Macmillan, 1948.

ARTICLES

Beneš, Edvard. "The Organization of Postwar Europe." *Foreign Affairs* 20, no. 2 (January 1942): 226–42.

Cohen, Barry Mendel. "Moscow at Munich: Did the Soviet Union Offer Unilateral Aid to Czechoslovakia?" *East European Quarterly* 12, no. 3 (September 1978): 341–49.

Firt, Julius. "Záznamy-I." *Svědectví* 10, no. 40 (1971): 517–39.

————. "Cestou k únoru: Počátky byly v Londýně. Záznamy-II." *Svědectví* 12, no. 46 (1973): 211–51.

Griffith, William. "Myth and Realities of Czechoslovak History." *East Europe* 11, no. 3 (March 1962).

Hauner, Miloš. "Září 1938: Kapitulovat či bojovat?" *Svědectví* 13, no. 49 (1975): 151–77.

"K politice Sovětského svazu na obranu Československa v roce 1938." *Dějepis ve škole*, no. 1 (September 1970): 6–10.

Kaplan, Karel. "Úvahy o nevyhnutelnosti února." *Svědectví* 14, no. 55 (1978).

Krajina, Vladimír. "Byl president Beneš skutečně vinen?" *České slovo* 1977, no. 5 (May): 5.

Král, Václav. "Československo a Mnichov." *Československý časopis historický* 7, no. 1 (1959): 25–48.

Lockhart, Robert Bruce. "The Second Exile of Edward Beneš. *Slavonic and East European Review* 28, no. 70 (November 1949): 39–59.

"Londýnská emigrace Benešovýma očima." *Predvoj*, no. 39 (September 30, 1965): 10–11.

Lukeš F. "Poznámky k československo-sovětským vztahům v září 1938." *Československý časopis historický* 16, no. 5 (May 1968): 703–32.

Lvová, Míla. "Mnichovská křižovatka." *Svět práce*, no. 38 (September 24, 1959): 4.

Mastný, Vojtěch. "Benešovy rozhovory se Stalinem a Molotovem." *Svědectví* 12, no. 47 (1974): 467–98.

———. "The Beneš-Stalin-Molotov Conversations in December 1943: New Documents." *Jahrbücher für Geschicte-Osteuropas* 20, no. 3 (1972): 367–402.

Pfaff, Ivan. "Jak tomu opravdu bylo se sovětskou pomocí v mnichovské krizi." *Svědectví* 14, no. 56 (1978): 566–85; 15, no. 57 (1978): 51–68.

Smutný, Jaromír. "Edvard Beneš a čs odboj za druhé světové války." *Svědectví* 6, no. 21 (1963): 50–60.

Sipols, V., and Pankrashova, M. "Preparation of the Munich Deal." *International Affairs* (Moscow), 1973, nos. 4, 6, 7, 10.

Taborsky, Edward. "Beneš a náš osud." *Svědectví* 15, no. 57 (1978): 17–50.

———. "Beneš and Stalin: Moscow, 1943 and 1945." *Journal of Central European Affairs* 13, no. 2 (July 1953): 154–81.

———. "Beneš and the Soviets." *Foreign Affairs* 27, no. 2 (January 1949): 302–14.

———. "Benešovy moskevské cesty." *Svědectví* 1, no. 3/4 (1957): 193–214.

———. "A Polish-Czechoslovak Confederation: A Story of the First Soviet Veto." *Journal of Central European Affairs* 9, no. 4 (January 1950): 379–95.

———. "President Edvard Beneš and the Crises of 1938 and 1948." *East-Central Europe (L'Europe du Centre-Est)* 5, no. 2 (1978): 203–14.

———. The Triumph and Disaster of Eduard Beneš." *Foreign Affairs* 36, no. 4 (July 1958): 669–84.

Voigt, F. A. (editor). "Constants in Russian Foreign Policy." *Nineteenth Century and After* 134, no. 801 (1943): 193–200, and no. 802 (1943): 241–47.

Wallace, William. "New Documents on the History of Munich." *International Affairs* (London) 35, no. 4 (October 1959): 447–54.

Weinberg, Gerhard L. "Secret Hitler-Beneš Negotiations in 1936–1937." *Journal of Central European Affairs* 19, no. 4 (January 1960): 366–74.

Winters, Stanley B. "Document. The Health of Edvard Beneš: An Unpublished Letter from 1948." *East-Central Europe (Europe du Centre-Est)* 4, no. 1 (1977): 60–66.

Zinner, Paul E. "Marxism in Action: The Seizure of Power in Czechoslovakia." *Foreign Affairs* 28, no. 4 (July 1950): 644–58.

Index